A TIME OF SIFTING

 PIETIST, MORAVIAN, AND ANABAPTIST STUDIES

EDITOR

Craig D. Atwood
*Director of the Center for Moravian Studies, Moravian Seminary*

Volumes in the Pietist, Moravian, and Anabaptist Studies Series take multidisciplinary approaches to the history and theology of these groups and their religious and cultural influence around the globe. The series seeks to enrich the dynamic international study of post-Reformation Protestantism through original works of scholarship.

ADVISORY BOARD

Bill Leonard, *Wake Forest University*
Katherine Faull, *Bucknell University*
A. G. Roeber, *Penn State University*
Jonathan Strom, *Emory University*
Hermann Wellenreuther, *Georg-August-Universität Göttingen*
Rachel Wheeler, *Indiana University–Purdue University Indianapolis*

BOOKS IN PRINT

PAUL PEUCKER, *A Time of Sifting: Mystical Marriage and the Crisis of Moravian Piety in the Eighteenth Century*

PAUL PEUCKER

# A TIME OF SIFTING

Mystical Marriage and the Crisis of Moravian Piety
in the Eighteenth Century

The Pennsylvania State University Press
University Park, Pennsylvania

Some of the material in this book was first published in an earlier form:
   Paul Peucker, "'Inspired by Flames of Love': Homosexuality, Mysticism, and Moravian Brothers Around 1750," *Journal of the History of Sexuality* 15, no. 1 (2006): 30–64. Copyright © 2006 by the University of Texas Press. All rights reserved.
   Paul Peucker, "Wives of the Lamb: Moravian Brothers and Gender Around 1750," in *Masculinity, Senses, Spirit*, ed. Katherine Faull (Lewisburg: Bucknell University Press, 2011), 39–54.
   Paul Peucker, "The Songs of the Sifting: Understanding the Role of Bridal Mysticism in Moravian Piety During the Late 1740s," *Journal of Moravian History*, no. 3 (2007): 51–87.
   Paul Peucker, "'Blut' auf unsre grünen Bändchen: Die Sichtungszeit in der Herrnhuter Brüdergemeine," *Unitas Fratrum: Zeitschrift für Geschichte und Gegenwartsfragen der Brüdergemeine*, no. 49/50 (2002): 41–94.

LIBRARY OF CONGRESS CATALOGING-IN-PUBLICATION DATA

Peucker, Paul, 1963– , author.
   A time of sifting : mystical marriage and the crisis of Moravian piety in the eighteenth century / Paul Peucker.
        pages      cm — (Pietist, Moravian, and Anabaptist studies)
   Summary: "Examines the eighteenth-century crisis in the Moravian Church known as the Sifting Time, and the church's subsequent shift from radical beliefs and practices to conservative mainstream Protestantism"—Provided by publisher.
   Includes bibliographical references and index.
   ISBN 978-0-271-06643-1 (cloth : alk. paper)
   ISBN 978-0-271-06644-8 (pbk. : alk. paper)
   1. Moravian Church—History—18th century.
   2. Piety—History—18th century.
   3. Marriage—Religious aspects—Moravian Church—History—18th century.
   I. Title.

BX8565.P48   2015
284'.609033—dc23
2014045755

Copyright © 2015 The Pennsylvania State University
All rights reserved
Printed in the United States of America
Published by The Pennsylvania State University Press,
University Park, PA 16802–1003

The Pennsylvania State University Press is a member of the Association of American University Presses.

It is the policy of The Pennsylvania State University Press to use acid-free paper. Publications on uncoated stock satisfy the minimum requirements of American National Standard for Information Sciences—Permanence of Paper for Printed Library Material, ANSI Z39.48–1992.

*For Jeffrey*

CONTENTS

*List of Illustrations* .......................ix
*Prologue: The Hole* ......................xi
*Acknowledgments* ......................xiii
*List of Abbreviations*.....................xv

    Introduction ............................1
1  Herrnhut and Herrnhaag ................11
2  Historiography ........................33
3  The Crisis Revealed ....................46
4  Characteristics of the Sifting.............58
5  Songs of the Sifting....................93
6  The Actual Sifting.....................104
7  The Aftermath of the Sifting............135
8  The Post-Zinzendorf Era ...............147
9  What Was the Sifting Time?............165
10  The Sources ..........................172

*Notes* ................................187
*Bibliography* ..........................225
*Index* ................................243

ILLUSTRATIONS

1 View of the community of Herrnhaag . . . . . . . . . . . . . . . . . . . . . . . . . . . . . . . .22
2 The former sisters' house and *Grafenhaus* in Herrnhaag. . . . . . . . . . . . . . . . .43
3 Portrait of Joachim Heinrich Rubusch (1717–1773). . . . . . . . . . . . . . . . . . . . .51
4 *Ohne Kopf und Ungescheid*. . . . . . . . . . . . . . . . . . . . . . . . . . . . . . . . . . . . . . . 70
5 Two Moravian sisters in the grave with Jesus . . . . . . . . . . . . . . . . . . . . . . . . .87
6 *Singet, springet, klopfet in die Hände*. . . . . . . . . . . . . . . . . . . . . . . . . . . . . . . . 103
7 A Moravian Communion service in 1753 . . . . . . . . . . . . . . . . . . . . . . . . . . . 108
8 Circle of Moravian men with their arms linked together . . . . . . . . . . . . . . . 125
9 Portrait of Christian Renatus von Zinzendorf (1727–1752). . . . . . . . . . . . . .140
10 *Zinzendorf as the Teacher of the Nations* . . . . . . . . . . . . . . . . . . . . . . . . . . . . . 145

PROLOGUE: THE HOLE

At the south end of Main Street in the historic district of Bethlehem, Pennsylvania, sits the single brothers' house. This large stone building was completed in 1748 as the residence for the single men of the Moravian community. When I first saw the building while visiting Bethlehem with my parents in the 1980s, a large, gaping hole was prominently visible in the center of the north façade, above the two entrance doors. It marked the location of a stone with an inscription that adorned the brothers' house when it was first built. The original inscription read, "Vater und Mutter und lieber Mann, habt Ehr vom Jünglings Plan" (Father and Mother and dear husband, be honored by the young men's plan). On the south side of the brothers' house a sun dial was placed with the text "Gloria Pleurae" (glory be to the side wound).[1]

Both texts summarize the theology of the Moravians at the time of construction of the brothers' house: the Trinity was described as the Holy Family, with God the Father, the Holy Ghost as the Mother, and Christ as the husband. Christ's side wound, the last wound Christ suffered on the cross when the Roman soldier pierced his side to see if he had already died (John 19:34), was the focus of Moravian devotion at the time.

Soon, however, Moravians became embarrassed by the text. A Swedish visitor in 1754 noted how Thomas Benzien, one of the Bethlehem pastors, evaded questions about the text of the inscription.[2]

> Pastor Unander came forward with the serious question, "What is the meaning of the inscription which is read over the door of the unmarried Brethren's house, *'Vater und Mutter und lieber Mann,'* etc.?"
>
> "Ah," answered Mr. Benzien, "that is something that he devised who built the house. I, for my part, have never approved of it."
>
> I fell into the conversation, and said, "Be assured, gentlemen, that although the words are altogether mystical, yet we well understand their meaning."
>
> "I doubt not, gentlemen," he answered, "that you do indeed understand it, and that you are not ignorant of the Brethren's arrangements in other places."

"But," said Pastor Unander, "would it not be better if those words did not stand there?"

"Yes," said he; "so I also think that it would be better. Yet no one can doubt that the man who first put that up had a good meaning with it."

It was undoubtedly Mr. Benzien's idea that that should be kept among the secrets of the Brethren, and not stand before the eyes of every one, whereby their Society might be misjudged. For that he is one of their chief men, who approves of all their inventions, cannot be doubted.[3]

Did Brother Benzien's uneasiness relate to the fact that the Holy Spirit was called Mother or was it the fact that Christ was referred to as the husband of the single men? In any case, at some point during the eighteenth century the stone was removed so that no one would be offended by the text, leaving a gaping hole in the façade. In later years the brothers' house was stuccoed over, and the hole disappeared from sight.

When the brothers' house was restored to its original appearance in the 1960s and the stucco was removed, the empty hole reappeared. For many years the hole remained prominently visible, reminding passersby of the way Moravians treated the history of the late 1740s.

When I moved to Bethlehem in early 2004, I noticed to my surprise that the hole had been filled with a replica of the original stone, bearing the same inscription that once caused such great embarrassment to the Moravians. Today the inscription is incapable of causing much discomfort: the number of people in Bethlehem who can read German is limited nowadays, and who would really understand the meaning of such a cryptic text?

The tablet, however, is representative of how Moravians have dealt with their history and theology of the late 1740s. After first giving it one of the most prominent locations in the community, Moravian leaders chipped the stone away and discarded it, leaving an empty hole of taboo and ignorance. The stone was later replaced, at a time when few people could grasp its meaning except for those interested in unraveling one of the enigmas of Moravian history.

It is the piety of the late 1740s and the subsequent embarrassment about this piety that form the subject of this book.

ACKNOWLEDGMENTS

Over the years, many people have helped me, knowingly or unknowingly, to write this book. My study of the Sifting Time began when I was archivist at the Unity Archives in Herrnhut. Many relevant finds were made unexpectedly while I was assisting researchers or processing collections. Ursula Hommel brought the manuscript hymnbook from 1749 to my attention. I also thank Karl-Eugen Langerfeld, assistant archivist at the time, for his useful comments. Current Unity archivist Rüdiger Kröger, and especially staff member Olaf Nippe, have been very supportive and provided numerous useful sources and images. Michael Kießling digitized paintings and drawings. Lanie Graf Yaswinski, former assistant archivist at the Moravian Archives in Bethlehem, Pennsylvania, and Thomas McCullough, current assistant archivist, have helped me in many ways. Nancy Strobel and Debbi Gaspar, interlibrary loan assistants at Reeves Library of Moravian College, have ordered numerous books and articles for me.

I am grateful to Jonathan Yonan for encouraging me to write this book. For sharing valuable insights I thank Katherine Carté Engel, Katherine Faull, Arthur Freeman, Aaron Fogleman, Scott Gordon, Markus Gill, Colin Podmore, Beverly Smaby, and Peter Vogt.

I thank Pennsylvania State University Press for publishing this book. I am especially grateful to Craig Atwood, editor of the series in which this study appears, whose advice has proven invaluable in the realization of this publication, as well as to the anonymous reviewers for providing constructive and helpful comments on an earlier version of the manuscript. It was a pleasure working with acquisitions editor Kathryn Yahner and copyeditor John Morris.

My greatest gratitude, however, is for Jeffrey Long, who has accompanied this project from the beginning. He shared in my enthusiasm for new discoveries; he helped me photograph hundreds of documents; he allowed me to work on this project for so many evenings and weekends; and he tirelessly edited the entire text before it went to anyone else.

Moravians were German speakers, and most of the sources used for this study were written in German. All translations are my own if not mentioned otherwise. If contemporary translations exist and are useful, I used these and indicated the source in the notes. The original German is generally included in the notes, especially if the original wording is particularly important for a correct understanding. If the source is printed or otherwise easily accessible, or if a translation into English is sufficient, the original German is left out.

Moravian texts frequently use diminutives. These are often translated into English as "little" or "small." However, Moravian diminutives express tenderness and it is more appropriate to translate them accordingly. Therefore, a *Seitenhöhlchen* is not a "little side hole" but rather a "dear side hole."[1] In quoting Bible verses or translating biblical terms I have used the King James Version as coming closest in connotation to the 1545 Luther translation used by German-speaking Moravians at the time.

ABBREVIATIONS

BethSB      Records of the Single Brothers' Choir in Bethlehem in MAB
EBG Zeist   Archives of the Moravian congregation at Zeist, Netherlands, held at the Utrechts Archief in Utrecht, Netherlands
*JMH*       *Journal of Moravian History*
MAB         Moravian Archives, Bethlehem, Pennsylvania
PP Zdf      Zinzendorf Papers at Moravian Archives, Bethlehem
*PuN*       *Pietismus und Neuzeit: Ein Jahrbuch zur Geschichte des neueren Protestantismus*
*TMHS*      *Transactions of the Moravian Historical Society*
UA          Unity Archives, central archives of the worldwide Moravian Church in Herrnhut, Germany
UEC         Unity Elders' Conference
*UF*        *Unitas Fratrum: Zeitschrift für Geschichte und Gegenwartsfragen der Brüdergemeine*
*ZBG*       *Zeitschrift für Brüdergeschichte*

INTRODUCTION

The Lord led us into a sifting that
admittedly is a most severe punishment,
of which one cannot think but with horror.
—*Interim constitution 1762*

## The Ceremony of December 6, 1748

During the afternoon of December 6, 1748, the single men in the Moravian community of Herrnhaag took part in an unusual ceremony. Their leader, Christian Renatus von Zinzendorf, son of the leader of this new controversial international religious movement, gathered the men in the chapel, where he declared them all to be women. No longer were they to consider themselves men, but from then on they would all pass as "sisters." The following day, Christel, as most Moravians affectionately called him, together with his fellow elder Joachim Rubusch, went to nearby Marienborn, seat of the church's theological seminary, and repeated the ceremony with the single men present there. What followed was a scandal that caused great embarrassment among many in the church, prompting Count Zinzendorf to intervene when he learned about it.

Even though three independent sources for the gender-changing ceremony exist, this event has not been discussed in any studies of eighteenth-century religion. The happenings of December 6 and 7, 1748, however, form a crucial moment in the history of the Moravian Church. Examining the developments leading up to the events as well as the reactions that soon followed will give us a good understanding not only of the Moravian movement but also of the vitality and diversity of Christian religion in the Atlantic world of the eighteenth century. In declaring the men to be women, Christel built on various aspects of his father's theology relating to bridal mysticism, salvation, the Lutheran understanding of justification by faith, ideas on gender roles and gender identity, the ideal of *imitatio Dei*, sexuality, and eschatological expectations.

During the 1750s Moravians began to speak about a crisis that had recently occurred within their communities, of which the gender-changing ceremony of 1748 was the most dramatic and, to many, the most disturbing aspect. They called this crisis a time of "sifting," believing the strength of their faith had been tested by Satan: "And the Lord said, Simon, Simon, behold, Satan has desired to have you, that he may sift you as wheat" (Luke 22:31). The idea of a sifting occurring in the 1740s shaped later Moravian historiography, but no one has given a suitable definition or description of this Sifting Time.

I will argue that this so-called Sifting Time was a culmination of Moravian theology of the 1730s and 1740s. It was a combination of Lutheran theology, with its emphasis on justification by faith alone; of bridal mysticism; and of traditional passion symbolism. It was also a reaction against the austere Pietism of the time, resulting in provocative playfulness. At the end of the 1740s these elements, combined with the belief that the union with Christ could be experienced during sexual intercourse, culminated in antinomianism and perfectionism. The actual Sifting occurred when Moravians began to believe that the union with Christ could be experienced not only during marital intercourse but during extramarital sex as well. This undermined notions of marriage as a sacred bond that lay at the core of Moravian theology. The crisis revealed deficiencies of Moravian teaching and eventually led to a transformation of Moravian piety. After Zinzendorf's death in 1760, Moravians were faced with a chaotic situation left behind by their leader: they were under attack from Lutheran and other Protestant opponents and faced with internal turmoil caused by Zinzendorf's lack of leadership as the crisis of the Sifting peaked and by his refusal to acknowledge that his own theology had led to the crisis. In the end, Moravians distanced themselves from any radical elements in their teaching and adapted to more generally accepted forms of Protestantism.

The main geographical focus of this study will be the community of Herrnhaag, the Moravian center of the 1740s, located north of Frankfurt am Main, but the geographical spread of ideas and practices connected to the Sifting extended far beyond Herrnhaag.

Religion and Sexuality

The crisis of the Sifting Time was connected most of all to eighteenth-century ideas on religion and sexuality. As recently as 1997 the study of religion and sexuality could still be called "an underdeveloped area of research," but historians have since worked to fill this gap.[1] Among scholars of Pietism as well, interest in questions of sexuality and marriage has increased in recent years.[2] Religious concepts such as original sin, purity, marriage, and celibacy had an impact on sexuality, and Christian ideas and institutions shaped sexual attitudes, as religious leaders attempted to control the sexual lives of their followers. But sexuality also influenced religion: around the turn of the eighteenth century several religious people and communities separated from the established church because of the issue of sexuality.

A. G. Roeber draws attention to the debate among early modern Protestants about the nature of marriage: is marriage a legal bond that asserts the authority of men as heads of the household, or is it a partnership in which husband and wife together pursue the ideal of holiness, reflecting the relationship of Christ with the church? Luther as well as Spener tended to the latter view, while other theologians, among them Pietist leader August Hermann Francke, rejected the "quasi-sacramental friendship marriage."[3] Willi Temme has pointed out that around the turn of the eighteenth century many Pietists raised questions regarding marriage, gender, physicality, and sexuality.[4] For them these were pressing problems, solved in diverse ways. Traditionally, lust (concupiscence) was considered a sin, by which original sin passed from one generation to another. The question therefore was, if sexual lust was sinful, how could sexual intercourse be acceptable?

For most Protestants of the Reformation, as well as for most nonseparatist Pietists, the purpose of sex within marriage was procreation, and it was consequently sanctified. Many radical Pietists did not accept such reasoning. For them, sex remained sinful, be it within or outside marriage. Some radical Pietists had high regard for so-called virginal marriages, in which both partners abstained from sex by mutual agreement. Others, such as Johann Georg Gichtel in the Netherlands and Conrad Beissel in Pennsylvania, taught strict celibacy, believing the truly converted should not defile themselves with sex.[5] Gottfried Arnold, who in his earlier works promoted celibacy, did not find much sympathy among his former admirers when he married in 1701, seemingly abandoning his earlier ideals of purity.[6] Some groups, in fact, believed sexuality could be cleared of any sinfulness. Followers of Eva von Buttlar, united in the Society of Mother Eva, believed they could be purified from earthly desire and could thus "blend" together with the body of Christ while having sexual intercourse among each other.[7] Similar ideas about sinlessness and perfectionism existed among Moravians during the late 1740s.

Sexuality was an important question among eighteenth-century Moravians.[8] Like other radical Pietists, Zinzendorf had struggled with the question of whether a true Christian could marry or not. It has been suggested that he was influenced by the ideas of Ernst Christoph Hochmann von Hochenau on marriage.[9] On the question whether marriage was a legal institution or a holy bond, Hochmann distinguished between the marriage of ordinary (unconverted) people and true Christians. Hochmann believed secular people did not need to have their marriages legitimized by the church; a strictly secular performance of their marriages was sufficient. Church weddings should be reserved for Christian believers, whose bond was to be a reflection of the love of Christ for the church. Representing a higher degree of marriage, according to Hochmann, were the "virginal marriages" for true Christians, who together committed their lives as warriors for Jesus. The highest degree of marriage was celibacy, where the individual believer was betrothed to Jesus.[10]

Zinzendorf came to the conclusion that a Christian was able to marry. He agreed with the radical Pietists that lust by definition was sinful, even within marriage. His solution was not to abstain from sex but to remove lust from sexual intercourse. When sex was performed without lust, it was not merely acceptable, but became a divine, sacramental act. Zinzendorf taught his followers to have sex without lust, during which they were able to experience the union with Christ.[11] Zinzendorf's teachings on marriage, especially his concept of sexual intercourse between husband and wife as a sacrament, placed the Moravians at the center of the ongoing Protestant discussion on marriage.[12] Eventually, these same teachings, as I will argue, resulted in the crisis of the Sifting Time, when Moravians began to celebrate the bond between Christ and the church outside of sanctioned, marital relationships.

The Sifting Time

The Moravian Church began in 1722 when a small group of refugees and descendants of the old Unitas Fratrum (Unity of Brethren), a pre-Reformation Protestant church in Bohemia that had suffered under severe persecution during the seventeenth century, settled on the estate of Nikolaus Ludwig, Count Zinzendorf in eastern Saxony, founding the community of Herrnhut. The count was not only their secular lord but also the spiritual leader of the movement that emanated from the Herrnhut community. Awakened Christians from various parts of Germany and beyond joined the Herrnhuters and founded new communities on the European continent, in Britain, and in North America. Missionaries went out to the slaves in the Caribbean, to the Inuit in Greenland and Labrador, to various tribes in Africa, and to non-

Christian nations in the East. The Moravians claimed to be a continuation of the Unity of Brethren, and in fact the British Parliament passed an act in 1749 acknowledging this claim. Central to their ideas was a personal surrender to Christ, whose suffering and death on the cross were to touch the heart of the true believer. Chapter 1 will explain how the Moravians (named after the country of origin of some of the first settlers) grew into a transatlantic religious movement of thousands of people. Like the Methodists, the Moravians were one of the significant religious renewal movements of the eighteenth century. But while eighteenth-century Methodism was predominantly an Anglo-American movement, Moravianism attracted Germans, Scandinavians, English, Dutch, Caribbean slaves, American Indians, and Balts, as well as the odd Italian, Persian, and Frenchman.

In recent years historians have studied many aspects of the eighteenth-century Moravians, such as art, education, music, sexuality, autobiographies, theology, linguistics, cross-cultural exchanges, and transatlantic economics.[13] Many of these studies imply that Moravians had a "dark side," a period of crisis when things got out of hand, during which the use of bizarre and repulsive language alienated previous sympathizers. The Sifting Time is primarily a historiographical construct, invented by contemporaries to label a crisis in their recent past. Over time, the meaning of the Sifting Time as a historical category shifted. As we will see in chapter 2, later historians, unaware of exactly what this crisis had entailed, began applying the term to their own interpretation of anything unorthodox and out of the ordinary found in the records. The further away an observer stood from the original crisis, the longer and more comprehensive he or she considered the Sifting Time to have been.

What was the Sifting Time, and why did Moravians perceive it as a crisis? What role did the concept of a Sifting Time play in the development of Moravian self-identity and historiography? How do the ideas and practices of the Sifting Time relate to other religious groups of the time? This study of this relatively short crisis will touch upon questions of gender, masculinity, marriage, sexuality, and religion in the eighteenth century. We will examine the place of Moravianism within the world of radical Pietism and the influence of mysticism on a transatlantic movement during an age before national-confessional cultures dominated the stage. Examining the nature of the Sifting Time will help us get a better understanding of the vitality and inventiveness of religion during the eighteenth century.

While most historical narratives on the Moravians include the Sifting Time, its exact nature remains vague. A general sense of embarrassment discouraged early Moravian historians from describing the precise character of the crisis and led them to destroy any archival evidence documenting it. Later generations of historians therefore found it increasingly difficult to define the Sifting Time. Thus, the Sifting Time evolved from a taboo subject into an unsolved mystery of Moravian historiography. Due to the lack of adequate source material, many previous interpretations made the mistake of inferring that anything unusual and unorthodox during the 1740s was an element of the Sifting Time.[14]

Often the Sifting Time has been interpreted as a period defined by an excessive focus on the blood and wounds of Christ. Such an interpretation can hardly suffice. If the Sifting Time was really about intensive blood-and-wounds language, exuberant festivities, and playful silliness, why was the reaction from Moravian leaders so severe? The strong rejection of the Sifting Time must have been connected to something larger than we previously thought it to be.

In 1996 Craig Atwood argued that in order to understand the Sifting Time one must study how contemporaries defined it. He was able to demonstrate that "those aspects of the theology and piety of Zinzendorf and the Brüdergemeine in the mid-eighteenth century which later scholars have considered the essence of the Sifting Time are almost absent from Zinzendorf's rebuke to the community."[15] Consequently, blood-and-wounds theology, the adoration of the Holy Spirit as Mother, the language of the Litany of the Wounds, and an "over-emphasis on religious devotion" should be seen not as particular aspects of the Sifting Time but as general characteristics of Moravian piety in the eighteenth century. This book will follow a similar methodology and attempt to establish which developments in the 1740s contemporaries found so disturbing that they perceived them as a crisis. We will consider texts by contemporaries and examine how they defined the crisis. Based on a close reading of these descriptions and statements, we will look at the preceding years and analyze how the crisis developed. It will also be important to place the ideas of the Sifting Time in the context of other religious traditions. By finding an answer to the question of what the Moravian Sifting Time entailed, we will gain better insight into the Moravian movement of the eighteenth century and how it adapted to notions of reasonable religion and to changing gender roles.

In chapter 3 we will lay out the chronology of events, from the moment Moravians realized something had gone wrong, to the issuing of Zinzendorf's letter that defined the crisis, and finally to dealing with the crisis. We will also discuss the terminology used to describe the crisis and consider the question of how the crisis should be dated. The crisis only became a crisis when it was named as such. By writing his letter of reprimand in February of 1749, Zinzendorf publicly admitted something had gone wrong, and based on his letter and other contemporary texts looking back on the crisis, we will attempt to detail and explain the various elements that Zinzendorf and his contemporaries believed defined the crisis. Chapter 4 will begin to lay out these aspects, although a full understanding of the crisis cannot occur until chapter 6.

Hymns played an essential role in Moravian life and worship. Before turning to the height of the crisis, in chapter 5 we will pause to examine the hymns that were used during the late 1740s and their connection to bridal mysticism. Some of these hymns were never published but rather distributed in handwritten hymnbooks that were destroyed after the nature of the crisis had been revealed. In chapter 6 we will turn to the crisis itself and try to discern what the Sifting Time comprised and why it was considered so scandalous that most related records were destroyed.

In chapters 7 and 8 we will treat the church's reaction to the crisis, both in the immediate aftermath and over the decades that followed. As I will argue, the transformation of the Moravian Church during the second half of the eighteenth century is a consequence of the crisis of the late 1740s. The Sifting Time caused the Moravian Church to change course radically and become a noncontroversial mainline church, closely related to the official German Protestant churches (*Landeskirchen*) but with obvious Pietist leanings and a separate identity.

In the final chapter we will discuss Moravian record keeping, the symbolic role archives played for Moravians, and how Moravians constructed their history by consciously collecting as well as by purposely destroying historical records. We will discuss what source material survives and how these resources were able to provide an understanding of the Sifting.

The crisis of the Sifting Time was a defining moment in the history of the Moravians. It was the culmination of Moravian piety of the late 1730s and 1740s, and its aftermath determined the development of the church for many decades. In order to fully understand the Moravian movement during the period of its rapid expansion from a local phenomenon (Herrnhut) into a worldwide religious network, it is necessary to study the Sifting. In this study I want to consider the theology and practices of the 1740s seriously rather than dismissing them as nonsense or aberrant theology. Moravian piety of the 1740s needs to be studied in its own right. Studying these years will also give us better understanding of Zinzendorf himself. We will see that the idea of a Sifting Time later served as a historiographical construct to either alienate

Zinzendorf from the "true" Moravian Church or separate him from his own theology. Atwood argues that the traditional understanding of the Sifting Time has "in fact distorted our understanding of the entire Zinzendorfian era and the evolution of Moravian theology and piety."[16]

At the same time, the Sifting Time was an expression of eighteenth-century Christianity. Thousands of people, Europeans and non-Europeans alike, were attracted to the Moravians during the late 1740s, and many of them, to varying degrees, participated in what we would now label as aspects of the Sifting Time. Thus, this is not a German story but rather a European and even a transatlantic story: European religion manifested in the Atlantic world.

Zinzendorf's theology was perhaps not as unusual for eighteenth-century Europeans as is sometimes suggested.[17] The Moravians were but one example of radical Christian social experimentation. Other groups, such as the Shakers, the Inspirationists, the Society of Mother Eva, the French Prophets, and Beissel's community at Ephrata, to name but a few, practiced similarly unconventional ideas, but they left few detailed records. The Moravians, with their tradition of detailed record keeping, provide a unique nuanced perspective on radical religion in the period of the Enlightenment.

Another reason for studying the Sifting Time is the resulting consequences and what they tell us about the transformation of radical religious movements over time. Traditionally, Moravians have presented the Sifting Time as an aberration, a short but exceptional phase that was sometimes not even worthy of mention, after which the church regained its true calling. I will argue instead that the Sifting Time was a crucial period in the history of the Moravian Church as it developed from a radical-Pietist group into a noncontroversial evangelical group, the culmination of developments that began early in the church's history. At the same time, for many contemporaries inside the church the Sifting was also proof that certain aspects of Zinzendorf's theology and practice had undesirable consequences.

The specter of their recent history continued to loom over the Moravian congregations until the end of the eighteenth century. The fear of anything out of the ordinary and the desire to turn to the safety of mainstream Protestantism led to the conservatism of the second half of the century. As a consequence, Moravians revisited their theology regarding marriage. From a sacramental act by which the believer could experience union with the divine, Moravian marriage became a much more conventional institution. Without the Sifting Time Moravian leaders would not have changed their course so radically. We cannot understand the Moravian Church of the second half of the eighteenth century without understanding the effects of the Sifting Time. Nor can we fully understand Moravian piety and practice of the first decades of the eighteenth century from the perspective of the second half if we are unaware of the changes that occurred after 1760.

## The Moravians Within the Context of Radical Pietism

Radical Pietists are usually defined as those individuals or groups who separated from the established church, as opposed to ecclesiastical Pietists, who remained within the church.[18] Schneider calls the formation of established groups within radical Pietism a new phenomenon in the eighteenth century.[19] In addition to the Moravians, such groups included the seventeenth-century Labadists, the Society of Mother Eve, the Schwarzenau Brethren, and the Inspirationists; although the last two still exist in the United States, they never matched the size and spread that the Moravians achieved within only a few decades of their origin.

Zinzendorf and his followers would not have agreed with either classification: they distanced themselves from the ecclesiastical Pietists of Halle at an early time, and they categorically denied any separatist intention. However, from its beginning, the community at Herrnhut developed its own organization and held its own church meetings independent from the parish church of Berthelsdorf, to which Herrnhut officially belonged. Zinzendorf and the Moravians disguised their separatist intentions by proclaiming themselves an ancient pre-Reformation church, the Unity of Brethren or Unitas Fratrum; as such, they gained official recognition from various European governments.[20]

Radical Pietists often shared features beyond separatism. Both Schneider and Wallmann consider Philadelphian ideas the binding element of radical Pietism,[21] and Shantz lists several additional common features: the language of personal and cosmic renewal as found in the works of Jakob Böhme and Johann Arndt; a migratory lifestyle; an eclectic way of drawing from other traditions such as Lutheranism, mysticism, and alchemy; an indifference to the importance of confessional differences; a greater role for women; and the ideal of forming communities of true Christians. Some groups had charismatic leaders whom they considered divinely inspired.[22] In his fourfold typology of radical Pietism, Shantz places the Moravians under the category of the "sect model."[23]

Moravians have not always been recognized as a radical Pietist group; sometimes Moravianism been treated as its own form of (ecclesiastical) Pietism.[24] There are two reasons for this. First of all, Zinzendorf and the Moravians deliberately avoided the impression of separatism; they insisted that their community was the continuation of the ancient Unity of Brethren, while Zinzendorf tried his best to place his movement on a Lutheran foundation. In addition, during the last decades of the eighteenth century the Moravians explicitly distanced themselves from their radical past, promulgating a reinvented, nonenthusiastic identity that has somewhat distorted the view of their earlier history. Certain aspects of Moravian theology and practice during the first half of the eighteenth century were simply overlooked, ignored, or dismissed as premature aberrations that were not important in the long run. The historiographical concept of a Sifting Time as a (brief) period of deviation conveniently made it possible to group anything unconventional as a feature of the Sifting Time. This study will focus on some of these unconventional aspects of Moravian piety.

As Shantz recently pointed out in his study of German Pietism, there has been a shift in the historiography of Pietism. For most of the twentieth century, historians have downplayed mystical and radical influences in Pietism and emphasized the Lutheran roots of the renewal movement. In recent years, however, the study of radical Pietism has thrived.[25] New studies have been published on groups like the Ephrata community, the Schwarzenau Brethren, and the Mother Eva Society.[26] A similar shift can be seen in Moravian studies. Scholars of Moravian history, including Hans Schneider, Craig Atwood, Katherine Faull, Beverly Smaby, Aaron Fogleman, Peter Vogt, Marsha Keith Schuchard, and, most recently, Seth Moglen and Derrick Miller, have become more interested in questions of gender, sexuality, the role of mysticism, and the less conventional aspects of Zinzendorf's theology.[27]

This is a study about Zinzendorf's theology and how it was received by his followers. Zinzendorf's theology was authoritative and dominant among Moravians, but his followers developed his ideas further and sometimes came to conclusions that revealed undesired consequences. The Sifting Time was the logical consequence of Zinzendorf's teachings. The relationship between Zinzendorf and his followers began on his estate during the 1720s.

# 1

HERRNHUT AND HERRNHAAG

Herrnhut shall remain in a constant bond
of love with all brethren and children of
God in all denominations.
—*Brotherly Union and Agreement of Herrnhut, 1727*

Shortly before Christmas of 1722, the young Count Zinzendorf and his new wife were making their first trip together from Dresden to their estate in Berthelsdorf, located in a part of eastern Saxony called Oberlausitz (Upper Lusatia). On May 15 of that year, Zinzendorf had purchased Berthelsdorf from his grandmother, Henriette Katharina von Gersdorf, whose estate, Grosshennersdorf, was nearby. In August he became engaged to Erdmuth Dorothea Reuss, and on September 7, 1722, they were married in Ebersdorf, the home of her family in Thuringia. Their wedding anniversary would later become the festival day of all married couples in the Moravian Church. They took up residence in Dresden, where he had accepted a position at the court of the king of Saxony.

As the carriage entered the forest belonging to the estate, Count Ludwig noticed the lights of a house that had not been there the previous time he had traveled this road. Twenty-five years later, on the anniversary of the founding of Herrnhut, Zinzendorf would recall: "I asked and was told this was my house; the people from Moravia had built it. We then entered the house and visited Augustin Neisser and his family."[1] This was the Zinzendorfs' first personal encounter with a small group of Protestant refugees from Moravia who would form the core of the Herrnhut community.

Within twenty years the unconventional union between an imperial count and a group of propertyless religious exiles developed into a transatlantic religious movement that affected the lives of thousands of people in different parts of the world. The refugee settlement on the road between Löbau and

Zittau grew into the town of Herrnhut, the center of the Brüdergemeine or, as it became known in English, the Moravian Church. Similar communities based upon the model of Herrnhut were founded in other parts of Germany, in England, in the Netherlands, as well as in Pennsylvania and North Carolina. Missionaries, mostly untrained lay people, went out to remote places such as the Caribbean, Greenland, South America, and southern Africa to preach the gospel and to establish mission stations. Thousands of Europeans joined the Herrnhuters to live in their church-controlled communities; many others had to be turned down. This chapter will examine how Moravian theology was rooted in radical-Pietist Philadelphian thought and how Moravians chose the identity of an ancient church in order to avoid suspicions of separatism. It will also explain how Moravian devotion of the blood and wounds of Christ in combination with mysticism formed the basis for the ideas of the Sifting Time.

## Zinzendorf

During his upbringing in the house of his grandmother, Nikolaus Ludwig, Count von Zinzendorf, was exposed to a variety of religious ideas. His grandmother, Henriette Katharina von Gersdorf, was a well-educated woman who had published her first book, a poetic meditation on the suffering of Christ, when she was only seventeen years old. An analysis of a recently discovered inventory of her library indicates that she had a broad interest in theology (including radical Pietist authors such as Johann Wilhelm and Johanna Eleonora Petersen, Jane Leade, Gottfried Arnold, and Christian Hoburg), literature, alchemy, languages, and history.[2] Six weeks after Ludwig's birth in the Saxon capital city of Dresden on May 26, 1700, his father died.[3] His mother remarried, but because of the amount of time her second husband, a Prussian field marshal, spent on campaign, she continued to live with her mother, and when she was able to join her husband she left Ludwig behind in Grosshennersdorf. When Ludwig was ten years old, his family sent him to Halle to be educated in Francke's school for the nobility. After spending six years in the center of Pietism, he went to Wittenberg. Although he was formally a student of law, Ludwig's main interest was theology. In Wittenberg he read a great number of theological works and met with leading theologians. His education culminated in a grand tour that took him to the Netherlands and France.

Hans Schneider points out that the key to understanding Zinzendorf's activities and his ecclesiology is his Philadelphian ideal of uniting the true children of God.⁴ Throughout his life, Zinzendorf strove to overcome denominational differences and to bring together different confessions within one movement on the basis of brotherly love rather than confessional uniformity. The Philadelphian ideal, as Schneider argues and as will be discussed in more detail below, underlies the founding of Herrnhut and remained a deciding factor in Zinzendorf's plans throughout his life.

The Philadelphian ideal originated with John Portage and Jane Leade in England during the 1670s and 1680s and soon became popular among radical Pietists in Germany as well. The term "Philadelphia" refers to one of the seven churches mentioned in the biblical book of Revelation as well as to the "brotherly love" shared by the true children of God among each other. The seven churches in Revelation are all identified according to their specific characteristics, which the supporters of the Philadelphian movement applied to different phases in history. For example, they believed the Protestant churches of their own time lived in the era of Sardis, when Christianity, despite knowing the truth of the gospel, was spiritually "dead" (Rev. 3:1). After the era of Sardis, the era of Philadelphia would follow, when the true children of God who had kept the word and had patiently endured (Rev. 3:7–13) would be gathered "from the four winds" (Matt. 24:31) to be the wife of the Lamb (Rev. 21:9). A crucial biblical text to the Philadelphians—including Zinzendorf—was John 17:21: "that they all may be one"; that is, the dispersed children of God would be gathered and become one. According to Schneider, the Philadelphians believed their religion of the heart, which concentrated on the essentials, was impartial, unlike the divided theologies of the denominations. Philadelphians believed themselves to be part of a transdenominational community of true believers, as opposed to the corrupted institutional churches ("sects"), which were too much caught up in the world. They also believed this transdenominational church would soon be realized on earth. Zinzendorf's community of Herrnhut, too, was founded with strong eschatological expectations,⁵ as became even more evident during the late 1740s.

Many radical Pietists followed the call to "exit from Babel" and leave the institutional church.⁶ Separatist groups started in different parts of Germany and among German emigrants in Pennsylvania. In Ebersdorf, Thuringia, the home of Zinzendorf's friend Heinrich XXIX, Count Reuss, who had accompanied him on parts of his grand tour, Zinzendorf encountered one of these groups.⁷ Zinzendorf had been exposed to Philadelphian literature as an adolescent at his grandmother's house as well as in the Netherlands during his grand tour, and now for the first time he experienced a congregation consisting of awakened representatives from different religious movements living together in harmony. It made such an impression on the young man that in the following years he modeled the communities in his manor house in Berthelsdorf and in Herrnhut after this example.

The importance of Zinzendorf's experience in Ebersdorf can hardly be overstated. Not only was Ebersdorf a formative influence on the Philadelphian character of his ecclesiology, but he also encountered there a form of blood-and-wounds piety that made a deep impression on him. In Ebersdorf he was first confronted with the ideas of Ernst Christoph Hochmann von Hochenau, which would have a lasting impact on his views on sexuality and marriage.[8] And in Ebersdorf Zinzendorf also met his future wife, Erdmuth Dorothea Reuss. Born on November 7, 1700, Erdmuth had grown up in the Pietist congregation of the manor house in Ebersdorf.[9]

The Early Years of Herrnhut

In 1722, shortly after purchasing his estate, Zinzendorf gave permission to a small group of religious refugees from Moravia to settle there. They came from Zauchtenthal, or Zauchtel (Czech: Suchdol nad Oudrou), and their leader was Christian David, a carpenter who had converted to Protestantism and become an itinerant preacher in the area around his hometown of Söhle.[10] David reached out to Zinzendorf through connections with a Pietist group in Görlitz. Within five years Herrnhut grew to a community of around thirty houses inhabited by 133 adults and 87 children.[11]

Since the defeat of the Protestants at the battle of White Mountain in 1620, groups of Bohemians had repeatedly settled in Saxony and other neighboring Protestant lands. Grosshennersdorf, the estate of Zinzendorf's grandmother, was home to a relatively large colony of Czech-speaking Protestant refugees.[12] The Schwenkfelders from Silesia also found a (temporary) home on Zinzendorf's estate.[13] Protestants from other parts of Europe settled in Herrnhut as well; in 1727 about a third of the adults (forty-four people) had come not from Moravia but from various German territories.

Surprisingly, no study of the early years of Herrnhut has been written; consequently, we do not have a good understanding of how this settlement of refugees developed into the center of a worldwide church.[14] What made Herrnhut different from other colonies of religious exiles? An important factor was Zinzendorf's leadership, his theology, and his connections with German nobility. He intended to incorporate the Moravian immigrants into his plans to develop a Philadelphian community.

As Herrnhut grew in the five years that followed its founding, so did the diversity of ideas and expectations among its people. In order to bring unity, Zinzendorf, as lord of the manor, introduced rules and regulations for all inhabitants of the new village. Furthermore, bylaws were presented by Zinzendorf for those Herrnhuters who wanted to be part of a voluntary association modeled on the primitive church, consisting of "brethren" living in unity with the "children of God" in all denominations.[15] In May of 1727 most of the inhabitants signed the bylaws. Life in Herrnhut was now placed on a formal footing. More important to the self-understanding of the Herrnhuters, however, was an event that took place that summer. On August 13, during a communion service in the parish church at Berthelsdorf, a revival occurred that formed the people of Herrnhut into a tight religious community. From then on Herrnhut was the center of the Renewed Moravian Church. Traditionally, the early years of the village are told through the lens of this revival.

A Renewed Church or a New Church?

The continuity of the Herrnhut church with the Unity of Brethren (Unitas Fratrum) has traditionally been treated as a given in Moravian historiography. However, many historians question whether this continuity was not merely a historical construct, expressing a wish of the early Herrnhuters.[16] The Unity of Brethren originated in 1457 or 1458 among moderate followers of the Czech reformer Jan Hus and spread throughout Bohemia and Moravia.[17] With the defeat of the Protestant nobility at the battle of White Mountain in 1620, however, the Unity of Brethren, like all other Protestant groups, was outlawed. Some members left and went to neighboring countries such as Poland, where a branch of the Unity of Brethren survived well into the twentieth century. Those Brethren who had remained within the Habsburg Empire had the choice of converting to Roman Catholicism or going underground. Those who chose the latter would play an important role in the traditional narrative of the Moravian Church. Remaining faithful to the Protestant faith and practices of their ancestors, they continued to meet in houses, barns, and guarded places in the mountains. They were called the "hidden seed," a seed that would lie dormant until a century later, when it brought forth the awakened Christians who left their homes and farmsteads in Moravia to renew the church of their ancestors in Herrnhut.[18]

As we have seen above, Zinzendorf's ecclesiology was characterized by Philadelphian ideals. Schneider argues that Herrnhut from its early beginnings was organized as a Philadelphian community, modeled on Zinzendorf's experiences in Ebersdorf. The bond of brotherly love with other denominations was firmly established in the statutes of Herrnhut from May of 1722. From early on, Herrnhut considered itself to be an independent congregation, even challenging the authority of the pastor in Berthelsdorf, to whose parish Herrnhut officially belonged.[19]

The early Herrnhuters patterned their community on the example of primitive Christianity. As their guide they used *The First Love*, an exhaustive work on the early Christians written by Gottfried Arnold, a declared Philadelphian. Arnold believed "the first love," which the church of his own time had lost (Rev. 2:4), could be regained by returning to the faith and practice of the early Christians. The example of early Christianity and the Philadelphian ideal went hand in hand. For Philadelphians, the primitive church served as the example of true, uncorrupted Christianity. Although the Herrnhuters were required to attend Sunday worship at the parish church in Berthelsdorf, they developed a range of additional religious meetings held in the *Saal* (hall) of the boarding school on the town square in Herrnhut. These meetings (singing meetings, love feasts, foot washings, prayer meetings, etc.) were modeled after descriptions of the early Christians by Arnold and other authors. Many of the offices in Herrnhut were also patterned after this ideal.[20] Soon, however, the ideal of primitive Christianity was complemented by another concept: the renewal of the ancient Unity of Brethren.

We do not know how much the early immigrants from Moravia were aware of their religious history, nor do we know what their expectations of the community in Herrnhut would have been.[21] It seems highly unlikely that from the outset they strove to reinstate the church of their fathers; this idea must have originated relatively late. When confronted with the differing views of others living in Berthelsdorf and Herrnhut, the Moravian immigrants would have become increasingly aware of their separate identity and the history of their ancestors.[22]

In order to inform himself better about the history of the Unity of Brethren, Zinzendorf borrowed Comenius's *Historia Fratrum Bohemorum* (1702) from the library in the nearby town of Zittau and took it along with him on a journey to Silesia at the end of July 1727. In it he discovered similarities between the organization of the Herrnhut community and the ancient Brethren. Like the Unity of Brethren and other reform movements within the Christian church, the Herrnhut community intended to model itself after the apostolic example of the early Christians, using the descriptions of the early church in the Bible as their guide. Upon hearing Zinzendorf's findings after his return in early August, the Herrnhuters considered it "miraculous" that they had unknowingly adopted the constitution of their ancestors.[23] It appeared to them that God had reinstated the order of the Unity of Brethren in Herrnhut. Only a few days after Zinzendorf's return from Silesia, the congregation in Herrnhut was "so much beside itself" that the Sunday worship continued until midnight. Impressed with what was taking place among the Herrnhuters, Pastor Rothe, the minister of the parish, called for a Communion service the following Wednesday, August 13, 1727. This service became known as the spiritual birthday of the Moravian Church.[24] The Herrnhuters had found a new identity as the renewed Unitas Fratrum.

In subsequent years, aspects of the organization of the Unity of Brethren were consciously copied by the Moravians. In 1735 the first Moravian from Herrnhut was consecrated a bishop of the Unity by Daniel Ernst Jablonski, grandson of Comenius and *senior* of the Polish branch of the Unity. In 1745 the Moravian Church adopted the office of acolyte as well as the threefold orders of ministry (deacon, presbyter, and bishop).[25]

Despite the claim to be renewing the Unity of Brethren, little theological continuity existed between the eighteenth-century Moravian Church and the Brethren. At synods Zinzendorf repeatedly declared his dislike of the teachings of Hus and the confession of the Bohemian Brethren, which for him were inferior to the Augsburg Confession. He declared in 1746, "We are not founded on any Bohemian *creed* but only on Moravian *discipline and order*."[26]

Nevertheless, reviving the Unitas Fratrum enabled Zinzendorf and the Moravians to hide the fact that their church was indeed a new religious community, and to introduce many distinctive practices and teachings without raising suspicions that they were separating from the church and founding a new religious body. Establishing a new church was not permitted within the Holy German Empire, and very difficult even within the most tolerant of the European states. So the Moravians became "Philadelphian brethren, speaking with a Lutheran tongue and appearing in a Moravian cloak," as Zinzendorf explained in 1743.[27] In fact Herrnhut was not simply a Pietist *ecclesiola* within the Lutheran parish of Berthelsdorf, nor was it exclusively a community of runaway Protestants from Moravia. It was a new religious body, independent and separate from the existing churches.

Herrnhut and Halle

The relationship with Halle and the Moravians' rejection of Halle Pietism were important factors in the ensuing Sifting Time. Herrnhut became the center of a new and vibrant form of Pietism.[28] But although Moravians are considered Pietists by most historians, Zinzendorf would not have agreed with this categorization. For him, the term "Pietism" equaled "Halle Pietism." "We are the direct opposite of Pietism," Zinzendorf stated in 1745,[29] when his relationship with Halle Pietism had deteriorated beyond repair. Nonetheless, Zinzendorf's relations with Halle Pietism had started out quite differently.

Although the claim that Philipp Jacob Spener, father of Pietism, was Zinzendorf's godfather has proven to be a myth,[30] Zinzendorf's family did have close ties to Halle Pietism. Henriette Katharina von Gersdorf and her husband had friendly connections with Spener and generously supported August Hermann Francke and his projects in Halle. Zinzendorf saw Francke for the first time in 1704, when he was only four years old, during a visit by Francke to Grosshennersdorf. Between 1710 and 1716 Zinzendorf attended Francke's *paedagogium* for aristocratic boys in Halle, where, due to his status as imperial count, he ate at Francke's table. In his younger years Zinzendorf identified himself as a Pietist, and Herrnhut initially was intended as a copy of Halle, with an orphanage, a *paedagogium*, a print shop, and an apothecary. During the 1730s and especially during the 1740s, however, a rift between Halle and Herrnhut developed.

In Moravian historiography this rift has traditionally been explained in terms of differing theologies.[31] Francke taught that the way to saving grace was a "penitential struggle" (*Busskampf*) within the soul: when the believer had become sufficiently aware of his shortcomings, he would desperately call out to God for help and consequently be converted. Zinzendorf, on the other hand, taught that conversion could happen in an instant, when the believer realized in his heart he was saved by Christ's suffering and death. One could be saved not by leading a pious life, as Zinzendorf paraphrased Hallensian theology, but by experiencing the blood and grace of Christ in one's heart. The Hallensians, according to Zinzendorf, stressed the importance of holiness of one's way of life as the way to salvation, whereas the Herrnhuters preached only grace. Christ's suffering and death were sufficient for an individual's salvation; a serious and strict lifestyle could not accomplish salvation, but only "the blood of Christ."

Other factors also played a role in the split. Hans Schneider, in his recent analysis of the relationship between the Halle Pietists and Zinzendorf, argues that Zinzendorf, though aspiring to be part of Halle's undertakings, was repeatedly turned down by Francke, Francke's son Gotthilf August, and other Halle leaders. Zinzendorf's unpredictable and headstrong personality, his unconventional theology, his departure from Lutheran liturgy and practice, his close connections with Inspirationists and other radical Pietists, and his apparent deafness to any form of advice from Halle all caused great concern in Halle. Furthermore, Zinzendorf's involvement with the Protestants from Moravia interfered with Halle's activities in that same region, and when Herrnhut began to send out itinerant evangelists throughout Germany and missionaries to overseas destinations, some Hallensians saw this as a sign of open competition. As a result, Zinzendorf's repeated approaches for cooperation with Halle were met with open rejection or, at best, with silent disregard.[32]

During the subsequent years Zinzendorf and the Herrnhuters distanced themselves from Halle Pietism. Zinzendorf realized that a certain amount of envy and competitiveness existed between Halle and Herrnhut, both in Europe and overseas,[33] but he also believed the teachings of Halle were fundamentally different from those of Herrnhut. Zinzendorf went so far as to claim that Halle Pietism, with its alleged justification by works, was not Lutheran, while the Moravians, who stood fully on the foundation of justification by faith, were true Lutherans.[34] Zinzendorf caricatured the Halle Pietists and their preoccupation with righteous behavior: "The Pietists have their own plan that is opposed to ours; and they know that. The main points [for the Pietists] are not to wear cuffs, not to powder one's wig but otherwise to dress very properly, no dancing, no playing, to disapprove of tobacco, to speak badly of the *theologis irregenitis* [theologians who are not born again], etc."[35]

During the mid-1740s Moravians became convinced that they had found true joy in salvation through the death of Christ, while the Hallensians, with their somber outlook, were occupied with worries about the right way of life. A Pietist, according to Zinzendorf, "limps along the way while we are dancing."[36] After 1745 the anti-Pietist attitude of the Moravians escalated. Not only did they celebrate their joy about salvation and deem good moral behavior unnecessary, but, as a reaction against their own former Pietist identity, they engaged in playful and silly behavior explicitly disapproved of by Pietists. This anti-Pietist attitude was a major contributing factor in the Sifting Time, which to a large extent was a reaction against Halle Pietism, a deliberate provocation against Pietist values and ideals.

Expansion

The incredibly rapid expansion of the Moravians confirmed to them that their objectives were in accordance with divine plans. In 1752 Zinzendorf claimed that as early as 1723 he had seen it all in a dream revealing to him a landscape with many Christian towns similar to the community of Herrnhut.[37] The Moravian movement soon spread beyond the immediate area of

Herrnhut, and in order to gather other like-minded "true children of God," Herrnhuters went out and established contacts in other regions of Europe. Some of the (ethnic) Moravians regularly went back to their homeland in order to encourage others to move to Herrnhut as well. As a result, the population of Herrnhut kept growing.

In 1732 two missionaries, Leonhard Dober and David Nitschmann, carried out the first overseas mission of the Moravian Church when they traveled to the Caribbean island of St. Thomas to preach the gospel to the enslaved Africans. Other destinations soon followed: Greenland, South Africa, Suriname, and the American colony of Georgia.[38] Moravian missionary activity was closely related to their Philadelphian ideas, as Wolfgang Breul has recently argued.[39] In accordance with these ideas and their eschatological expectations, Moravians set out to gather true Christians from all nations. Moravian missionaries did not promote a particular denominational identity, as they did not want to transplant the confessional differences of Europe to other parts of the world.

Sometimes, as in Georgia, the missionary attempts were combined with colonizing efforts. As immigrants, especially from the Habsburg Empire (to which Moravia belonged), continued to arrive in Herrnhut, the Saxon government kept a watchful eye. The Lutheran Church in the Oberlausitz, too, was greatly concerned about the independent activities of the Herrnhut community. In order to avoid government intervention, Zinzendorf looked for alternative locations for Moravian immigrants to settle. In addition to Georgia, new Moravian colonies were founded in Pilgerruh near Oldesloe in northern Germany and Heerendijk near IJsselstein in the Netherlands.

While Zinzendorf was visiting the Netherlands in early 1736 to negotiate with Maria Louise, Princess of Orange, about the Heerendijk community and to explore the great variety of religious groups in the Netherlands, the Saxon government in Dresden issued a decree expelling him from Saxony. Unable to return to Herrnhut, Zinzendorf chose to move his headquarters to the Wetterau, a religiously tolerant and diverse region north of Frankfurt am Main, known as a place of refuge for radical Pietists.[40]

For the next fifteen years, the Wetterau would be the center of the Moravians, replacing Herrnhut. The Moravians rented parts of the Ronneburg, a medieval castle near the town of Büdingen, and leased Marienborn, a former monastery in the same region. Marienborn became the seat of Zinzendorf and his staff, the "pilgrim congregation" (*Pilgergemeine*). But from now on Zinzendorf would not stay in one place for very long. Like other radical Pietist leaders, such as Johann Wilhelm Petersen and Johann Friedrich Rock, who traveled extensively to keep in touch with their followers, Zinzendorf led a wandering existence. He believed that as a pilgrim he was following the example of Jesus, who during his earthly life did not have a permanent home.[41] In between travels, Marienborn was the seat of the pilgrim congregation. Many synods and conferences were held there, and it was where the seminary, chancellery, print shop, bookstore, library, and archives were housed.

In the Wetterau the Moravians engaged in their most daring and most original architectural experiment. Six miles from Marienborn they built the communal town of Herrnhaag. Between its founding in 1738 and its abandonment in 1753, Herrnhaag was the place where Moravianism attained full development. Herrnhaag also served as the main stage for the Sifting Time.

Herrnhaag: Life in a Moravian Town

Herrnhaag, just north of Frankfurt am Main, was the first community planned and built entirely according to Moravian architectural principles, the first true congregational town. Other settlements, such as Heerendijk (1736), Pilgerruh (1737), and Bethlehem (1741), originally had the character of an *Anstalt* (institution, establishment) and consisted initially of a main building (*Gemeinhaus* or *Anstaltshaus*) around which additional buildings were grouped. Herrnhaag, by contrast, was a planned city, with large communal structures constructed around a central square. In the center of the square stood a springhouse, providing the community with a fresh water source. A carillon in the springhouse played Moravian tunes throughout the day. Around the square stood seven large buildings: the *Gemeinhaus* (community house), the widows' house, various private houses, and Zinzendorf's house, the *Grafenhaus*, also called the *Lichtenburg* (castle of lights) because of the many festive illuminations inside. Each building on the square had a very similar façade, providing the settlement with a uniform appearance. The brothers' house and the sisters' house were located in side streets off the square, as were smaller, private houses.

No separate church building existed in Herrnhaag, but there were several chapels inside other structures that served as religious gathering spaces. The most important *Saal* (hall) was on the second floor of the Lichtenburg. The first *Gemeinhaus* as well as the choir houses in which members lived also contained a *Saal*.

A Moravian congregation was typically divided into various groups called choirs.[42] Although such choirs were typical for the Moravians during the eighteenth century, no systematic studies have been made of the choir system.[43] Membership in the choirs was based upon age, gender, and marital

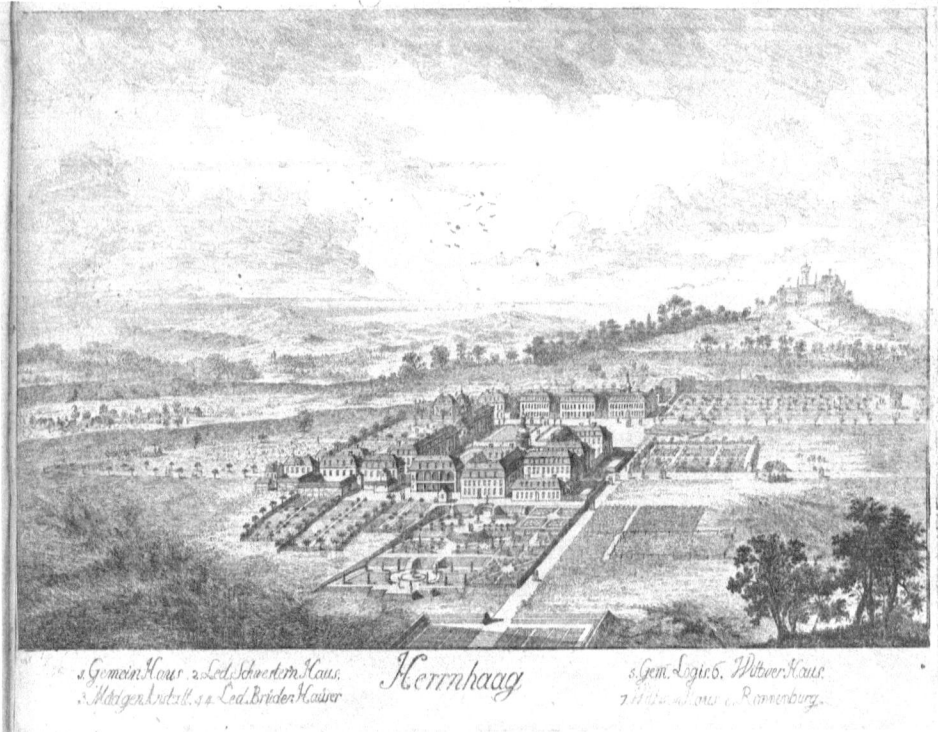

*Fig. 1* View of the community of Herrnhaag. Copper engraving, 1757. Moravian Archives, Bethlehem.

status. There was a children's choir, as well as a choir of the older boys, of older girls, of single brothers, of single sisters, of married people, of widowers, and of widows. The choir of the single brothers in Herrnhaag plays a major role in this book, since its members seem to have taken the lead during the Sifting Time. The transition from one choir to another was observed with great care and ceremony. Choir ribbons were visible signs of one's choir affiliation. Women wore their choir ribbons under their caps; men tied theirs into their shirt collars or wore them around their necks.[44] The single brothers, single sisters, and widows had their own choir houses, where choir members lived, worked, and worshipped together and where most choir meetings were held.[45] Each choir member had an assigned task, and each choir had its own pastoral leader (*Pfleger*) and sometimes also a financial head (*Diener* or *Vorsteher*).

Each choir was to represent a specific aspect of Jesus's life. The single men, for example, were told to model their lives after that of Jesus, who was himself a single man, while married couples were to represent the bond between Christ and his earthly bride.[46] Zinzendorf considered his teaching on marriage and sexuality the central point in his theology, calling it "a primum principium," "the root of the church tree," and "the biggest secret" Christ had revealed to the Moravians.[47] Unlike other radical Pietists, who rejected sexuality and considered a life of abstinence to be the ideal for the truly converted, Zinzendorf regarded sexual intercourse as a most holy act and a duty for each married couple. While some radical Pietists believed a sexual relationship would prevent the believer from attaining union with divine wisdom, Zinzendorf considered sexual intercourse a way to experience union with the divine. In accordance with traditions dating back to the thirteenth century, Zinzendorf applied mystical imagery of Christ as the bridegroom and the soul of the believer as the bride to marriage. The husband took on the role of Christ the bridegroom, while the wife symbolized the bride, so that in intercourse they symbolically performed on earth what was to come in heaven: the unification of Christ and his bride. Zinzendorf's marital theology (*Ehereligion*) played a crucial role during the developments of the late 1740s.[48]

Life in the choir houses was not only characterized by *imitatio Dei*; it was also determined by a strong mystical desire for union with Christ. Single persons eighteen or older lived in the brothers' or sisters' house; during the mid-eighteenth century most of the residents of these houses were in their twenties and thirties. Each choir house had a large dining hall for common meals and a dormitory where most of the choir members slept. The dormitories were significant spaces with an almost sacred function. The assignment of the individual beds occurred by lot, and choir members were supposed to sleep in a chaste, liturgical manner, as illustrated by a painting of the corpse of Jesus hanging in the dormitory of the single brothers in Herrnhut: just like Jesus's corpse, one was to mortify all desires of the flesh. In 1744 Johannes von Watteville instructed the single men in Herrnhut to place their hands on top of the sheets and keep them folded together throughout the night.[49] Sleeping was considered a sacrament during which the believer pictured himself as lying in the side wound of Jesus.[50]

Daily choir meetings, such as morning devotions, evening meditations, and the celebration of Holy Communion, were held in the *Saal* of the respective choir houses. A highlight in the life of the choirs was the annual choir festival. During the day the choir house was elaborately decorated with greenery and paintings; there was music and hours-long worship, special hymns were written for the occasion, and festive illuminations lit up the buildings at night.

Each choir was divided into classes reflecting the spiritual growth of each member. The classes met every afternoon or evening. Herrnhaag also divided members into companies (*Gesellschaften*); the distinction between the classes and the companies requires further investigation. In order to oversee the great number of people and groups, "laborers" (*Arbeiter*) were appointed: in 1746 and 1747 there were forty laborers among the approximately three hundred single brothers in the Herrnhaag brothers' house.[51]

Members of a Moravian congregation were subject to a strict spiritual hierarchy, presided over by helpers and elders in each choir, as well as by congregational elders and overseers. During Zinzendorf's lifetime the offices and their holders were very much in flux, with changes occurring on a regular basis. At the top of the hierarchical pyramid stood Count Zinzendorf himself, whose secular power as lord of the Berthelsdorf estate (where the original community of Herrnhut was located), standing as imperial count (*Reichsgraf*) among European nobility, charismatic personality, and, above all, alleged direct relationship with Christ, who continued to reveal his plans through Zinzendorf, made him the undisputed leader of the church. Zinzendorf was considered the "Disciple" (*Jünger*) and was usually addressed by members of the church as Papa. His wife, Erdmuth, was addressed as Mama. Although she had important administrative responsibilities for the Berthelsdorf estate, she remained mostly in the background. More visible as spiritual leader was another woman. Anna Nitschmann, who was called *Mutter* (Mother), had been noted for her remarkable spiritual gifts ever since she was appointed as head of the single sisters in Herrnhut in 1730, when she was fifteen years old. During Zinzendorf's journey to Pennsylvania she became his closest confidant, a position she would retain until her death only twelve days after Zinzendorf's passing in May of 1760. In December of 1756, after Erdmuth's death, Anna received the title "Discipless" (*Jüngerin*), placing her on almost equal footing with Zinzendorf. Her main responsibilities involved overseeing women within the church.[52] She and Zinzendorf were married—despite their fifteen-year age difference and the unbridgeable gap in social standing—in 1757.

During the 1740s and the 1750s a form of religious court culture developed within the Moravian Church, mirroring the culture of secular courts and setting them apart from other religious movements of the early modern period. Around Zinzendorf was an entourage of family members and confidants, who often had high offices within the church. For example, when Zinzendorf paid a visit to the brothers' house in Herrnhaag during March of 1747 he was accompanied by a suite consisting of Erdmuth, Anna, his daughter Benigna, son-in-law Johannes von Watteville, and several servants. A detailed overview from 1744 lists fifty-three members of his immediate household plus thirty servants.[53]

Like other Christians, Moravians considered Christ the head of the church. But Moravians went further. They believed that Christ, by accepting the office of chief elder on September 16, 1741, had forged a special bond with the Moravian Church.[54] Every year Moravians celebrated Christ as chief elder and paid renewed homage to him. To the outside world they tried to play down the special nature of Christ's chief eldership, but in reality they believed Jesus was actively involved among his people.[55] At meetings an empty chair signified his presence, and all major decisions had to be made by Christ or at least approved by him. Moravians used the lot in order to let Christ actively decide issues that were put before him. After careful deliberation by the elders, a preliminary decision could be approved by a "yea" lot being drawn, or denied by a "nay" lot. A third, blank lot would indicate that the question was incorrectly phrased or the timing was not opportune. Alternatively, they could write possible resolutions to a question on slips of paper (including a blank one) that were then drawn from a box.[56]

A strict sense of order was important to Moravians. Comments in the Herrnhaag single brothers' diary such as "everything occurred in the most beautiful order" express this sense.[57] Moravians observed a similar order during worship: each *Saal* had one side for men and one for women. Visitors praised the quality of the singing and the music as well as the disciplined behavior of the congregation.

Singing as an expression of the religion of the heart had an important place at each of the worship meetings. Some meetings, such as the singing meetings (*Singstunden*), consisted almost exclusively of singing. The spoken word had an important place as well, but meditations were often short; some services were even called "quarter-hours" (*Viertelstunden*). On Sunday morning the full congregation assembled to hear a sermon, usually in the local parish church. In Herrnhut this was the church in Berthelsdorf, and in Herrnhaag it was the nearby Marienborn chapel. Moravians celebrated the various liturgical rituals in separate services. Holy Communion was normally celebrated once a month on Saturday evening. There were special services for prostrate prayer (*Anbeten*) and for foot washing. Love feasts occurred frequently: on birthdays, to celebrate the Sabbath as a commemoration of Jesus's resting in the grave, to celebrate the reception of new members, to discuss important matters, to welcome or to see off travelers, or to simply strengthen the fellowship among the members.

Life in a Moravian town, and especially in Herrnhaag, was characterized by festiveness, combined with a sense of elegance and splendor: instrumental music, singing, paintings, architecture, and landscaping testified to great religious joy. A celebration would often last deep into the night. For example, the diary of the single brothers in Herrnhaag notes on the day of the feast of all choirs in 1747, "At four o'clock in the morning at the conclusion of this blessed day we had a general evening devotion and then . . . we went to sleep for a few hours."[58]

For Moravians, itinerancy was an ideal.[59] In their litany they prayed, "teach us to be everywhere at home!" They felt themselves to be part of a larger, imagined community beyond their local congregation, a community made up of brothers and sisters in Europe, in North America, in the mission stations in South America, Greenland, southern Africa, and elsewhere. Herrnhaag was a busy hub of travel activity. Frequently, the Herrnhaag single brothers' diary records ceremonies where travelers were sent off to multiple destinations. On April 11, 1746, for example, brethren headed to thirteen destinations, including Marienborn, Herrnhut, and Silesia, and farther abroad to places such as England, Latvia, Persia, and Berbice.[60] Moravians especially thrived in the Atlantic world, where they spread their ideas in print and in manuscript but even more so in person. Moravian leaders regularly traveled across the Atlantic, and at times the church even had its own ship for transporting people and goods between Europe, Greenland, the Caribbean, and North America.

The people in Moravian communities came from different regions and countries, different classes, and different races. In Herrnhaag lived former African slaves from the Caribbean, two Arawak Indians from Berbice, a Tatar, and a man from the Malabar Coast.[61] Moravian language reflected this international makeup. Zinzendorf purposely used many loan words in his discourses and hymns. Sometimes Moravians sang hymns in twenty or more languages at the same time.[62] This multilingualism reflected their eschatological outlook. By using words from different languages and singing hymns in different tongues, they prefigured the biblical multitudes that would gather around the throne of the Lamb and canceled the confusion of tongues that, according to the Bible, had existed as a consequence of human hubris since the Tower of Babel. Moravians believed the time was almost fulfilled and the end was near.

Blood-and-Wounds Devotion

Although Moravian blood-and-wounds devotion has traditionally been considered a typical feature of the Sifting, it was in fact an important feature of Moravian piety before and after the Sifting Time. Nevertheless, the 1740s saw its most drastic manifestations. During that time Moravian religious language increasingly concentrated on the blood and wounds of Christ as the symbols of his passion.

Such devotion was, of course, not unique to the Moravians, and can be traced back to the High Middle Ages. Caroline Walker Bynum finds that during the fourteenth and fifteenth centuries an intense devotion of the blood of Christ evolved in various locations in northern Europe. Unlike earlier scholars, she does not see it as an expression of a violent society: "The wound or wounds of Christ are more frequently hymned as doorway and access, refuge and consolation, than as violation; to penetrate is to open the way."[63] The parallels with Moravian piety will become clear throughout this book. For Luther, the Puritans, Methodists, and many other Christian traditions, the blood was an important tangible symbol of Christ's passion and of salvation.[64]

Moravians believed salvation was accomplished through the sacrificial death of Christ. The believer was to appropriate the atonement through intense contemplation of all aspects of the humanity and suffering of the Savior, which was the predominant topic of meditations, hymns, and liturgies and depicted in words and images alike. The expressions used to describe the blood and wounds as symbols of Jesus's passion became increasingly graphic and blatant. This did not happen without dissent, however. A 1742 letter from Andreas Grassmann, elder of the Herrnhut congregation, to Zinzendorf, who was in Pennsylvania at the time, gives insight into the differing views regarding the emergence of blood-and-wounds devotion. Grassmann complained that Johann Langguth (later Johannes von Watteville), elder of the single brothers in Herrnhut, had made the wounds of Christ the sole topic of his preaching: "Langguth only gives one kind of address. Even when he holds three meetings a day or when he interprets the watchwords—be it appropriate or not—he will use this expression twenty times: 'One has to fully get into the wounds of Jesus, etc.' Whoever is simple will receive a blessing from it, but whoever uses his mind and wants to get to the core of the Bible will not agree with all of these expressions and phrases."[65]

Despite some initial resistance against this form of piety, blood-and-wounds devotion soon prevailed. An outstanding example is the Litany of the Wounds, which consists of various petitions with responses, contemplating each aspect of Jesus's humanity and the qualities of his wounds.[66] The litany, following traditional Roman Catholic and Lutheran examples, was written in March of 1744 by Zinzendorf, Langguth, Polycarp Müller, Johann Jakob Müller, and Christian Renatus. It soon became a popular text among Moravians; in Bethlehem it was used for the first time before the end of the same year.[67] In 1755 the Litany of the Wounds was divided into the Litany of the Life, Sufferings, and Death of Jesus and the Hymn of the Wounds of Jesus. These liturgical texts remained in use throughout the eighteenth century and survived the attempts by post-Zinzendorfian leaders to rid the Moravian Church of all features of its enthusiastic past. The language of the Litany of the Wounds can therefore hardly be considered a feature of the Sifting Time.

During the nineteenth century Moravians no longer understood blood-and-wounds devotion and dismissed its language as nonsensical and absurd. Bettermann, however, argued that blood-and-wounds devotion was an expression of the doctrine of justification by grace alone.[68] Atwood, in his study of Moravian piety in Bethlehem, states, "Blood is a symbol of immersion in the divine life; it is a fountain in which the believer swims and from which she drinks. It is a fluid symbol of vitality and strength."[69] For Moravians, as for generations of believers before and after them, the wounds were a symbol of salvation and the object of contemplation, places to go into and to unite with the divine. By entering the wounds of Jesus, the believer was able to become one with Christ as the object of devotion. During the 1740s there was a tendency to concentrate on the wound in Christ's side, the *Seitenhöhlchen* (side hole).

Zinzendorf's bridal and passion mysticism were connected to his Philadelphian ideas. He believed that throughout the ages there had always been a "holy church" of true believers. The characteristic feature of their faith, as he stated in 1748, was "the doctrine of the passion of Jesus." For Zinzendorf, the devotion of the suffering of Christ was a feature of true Christianity. As historical examples Zinzendorf named Bernard of Clairvaux, Johannes Tauler, the Bohemian Brethren, Luther, and the Herrnhuters of his own time.[70]

Mysticism

As should be evident by now, mystical traditions played an important role in Moravian theology and piety. Bernard McGinn defines mysticism as "the preparation for, the consciousness of, and the reaction to what can be described as the immediate or direct presence of God." It is found in many religions and can be generally described as the pursuit by which the believer seeks to become one with the divine.[71] An important figure for Christian medieval mysticism was Bernard of Clairvaux (1090–1153), who taught that man could restore his original similarity with God, which was lost through the Fall. Mystical ideas also played a role within Protestantism, especially among early Pietists and Puritans. Johann Arndt, whose work became the inspiration for many later Pietists, made the works of mystical authors available by editing and translating them. His widely read *Four Books of True Christianity* spread mystical thought throughout Protestantism. Surprisingly, Bernardine bridal mysticism, although an unmistakable component of Arndt's later works,[72] was treated with reservations by many Pietists of the seventeenth and eighteenth centuries, but among the Moravians and radical Pietists it played an important role.[73]

Zinzendorf's position regarding mysticism is somewhat controversial. Although its influence on him as a young man is undisputed, some Zinzendorf scholars assert that, as he himself claimed, he turned away from mysticism in 1734.[74] Others doubt that this so-called turn to Luther was truly an abandonment of mystical ideas. According to W. R. Ward, Zinzendorf merely traded one form of mysticism for another form: "it is impossible to overlook his indebtedness to the Bernardine bride- and passion-mysticism with which he had grown up and which had come to him out of the devotional traditions of Lutheran Orthodoxy. No one emphasized more than he the experiencing and feeling, the enjoying and tasting of the work and the body of Christ."[75] Meyer believes the term "mysticism" had negative connotations for Zinzendorf because of its methodology of working oneself closer towards God. Zinzendorf rejected this aspect of mysticism. However, he considered the bridal mysticism of such people as Bernard of Clairvaux not as mysticism but rather as orthodox Lutheran theology. According to this reasoning, it is possible to regard Zinzendorf as a Lutheran theologian without excluding the more mystical elements of this theology. To Ward, Zinzendorf's misleading definitions of Lutheranism and mysticism conceal important aspects of his theology. As stated above, the desire among some scholars to argue that Zinzendorf was a true Lutheran (i.e., a sound Christian) resulted in a rather one-sided reading of his theology.[76]

Moravian View of History

Zinzendorf believed that history was characterized by progress: God's revelation increases from generation to generation, and history leads us ever closer to the truth in Christ. He distanced himself from church historians like Gottfried Arnold who saw not progress but decline throughout the history of the church. It was not unusual for eighteenth-century historians to see progress in history, but Zinzendorf's view of history differed decidedly from that of other thinkers during the age of Enlightenment. He was not interested in progress regarding human reason and knowledge, but rather in a progressive manifestation of divine revelation. This manifestation had taken place over the centuries but gained considerable momentum during the 1740s among the Moravian community, who believed they had gained an ever deeper understanding of the nature of Christ and his redemption.[77]

Moravians during the 1740s were well aware of the changes taking place regarding piety in their midst. They realized that it was markedly different than in the 1730s and was undergoing a rapid succession of different phases. They did not consider this a sign of erratic inconstancy but instead believed they were witnessing a progressive divine revelation. The references to this awareness are so frequent and widespread that they suggest it must have been much more a part of Moravian consciousness than has previously been realized.

In 1747 Martin Dober wrote a history of the consecutive themes in Moravian doctrine since 1725 that was found among his papers after his death on December 10, 1748.[78] His account is especially interesting because of the insight it provides into the increasingly playful style of Moravian piety. Although Dober resisted the playfulness for some time, he eventually gave in and came to see it as the culmination of the themes of the previous years. Another example is Christian Hart, who gives a detailed description of the various phases he experienced during his involvement with the Moravians. When he first joined in 1744, the focus of Moravian piety was the Lamb and the blood and wounds of Christ. The next period began in 1746, when the topic of meditations and songs was the "air around the cross" and the "cross-air birds." This period was followed by a time when everything revolved around the "pleura" and the "side hole" of Christ. After that, Moravians spoke exclusively about the "husband," the "marital bed," and the "marital cabinet." This phase was succeeded, according to Hart, by a time when the single brothers "were declared to be single sisters."[79]

Several instances from the 1740s confirm the Moravian belief that they were witnessing an increased progression of insight into divine secrets. On March 26, 1747, Zinzendorf explained to the single brothers of Herrnhaag the difference between that former Moravian idea of being "warriors" (*Streiter*) for Christ, and the "current plan" of aiming to become similar to Christ in everything they did.[80] In May of the same year Zinzendorf announced the beginning of a new period during which men would still have male bodies but would spiritually have become female.[81] In May of 1748 the single brothers in Bethlehem were told a new period was to begin among them whose central theme was the side hole.[82] And the diary entry of the single men in Marienborn for November 29, 1748, mentions the beginning of yet another "blessed period."[83]

Not only were Moravians aware of the progression of the phases of their own history as these occurred, but they even anticipated a succession of different phases to come. This is made clear in a 1744 document that predicts four successive periods in the years leading up to 1750:

> (24) Until 1750 there will be four main periods, the first of which will begin on January 1, 1742, and will pause a little in the middle. The time from 1741 on is not to be divided into eras of equal length. It will become self-evident when a new one begins. 1741, month of March.
>
> (25) Until now we represented the merchant who found the pearl [Matt. 13:45–46]. The next periods will be (1) the mustard seed [Matt. 13:31] until into the second period; (2) around the middle [of the time up to 1750?] the net [Matt. 13:47], and toward the end the character of the leaven [Matt. 13:33] will be revealed. Month of March 1741.[84]

Because of the prophetic character of this document—it appears to be a list of earlier predictions with their dates—the exact meaning of the text is somewhat elusive. Be that as it may, the document confirms that Moravians were expecting a continuous manifestation of divine wisdom throughout the years to come and were consciously seeking new insights. One observer mentioned this eschatological worldview after he had left the Moravians: "These people call themselves of the new Period."[85] Moravians during the 1740s had a strong sense of living in a new age, if not during the end time. This belief contributed to the expectation that more revelations were to follow and added to the highly suggestive atmosphere of the 1740s. Against this background, it may not be surprising that many rejoiced when yet another period was announced at the end of 1748. This period soon became labeled the "Sifting Time."

After the Sifting was over, Moravian perception of their own history changed profoundly. They still saw their history as a succession of different periods, but no longer did they believe the succession was a continuous progression leading them ever closer to Christ. At a synod for single brothers in London in 1752–53, Johannes von Watteville said, "We have passed through many periods in our choirs. For a while there was a legalistic course, after which followed a truly frivolous time. Now the choirs have arrived at more of a sinners' sense again."[86] By then it had become clear that the phase previously hailed as yet another highlight in their history had turned out to be a time of crisis in which Satan tried to "sift" the Moravians. Moravians had concluded that their history could also go in the wrong direction. This conclusion came as an immense shock to a community that, only a short time earlier, believed it had realized heaven on earth. Instead, it was abruptly brought down to earth.

Under Zinzendorf's leadership the Moravians drew from a variety of different sources, including Lutheranism, German Pietism, medieval mysticism, and the traditions of the ancient Unitas Fratrum, to develop their own form of piety. One author calls Moravian beliefs a "philadelphian reconciliation of mysticism, Pietism, and orthodoxy."[87] In Moravian theology the main focal point was the incarnation, suffering, and death of Christ. Zinzendorf taught that each believer was to be touched in his or her heart by the love of God shown in Christ's humanity, and was thus to achieve a personalized relationship with Christ the Savior. The manner by which this faith was expressed changed throughout the first few decades of the existence of the Herrnhut movement. Within this dynamic and expanding religious group new ideas developed rapidly and replaced older traditions. The period of the late 1740s was a culmination of developments that had begun a decade earlier.

# 2

## HISTORIOGRAPHY

Should an Historiographer
Arise some future Day,
Who all Events and Men with Care
Would in just Light display,
And should his Theme Church Matters be
Of the now-current Century,
And at last *Fratrum Unitas*;
How shall he paint their Case?
—John Gambold, 1752

### Eighteenth-Century Moravian Historiography

The term "Sifting Time" is obviously a historical concept, a periodizing label. In this chapter we will look at the manner in which historians have "painted the case" of the Sifting Time and discover how the intentional vagueness of the early Moravian historians made it possible for later generations to invent their own Sifting Time.[1] Often, the problem of the Sifting Time has mistakenly been identified with the excesses of the blood-and-wounds theology.

The first generation of Moravian historians—Cranz, Spangenberg, and Schrautenbach—had all witnessed the Sifting Time themselves, but none of them offer a precise description of what happened. David Cranz's (1723–1777) explanation of the excesses of that period is ambiguous: rejection of legalistic methods of sanctification, resulting in a playful evangelical freedom that eventually led to inventive jargon about the side wound of Christ, combined with mystical and enthusiastic ideas, while losing sight of the merits of the life and death of Christ. But Cranz does not give a clear description of what actually happened. He merely calls it "excesses in doctrine and practice" or "abuse and excesses in word and acts," which were "spreading like wildfire through several congregations." But he refuses to give any more detail, except to assure the reader that these had not led to any "punishable offenses and works of the flesh."[2]

August Gottlieb Spangenberg (1704–1792) is even vaguer. He blames the problem on the influx of new people who brought "mystical and enthusiastic principles" into the church, and he downplays the seriousness of the Sifting: whatever happened, although "ordinary" and "unpunishable" in the world, was still unsuitable for a child of God and a servant of Jesus.[3] The imprecision of both Cranz and Spangenberg should not surprise us if we realize their publications were intended to assure the public that Moravians had nothing to do with the radical enthusiasm that earlier publications had accused them of.

Ludwig Carl von Schrautenbach's account, on the other hand, was not intended for publication. Although Schrautenbach (1724–1783) had distanced himself from the Moravians during his thirties, the section on the Sifting Time in his biography of Count Zinzendorf can be read as an insider's account. We know that Schrautenbach, after initially resisting the wave of playfulness that came over the single men in the Wetterau, had become an enthusiastic player himself.[4] He writes, "One is drunk with delight, one feeds on ideas, one dreams of sensations, one simulates them. With one's light-footed pace one touches the visible ground only slightly. One finds oneself richer in insights and more blissful than anyone else." But about the nature of the crisis he remains as vague as Cranz and Spangenberg. He defines it as "playing around, indecency in word and deed ... a kind of sensitivity—sentimental nonsense, ... enhanced by a layer of mysticism."[5] The lack of details offered by the first generation of Moravian historians would become a problem for later historians.

Nineteenth-Century Historiography

Moravian archivist and historian Johannes Plitt (1778–1841) was aware of the shortcomings of the printed histories as well as of the surviving archival records. In his monumental "Geschichte der Brüder-Unität alter und neuer Zeit" (History of the Moravian Church of old and new times) (1828–41) Plitt complains repeatedly about the lack of sufficient reliable sources on the Sifting Time, which made it impossible to write a "comprehensive history of the enthusiastic course" the church took during the 1740s. Although he refers to the continued existence of oral anecdotes about the Sifting Time within the Moravian community of his day, he unfortunately refuses to include these "legends" in his writing. Still, Plitt attempted to put together what he was able to find about the Sifting Time. Like many historians after him, he fell victim to the method of categorizing anything that appeared unusual to him as part of the Sifting, which for him consisted of frequent festivities with elaborate decorations, playful activities, and consequently a neglect of work duties and waste of money. Wanting to let the sources speak for themselves, he gives long quotes from which the reader is to form his own understanding of the Sifting Time. But a definitive explanation of the Sifting Time is difficult to find in Plitt's work, which served as the main resource for many subsequent histories of the Moravians.[6]

Like earlier Moravian historians, Plitt connected the Sifting Time with the end of Herrnhaag that followed. When the directive from the government of Büdingen to leave Herrnhaag came in early 1750, Moravians readily accepted it as a punishment from God for what had happened. Ten months later, on New Year's Eve, Zinzendorf stated, "the emigration from Herrnhaag saved us from all peril," and called it both a "blessing" and a "punishment" for the previous Sifting.[7] Soon the Sifting and the subsequent survival of the church were interpreted as evidence of the special bond between Christ and the church. Cranz writes, "Our rescue from this peril was one of the most evident proofs to many undecided friends and observers that our Moravian Church was not the work of man but the work of God, because otherwise the whole thing would have fallen apart."[8]

By linking the Sifting Time with the end of Herrnhaag, Moravians were able to interpret the crisis as "a wholesome school of humiliation," as Ernst Wilhelm Cröger (1811–1878) put it in 1853 in an official church history. Cröger saw the Sifting Time as a period of enthusiasm, of frivolous festivities, and of childlike playfulness through which the church was led astray from the right path of Scripture "to impure and carnal things." At the same time, it was for him God's "beneficial punishment for his children."[9] Like other Moravian historians before and after him, Cröger gives little detail about the nature of the Sifting "as not to feed punishable frivolity or to cause unnecessary offense."[10] This intentional vagueness, combined with what Atwood calls a silence in the sources, caused later historians "to create a *Sichtungszeit* that may or may not be accurate."[11]

Another recurring theme in these historical narratives is the question of Zinzendorf's role in all of this. This developed into one of the main questions in the historiography of the Sifting Time. Atwood shows how German historians and British and American historians found different approaches to this issue. German historians used the concept of the Sifting Time to separate the "real" Zinzendorf from that of the 1740s, while in England and America the Sifting Time was often used to separate the "true" Moravian Church from the impositions of Zinzendorf's "bizarre" theology.[12] In this context, German theologians were also concerned with how "Lutheran" (i.e., orthodox) Zinzendorf really was, a question that left most British and American scholars cold.

Early Moravian historians Cranz and Spangenberg tried to shield Zinzendorf from any appearance of involvement with the Sifting Time by blaming unspecified groups of people for introducing mystical and enthusiastic principles into the church.[13] Schrautenbach, on the other hand, attributed more responsibility to Zinzendorf: "The count may not have foreseen the effect of some of his statements, but these people have nevertheless received their first impressions as well as the occasion for their excesses from him."[14]

Plitt did not accept the apologetic explanations by the previous authors. He called Zinzendorf's attitude "enigmatic" (*rätselhaft*) and the letter of reprimand "meaningless." Plitt attributed the count's misjudgment of the situation to his character and personality but had to admit that "for us later readers, much need for further clarification remains."[15] Although he was not able to find a satisfactory explanation, Plitt clearly assigned Zinzendorf a much greater responsibility for the Sifting Time than any of the previous authors had.

Plitt's son Hermann (1821–1900) wrote the first academic treatment of Zinzendorf's theology. The second of its three volumes, tellingly titled *Die Zeit krankhafter Verbildungen in Zinzendorfs Lehrweise, 1743–1750* (The time of pathological deformations in Zinzendorf's teaching, 1743–1750), is entirely dedicated to the Sifting Time. Hermann Plitt distinguished between the "true image of the Moravian Church" and the Sifting Time as a period of "distortion" during which Zinzendorf fell victim to "aberrations" in his theology. He aimed to prove to the academic world that Zinzendorf's theology was not what was known from the 1740s, "but a very different, yet original but essentially pure and biblical Protestant" theology. His approach of separating Zinzendorf from important aspects of his theology became dominant for years to come, and his work also marked the beginning of a tradition among German Moravian scholars of trying to prove that Zinzendorf, despite his eccentricities, was basically a Lutheran theologian.[16]

The question of the Lutheran nature of Zinzendorf's theology took on renewed life after 1910 when Oskar Pfister (1873–1958), a Swiss pastor and psychoanalyst who had spent part of his youth in the Moravian community of Königsfeld, applied the methods of Sigmund Freud's psychoanalysis to

Zinzendorf. Pfister defined the 1740s as Zinzendorf's "eruption period," when Zinzendorf's "dormant sadistic and masochistic, homosexual-oriented desires" were released and fully displayed in the guise of piety. For Pfister, the 1740s, Zinzendorf's *Schwarmperiode* (time of zealotry), as he calls it, was not a period of abnormality, but is the key to understanding Zinzendorf's personality.[17] Moravians did not wait long with their response. Gerhard Reichel (1874–1953), professor of church history at the Moravian Theological Seminary in Gnadenfeld, published his reaction the following year. He demonstrated that most of Zinzendorf's terminology and imagery were in fact not invented by the count but had a long tradition in seventeenth-century German religious poetry.[18]

## British and American Scholarship

Unlike Moravian historians in Germany, many twentieth-century British and American historians considered Zinzendorf the main culprit of the Sifting Time. In this narrative Zinzendorf was not the founder and instigator of the Moravian Church but merely a patron who temporarily took the Moravians under his wing. During this time he forced his theology on them and tried to make them into something different from the true Moravian Church. The result of these attempts was the Sifting Time, but, fortunately, the church was able to free itself from Zinzendorf's influence and revive the true Moravian Church.

This view has to be seen in context with the growing desire among nineteenth-century American and British Moravians to present themselves as more independent from the German Moravians, who had overseen the worldwide church until 1857. Instead of finding their identity in the (German) story of Herrnhut and Zinzendorf, Moravians in America began looking at the earlier history of the Unitas Fratrum.[19]

Nineteenth-century Moravian historians, such as Holmes, Reichel, and Levering, defined the "time of Sifting" as a linguistic problem. John Beck Holmes (1767–1843), a Danish-born Moravian bishop in England who wrote the first overview of Moravian history in English, described the problem of the Sifting Time as "turgid, puerile, and fanatical" language.[20] Levin Theodore Reichel (1812–1878) also characterized the Sifting as a lapse of religious language, which, he was quick to reassure readers, only lasted a short time. Other phenomena of the Sifting were graphic depictions of Christ's sufferings, frequent festivities with their elaborate decorations, and costly love feasts, all resulting in great expense and financial debt for the church.[21]

Joseph Mortimer Levering (1849–1908) blamed Friedrich Cammerhoff for introducing the language of the Sifting Time to America. Like Holmes and Reichel, Levering defined the Sifting Time as a linguistic problem, while including other characteristics: overelaborate liturgical practices, frequent expensive festivities, grotesque depictions of the sufferings of Christ, and—a characteristic he introduced—a sense of being "the special, selected favorites of Jesus."[22] None of these authors tried to understand how contemporaries originally defined the Sifting Time; they all defined it from their nineteenth-century perspective and standards.

John Taylor Hamilton (1859–1951), professor of church history at Moravian Theological Seminary in Bethlehem, wrote a general overview of Moravian history that remained a standard text throughout the twentieth century. Like other historians before and after him, Hamilton listed aspects of Moravian piety from the 1740s that seemed unusual to him but that were not necessarily aspects of the Sifting Time, when the term was originally coined: the use of endearing diminutives and other sensuous language, mysticism, a "sentimental and extravagant" focus on Christ's physical wounds and an exaggeration of the "material efficacy" of the blood of Christ, a "figurative theory of the Trinity" (probably referring to the concept of the motherhood of the Holy Spirit), and complete control of the church over individuals' lives. Hamilton's definition of the Sifting Time is based on his own reading of the 1740s; in no way does it explain what made Zinzendorf so upset as to write his letter of reprimand. Unlike later historians, Hamilton did not hold Zinzendorf responsible for the Sifting Time. Zinzendorf's exaggerated expressions and ideas had been carried to the extreme by others, such as "Pietists" from Frankfurt, Jena, and Livonia who joined the Moravians in the Wetterau, bringing with them a "predilection for morbid sentimentalism." Zinzendorf had no knowledge of any of this, according to Hamilton, until his confidants opened the count's eyes and he forcefully ended everything.[23]

Hamilton introduced a new element to the narrative: the idea of the pure piety of the original refugees from Moravia as it existed in Herrnhut between 1722 and 1727.[24] According to Hamilton, the piety of early Herrnhut, with its sense of "warriorship for the Lord," had been replaced by a mystical *imitatio Christi* during the Sifting Time. The period afterwards was characterized by "the absolute return of the Brethren to simplicity and a scriptural form of thought." With the end of Herrnhaag, fanaticism within the Moravian Church had been "completely sublimated" and all extravagances completely disappeared, making way for the true Moravian spirit of early Herrnhut.

Hamilton's concept of the true Moravian spirit as distinct from the distortions of the Sifting Time became even more pronounced when authors such as Joseph Hutton (1868–1937) and John Jacob Sessler (1906–1983) identified Zinzendorf as the person who led the Moravians astray. Hutton, minister of the British Moravian Church and author of a widely circulated history of the Moravian Church, lacked any understanding of Zinzendorf's ideals and theology. "The chief sinner was the Count himself," Hutton states in his chapter on the Sifting Time. By "throwing his common sense overboard," Zinzendorf called down the disastrous Sifting Time on his followers: "For seven years these Brethren took leave of their senses, and allowed their feelings to lead them on in the paths of insensate folly." This "folly" consisted of excessive use of diminutives, the metaphor of a family for the Trinity, blood-and-wounds theology, and a lifestyle of feasting and festivities at Zinzendorf's expense: "It was a luxury, an orgy, a pastime." Worst of all was Zinzendorf's candid discussion of sexual matters. But at long last "the Count saw ... the damage he had done." Zinzendorf ended the madness, and the Moravians emerged as a better church: "They became more guarded in their language, more Scriptural in their doctrine, and more practical in their preaching."[25] This account leaves the reader with unanswered questions: why was Zinzendorf so successful, and why did so many people join the Moravians, especially during the 1740s? It may be evident that Hutton's explanation of collective insanity is absurd.

Sessler, who was minister at the Reformed Church in Middletown, New Jersey, when he wrote his book, went even further in trying to prove that Zinzendorf and his followers were different from the true Moravians. In Sessler's narrative, Zinzendorf was not the promoter but rather an obstructor of the cause of the church: "Because he tried persistently to instill his own ideas into the Brethren, he caused many of the serious divisions and disturbances which were a hindrance to the progress and widening of the activities of Moravianism both in Europe and America."[26] He was "a dictator, a theocrat ruling directly under the Invisible King." Ever since his banishment from Saxony in 1736, Zinzendorf had been surrounded by a group of separatists of different background, class, and nationality who were "decidedly different from the Moravians in Herrnhut and were indeed not Moravians at all." Sessler showed a remarkable aversion to the diversity of nationalities in Herrnhaag: "Of seven who were taken into the membership of the settlement on a single day, one was from Poland, another from Hungary, a third from Switzerland, a fourth from England, a fifth from Livonia, a sixth from Germany, and the last from Sweden." This "medley of beliefs and nationalities and the unexpected prosperity," combined with Zinzendorf's "extravagant imagination," formed the breeding ground for "the illegitimate child of Moravianism," the Sifting Time.[27] By encouraging the Moravians to concentrate on the atonement in Christ, Zinzendorf made them into "a group of enthusiastic fanatics." Believing, like Hutton, that Zinzendorf suffered from a "pathological condition," Sessler presented many examples of what he considered the language of the Sifting Time, using descriptions such as "repulsive," "flourished with morbid sentiments," "meaningless words," "unintelligible," "morbid," and "objectionable."[28] For Sessler this form of piety was an alien element in the theology of the Moravians: "This extravagant fanaticism was never characteristic of Moravianism at its best."[29] But if Sessler is correct, we may ask, how was it possible that a single person was able to hold hostage an entire church, spread over continents, for such a long period of time?

The various strands in Anglo-American historiography about the Moravians and specifically about the Sifting Time culminated in a new concept, summed up by Samuel H. Gapp (1873–1962), bishop and archivist at the Moravian Archives in Bethlehem, who wrote that Zinzendorf was "never a Moravian, though their patron."[30] In an intriguing attempt to manipulate their own historiography and to dissociate themselves from the theology of their ancestors, American Moravians cut their church loose from its founder. Moravian historiography, with its undefined concept of a Sifting Time, enabled historians to label anything incomprehensible an aberration and a (temporary) departure from the ways of the true, pure Moravian Church. Eventually, Zinzendorf himself was seen as the personification of this deviation.

A different reading of the Sifting Time is found in the work of Gillian Lindt Gollin. In addition to characteristics of the Sifting Time given by other authors—antirationalism, an intense preoccupation with the physical and emotional details of Christ's death resulting in a "blood-sodden adoration of Jesus' wounds," and a sense of being the elect children of God—another aspect was the most defining for Gollin: because Moravians spent so much time in worship, they neglected their work; as a result, outsiders had to be hired as servants. Moravians also forgot their ideal of simplicity and began to live in luxury: some wore silk, and the women "flaunted gay ribbons and ornate bonnets and vied with their aristocratic members for elegance of dress." Although "religious enthusiasm" in Bethlehem was similar to that in Herrnhut, Gollin writes, American Moravians were not as preoccupied with religion as their German counterparts. Consequently, in Bethlehem there was not as much of a "disregard for day-to-day affairs of the world."[31]

A positive change in the assessment of the Sifting Time among Moravian historians occurred in 1967, when Kenneth G. Hamilton (1893–1975), son of John Taylor Hamilton, published a modified version of his father's book, expanded to the year 1957. Although he included most of his father's account of the Sifting Time, Kenneth Hamilton added a positive twist: "no period in Moravian Church history has been so creative of significant ritual, customs, hymns, or liturgical elements, as was this 'time of sifting.'"[32] Kenneth Hamilton's addition, while counter to the rest of the book's narrative, reflected a new appreciation for the 1740s that had developed in German scholarship during the previous decades.

New Appreciation

This appreciation of the 1740s can be traced to around 1900. Guido Burkhardt (1832–1903) wrote, "We have to perceive this time in its entirety and should not judge it according to the aberration of the later years. The time of Wetteravia [i.e., the Sifting Time] is rather a memorable and meaningful part of the history of the Moravian Church." During these years a form of legalistic Pietism was overthrown; it was a time of rapid expansion of the church as well as of a "childlike, joyful faith."[33]

In 1900, in a lecture at the commemoration of the two hundredth anniversary of Zinzendorf's birth, Paul Kölbing (1843–1925), professor of systematic theology and the New Testament at Moravian Theological Seminary at Gnadenfeld, called for a more integrated treatment of Zinzendorf's theology. Whereas Hermann Plitt had isolated the 1740s as a period of aberration in Zinzendorf's theology, Kölbing wanted to treat Zinzendorf's theology as a unified whole. He called the 1740s Zinzendorf's theologically "most productive" period and the sermons from these years his "richest." For Kölbing Zinzendorf's "sensuous style" was not "a product of his overproductive imagination" but an integral part of his theological thinking. In his lecture, in which the term "Sifting Time" does not appear, Kölbing qualified Zinzendorf's statements from the later 1740s as "the most extreme expression of a characteristic quality of the count's entire theology." Several new studies of the 1740s followed Kölbing's positive assessment.[34]

For Wilhelm Bettermann (1879–1939), Unity archivist, the 1740s were Zinzendorf's most creative period and are important for a full understanding of Zinzendorf's theology.[35] Like Gerhard Reichel before him, Bettermann showed that many parallels in earlier traditions could be found for

Zinzendorf's language and ideas. He argued that Zinzendorf's blood-and-wounds theology was genuinely Lutheran and praised Zinzendorf for leading Pietism back to Luther.[36] He purposely left out one important area, however, feeling he could not deal with the imagery derived from sexuality before a thorough study of Zinzendorf's ideas on sexuality had been written.[37] As we will see, those ideas were significant for what happened during the 1740s.

The question whether Zinzendorf's theology was Lutheran became a leading issue among European Zinzendorf scholars during the twentieth century. In the 1930s, Heinz Renkewitz (1902–1974) and Samuel Eberhard, similar to Bettermann, argued that Zinzendorf was a true Lutheran.[38] The question became relevant again after World War II when scholars like Gösta Hök (1903–1978) in Sweden, Leiv Aalen (1906–1983) in Norway, and Pierre Deghaye in France stressed spiritualist and mystical influences on Zinzendorf.[39] From what follows here, it will become evident that Zinzendorf and the eighteenth-century Moravians were definitely influenced by spiritualistic and mystical ideas. It appears that the question about Zinzendorf's alleged Lutheranism is in fact a question about Zinzendorf's orthodoxy: if it can be proven that Zinzendorf's ideas—however eccentric they may appear—were in fact Lutheran, his doctrine can be approved as theologically sound. Perhaps not surprisingly, this question was particularly important to scholars within the Moravian Church, for whom an orthodox Zinzendorf implied an orthodox Moravian Church, even during the eighteenth century. For scholars in America, where Lutheranism is not by definition the criterion of sound Protestantism, the question about Zinzendorf's Lutheranism played only a minor role.[40]

Postwar historian Gerhard Meyer (1900–1984) labeled the Sifting Time "the most significant period in the life of Zinzendorf and Herrnhut," and Erich Beyreuther (1904–2003) called the 1740s "Zinzendorf's most creative period."[41] Beyreuther mentioned the "not harmless" linguistic developments of the 1740s, resulting in the creation of a congregational jargon; the blood-and-wounds theology, culminating in the "cult" of the side wound; the playfulness; and the festivities with their extravagant decorations. But he also mentioned the great number of people joining the church during these years and the many Moravians who went out as missionaries, preachers, and colonists. For Beyreuther, the point at the height of the Sifting when people believed the line between earth and heaven was beginning to disappear and they were no longer earthly sinners was the "great aberration." "Ecstatic" and "tasteless" things happened, but, Beyreuther insists, no sexual immoralities

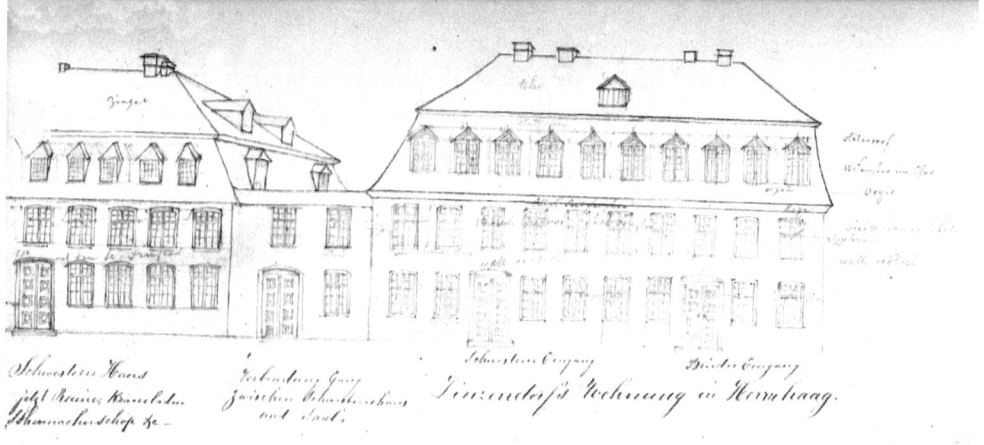

*Fig. 2* The former sisters' house and *Grafenhaus* (Zinzendorf's house with main meeting hall) in Herrnhaag. Pencil drawing by an American Moravian during a visit in 1848. Herrnhaag continued to attract Moravians throughout the nineteenth and twentieth century as a *lieux de mémoire* or space of shared memory. Moravian Archives, Bethlehem, DP vol. 2.5.

took place.[42] Beyreuther's reading of the Sifting Time is ultimately contradictory and leaves questions. If the Sifting was completely Zinzendorf's work, as Beyreuther claimed,[43] why did the count suddenly end it with such force? Why did Zinzendorf consider the occurrences so appalling that he called them "a sifting by Satan"? This does not make sense, unless something else happened. Perhaps the real problem of the Sifting Time lay elsewhere.

In 1988 Moravians in Germany celebrated the 250th anniversary of the founding of Herrnhaag. By that time the place had lost most of its negative connotations; in 1960 a group of Moravians had purchased two of the four remaining buildings in the abandoned community and made it into a center of Moravian activity once again. At the anniversary celebration, Hans-Walter Erbe spoke about the question, Herrnhaag—low point or high point in Moravian history?[44] Also in 1988, the Arbeitskreis für Brüdergeschichte (Study Group for Moravian History) published their detailed analysis of the 1740s, with a special focus on Herrnhaag from the perspectives of theology, sociology, psychology, and linguistics.[45] Without any inhibitions or deprecating assessments, the piety and practice of these years were discussed and explained. The 1740s were now fully rehabilitated into Moravian historiography. No longer a period of "pathological deformations" or "appalling aberrations," the

1740s and Herrnhaag stood for creativity, originality, religious experimentation; in short, the 1740s were a "period of genius."[46]

With this rehabilitation every sense of the Sifting Time as a crisis also disappeared. It was now seen simply as a natural end to the developments of the previous years: "That was the Sifting Time. Herrnhaag had radiated out to all continents. It was a concentration of art, poetry, music, painting, liturgy, social design, and of a special form of piety. Now it had passed its peak and was on the brink of decline. Could it be saved?"[47] Dietrich Meyer discusses the Sifting Time—or as he prefers to call it, the "Wetteravian Period"—in similarly mild terms. For him, the "blood-and-wounds cult" was a reaction against the legalistic nature of Pietism, and he almost trivializes the Sifting in his conclusion that in the end merely "mischievousness, indifference and factionalizing occurred."[48]

Aaron Fogleman defines the Sifting Time as an "episode of extreme mystical spiritualism and 'blood and wounds' beliefs, . . . a time in which virtually anything was possible in the realms of gender, sex, and spirituality."[49] W. R. Ward understands the influence of Bernardine mysticism on Zinzendorf, but his definition of the Sifting Time is rather vague: "The *Sichtungszeit* was that rather ill-defined period in the 1740s when the overflow of Zinzendorf's baroque enthusiasms seemed to burst all bounds, and was spectacularly exemplified in the feasting and fireworks in the settlement of Herrnhaag."[50]

These definitions of the Sifting Time are not sufficient. A positive assessment of the 1740s is appropriate and justified, but the question remains: what happened at the end of the decade that caused Zinzendorf and other leaders to intervene? Why did contemporaries who themselves had been involved or were even instigators of the piety of the 1740s suddenly distance themselves and reprimand those who were held responsible? If the 1740s were actually the most creative period in the history of the Moravians, the Sifting was simply the moment the church realized it had done enough experimenting. It was now time to move on.

In 1996 Craig Atwood raised similar concerns. "It is necessary," he wrote, "to examine how Zinzendorf and his community defined the temptations of the Sifting Time, not simply to quote long passages which may repulse or even titillate us today."[51] Atwood drew attention to Zinzendorf's letter of reprimand from February 10, 1749, which was written to end the ongoing abuses. This text, Atwood pointed out, should be the starting point for our understanding of the sense of crisis that had captured Moravian leaders at the beginning of 1749. Atwood thus placed the problem of the Sifting Time back on the table. While in previous decades historiography seemed to suggest that the Sifting was not much of an issue, Atwood made clear that contemporaries certainly felt something had gone wrong.

There truly was a sense of crisis during the late 1740s. By looking at texts by Zinzendorf and other Moravian leaders about the crisis, including Zinzendorf's letter of reprimand that ended it, we will investigate the cause of their disapproval.

# 3

## THE CRISIS REVEALED

Trust me, if I had known anything I would
have thundered, ranted and raved, and
blown away half of the congregation; I
would have whipped twenty to thirty
people to the utmost; others I would have
thrown into prison for two or three years.
—*Zinzendorf at Barby synod, September 26, 1750*

In order to comprehend the crisis of the Sifting Time, we need to know how contemporaries perceived and defined this crisis. Understanding what they considered objectionable and using that as the starting point for our definition of this period, we may steer away from the anachronistic interpretations of later historians who labeled anything unusual from the 1740s a feature of the Sifting Time. Therefore, in our study of the Sifting Time we have to begin at the end, at the moment when Moravian leaders, realizing that things had gone wrong, stepped in and forbade their members from continuing certain behavior. By identifying what was objectionable, they inherently also defined what the crisis was about.

This moment came when Zinzendorf wrote his letter of reprimand to all the Moravian congregations on February 10, 1749. In this chapter we will look at the events leading up to the writing of this letter, how the letter was received in the church, and subsequent attempts by Moravian leaders to end the crisis and deal with its consequences. An analysis of the contents of Zinzendorf's letter, as well as an examination of the discussions at synods, along with the sermons and other letters in which the crisis was addressed, will follow later in the book.

"According to the power to reform, as given to me by the Lamb, I order you in the name of Jesus Christ"—with these powerful words Zinzendorf began a long letter of reprimand (*Strafbrief*) to all the congregations and missions of the Moravian Church on February 10, 1749.[1] According to the instructions attached to the letter, this detailed missive was to be read first of all by the local leaders to the general choir leaders and members of the elders' conferences, then, "if needed," to the helpers, and finally to the full members of the congregation. "If this does not work," the instructions conclude, it was to be read to the congregation at large. The letter is regarded as the first attempt by the count to end the abuses that he soon would call a "time of sifting." The same day Zinzendorf wrote this public letter, he also wrote a private letter to his son, Christian Renatus, whom he considered responsible for the crisis. Without giving Christel an opportunity to respond in his own defense, Zinzendorf removed him from office as his representative ("von meinem Vicariat"). Anna Nitschmann, Zinzendorf's closest assistant and second-in-command, wrote a letter to Christel as well: "God in heaven! Are you all crazy or what?"[2] These letters form the basis of our understanding about what Zinzendorf initially considered to have gone wrong within the Moravian Church.

Zinzendorf's Letter of Reprimand

What were the reasons for Zinzendorf and Anna Nitschmann to write such letters? What had happened to cause the leaders of this transatlantic religious movement to intervene in a situation that had been developing over the past months, if not years?

Zinzendorf wrote his letter of reprimand from London, where he had arrived only a few weeks earlier. The previous year had been busy for him. In early March he left Herrnhaag for Herrnhut and on to Silesia. After an engagement with the Royal Saxon Commission of Inquiry in Grosshennersdorf in late July and early August, he returned to Herrnhaag on August 31, only to leave again for Zeist in the Netherlands on September 17. On December 31 Zinzendorf boarded a ship to England from Hellevoetsluis, and on January 4, 1749, he arrived in London.[3] Thus, even though Zinzendorf would later claim he had no idea about the matters he mentioned in his letter, he had ample opportunity to see for himself what was brewing in the various Moravian congregations.

In later years Zinzendorf recounted how he was informed about what was going on in the church: from a note from an unnamed single brother, a conversation with Carl Heinrich von Peistel, and a letter from Johann Friedrich Köber.[4] We do not know the contents of the note from the single brother.

Peistel was the minister of the Herrnhut congregation at the time. Writing his memoir many years later, he prided himself on being the one who had enlightened Zinzendorf about the situation in the church while sailing from Holland to England: "My journey with the count to London caused his earnest letter to all congregations of February 10, 1749."[5] It is significant that Peistel, of all people, warned Zinzendorf; a few years earlier Zinzendorf had put Peistel in charge of investigating a situation in Herrnhut that was similar in some ways to the crisis of 1748. That situation, however, appears to have been "only" a matter of sexual misconduct, whereas in 1748 the offenders justified their behavior with Moravian theology.

As unsettling for Zinzendorf as his conversation with Peistel was the letter from Johann Friedrich Köber, his agent in Dresden, who was pursuing negotiations with the Saxon government about the recognition of the Moravian Church in Saxony, where Herrnhut was located. Zinzendorf was horrified to learn from Köber how public opinion in Dresden had turned against the Moravians. Köber recounted how Count Hennicke, representative of the Saxon government, had read the latest slanderous publication against the Moravians and how other reports were creating anti-Moravian sentiment in Dresden: "The Revealed Secret of the Malice of the Herrnhuters, this shameless *chartèque*, has done much damage. H[ennicke] has read it also and he said: it deserved to be burned. Furthermore, there is Wittenberg superintendent Hofmann's new tract about the fundamental errors he attributes to us in the doctrine of the Trinity, plus the news of a new ban in Hanover on all publications of the [Moravian] church and on private meetings on heavy penalty."[6] Köber mentions several anti-Moravian texts circulating in Dresden: the *Gegründete Anzeige* by Carl Gottlob Hofmann, superintendent in Wittenberg,[7] and, most importantly, the *Revealed Secret* by Büdingen clerk and former Moravian Alexander Volck. Zinzendorf's letter to his son Christel, written on the same day as the reprimand, refers to Köber's letter: "Would you want to see more such church histories printed like the one in which your name so frequently appears, that is making its rounds in Dresden and that perhaps will deprive the congregation of its recognition? Recently I was ashamed that Count Hennicke said the book should be burned by the executioner; it [the book] is by far not as untrue as it seems!"[8] Zinzendorf's concern over the change of public opinion in Dresden is apparent, especially now the Moravians were seeking official recognition from the Saxon government. The last sentence is especially revealing. Although men like Hennicke may have thought Volck's writings too outrageous to be true, Zinzendorf knew these publications in reality were not far from the truth.

At the time, the Moravians' position in various parts of Europe was critical. On November 22, 1748, a decree had been issued banishing all Moravians from the electorate of Hanover. Although only a handful of Moravians had been living in the electorate, it was obvious that the decree could have undesirable consequences because of the close ties between Hanover and Great Britain through the House of Hanover. Upon hearing of it, Zinzendorf decided his campaign for recognition by the British Parliament could no longer wait. A first petition was presented to the House of Commons on February 9, the day before Zinzendorf wrote his letter of reprimand.[9] The procedure with the Saxon government seemed equally at risk. A failure of the talks in Dresden could even result in an expulsion from Saxony, Zinzendorf feared.[10] And from Stockholm a similar change of public opinion was being reported.[11]

In light of such negotiations, Zinzendorf wanted to prevent any negative press regarding the Moravians. Although it may have seemed that the unending stream of anti-Moravian publications had little effect on the Moravians—Volck even complained about the lack of reaction his publications provoked—it will become evident how much effect the polemical publications had within the Moravian Church.[12] Equally important is to realize that Zinzendorf implicitly admitted the truth of many of Volck's allegations—as will be confirmed when we compare Volck's book with Moravian sources.

An additional occurrence may have contributed to Zinzendorf's decision to issue the reprimand. Three single brothers from Herrnhaag—Johann Heinrich Andresen, Samuel Hunt, and Thomas Stach—arrived in London on February 8, as recorded in the official diary of Zinzendorf's staff under February 9. It seems likely that they met with Zinzendorf on that day and provided him with the latest news from Herrnhaag, once more confirming his worst fears.

On February 10, Zinzendorf, having ignored earlier indications that something was amiss, at long last drafted a reprimand to all the congregations as well as a letter to his son. Zinzendorf took what looked like firm action, removing his son from office and calling him to London, away from Herrnhaag and the other German congregations, and telling him to break off immediately his official correspondence with local leaders of the congregations and with individual members of the church.

In London, Christian Renatus would become Zinzendorf's "right hand." It is not clear if that means he was placed under his father's supervision or if he was to continue his leadership from England. The question is justified because as stern as Zinzendorf seems to be at the beginning of the letter, in other places his tone is more appeasing and consoling. The letter starts out forcefully by suspending Christel from his position as Zinzendorf's substitute, but toward the end his anger appears to have softened considerably. Zinzendorf addresses his son by his pet name, "Christel," and even by the double diminutive "Christelgen"; diminutives were used by many members of the church to express close affection. Christel was allowed to bring his "dearest hearts" along with him to London, with whom a "new congregation" would be formed. Zinzendorf concludes by saying, "Well, dearest Christelgen, I cannot be harsh with you, although you have made very big mistakes."[13] Thus it may not be surprising that Christel did not follow his father's wishes immediately, but remained in Herrnhaag three more months, until May 9, 1749. Accompanied by fellow elder Rubusch and eleven other men, on the way to England he stopped for a few days in Zeist, the Moravian center in the Netherlands, where they proclaimed similar ideas as in Herrnhaag during the previous months. The official diary notes that when he and his travel party finally arrived in London on May 23, his father received him "somewhat harshly."[14]

A month after the letter of reprimand, Zinzendorf wrote a letter to his son-in-law Johannes von Watteville, who was on an official visit to the Moravian communities in Pennsylvania at the time. Surprisingly, he gives an optimistic depiction of the congregations in Europe. Only once does he refer to any problems, when he defends his son and puts the blame on others: "Christel is the sweetest angel and closest to the dear Lamb, but I hate most of his collaborators: Rubusch, Caillet. Cook died as punishment because he stirred up Herrnhut and Herrnhaag."[15] (John Cook, who preceded Caillet as leader of the single brothers in Herrnhut, had passed away unexpectedly on February 15 while on a visit to Herrnhaag.) Soon Zinzendorf would defend the innocence of the entire Zinzendorf family (including himself) and label what happened as an attack against his position of leadership within the church.

In the meantime the reprimand was read in the various Moravian congregations. From the records we learn about the reactions. The leaders of the Berlin congregation wrote that they humbly accepted the admonishment, and the elders in Copenhagen read the letter "with respect."[16] Johannes von Watteville wrote from Pennsylvania how relieved he was to learn that Rubusch had finally been removed from Herrnhaag: "Only my dear Lamb knows in what great anxiety I have been ever since I received certain letters about last year's celebrations of the Single Brothers' and Single Sisters' Festivals and about what happened around Easter in Herrnhaag."[17] These festivals will be closely analyzed in a later chapter.

*Fig. 3* Portrait of Joachim Heinrich Rubusch (1717–1773). Oil on canvas, attributed to John Valentine Haidt. Unity Archives, Herrnhut, Germany, GS 165.

In Herrnhut the letter of reprimand was read, it was reported, with "a melancholy feeling of sinfulness." On the evening of the same day that it was read, a memorial service was held in Herrnhut for John Cook, who was considered one of the main culprits of the Sifting Time. The service began with a hymn: "Forgive us our trespasses as we forgive those who trespass against us." Was this hymn a deliberate choice for the Herrnhut congregation, recognizing Cook's role in instigating the practices Zinzendorf had banned in his reprimand? But then the service continued with verses about the side hole and about kisses from "the husband"—verses typical of the Sifting Time. Apparently the message of Zinzendorf's letter had not quite sunk in yet. Not until the spring of 1750 did Johannes von Watteville address the spirituality and practice of the Sifting Time with individual members in Herrnhut and in the other congregations.

In April of 1749 Zinzendorf replaced François Caillet, the leader of the single brothers in Herrnhut, with Urban von Luedecke. Caillet was born in Erlangen in 1718 as the son of Huguenot refugees.[18] Moravian critic Andreas Frey characterized him as "a short little Man in Person, [but] of an enormous Size in Profaneness."[19] He learned the trade of wigmaker in Geneva, where he heard Zinzendorf preach in 1741 and decided to join the Moravians. He arrived in Herrnhaag in 1742 and was soon promoted to responsible positions.

He was one of the helpers in Marienborn in 1746, and a year later he became warden of the Theological Seminary. He left Herrnhaag on January 2, 1749, and arrived in Herrnhut eleven days later as the new head of the single brothers' choir. Zinzendorf considered Caillet one of the instrumental forces in the crisis. Christian Renatus, against his father's will, made him pastoral head of the Herrnhut single brothers after Cook's death, but Zinzendorf was quick to replace him with Luedecke, to the great surprise of the Herrnhut brothers, who thought it was all a big "misunderstanding." The day after Luedecke arrived in Herrnhut, Caillet quietly left for Silesia.[20]

After the Uncovering

Aside from a few personnel changes in Herrnhaag and Herrnhut during the first months of 1749, nothing seemed to happen for a while. In September of 1749 Zinzendorf held a synod in London for the chief leaders of the Moravian Church. Christian Renatus as well as Rubusch, the other main instigator of the Sifting Time, were among the official delegates. Interestingly, the problems Zinzendorf had addressed in his letter of reprimand a few months earlier did not come up. Zinzendorf was worried about how the attacks against the Moravians in various publications could endanger the desired official recognition in Saxony (which did occur on September 20). This peculiar period of silence and inactivity in regard to the problems of the Sifting lasted until Johannes von Watteville's return from America.

During the following years Zinzendorf repeatedly claimed ignorance of the full circumstances: "I did not have the slightest idea of the matters written in my letter. I simply wrote it in my usual manner, which is that when I hear about a matter, I imagine twenty-four other possibilities." Zinzendorf even claimed not to have known anything about Volck's book until May or June of 1749.[21] We have already noted that as early as February he was very well aware of Volck's book and that it was one of the immediate causes for the letter of reprimand. Furthermore, Zinzendorf already knew the crisis was of a sexual nature when he wrote the letter.[22] At a synod in Gnadenberg in 1750 Johannes von Watteville affirmed Zinzendorf's claims of ignorance and made it sound almost like a miracle that the count, without really knowing what he was writing about, was able to address the issues of the Sifting.[23] Zinzendorf's alleged ignorance probably served to justify his inactivity. Whatever the reason, he left it to his son-in-law to deal with the matter and solve the problem.

Johannes was absent from Herrnhaag for almost two years. Together with his wife, Benigna née Zinzendorf, he had left Herrnhaag in January of 1748 to visit the church in America and the West Indies. Because of several delays and changes of plan along their way, they did not sail from England until the end of July. One goal of their visit was to ground the Moravians in Bethlehem and elsewhere in America in the theology of the side hole and the style and teaching so typical of Moravianism of the late 1740s. In July of 1749, after their return to Bethlehem from the West Indies, they learned about Zinzendorf's reprimand. Now Johannes himself had to change his tone: the references to the side hole, of which his earlier letters were full (and which a later editor carefully marked through), suddenly disappeared from his letters.[24] In October Johannes and Benigna left America, and they arrived in England on November 9, 1749. After staying with Zinzendorf in London for two and a half months, they set out for Herrnhaag and the other continental congregations. Johannes's mission was to deal with the crisis and put things in order.[25]

In the meantime, additional problems for the Herrnhaag congregation were developing. Not only was Herrnhaag the center of a series of religious excesses that shocked the church, but now the very existence of the community became uncertain as the government in Büdingen threatened to evict all inhabitants from Herrnhaag. Reichel claims this threat was "as unexpected as a thunderstorm during winter."[26] In reality, difficulties had existed between the government and the Moravians for several years. A year before the edict of eviction, Zinzendorf had already alluded to the possibility that Herrnhaag would be completely abandoned.[27] Christoph Friedrich Brauer, counsel to the Count of Büdingen, had proven extremely critical of the community at Herrnhaag, seeing them as loyal foremost to their Moravian elders and wardens, and especially to Zinzendorf, much more than to their legitimate secular lord, the Count of Büdingen. He believed the Herrnhaag community had become a state within the state where the count could not fully exercise his power.[28]

When Johannes and Benigna arrived in Herrnhaag on February 8, 1750, the crisis was in full swing. With the death of Count Ernst Casimir zu Ysenburg and Büdingen on October 15, 1749, Brauer, as well as the new count, Gustav Friedrich, saw an opportunity to make demands on the inhabitants of Herrnhaag to pay homage to the count in Büdingen. This would not have been problematic had not the text of the homage, as determined by Brauer, required renouncing any allegiance to Zinzendorf and the other Moravian elders and overseers. On February 2, 1750, the inhabitants of Herrnhaag were ordered to unconditionally accept the wording of the homage and renounce their Moravian leaders. When they refused, they were told to leave Herrnhaag within the next three years.[29] Many Moravians immediately declared their willingness to leave, and on February 21 thirty single brothers left Herrnhaag for Pennsylvania. For the Herrnhaag congregation the ordeal of emigration proved to be a way to overcome the stigma of the extravagances they had engaged in during the previous years; now they could take up their cross and become "pilgrims." The idea that God had punished Herrnhaag for its excesses and that the Moravians willingly accepted the ordeal soon became an integral part of the historical narrative. Zinzendorf's wife, Erdmuth Dorothea, left Herrnhaag on April 26, and others followed soon thereafter. By July of 1753, Herrnhaag was completely empty.

Besides having to deal with the situation created by the eviction notice, the real purpose of Watteville's visitation was to take on the persisting ideas of the Sifting. During his stay in Herrnhaag, he addressed, sometimes together with Benigna, all groups: married people, single sisters, single brothers, and even children; with many members he had individual conversations. On March 3 he addressed the congregation in Herrnhaag during the evening meeting, and the next day he spoke to the single brothers in Marienborn. His address there survives and is an important source for our understanding of the Sifting.[30]

The Wattevilles left Herrnhaag on April 13 and went on to Gnadenberg, a Moravian community in Silesia, where Johannes held a synod for the congregations in Silesia (Gnadenfrei, Gnadenberg, Neusalz) and the Oberlausitz (Herrnhut, Niesky).[31] During this synod, Johannes spoke extensively about what had gone wrong in the previous years. From Gnadenberg he returned to Herrnhut, where he held similar conversations ("speakings") as in Herrnhaag with the single brothers between May 21 and 23. In September of 1750 a General Synod was held for the Moravian Church in Barby. Zinzendorf, who had not been present at the Provincial Synod in Gnadenberg, attended, and on September 26 he held a "special conference" about the crisis of the previous years. Many of the leaders of the church also attended the special conference. Christian Renatus was there but—at least according to the minutes—did not say a single word. Equally interesting is that Rubusch, Christel's confidant and accomplice, was absent. Zinzendorf had allowed him to attend the synod in London the previous year, but he had since been demoted from his office as elder. Erdmuth Dorothea was also absent from the special conference, though she was in Barby and attended the general sessions.

During 1750 the problems of the recent crisis were addressed. Johannes's addresses in Herrnhaag in March, as well as the minutes of the Provincial Synod in Gnadenberg in May and of the General Synod at Barby in September, all give insight into how Moravian leaders thought about the recent events and what they considered to be part of the crisis. They began to define it and view it as a separate period, set apart from what came before and what followed afterwards. The term *Sichtung* (Sifting) was applied to the recent internal crisis for the first time at the Barby synod.[32]

Sifting Time: Term and Periodization

The reference to "sifting" is derived from Luke 22:31 ("And the Lord said, Simon, Simon, behold, Satan hath desired to have you, that he may sift you as wheat"), and the word is used with a similar meaning elsewhere in the Bible as well (e.g., Amos 9:9: "I will sift the house of Israel among all nations, like as corn is sifted in a sieve"). A sifting time was thus a time during which Satan tried to test them, a period of profound crisis.

The German words *sichten* (to sift), *Sichtung* (sifting), and *Sichtungszeit* (sifting time) are not exclusively Moravian terms, but had been used among other German Protestants during the seventeenth century, as documented by Hans Schneider. Hymn writers such as Johann Frank, Sigmund von Birken, and Johann Heinrich Schröder used *Sichtung*. German radical Pietist Heinrich Horch used *Sichtungszeit* to describe a process of purification the members of his own Philadelphian group had experienced. Zinzendorf and other people in close connection with the early Herrnhut community used the term as well.[33] As early as 1727, Zinzendorf called the serious division in Herrnhut in 1725–27 "a great sifting by Satan,"[34] and in his eighteenth-century biography of Zinzendorf Spangenberg called that same crisis a sifting time.[35] Zinzendorf also called the time following his return from America in 1743, when he saw his Philadelphian endeavors being undermined by those who administered the church during his absence, a sifting.[36] At a conference in Bloomsbury in London in 1749 Zinzendorf spoke about several siftings that the church had recently escaped from. Surprisingly, even though it was only eight months after his letter of reprimand, the crisis of 1748–49 was not among them; Zinzendorf in this case was referring to the financial difficulties and confusion during the second half of the 1740s and about the greater influence of erudition within the Moravian Church, to the detriment of the original simplicity of the brethren's theology.[37] Later, Zinzendorf called the financial crisis of 1753 a sifting.[38] In later Moravian historiography as well, "sifting time" was not always used exclusively for the crisis of the 1740s. Nineteenth-century Moravian historian Ernst Wilhelm Cröger, for example, spoke of a "new economic sifting" during the years 1769 to 1775.[39]

Generally, however, "Sifting Time" came to mean the late 1740s. Though he did not use the word "sifting," at the Provincial Synod at Gnadenberg in May of 1750 Johannes von Watteville applied the metaphor from Luke 22:31 to the recent crisis: "We have to admit: *Satan has desired us*, but the sweat of our Lamb did not allow it. Praise be to the Lamb!"[40] Four months later, at the synod in Barby, the "siftings of Satan" (*Sichtungen des Satans*) were mentioned frequently in discussing the problems of the recent past. This was the first time, as noted above, that "sifting" was used to describe the late 1740s. On New Year's Eve that year, Johannes spoke of the *"previous* Sifting Time," and the same night Zinzendorf declared, "The time is over when Satan wanted to sift us as wheat."[41]

Other terms in use among Moravians, some as late as the nineteenth century, say something about the character of the crisis. *Schätzelperiodus* refers to the companies of "sweethearts" (*Schätzel*) that were dominant among the single choirs during these years. *Seitenhöhlchenszeit* (time of the side hole) refers to the central role played by the side wound of Christ during the late 1740s. Other terms have to do with the playfulness and frivolity that was prominent during these years: *leichtsinniger Periodus* (frivolous period), *Spielzeit* (playtime), and *lustige Zeit* (jolly time).[42] For the most part, unlike "Sifting Time," these designations have positive connotations.

Many historians read "Sifting *Time*" as synonymous with "Sifting *Period*" and consequently try to define this period. Some date it simply as the 1740s,[43] but most attempt to be more precise. Many place the beginning of the Sifting Time in 1743 with Zinzendorf's return from America.[44] Some take 1745 or 1746 as the starting year.[45] And a few authors put it as early as in 1738.[46] There is more agreement about the end: usually 1749 or 1750, although 1752 or 1753 is sometimes mentioned.[47] Johannes Plitt is very specific: he sees 1738–43 as the "preparation," 1743–48 as a "period of transition," and 1748–49 as "the actual Sifting Time."[48]

When the Sifting Time is interpreted as an era, everything that happened during it is considered to be a feature of the crisis. For example, Jörn Reichel uses "Sifting Time" as a chronological term in his study of poetry and language in appendix 12 of the Herrnhut hymnal. For him, the Sifting Time lasted from 1743 until 1750, and consequently the hymns written during these years contain language and theology typical of the Sifting.[49] American scholar Gillian Lindt Gollin argues in a similar way, although for her the Sifting Time lasted from 1738 to 1752.[50]

It is incorrect, however, to read the Sifting Time as a well-defined period. It was primarily a situation, a crisis. *Zeit* (time) has to be read not as indicating a period of time but rather an *occurrence* or a *moment*; Zinzendorf sometimes used the term *Sichtungsstunde* (hour of sifting).[51] By examining how immediate contemporaries defined the Sifting, we will see that a sense of real crisis did not exist before 1748. By the end of that year a point had been reached when leaders such as Peistel and Weiss could no longer hold back and asked Zinzendorf to act.

Of course, in hindsight the contemporary witnesses claimed to have seen the origins of the crisis earlier in the 1740s. Johannes claimed he had seen the first indications of "a bad period" in 1744, when "several frivolous people" abused Christian Renatus's "innocence," without envisioning "what later came of it."[52] In September of 1749 Zinzendorf claimed he had known a sifting was to come over the church ever since Luke 22:31 was the daily watchword (*Losung*) on his birthday in 1746. He also trusted the crisis would soon be over when he read the hymn verse under the daily watchword for January 3, 1750: "We Have Been Saved from All Peril."[53]

Zinzendorf's letter of reprimand serves as our primary source for understanding the nature of the crisis. Now we need to examine the content of the count's letter, in combination with other texts related to the end of the Sifting.

# 4

## CHARACTERISTICS OF THE SIFTING

A congregation without play is nothing.
—*Zinzendorf, address to the single brothers in Marienborn, January 8, 1747*

"With today's mail a serious letter by the ordinary [Zinzendorf] was dispatched to all the main congregations regarding some disorders that had taken hold," the general diary of February 11, 1749, noted, with some understatement.[1] This chapter will examine this "serious letter" in order to gain an understanding of what Zinzendorf and his contemporaries considered to be aspects of the crisis. What were these "disorders that had taken hold"? Although the letter of reprimand is a crucial text for our understanding of the nature of the crisis, it is not the most explicit text. By merely alluding to the various problem areas, Zinzendorf hoped that those in the know would understand what he was referencing, without giving away too much to those unaware of the details. For insight into how Moravian leaders around 1750 defined the crisis, we need to include other texts in our examination as well: the minutes of the Barby synod and the Provincial Synod at Gnadenberg; the diary of the Theological Seminary at Marienborn; Johannes von Watteville's discourses when addressing the problems of the previous years; as well as polemical writings by non-Moravians. An important aspect of the developments during the 1740s was the intentionally provocative behavior of some Moravians. We will find that the letter of reprimand and the additional texts suggest that the crisis of the Sifting was related to the idea of becoming sinless and to sexual transgressions.

## Authority and Power

Zinzendorf's letter of reprimand starts forcefully: "According to the power to reform, as given to me by the Lamb, I order you in the name of Jesus Christ...." After identifying various areas of abuse, the letter concludes with equally powerful language: "If you do not follow me, I will not only lay down my office over all the congregations and form a new selection from the congregations according to Jesus's heart, I can also assure you in advance that the Savior's office of chief elder will cease as well." So if the Moravians defied Zinzendorf, not only would the count leave the Moravians and take with him a select group of followers to form a new church, but Christ would cease to be chief elder of the remaining Moravian Church.[2]

Of the twenty-three points in the letter, eleven deal with issues of authority: collecting notes with confessions by fellow brothers and sisters and using these against them; reporting internal matters to outsiders without permission (often used as sources by anti-Moravian publicists); setting up private societies without knowledge of the general leaders of the church and holding private meetings without permission of the congregational elders; unauthorized public preaching, especially about marital matters; holding offices within the choirs without having been called by the elders of the congregation; using the lot without approval; unauthorized meddling in marital matters; and using hymns that were not authorized by Zinzendorf.

Zinzendorf considered the crisis the result of his loss of control over the church. Incapable people had taken over offices and positions within the church without being authorized by the general leadership. In the letter, Zinzendorf reasserted his power. He removed his son, Christian Renatus, from office and called him to London. Others in lower offices were also removed by Zinzendorf or stepped down themselves. Later, at the Barby synod in September of 1750, Zinzendorf considered the crisis a personal attack on the position of the entire Zinzendorf family: "I consider all these things as a cabal to depose me, my son-in-law, my son, and family."[3]

In fact, there are no indications to confirm the existence of such a "cabal." To the contrary, the developments of the late 1740s were the logical consequence of Zinzendorf's own teaching. It seems more likely that Zinzendorf, by blaming others, was trying to protect himself and his relatives against accusations that he may have caused the crisis himself.

During the meeting in Barby Zinzendorf complained about his fellow leaders, who had not fully informed him about the situation: "Where will this lead to when we hide such things from one another for such a long time?

How can we trust each other? Who can hold office within the church with a good conscience? Who can be a servant or an angel of such a church?"[4]

Garments

In point 10 of his letter of reprimand Zinzendorf criticized certain "extraordinary" practices regarding clothing. He admitted that these were probably introduced without ill intentions and were "not sinful" by themselves. It almost seems as if someone had brought this point to his attention and he felt obliged to mention it without really agreeing with the criticism. The critic probably noted the recent introduction of white surplices (*Talare*) as well, but Zinzendorf refused to forbid their use, and even explicitly defended them.

The white surplices had been introduced by Christian Renatus at the single brothers' festival of May 2, 1748.[5] At the beginning of the morning service in the worship hall of the Lichtenburg, Christian Renatus, Rubusch, and twenty-eight other men entered the space dressed in "long white robes reaching to the ground, with an award [*Orden*] of green ribbon around their necks and wreaths on their heads." The effect on the single brothers in attendance was overwhelming: "Of all of them, our dear Christel looked the most charming and venerable, like an angel and a prince of God. One could see a majesty on him not found with any king or emperor."[6] That night the thirty men wore their white surplices again during the Communion service concluding the choir festival. It was the first time the white surplices were worn during a Moravian Communion service, and they would soon become regular attire for Moravian ministers administering Communion and baptism.

Zinzendorf defended the surplices on several occasions, apparently reacting to strong resistance within the church against their use. "It is not a popish but an apostolic invention," he said later that same year, noting that not only had the Anglican Church preserved the white surplice in their tradition, but the Lutherans had as well.[7]

Christian Renatus and the other single brothers at Herrnhaag attached their own specific symbolism to the surplices. In a poem written around this time, Christel called the white surplice a wedding dress for their marriage with Christ.[8] If so, the wreath can also be read as a bridal wreath.[9] When Zinzendorf edited the report of the 1748 choir festival for publication in the Congregational Accounts, he inserted an explanation about the robes not found in the longer version of the report. Its defensive tone once again confirms that resistance existed within the church. But it also reveals what may have been close to the original intentions of the men: their festive dress symbolized the shroud Jesus wore in the grave and when he appeared to his disciples after the Resurrection.[10] Zinzendorf later called the surplice an expression of "our future bliss when we can become pure souls of the Savior" and added that it was "something the sisters already have with their white uniforms."[11] Thus the white robes served as the male equivalent to the white festive dress of the women.

To sum up, in addition to the reference to the white robes of Revelation 7:9, the eschatological nature of the surplices derives from the image of the burial shroud, the wedding dress, and the festive dress: the surplices were the dress of the believer who had mortified all sinful desires of the flesh, had become pure, and was ready to wed Christ. They enhanced the solemnity of the liturgical act and of the men who wore them, as the description of Christian Renatus as a prince of God, superior to any emperor or king, illustrates. And the wreath he was wearing that day certainly enhanced that effect. As will be shown below, the symbolism of the white surplices as the dress of the perfected believer, ready to unite with Christ, lies at the heart of the Sifting.[12]

The single brothers were experimenting with other types of garments as well. At a Communion service on December 4, 1748, Christel, Rubusch, and Johann Nitschmann wore red surplices.[13] Volck writes that Christel once wore a "purple-colored surplice, decorated with ribbons"; he also quotes from an anonymous letter of a visitor to Herrnhaag, describing a Communion service when Christel wore a purple surplice while twelve others distributed Communion in white robes, representing Jesus and the twelve apostles.[14] No other garb and decorations are mentioned in the records, but it seems likely that more was going on. Zinzendorf does not seem to have been too concerned, and even defended some aspects. Because of the inclusion of point 10 in the letter of reprimand, we may assume that during the activities of the Sifting special garments were worn.

Playfulness

"The first occasion for the short but dreadful moment of sifting among us I probably gave myself," Zinzendorf declared in 1757, "namely by the idea that there is nothing more blessed in his church than to become like a child and to behave as a still unspoiled Swiss peasant."[15] Childlike behavior, playfulness, anti-intellectualism, and silliness were a crucial aspect of the Sifting Time and would eventually lead to the more sexually related incidents. The diary of the Theological Seminary at Marienborn describes many love feasts as "jolly and cheerful" (*lustig und vergnügt*). In the entry for April 5, 1748, a later redactor crossed out the word *lustig*, probably because this reference to the exuberance of the time had become too much associated with the Sifting Time.[16] As it turns out, Zinzendorf did not address the playfulness in his letter of reprimand, nor in his letter to Christel of the same day. During the Barby synod this aspect was excused as a relatively harmless phenomenon of the Sifting Time, and Zinzendorf even strongly defended the "childlike character" and "foolish nature" of a true believer.[17] Only later did Zinzendorf realize that the playfulness had led to the excesses.[18]

The focus on playfulness had its roots in the Order of Fools, founded by Zinzendorf on Pentecost Sunday, June 2, 1743, shortly after his return from America. Zinzendorf was dissatisfied with the course of the church during his absence. He felt that its leadership had departed from the Philadelphian ideals by engaging in negotiations with several European governments about recognizing the church. He also sensed a tendency toward self-importance among church leaders as well as disagreement on matters of piety. His reaction was to found the Order of Fools. The name was based on Matthew 11:25: "I thank thee, O Father, Lord of heaven and earth, because thou hast hid these things from the wise and prudent, and hast revealed them unto babes." In the original Greek, the word "babes" is the nominalized adjective νηπιοι (childlike), which Zinzendorf translated as "fools" (*Närrchen*). Other radical Pietists, such as Gottfried Arnold, who also wrote about the ideal of irrationality for the true believer in the light of divine wisdom, translated it as "idiots" (*Idioten*).[19] Believers, according to Zinzendorf, should simply put their trust in the Lord, in a childlike, uninhibited manner.[20]

In his 1771 history of the Moravian Church, Cranz claims that what he calls the "evil" of playfulness first came to light when Zinzendorf and the other leaders were away from Herrnhaag attending the synod at Zeist during May and June of 1746.[21] Although Cranz's assertion may initially seem an attempt to shield Zinzendorf from any responsibility for the playful behavior, other sources confirm that having begun earlier in 1746, it took on more extreme forms during Zinzendorf's absence.[22] In the regular elders' absence, Joachim Rubusch was made general leader of the single brothers in Herrnhaag, Marienborn, and Lindheim. This decision would have far-reaching consequences.

Heinrich Joachim Rubusch was born on the Baltic island of Oesel in 1717.[23] Both of his parents died when he was only two years old, and he was brought up by several of his twenty-three older siblings. Although he had a strong inclination and desire to become a minister, his family apprenticed him instead to a merchant in Reval (now the Estonian capital city of Tallinn).

When he was around twenty years old, he began to display a form of religious fanaticism. In an attempt to attain a state of perfection, Rubusch followed a regimen of fasting and praying. Soon, however, probably through his acquaintance with Moravians in Reval, he experienced a profound change. He realized his own human shortcomings in light of the sacrifice of Jesus's suffering and death; he knew he was saved not by his own works but solely because of Jesus's sacrifice. From then on he abhorred his earlier perfectionism and—according to his memoir—only wanted to know and hear about the merit of Jesus's death. Rubusch was a man of extremes, and this explains the developments within the single brothers' choir in Herrnhaag once he took charge of it. He taught the single brothers to despise anything that reminded them of Pietist seriousness and gloominess. Interestingly, he had not abandoned his perfectionism. At the end of the 1740s he believed that he and his Moravian brothers had indeed reached a state of perfection.

Rubusch joined the Moravians in Reval in 1741. That same year he encountered Countess Erdmuth Dorothea von Zinzendorf, and two years later he met the count himself when Zinzendorf came to see the developing work of the Moravians in the Baltic states. In January of 1744 Rubusch arrived in Herrnhut. After working as a private teacher for a few months, he was called as a servant and sick nurse for the single brothers. His qualities as a charismatic leader were soon recognized; in 1745 he became elder of the single brothers in Lindheim, and was ordained a deacon the same year. On May 3, 1746, Rubusch took the place of Johannes and Christian Renatus as general elder of the single brothers. In the coming years, Rubusch would be instrumental in the developments within the brothers' choir. His bridal mysticism, his experimental ideas and side-wound theology, as well as his creative use of language would greatly influence Moravians during the second half of the 1740s. Together with Christian Renatus, Rubusch was a central figure of the Sifting Time.

Religious play seems to have originated during the first few months of 1746. In the diary of the single brothers in Herrnhaag, meetings had previously been characterized as *blutig* (bloody) and *selig* (blessed), but with increasing frequency that year they were called *vergnügt* (cheerful, joyful) and especially *lustig* (jolly). A few examples:

> After everything we had a jolly and nice love feast. (February 9, 1746)
>
> In the evening we had a very jolly conference. (March 2, 1746)
>
> We were together until 12 o'clock quite blessedly and joyfully. (March 9, 1746)

The playfulness was connected to a new hymn cowritten by Johannes and Christian Renatus during the first months of 1746: "Was macht ein Creuzluftvögelein," or, in a contemporary English translation, "What Does a Bird in Cross's Air."[24] In the hymn birds fly in the air around the cross of Jesus and clap their wings for joy, representing, as the printed explanation in the English Moravian hymnbook puts it, "Christian Souls, in the Shape of happy little Birds in the Cross's-Air, or in the Atmosphere of the Corpse of Jesus."

> What does a bird in cross's air,
> When it flies up to the Lamb near,
> When round the Lamb it moves and sings,
> And claps the *Ave* with its Wings?
> Dear hearts! look, look, and see,
> Look, look, and see,
> The little bird finds presently
> Its nest in the dear cavity,
> From whence the church was dug.
> Within the hole, where blood casts rays,
> The bird itself entangled has;
> And round the Castle of the Side
> Are wound-swans in the canal wide;
> There learns the little piper
> In th' hole to be a dipper.

The cross-air birds were a joyful and playful lot of mostly single brothers, proclaiming their joy in the atonement through the death of Jesus on the cross. The ten verses in the printed German hymnal were written for various occasions: besides the general first stanza there were stanzas for getting up in the morning, for being at work, for going on a walk, for when one was melancholic, for going to bed, and also for dying. The individual stanzas must have given plenty of opportunity to play out the pleasures of the existence of a cross-air bird. Soon the metaphor appeared in other hymns as well.[25] During these months the playfulness must have primarily consisted of wordplay as new images for the cross-air bird were invented.

By May of 1746 the character of the playfulness was changing. With Zinzendorf, Johannes, and Christel gone, Rubusch had free rein as elder of the single brothers. On May 23 he insistently called on the brothers to play as cross-air birds "from the side hole." In his meditations and sermons during the following weeks and months he spoke about how to play "within the side hole" and how to enjoy the union with Christ on a daily basis.

A letter written by Friedrich Geller to Johann Nitschmann during the summer of 1746 informs us about the nature of the play.[26] Geller expresses great concern about what at first had seemed like a cheerful and enjoyable pastime in which he and his wife had participated ever since Zinzendorf's departure from Herrnhaag. But now, since the end of May, what seemed innocent amusement had turned into something objectionable: "Often I heard with amazement how brothers called one another beasts, scum, dogs, etc. and whatever else. Whoever did not want to play along was considered a confused fool and was ridiculed. They treated brothers this way and did not spare the laborers. They remarked about the quarter hours that they were too legalistic and so on."

Geller's dating of these events agrees with Cranz's dates and with the time frame in the single brothers' diary. His letter shows that an important element of the playful behavior was to express one's joy about the assurance of their salvation, which they saw as a defeat of their previous Pietist burden of sin. Many Moravians had been influenced by Pietist ideas of the *Busskampf* or penitential struggle. But Moravian theology as it was unfolding during the 1740s had taught them that they were redeemed solely through Christ's suffering. None of their own works, they learned, could contribute to their salvation.[27] During the summer of 1746 their joy turned into provocative behavior as they purposely engaged in all those things that they had previously disapproved of.

Other sources also mention name-calling of those who refused to play. Hart, the former Moravian from Zeist, claimed the players called those who did not feel comfortable joining in "Pietists and head hangers" (*Pietisten und Kopfhänger*) and accused them of despising the grace and mercy of God. The players mocked those they considered too serious in songs with such lyrics as "And when one looks into the brethren's house, one can see all Pietism is out."[28] Similarly, Frey writes that "they would not give over till they had driven Pietism out of the Community, Root and Branch."[29] It may not be surprising that Rubusch, who as a young man was one of the strictest Pietists himself, took the lead in this provocative playfulness. Hart claims that Moravian brothers engaged in games, something a serious Pietist would never approve of. They played nine-men's morris (*Mühle*), billiards, and a self-made card game with hymn verses written on cards numbered according to how they rated the importance of the verses. These cards seem similar to the sets of so-called side-hole cards that exist in the Unity Archives.[30]

Examples of fooling around and horseplay can be found in Moravian and non-Moravian texts alike. Geller writes,

> Many times I have seen how married brothers were so intimate with single sisters that they drove them from one corner into another, tickled each other, and the sisters even let them push them down to the ground; this happened just last Friday in the laundry room. I even heard the single sisters say that the brothers are much worse than the boys on the street. Many times have I happened on a particular sister in the evening who was waiting for a certain brother to come in order to play with him.[31]

At the Barby synod of 1750, jumping up and down staircases and "smashing everything that is in the way" were dismissed as relatively innocent phenomena of the Sifting.[32]

Volck, the disgruntled ex-Moravian from Büdingen, offers several instances of religious play among the men in the Wetterau. Although they may seem innocent to a modern audience, Volck expected his readers to consider such behavior scandalous; the pious were not to engage in idle amusement. Christian Brodersen, one of the students at the seminary, had trained his dog to smoke a pipe. One time during a love feast he placed the dog on a table with a lit pipe. Another time, in order to cheer up a "melancholic" fellow student at the seminary, Brodersen dressed up his dog with a band around his neck like a Protestant minister, put a pipe in the dog's mouth, and presented it to the depressed student. Volck also describes a prank with Christel as the main actor. The men put François Caillet, elder of the single brothers at the seminary, into a child's carriage, and Christel and another brother pushed him around in the garden until they had enough and dumped Caillet out into the mud. This last prank was a playful celebration of the childlike faith of the students and their leaders, but its symbolic meaning may have been lost on Volck's readers.[33]

One time a company of "cross-air birds" at the seminary decided to stage a confrontation between the side hole (Christ) and the devil. Christian Renatus played the side hole, and Ludwig Carl von Schrautenbach was chosen by lot to play the devil. So Schrautenbach blackened his face, took a fork from the fireplace, and went around the room while lots were drawn to determine which men belonged to the side hole or to the devil. It turned out, according to Volck's account, that the men claimed for the devil were those who did not appreciate the foolishness.[34]

A similar incident is reported from the Moravian group in St. Petersburg, Russia. It was the birthday of David Krügelstein, and the Moravian men and women were sitting around the table to eat a meal when Brother Köhler entered the room, wearing a long beard and dressed in Krügelstein's dressing gown. Köhler was playing the side hole (Christ), who ate with the birthday guests. The men and women kissed him and offered him an armchair. While he was eating with them, they felt "as if he [i.e., Christ] was there in person," one of the brothers later reported. After the meal the guests joined at the table, and while they were singing the "side hole began to beam so radiantly" that everyone cheered and jumped for joy.[35]

Volck describes an instance where a group of men were playing around while singing one of the popular songs of this period. "One of their love songs has the words 'It's thumping, it's hopping, it's throbbing,'[36] whereat the singers beat their breasts. Some time ago it came to pass that a few brethren were together jumping around in a room while singing these so-called love songs for fun and to pass the time. As they were beating their breasts, when they came to the words 'It's thumping, it's hopping, it's throbbing' one of the brothers present slapped his bottom and, while letting off an enormously loud fart, he said, 'It's cracking!'"[37]

Andreas Frey, a Moravian from Pennsylvania, was shocked by the pranks he witnessed during his stay at Herrnhaag between 1743 and 1747. "The young Folks began to grow wanton, laughing, sporting, jesting, leaping, throwing one another on the Floor, and strugling till they were quite spent and out of Breath, besides many filthy, gross Indecencies; once a Brother was drinking Tea in his Chamber, when in comes another, and lifting up his Leg, breaks Wind over the Brother's Tea-cup, so that a Brother and myself who were together in another Room heard it, upon which I said, such ranting Doings I never in my Life heard, not in a Guard-Room of Soldiers."[38] In June of 1748 a group of single brothers from Herrnhaag who had come to Bethlehem were asked about Frey's allegations. To the great dismay of the Bethlehem leaders, the brothers, who had left Herrnhaag in February, "only laughed about Frey's writing and said that in reality things were ten times worse but that they considered these things to be nice [hübsch]."[39]

Beginning in 1746, the single brothers in Herrnhaag, as well as the single sisters and the married couples, engaged in a form of religious play, which for them was an expression of the joy they had found in the doctrine of justification by faith alone. Zinzendorf and the other leaders did not disapprove of the playful activities that Rubusch had instituted in their absence. From Christian Renatus's return to Herrnhaag on November 8, 1746, he and Rubusch, his elder by ten years, worked closely together. Apart from a few days in November when he was only passing through on his way to Ebersdorf, Zinzendorf did not return to Herrnhaag until a few days before Christmas, when he unexpectedly stepped into the room as Christel, Rubusch, and a few other single brothers were having a "cheerful" gathering in Christel's room in the brothers' house. The men did not know how the count would react to their play, but they were apparently relieved to see Zinzendorf "surprisingly pleased."[40]

Zinzendorf fully supported the idea of playfulness as an expression of childlike, true faith in Christ. He preferred a silly person who truly loved the Savior over a bright, honorable, and reasonable man.[41] In a sermon on January 8, 1747, the watchword of the day was 2 Samuel 6:21: "I will play before the Lord." Zinzendorf unmistakably declared, "A congregation without play is nothing," and continued, "As soon as someone resists playing, then that is a sign he is either spiritually dumb or he is spiritually malicious." Everyone, he said, should play according to his stage of life: a child should play like a child, an adolescent like an adolescent, and an adult like an adult. Playing like children around the throne of the Lamb was an expression of true joy about their salvation. Playing was also a foretaste of heavenly joy: "One is already in eternity because one lives in Jesus." Therefore, those who had not attained this assurance in their hearts should not play; they would only be pretending to have found redemption, and their play would be a mockery. And those who had no understanding of the childlike players should not criticize or reprimand them.[42] Although a few days later Zinzendorf sent out a circular letter to all congregations warning them against play that was too nonsensical and clownish, he was undeniably a supporter of the playful manner of many Moravians.[43]

While it has been suggested that this playfulness may have resulted from an aversion to the rationalism of the Enlightenment,[44] it was actually a reaction against Halle Pietism and its emphasis, as Zinzendorf saw it, on a pious lifestyle and righteousness by works instead of justification by faith. Later, when dealing with the aftermath of the Sifting Time, Johannes von Watteville observed that it was those people who previously had been legalistic and strict in their faith who engaged in the most extravagant behavior.[45] It is thus not surprising that Rubusch, who as a young man was one of the strictest Pietists, was the leader of this provocative playfulness.

### Childlike and Headless

In one of his reports about the children in Bethlehem, Friedrich Cammerhoff wrote, "We also told them something about the cross-air birds, and we sang songs about them. That pleased them very much, and they were overjoyed. It is their greatest joy to think and talk with each other about going to the Lamb and kissing his wounds. And indeed they have no other concept of death than this one. What is more blissful on earth than being such a child?"[46] Atwood points out that Zinzendorf's theology of the heart was best expressed with the biblical image of the child.[47] To become like a child (Matt. 18:3, also John 1:12) is simply to accept the theology of salvation through Christ, without having to overcome obstacles of reason and education. During the 1740s Moravians observed and studied the behavior of children and recorded their observations in the children's choir diaries, which are full of anecdotes of how the children responded to the stories about the Lamb of God, the blood and wounds of Christ, and especially his side wound.

Adults also imitated the behavior of the children. In a booklet with hand-drawn images from the life of Elisabeth von Zinzendorf, an image illustrating the year 1748 depicts a group of children in a room clapping their hands, with the caption "Sing, jump, and clap your hands."[48] Volck prints an anonymous letter in which a visitor to Herrnhaag describes the children behaving in a similar manner.[49] And the adults too clapped their hands during the songs, such as when specific words like *Schätzel* (darling) were sung.[50]

The adults also imitated the language of the children, such as in their use of diminutives. In his 1749 letter of reprimand Zinzendorf listed the excessive use of diminutives in first place among abuses among Moravians, as will be discussed below.

The ideal of childlikeness found expression in the playfulness of the 1740s. The church had to play, Zinzendorf and other leaders repeatedly declared. In his address on playing of January 8, 1747, Zinzendorf said, "We *have* to play, we *have* to behave playfully. We have to be childlike, just like the Dutch say *kinderlijk*, that is, a little different than childish"[51] (emphasis in original). The single brothers especially followed this invitation with great enthusiasm.

Playing and childlike behavior became the appropriate expression for the joy Moravians experienced in their hearts, a joy to be shared with everyone. For Zinzendorf this joy was directly related to eschatology, as he compared a playing congregation with a group of children playing around the throne of the Lamb. Playing was also a sign of being grounded in the right doctrine: "He who has taken up his Abode in the Lamb's Wounds," as the Pennsylvanian Mennonite Frey summarized the theology he encountered in Herrnhaag, "cannot but live the Life of Nature, and be merry and jovial."[52] This emphasis on childlikeness and irrationality was not uncommon among mystics, as Gottfried Arnold stated in his history of mystical theology.[53] According to religious historian Philip Greven, evangelicals considered conversion a second chance to become a perfect child again.[54] Obviously Moravians took this quite seriously.

Closely connected to this ideal of childlikeness was the ideal of anti-intellectualism. Peter Vogt sees an anti-intellectual tendency among Moravians, their being "headless and un-erudite,"[55] as an integral part of Zinzendorf's theology and as an expression of Zinzendorf's opposition to the Enlightenment ideals of intellectual emancipation and responsible self-determination. The emphasis on irrationality among eighteenth-century radical Pietists was connected to the belief that God's hidden truth cannot be uncovered through reason.[56] For Zinzendorf, faith and reason were diametrically opposed. A true Christian believes with his heart, not with his head; the death of the Savior on the cross cannot be grasped by reason. The blood and wounds of Christ were repulsive to rational people, Zinzendorf argued, but they appealed to people who had truly experienced salvation. The Moravians' anti-intellectual attitude was especially pronounced among the single men in Herrnhaag and at the theological seminary in Marienborn.

On January 8, 1747, the same day that Zinzendorf gave his address on playing, a reorganization of the single brothers' choir in Herrnhaag was announced. Brothers who had not yet found their place inside the side hole would now form the third class. The second and largest class would consist of those who knew they had their place inside the side hole but were still insecure about it. And the first class would be made up of "those who could leave off their heads because of the side hole and who act according to their hearts."[57] Apparently it was considered the goal of each brother to eventually

*Fig. 4*  *Ohne Kopf und Ungescheid*. Drawing of a man with a side wound replacing his head, displayed inside a side wound. Watercolor on paper, ca. 1750. Unity Archives, Herrnhut, Germany, M.135.

reach the first class and "be inside the side hole," that is, with Jesus in eternity. In that state, which could not be reached by reason or logical thinking, one would leave rational thoughts behind and surrender completely to Christ (the side hole).

That year Johann Nitschmann's birthday was celebrated with a love feast in Zinzendorf's room in the Lichtenburg at Herrnhaag, where a picture was displayed "with only headless people; some had their heads under their arms, others in their pockets or under their feet."[58] And during the summer of the following year Christel spoke about the same issue in Herrnhut: "The Savior likes it when we treat his side hole very blatantly and without head and reason."[59] A similar image among the surviving holdings of the Unity Archives shows a person whose head has been replaced with a side hole.

The anti-Pietist attitude of Moravians during the 1740s was an expression of a deeply felt desire for a closer union with Christ. In this respect, the 1740s and the culmination at the end of the decade can be considered the result of a sincere endeavor for an intense personal experience of God. Such piety is not located in the rationality of the mind but in the sensitivity of the heart.

The Bible

There are persistent rumors that Moravians during the 1740s and early 1750s looked down on the Bible and even showed open contempt for Holy Scripture. This seems consistent with the provocative anti-Pietist attitude among Moravians during these years. Although no direct Moravian sources exist, there are enough references in anti-Moravian writings that the charge deserves investigation.

Of course, it was not unusual to accuse religious opponents of misinterpreting the Bible or of lacking of biblical grounds for their teachings. But opponents of the Moravians went further and claimed Moravians did not even care about the text of the Bible. Hart reported that Moravians rarely even spoke about biblical verses in their meetings, and then mostly only when guests were present. "During the past three years the Bible was not used," he wrote shortly after leaving the Moravians in 1751. Rather than preaching from a biblical text, according to Hart, they based their sermons on the hymn text printed under the daily watchword in their devotional booklets.[60] The surviving texts of meditations as well as entries in diaries from the 1740s indicate that Moravians indeed used hymn texts as the basis of their sermons and homilies, although not as exclusively as Hart claims.[61]

Other authors went further and claimed that some Moravians were openly opposed to the use of the Bible. Bothe, similar to Hart, wrote that among Moravians in Berlin the Bible was used only when visitors were present, and he claimed that "the pilgrims often laughed about the Bible and made fun of it."[62] Anton Rhode, Heinrich Melchior Mühlenberg's successor in the Lutheran church at Grosshennersdorf near Herrnhut, gave several examples of the Herrnhuters' open disdain for the Bible. Brother Gewinn, a stonemason from Herrnhut working on the orphanage at Grosshennersdorf, provoked bystanders by saying, "A stack of cards is sometimes better than the Bible. Many a man will do better by playing cards than by reading the Bible."[63] And a sister in the Herrnhaag sisters' house was allegedly reprimanded by her overseer for frequently reading the Bible. Much to the young woman's distress, the overseer angrily took the Bible from her "and threw it under the bench." The overseer dropped another pious book she was reading, Bayly's *Praxis Pietatis*, into the privy. She retrieved it, cleaned it, and kept it. Moravians, according to Volck, even tore out pages from the Bible to use as toilet paper.[64]

What can we make of this? In part, the antibiblical statements seem to have been yet another form of the provocative behavior employed by some Moravians to show the assurance of their salvation to others. The Pennsylvanian Frey, who lived several years in Herrnhaag, connected Moravian antibiblical speech with other forms of playful behavior and with the inner experience of faith. He explained why Moravians in Herrnhaag during the 1740s thought meditating on the Bible "so contemptible that it ought to be spit on." According to Frey's interpretation of Moravian thought, a true Christian was someone who knew the wounds of Christ and had experienced grace in his heart. In so doing, the believer had attained the goal of his search for God. In the words of the Moravians, he had "found Lodging, Bed, and Board in the Lamb's Wounds." There he could only be "merry and jovial," but anyone who still needed to meditate over the Bible had apparently not reached this goal, was not yet a true believer, and lacked the experience of the Savior's grace through his wounds.[65] Even though for Frey the Moravians' reasoning was proof of their wickedness, he seems to have understood them well.

During the 1740s at least some Moravians placed the individual experience of the divine above the study of the Scriptures. Hans Schneider points out that radical Pietists of the early eighteenth century believed a true believer did not need the outer word. According to their spiritualist ecclesiology, a true believer who has received the inner word can do without the Bible and the sermons of the confessional church.[66] Jonathan Sheehan argues that Pietists tried to free the Bible of a "theological superstructure" of confessional interpretation and replace it with the subjective experience of God's love. They tried to produce a text that would speak directly to the heart of the believer. Some radical Pietists produced literal translations that would give the ordinary reader of the Bible direct access to the original text, without the explanatory translation and filter of the ordained authorities. Others, such as in the Berleburg Bible, attempted to collect and unify all possible commentary and scholarship in one place and give the lay reader direct access to the text without the control of the scholarly theologians.[67]

Sheehan points out that while theologians like Johann Albrecht Bengel were trying to establish the uncorrupted text, radical Pietists during the early eighteenth century sought the true text of the Bible in their hearts.[68] On June 18, 1747, Zinzendorf, who in his earlier years had tried to produce a new Bible translation himself, spoke about the meaning of the Bible in an address on a petition in the Litany of Wounds: "Thy exact Ground in the Scripture, Make us all firm in the Scripture."[69] It is not necessary to have the most reliable version of the original text or the best translation of the Bible; the believer will be able to discern the divine truth if he is "firm in the Scripture" (*Bibelfest*), meaning he has the truth in his heart: "their heart feels or does not feel, their heart believes what is to be believed, their heart detects when something is not right or that is not important to them." But Zinzendorf was far from dismissing the Bible as irrelevant, as some of his followers in fact did. This discourse on the Bible may very well have been intended as an answer to what some of his followers, obviously influenced by spiritualist ideas, were saying at the same time about its irrelevance.[70]

Side-Wound Devotion

As the girls in the boarding school in Herrnhut were getting ready for bed one night in January of 1749, one of them spotted a curious sight in the sky. As she described what she saw, the other girls joined in her excitement. On the horizon, just above the Hutberg, an unusual cloud had appeared, and beaming from the center of the cloud was a bright red light. In this phenomenon the girls and their overseers all recognized an image of the side hole, the wound in Christ's side, and were so excited that they "devoured each other" and could not go to sleep for hours. The diarist commented that what the girls had seen was in fact caused by a rather unfortunate house fire in nearby Kemnitz, but that the longing of the children for the side hole was still "good and nice."[71] The girls' enthusiasm is understandable considering the great importance that Moravian piety during the second half of the 1740s focused almost completely on the side wound of Christ as the symbol of salvation that his death had provided each believer.[72] Numerous images in Moravian communities depicted the side wound, sometimes as a torso shining in the sky—which is what the girls in Herrnhut recognized that January evening.

In Zinzendorf's reprimand of 1749 he did not reject such devotion, but he addressed certain by-products of the devotion of the side wound in Moravian theology, such as the unnecessary use of the diminutive *Seitenhöhlchen*, as well as some nonsensical ideas (*Gewäsch*) that had developed.[73] In an undated letter to the congregation at Bethlehem he again told them not to use *Seitenhöhlchen*: "It is not a small hole, it is a large cleft, the mother city of all souls."[74] At the Barby synod he mentioned the "matter of the side hole" in one breath with the extravagances of the previous years, but, as in his 1749 letter, Zinzendorf did not distance himself from the core idea of side-wound devotion. He called the side wound "the most important wound" of Christ and the "birthplace of all souls."[75]

Peter Vogt points out that the term "side wound" or "side hole" appeared in Protestant hymns as early as the sixteenth century and that these hymns were known to the Moravians. He also shows that the frequency of the use of the term in Moravian hymns increased during the 1740s.[76] The image was also used in the immensely popular hymn written by Johannes and Christel, "What Does a Bird in Cross's Air," which initiated the period of playfulness in 1746.[77] According to this hymn, the birds in the air around the cross found a nest in the "blessed hole" (*selges Höhlgen*) of Christ. The diary of the single brothers in Herrnhaag indicates that the devotion of the side hole began around the same time the hymn was written. In the entry for Good Friday of 1746 the side wound is called "the great side hole into which one can go." The Herrnhaag brethren celebrated Good Friday as the anniversary of the origin of the side wound, as well as the birthday of their leader Rubusch.[78] During the next few weeks, left in charge of the single brothers when the other leaders left for the Netherlands, Rubusch spoke more and more about the side wound. In an address on May 23 he connected the playfulness of the cross-air birds with being inside the side wound. From then on the metaphor of the side wound had a prominent place in Moravian piety. When Johannes von Watteville, Christel, and Zinzendorf returned to Herrnhaag in the fall of 1746, they gladly participated in this form of piety, the basis of which they had laid themselves.

Throughout the following year the side-wound theology was further developed. Looking back at the end of the year, Zinzendorf remarked, "The teaching of this year has been the side hole."[79] The side wound of Jesus was the center of meditations, sermons, hymns, and anthems, as well as of the frequent celebrations that took place in Moravian communities. The brethren took any occasion, from religious holidays to birthdays of Moravian leaders, to stage elaborate festive displays. An examination of two of these festivals, the celebration of Good Friday and Easter of 1747 and the celebrations held in honor of Christel's birthday in September of the same year, will give us an understanding of the new side-wound devotion.

The topic of Johannes von Watteville's meditation on Good Friday 1747 was how the church was born from the side of Jesus. Accordingly, the day was celebrated as the birthday of the church and of the side wound. The single brothers prepared elaborate decorations. In the evening they displayed an image in Rubusch's room in their choir house showing the moment from John 19:34 when the soldier pierced the side of Jesus on the cross. At the same time, the display showed how believers were born from the side wound as water and blood were coming from his side. The image evoked almost ecstatic reactions among the onlookers. Jacob Schellinger, a former Mennonite from Amsterdam, wanted to kiss the soldier in the picture "for his effort." The following evening the single brothers displayed, in glowing red letters above the door of their choir house, the words "Honor to the side hole" (Ehre dem Seitenmal).[80]

By September of 1747 the focus had shifted from the actual physical wound in Jesus's side to a more metaphorical concept of the side wound, as the description of Christel's birthday in Herrnhaag and Marienborn on September 19 reveals. Christel was the chief elder of all single brothers, so his birthday was celebrated even though he was in Herrnhut at the time. The main theme of that year's festivities was the side wound. On the evening of September 19 the windows of the brothers' house in Herrnhaag were decorated with red and green stars and pyramids. Above the main door "side hole" was written in large letters. Around the windows of the third floor pictures of the "cross-air birds" were mounted. The main decoration was a giant image of the side hole in the shape of a heart on the second floor of the building. Inside this side hole were a freshly made bed and a table laden with food, as well as a depiction of Christian Renatus as a "dove looking like our dear heart Renatus." Around the side hole was a canal full of fish and swans, swimming in the blood and water coming from the side wound.[81]

Similar imagery was used for Christel's birthday celebration in nearby Marienborn that same day.[82] At one end of the hall a large man-made, three-dimensional rock was constructed. This was the rock from Isaiah 51 ("look unto the rock whence ye are hewn"), which was read as a symbol for the side wound. This image was combined with another image: the dove in the clefts of the rock from Song of Songs 2:14. Similar to the display on the Herrnhaag brothers' house, a portrait of Christian Renatus was placed inside the rock. Around the rock were a number of cross-air birds symbolizing the other brothers, similar to the birds around the third floor of the Herrnhaag brothers' house. But the Marienborn display had one additional element not found in Herrnhaag. In front of the rock was a lion. Based on Revelation 5:5–6, Moravians identified the lion of Judah with the Lamb of God and created the paradoxical image of the "lion-lamb" as a symbol for Christ.[83] So Christ protected Christel in a twofold manner: as the rock and as the lion in front of the rock. By locating Christel inside the side wound, both the Herrnhaag and the Marienborn displays illustrated that he was in close union with Christ.

These two festivals from 1747, Good Friday and Christel's birthday, provide us with insight into the symbolism Moravians connected with the image of Christ's side wound. Most of this symbolism traces back, as Vogt has argued, to older Christian traditions.[84] Important in the descriptions of both the Good Friday and the Herrnhaag birthday displays was the blood and water coming out of the side wound, which referred to the blood and water coming from Jesus's side on the cross when the soldier pierced his body to see if he had died (John 19:34). As early as the second century blood and water were interpreted as symbols for the sacraments of Holy Communion (blood) and baptism (water). Since the church was built on these sacraments, early Christian thinkers considered the church as metaphorically having been born from Jesus's side in a similar way to Eve having been taken from Adam's side (Gen. 2:22).[85] Moravians continued in that tradition when they referred to Good Friday as the "birthday" of the church. For Zinzendorf, all souls were born from the side wound to a new life in faith. He called the side wound of Christ a "central point" of his theology, from which all other ideas could be derived. Thus from this single symbol of the side wound the essence of the Christian faith could be explained.[86]

The Moravians added another layer of symbolism to the side wound. According to mystical traditions, the soul of the individual believer wants to come closer to the divine, the object of his devotions, and ultimately to become one with Christ. This union was expressed in the image of being inside the side wound. Moravians used graphic images such as a bed and a table inside the side wound. The bird that flies around the cross was attracted "like a magnet" to the side wound, where it found its nesting place. Thus, the side hole is a place of shelter and comfort but also a metaphor for the mystical union with Christ. The cross-air bird stood for the individual believer, seeking and longing for a closer union with Christ. Or the individual believer was symbolized by the fish or the swan swimming in the blood and water coming from the side hole. Being inside the side hole meant having attained the goal of the union with Christ. Moravians believed salvation of mankind had occurred through the suffering and death of Christ. The wounds were the symbols of his passion; the side wound was the terminal wound epitomizing his death. Only by believing in the wounds could one attain a full understanding of atonement, salvation, and grace.[87] Once the believer had attained this understanding, he was completely saved, or, to use Moravian language from the 1740s, he had "taken up his Abode in the Lamb's wounds."[88] So when Rubusch asked the laborers among the single brothers in Herrnhaag if any of them "was sitting inside the side hole," he wanted to know who among them had gained this insight. When none of the brothers dared to respond, Rubusch reprimanded them and instructed them how they could enter into the side wound and once inside could happily play.[89]

Because death meant being united with Jesus, the diary noted that, when someone had died, his or her soul had "flown into the side hole," and verses about going into the side hole were sung at funerals when the body was lowered into the grave. The dead had now attained their goal and were united with Christ; they were "inside the side hole." Reflecting the fact that sleeping and dying were closely related concepts, the diary described going to bed as "going to sleep in the side hole."

Moravian piety changed and developed rapidly during the 1740s. As images and symbols lost their initial appeal, they were constantly replaced with new ones.[90] The devotion of the side wound continued to develop after 1747. The report of the single brothers' festival of May 2, 1748, reveals yet another shift. From the physical wound in the side of Jesus (Good Friday, 1747) to the symbol of the union of the true believer with Christ (Christel's birthday in September 1747), the side wound had now become a synecdoche for Christ, replacing previous designations such as Lamb or Savior.[91] From then on, the brothers prayed to the side hole, they honored the side hole, and they wanted to unite with the side hole.

The report of the 1748 festival also illustrates the euphoric and rapturous mood that was now part of life in the Herrnhaag brothers' house.[92] The words *Vivat Gott Seitenhöhlgen* (Long live God side hole) were written in gold letters on the façade of the brothers' house and were illuminated at night. The same text was sewn onto the crimson banners of the trumpet players who played throughout the day. Christian Renatus addressed the brothers in highly suggestive sermons, creating an ecstatic atmosphere among them that increased in intensity throughout the day. After morning devotions and an early service in the brothers' house, during which Christel spoke about the ardent desire of the single brothers to be loved and caressed by the side hole, the single men from Marienborn joined the Herrnhaag brothers in the main worship hall in the Lichtenburg. Anticipation swelled as a soloist kept repeating the same hymn, until the door to the side room finally opened and Christel and Rubusch, together with thirty other laborers of the choir, entered the hall, all of them wearing long white surplices and head wreaths made of orange leaves. Christel announced that the side hole would embrace and take each brother into his arms that day. Then he and Rubusch stood and went through the rows to bless each man on behalf of the side hole: "It was as if the side hole was really standing in front of each brother, and he certainly presented himself in the person of Christel and of Rubusch before each brother." During the following prostrate prayer, several of the men broke down sobbing. Some were so beside themselves that they had to be helped by their neighbors. Then Christel exclaimed, "O side hole! Oh, kiss thou me!" Both Rubusch and Caillet repeated these words, and, after the singing of a hymn, the morning service was over. During the afternoon love feast, when Christel asked the men what they were eating, they responded, "Side hole!" And when he asked what they were drinking, "like little children" they repeated the same answer: "Side hole!" Rubusch, upstairs in the gallery around the hall, read a hymn written for the occasion. As he came to the line "He is here, can't you see it?" Christel could no longer hold back. He rose from his chair and sang, "Welcome among your flock of grace with joyful acclamation!" All men present stood up and joined in the hymn, welcoming Christ in their midst. During the singing of the words "Receive these kisses from the entire young men's choir" each brother kissed the man sitting next to him.

At the beginning of the day Christel had said, "Today is our festival, the festival of the originals and the copies of the side hole.... The single brothers want to resemble their dearest side hole, and they would like to look like the side hole. They want to be felt and loved, just like the side hole." In Moravian terminology of the late 1740s, Christel was describing the highest state of the mystical longing of a believer, that of becoming one and the same with the divine. By kissing the brothers next to them while singing that they were kissing the side hole, the men at the 1748 brothers' festival had made one another into side holes; in other words, they had become similar to Christ. What could be the next stage in this ecstatic buildup of religious emotion? Erbe, posing the same question, believed the situation was poised to topple over (*umkippen*).[93] As we will see, there was indeed a more drastic stage.

At eleven o'clock that night another festive decoration was revealed. Many people had assembled in front of the brothers' house, and when the main door was opened an effigy of the Savior under a triumphal arch appeared, smeared with blood and with his wounds clearly visible. Some of the men sang,

> In such a right Good Friday's Frame,
> As if the Spear's Thrust in the Lamb
> The Soldier but this Day had made,
> And I from Morn till Night had staid
> With him on Golgotha;
> As if our Jehova
> Still bodily hung on the Wood,
> And I like John and Mary view'd;
> As if that Torrent
> Flow'd plashing down this very Day,
> And foaming (bloody) like the Sea,
> And I should sit so happily
> Beneath, till all was red round me:
> Till I the very Incision
> May kiss, Lamb! keep this Vision.[94]

Meanwhile, a single brother dressed like a soldier walked up and pierced Jesus's side with a spear. Blood gushed out, foaming like seawater on the beach and splattering onto some of the bystanders. Christel approached the bleeding Christ figure, getting red blood on his green choir ribbon as he washed his hands in the blood. So far the installation had many similarities with the Good Friday display a year earlier. But there was an important difference. As the bleeding Savior became paler and paler, the following verse was softly sung:

> The manifold Savior
> about whom we used to sing
> has disappeared with all his wounds
> into the side hole.[95]

After the verse was repeated two more times, the effigy of the Savior disappeared and in its place appeared a large side hole, serving as an entrance into the brothers' house. Through the side hole and inside the house a table was visible on which the body of Christ lay carved (*tranchirt*) and neatly served in pieces. Christian Renatus passed through the side hole into the choir house, followed by Rubusch and the other members of the choir. The idea of the side wound as an entrance was not new; Johannes von Watteville had spoken about it more than a year earlier.[96] Through it, by implication, the entire choir had now entered into the side wound—that is, had been born again and attained a state of blessed union with the divine, which was the central message of the choir festival.

Another important element of the presentation should not be overlooked. Whereas previously ("weiland" in the hymn) the entire body of Christ was the object of the Moravians' devotion, now he had been reduced to one of his wounds. As the installation graphically showed, the side hole had become a universal symbol for the divine. As Christel would say to the single brothers in Herrnhut a few months later, "the entire bloody Savior with all his wounds and our entire choir plan and experience are united in the side hole as in a compendium [summary]."[97] Later, when dealing with the aftermath of the Sifting Time, Johannes von Watteville argued that this was a key error of the previous years: "The entire bloody Savior, his passion, and all his wounds belong together. Had the Savior not suffered so much for us in his body and soul, had he not suffered at all, we would not have a side hole from where new life and blood and water flowed, and the new birth from the *pleura* would not have been accomplished."[98] After 1749, Watteville, Spangenberg, and others appealed for a return to the blood-and-wounds theology of the earlier 1740s. They considered the abandonment of the devotion of Christ as the suffering Savior one of the main causes of the Sifting Time. The 1748 single brothers' festival is a graphic representation of this change in theology.

Let us now return to Zinzendorf's letter of reprimand. He criticizes side-hole devotion most explicitly in paragraph 17, but it is apparent that he did not dismiss the teaching of the side hole altogether, but only certain aspects. Paragraph 17 begins, "A single brother who can be found guilty of considering the holy side of the Savior the way our opponents describe, or of speaking about it—however innocent the explanation may be, he will be excluded from Communion for a year." A text-critical comparison of the different copies of this letter can help us understand what Zinzendorf meant by "the way our opponents describe." The original draft of the letter, written in Zinzendorf's hand, is in the Unity Archives (reference code R.3.A.8.13.1). There the passage in question reads "the way D[octor] Baumgarten describes." In the fair copy (R.3.A.8.13.2) Zinzendorf changed the words "D. Baumgarten" to the vague reference "our opponents," and this is how it remained in the final version of the text, which was distributed to the congregations worldwide. Thus Zinzendorf originally had a specific critic in mind: Siegmund Jacob Baumgarten (1706–1757), professor of theology at the University of Halle. Zinzendorf was undoubtedly referring to the following passage in Baumgarten's *Theologische Bedencken*: "that they pass off the [side wound of Christ] as the womb of the believers and that they consider this orifice as an image of the female genitalia; therefore they tried to place it in the abdomen and called it loin."[99]

Consequently, Zinzendorf was saying that someone who considered the side wound of Christ a vagina had to be excluded from Holy Communion.[100] Interestingly, Zinzendorf himself had compared the side wound to the female genitalia several times. For example, in his address to the married couples in Herrnhut on May 14, 1748, Zinzendorf said, "The sisters have the clear and uncontradictable image of the holy side of Jesus that was opened on the cross, whence he gave birth to our souls."[101]

What did Zinzendorf really mean in his letter of reprimand? Had he changed his mind and did he now think it had become objectionable to continue making this comparison? Or did he perhaps mean that some men were not just comparing the side wound to a vagina as figure of speech, but had actually gone further? As we will find, some Moravians during the Sifting Time believed they could experience the divine ("go into the side hole") through sexual intercourse, not only within but also outside marriage. It seems plausible that Zinzendorf's admonition had to do with the sexual transgressions that lay at the core of the crisis.

Erotic Mysticism

During the 1740s the language used by Moravians to describe their longing for the divine became increasingly eroticized. The union of the believer with Christ was described in terms of a sexual relationship. This becomes apparent, for example, in the prayer that Christian Renatus delivered at the choir festival of the single sisters in Herrnhaag on May 4, 1748. In it, he spoke as Christ in the first person: "All the kisses I will give to the church—you will receive them a thousand times. All embraces will be concentrated on you. I want to speak with each and every sister. I want to take each one into my marital temple, into the hole. And I want to kiss her, embrace her, hold her, and I want to take the body and soul of each single sister into my body and soul, and I want to be involved with them like never before."[102]

Similar erotic language was used two days prior at the single brothers' festival, when Christian Renatus used the image of the Old Testament prophet Elisha to describe the intimate physical embrace of Christ (the side hole) and the believer. As Elisha lay himself on top of the dead son of the Shunammite woman to bring him back to life (2 Kings 4:34)—mouth on mouth, eyes on eyes, and hands on hands—Christ would lay himself on the single men.[103]

In his prayer during the afternoon Christel said in his typical charismatic manner,

> O side hole, embrace each soul, hold this choir now and do it during this moment as Elisha did. We want to be the child, lay yourself stretched out on top of each single brother, on top of each member of each single brother. Rush into the veins of the single brothers' choir and drive through this choir, pass through, permeate, pervade, and penetrate this choir so indescribably and yet so bridegroom-nuptially as we have never received it before, as we will never feel it any more divinely until we will see you face to face.[104]

In this prayer Christel was preparing the men for the climax that was to come later that night. At midnight Holy Communion was celebrated among the single brothers. During the distribution of the bread the men continually repeated one hymn, made up of a single word: *Seitenhölchen* (side hole). The seemingly endless repetition must have brought the men into a trance-like state. When everyone had received the bread, Christian Renatus exclaimed, "O Lord Jesus, what kisses!" Then the men lay down on the floor and ate the bread. While they were lying prostrate, they pictured Christ as the side hole lying on top of them just like Elisha; they all embraced one another on the floor, and "everyone was completely gone" (es war alles ganz weg). A few hymns followed about marrying the side hole, kissing the side hole, going to bed with the side hole, and feeling the side hole inside their bodies when married to the husband. In this heated atmosphere it is not surprising that when the Communion wine was poured Christel declared it to be an antidote to the "paroxysm" of the "cold and hot fever." Through its highly erotic language the rising tension of the service became so intense that some outlet had to be found. By coincidence, just as the Communion wine was being poured, a heavy rain poured down upon the street outside and on the windows, cooling down the air as well as the hot heads of the men. The Communion service concluded with the usual kiss of peace, when each brother kissed his neighbor. With their arms tightly linked crosswise together, the brothers left the hall, "completely beside ourselves" (ganz ausser uns).

Moravian ideas on "marital relations with the husband" (ehelicher Umgang mit unserm Manne) drew on older traditions. Picturing Holy Communion as an embrace with Christ and using erotic language to describe the longing for and union with Christ was not unusual within Christianity. McGinn points out that Christians had used such language for centuries.[105] Bernard of Clairvaux explained the Song of Songs as the love song between Christ and the soul of the individual believer; the soul reaches the highest stage when it becomes one with God. He compared the *unificatio Dei* to the relationship between a man and a woman and described it in terms of a courtship. Inspired by Bernard, who used the metaphor of sexual intercourse for the mystical union, later mystics also used erotic language. Based on the Song of Songs, images of the beauty of the lover, of longing and lovesickness, of embraces, kisses, and intercourse were used. And among other Protestants, such as Puritans and eighteenth-century American Presbyterians, the metaphor of sexual union was used in connection with Holy Communion.[106]

The diaries of the single brothers in Herrnhut and Herrnhaag indicate that marital imagery for Communion had become increasingly popular since the mid-1740s. In October of 1745 Johannes told the brothers in Herrnhut that "the Savior wanted to enter into matrimony and penetrate them sacramentally, young-men's-choir-like, and maritally and hold them in his embrace."[107] We find entries such as "Rubusch spoke much about the marital relations with the Lamb" or "In the evening our dear Rubusch gave a tender Bible lesson about having the husband near and embracing him and becoming feverish about that, etc. etc. The brothers who understood him felt very well." On May 9, 1746, Rubusch explained how the Savior made the "communicant brothers truly fall in love with him and that a true communicant brother had to be like a husband to his wife (and much more so), etc., etc."[108] During the following months this imagery was further developed, with terms such as "embrace," "caresses," "kisses," and "marriage." The diary notes that on April 14, 1747, Zinzendorf explained how "we can not only put our fingers in his nail marks and our hands into his side, now we are even known [in the biblical sense] by him and his sweat and corpse's vapor permeates us and we attain the closest and most essential union with his person."[109]

In this nuptial imagery Christ was always the initiator. Christ held and embraced the believer, he kissed him, penetrated him, and made love to him. Hessel-Robinson points out, in the context of similar imagery among seventeenth-century Puritans, that the passivity of the believer is consistent with the Reformed understanding of election: grace is bestowed on the believer as a gift by God's choice, and therefore it is God who initiates the relationship with the believer.[110] The topoi of waiting for Christ, lying still, and being passive are further developed in Moravian hymns written during 1748.

By the time of the choir festival of the single brothers in 1748, as we have seen, bridal imagery had become predominant in Moravian piety. Immediately after the celebration in Herrnhaag, Christian Renatus left for Herrnhut, where the single brothers had postponed their choir festival in anticipation of his arrival. The Herrnhut single brothers' diary gives us insight into how

Christel brought to Herrnhut the erotic mysticism that had become so popular in Herrnhaag. It also shows how another element, the "daily enjoyment" of Christ, became increasingly popular during 1748.

Christel arrived in Herrnhut on May 17 and remained there until August 19. During these months Christel introduced the Herrnhut single brothers step by step to what the men in Herrnhaag had already learned about the marital relationship with Christ. Fortunately, though the Herrnhaag single brothers' diary for 1748 and 1749 has been lost, the text of the single brothers' diary from Herrnhut survives.[111] It gives us relevant details about the way concepts developed among the single men during 1748, especially since the author of the diary, Christian Gregor, wrote relatively informative entries.

Not long after his arrival, Christel introduced the men in Herrnhut to a new concept: they no longer needed the sacrament of Communion; instead, they could enjoy the side hole "every day, every hour, and every moment."[112] It was not unusual for radical Pietists to believe the outer sacraments were unnecessary for salvation because true Christians can receive anything they need for salvation without them.[113] We find references to this idea of the daily and constant joy of the marriage with Christ in the earlier Herrnhaag diary as well.[114] This joy was to be bestowed upon those brothers and sisters who "were inside the side hole," that is, who had attained the highest state of their union with Christ. By 1748 the concept of daily Communion had further developed, as Gregor's entries in the Herrnhut diary from the week of July 28 reveal. During this week Christel summarized his doctrine in daily meditations. On Sunday, July 28, he preached about the "*real* relations with the dear side hole" and said that "to be inside the side hole was not to be understood spiritually" but that they could enter *realiter* (actually), with body and soul.[115] How they could *physically* enter into the side hole is revealed in the entries for the following days. Christel spoke about how the brothers had become similar to, if not the same as, the side hole. On Monday he said, "May our body be filled so thoroughly with our husband's soul, body, and spirit that it can hardly be more perfect and complete in the perfected church."[116] And the next day he revisited this topic by meditating on the "equality between us and our husband." From the moment one believes oneself reborn from the side hole "the husband frames himself so thoroughly into us that we become side holes and the side hole becomes us, etc."[117] Phrased in Moravian vocabulary of the 1740s, this is the typical ideal of a mystical believer: to become one with the divine, to become whole, and to be perfected. By believing in the side wound of Christ as the center of all theology, Christel told the single men in Herrnhut, they would be reborn in the image of Christ. Thus, they would become like him ("copies"), the object of their belief. On Thursday he told them that it was the goal of "our husband" eventually to marry us; in order to prepare us here on earth for the heavenly marriage, he permeated our bodies as thoroughly "as a husband penetrates his wife." Our bodies would be almost ready and would not need "much time in the grave." Until then, Christel said on Wednesday, "his daily embraces and his manly presence" could replace Communion so that "each day and moment could have its own meal from the side hole."[118]

If these "daily embraces" could replace Communion, then they must certainly have been something different than Communion. The question arises, who could give these daily embraces? In other words, who was able to administer this form of Communion? Christel's meditation from July 29 sheds light on this question. He described how the bodies of the true believers were to be filled with Christ so that "we can pass it on to each other" or "infect each other with it," similar to a contagious disease. Did Christel mean that the nuptial love and caresses of Christ could be administered by the brothers among each other now that they had become just like him? If so, then Christ wants to love the believer and the believer has become equal to him; nothing prevents believers from passing on the love of Christ among one another.[119] The closing sentence of the diary entry for that day confirms that Christel's message was to be understood in a physical way: "These are the *bodily* blisses that have begun during this 1748th year, especially among the single brothers' choir, and that the side hole wants to give *to our bodies* to enjoy" (emphasis added). Twice in this sentence Christian Renatus, as reported by the diary writer, uses the word "body" (*Hütte*). No longer is the joy of the union with Christ a joy for the soul; it has become a physical experience and delight.[120]

Where, then, does this leave us? On September 26, 1750, during the meeting in Barby about the Sifting Time, Zinzendorf complained that "the false teachers began to aim *at the flesh* and to clothe themselves with coarseness." And in seven of the paragraphs of his 1749 letter of reprimand Zinzendorf indeed addressed the free relations between the genders (11), the bold and loud kissing (19, 20), the "carnal and carnally sounding" conversations (3), and the unauthorized discussions about marital matters (12, 16, 18). Based on these observations, we may conclude that the Sifting Time was very much about physical matters and carnal trespasses.

Mortification, Death, and the Grave

The single brothers' festival of 1749 took place shortly before Christel, Rubusch, and several others left Herrnhaag for London, heeding Zinzendorf's instructions a few months earlier. Unfortunately, no detailed description of the festival has been uncovered, only a brief description in the diary of the single brothers in nearby Marienborn. But the diary entry does mention another aspect of the theology and practice of this period that needs further attention. Various passages in the diary were later crossed out because they were considered to be related to the Sifting Time. The entry, including the redacted words (some of which cannot be deciphered), reads, "Afterwards we ended this important day with various blessed services, with a beautiful illumination representing the sickly and dying body, after which the entire choir went to the xxxx made grave xxxxxxx with a blessed although small Communion for some of the laborers."[121] The deleted words refer to a display of a dying body as well as to a visit to a grave—matters that were obviously considered to be connected to the ideas and practices of the Sifting Time. From this short and only partially legible entry it is impossible to fully understand what is meant here, except that a celebration is being described that included an image of a dying body and a visit to a grave.

Other texts from these same years also refer to dying, death, and graves. We have a description of how the teachers of the Moravian school at Peilau, Silesia, celebrated Christel's birthday on September 20, 1749. For this occasion they constructed an elaborate diorama, placed on a table in a door opening, consisting of different scenes representing Christian Renatus and Christ. The central scene of the display was situated in a grave in which a wax figurine of Christ wearing a white surplice with a red sash was placed. Lying on top of Christ was another wax figurine representing Christian Renatus. Above the scene was written, "Oh, sweet love in silence! He and his husband all alone. He feels, he feels, he feels, he feels! See, he even dies of lovesickness."[122]

During the second half of the 1740s a preoccupation with the corpse and the grave of Christ developed among Moravians. By the end of 1744 the Moravians in Herrnhaag celebrated the resting of Christ in the grave during weekly Sabbath love feasts, a custom that quickly spread to other Moravian congregations.[123] During the time when the single men in Herrnhaag were discussing the mystical relationship with Christ as their husband and the side hole as the place where Christ and the believer would unite in a holy embrace, they also learned about the transforming power of the corpse of Christ. In April of 1746 Rubusch spoke about how the entire brothers' choir would turn into a swarm of bees around the corpse.[124] By November of 1746 the "cross's air" had become a fragrant atmosphere filled with the scent of Christ's decaying body. For example, before the men went to bed on November 27, 1746, Johannes von Watteville gave a "juicy and savory meditation about the corpse and its fume, smell and cross's air, wounds and stigmata."[125]

The effect of the corpse of Christ on the brothers was illustrated in a discourse by Zinzendorf on Good Friday in 1747.[126] According to Zinzendorf,

*Fig. 5* Two Moravian sisters in the grave with Jesus. Watercolor on paper, ca. 1750. The text reads: "Do not ask me how I do it; I have enough when I can be more than one day in the grave where I can see, kiss, have, and embrace Jesus's dear corpse." Unity Archives, Herrnhut, Germany, TS Mp.376.10.

by approaching the dead and senseless body of Christ, the believer too could become "cold and stiff" against sin: "By the true *effluvia* [odors] and vapors [from the corpse] and by the air from the clefts of the rock all carnal desires, false stirrings, and evaporations are dried up. This occurs especially when our husband stretches himself with his deathly cold body over us, member by member, when he enters into us during Holy Communion and extracts the poison from the last bit of rot so that our bodies resemble his corpse."[127]

A popular hymn verse from these years was the short couplet "Dass der Sinn des Lamms Sinn gleiche, / und die Hütte seiner Leiche," translated by an anonymous English Moravian as "That our Mind the Lamb's resemble / And his Corpse our Body's Temple."[128] The couplet expresses the same desire as Zinzendorf's discourse: by becoming like Christ and especially like his dead body, the believer could mortify all carnal desire and free himself of sin. Mortification was an ongoing process, leading to perfection. The Litany of

Wounds contains the petition "Broken Eyes, Appear even in ours!"[129] The broken eyes are the eyes of the dead Christ, appearing in the eyes of the believer as a sign that he, like Christ, has died to sin. Since Christian Renatus was considered to have reached this stage of union with Christ, one of his portraits depicts him deathly pale and holding a slip of paper in his hands with these very words from the German Litany of Wounds: "Gebrochene Augen, seht uns zun Augen heraus!"

During the 1740s Moravians mortified their flesh, not by abstention, fasting, or self-inflicted pain, but by meditation and concentrating on the side hole. In order to enter the side hole and become one with Christ, one needed to have died to sin and buried "the old man." It was especially during Holy Communion that one was able to become one with Christ.[130] During Holy Communion the Moravian believer of the 1740s imagined that Christ's body was stretched out over him and that he was penetrated by Christ. The believer became filled with Christ, and Christ took possession of him. "The more often this happens, the more Jesus-like and the more corpse-like we become," said Zinzendorf, "until finally the sinful body ceases." By mortifying one's flesh one would become like Jesus, without sin and sinful thoughts. Zinzendorf held it possible for his followers to actually become free from sin and sinless: "One cannot sin, one is dead. The sinful members are dead. One cannot sin because the old man has been buried in Jesus-likeness, in Jesus-like character, and sinning is incompatible with that."[131] This observation is especially important in light of the gender-changing event of December 1748.

By 1749 Christ's grave was no longer only the resting place of the Savior; it had become the place where man was to unite with Christ. In the grave, a person had lost all temporal, earthly qualities and become pure. The image of the grave was combined with the image of the side hole, as when Zinzendorf applied Isaiah 51:1 to the side hole: "look unto the rock whence ye are hewn, and to the hole of the pit whence ye are digged." As described above, the display for Christel's birthday in Marienborn in 1747 had depicted the side hole as a giant rock, while according to the Gospels, Jesus's grave was hewn out of a rock.[132] In the following chapter about the songs of the Sifting Time, I will argue that the believer would not only die to sin but also die for love when he lay in Jesus's arms. Love for Christ would make the believer sick of love (Song of Songs 2:5, 5:8) while Christ, by his embrace, kisses, and caresses, would let the believer die in his arms.[133] The union with Christ was equated with dying; the grave became the marital bed.[134]

This imagery was visualized in a festive display for the birthday of Georg Ernst Heithausen, leader of the Herrnhaag single brothers after Christel's departure in 1749. When Heithausen went to bed in the dormitory in the attic of the brothers' house, he found that the other brothers had created a mound out of flowers and ribbons on top of his bed, "and on top of the mound there was a grave." In the grave were his initials, "G. E. v. H.," and the pillow and sheet were trimmed with a green ribbon. A canopy made from green branches stood over the head of the bed, and at the foot were placed two pyramids with red ribbons. The bed stood on white sheets strewn with green leaves, and on both sides of the bed were candles with red ribbons. The brothers had turned Heithausen's bed into both a symbolic grave and a marital bed. During the night the birthday boy could meditate on the embrace with his eternal husband.[135] We will return to the symbolism of death after examining Moravian ideas on gender in chapter 6.

Language

Zinzendorf opened his letter of reprimand with two paragraphs concerning language. In the first he prohibited the use of diminutives, and especially turning diminutives into verbs. Only a few years before, Zinzendorf had publicly defended the use of diminutives against his critics;[136] now he told his followers to use only diminutives that were found in the Bible.

The German language allows nearly every noun to be turned into a diminutive by adding an ending like *-chen* (or *-gen* in eighteenth-century spelling), *-lein*, or (in certain regions) *-el*. Moravians in the mid-eighteenth century had a special predilection for diminutives. They were intended less to diminish the size of the object referred to than as a term of endearment. For example, Jesus as the Lamb of God was not the *Lamm* but the *Lämmlein* (Lambkin), meaning not a small lamb but a dear lamb.[137] The examples that Zinzendorf specifically mentioned—*Schätzel* (sweetheart), *Seitenhöhlchen* (side hole), *Närrchen* (fool), *Bräutel* (bride)—were all connected to bridal mysticism and childlike playfulness, and thus essential for the piety of these years.[138]

In the second paragraph Zinzendorf forbade the use of new words. In his own sermons he used many neologisms and words borrowed from Greek, Latin, French, Dutch, and English. The mixture of languages seems to hint at the termination of the confusion of tongues caused by the sin of mankind at the Tower of Babel, suggesting that the end of times was near. But apparently some had taken their linguistic experimentation too far.

The purpose of special terms was twofold: it created an in-group language that defined and strengthened the identity of the Moravian community; and the childlike language gave expression to the desire to become like children.

After all, it was the children who would enter the Kingdom of God (Matt. 18:3).

At the single brothers' synod at London in 1752–53 the worship style of the previous years was discussed. Zinzendorf said, "I cannot fathom how the addresses held in the *Saal* during that time must have sounded." Delegates responded that sometimes a worship meeting consisted of a hymn verse, or just one line or even one word, being repeated over and over. The brothers at the synod also compared the preaching style of Christel and Rubusch. Christel, they said, preached with "his truthful and tender heart," while Rubusch spoke "with a certain force that is hard to define but that resembled an inspiration."[139]

Only a few letters and sermons by Christel, Rubusch, and other leaders from these years survive. On May 4, 1748, two days after the choir festival of the single brothers at Herrnhaag, Christel was invited to speak at the festival of the single sisters. Besides the typical language of these years, the text of his address reveals his style and the rhetoric he applied. He begins by speaking about the side hole (i.e., Christ) in the third person and to the sisters' choir in the third person plural: "On this day he will pervade, permeate, and penetrate every soul among them as never before. Today he speaks to his maidens' choir." But then he switches to speaking on behalf of Christ in the first person and addressing the choir in the second person singular: "I know that you love me; I found something good about you. I have felt the tenderness you feel for me all year round. I was able to truly penetrate into the choir with the beatitudes of the side hole that I let flow into the congregation. You collected it all, yea, even the smallest drop has made the choir so blessed, so manly as one can see now."[140] It is easy to picture how the single sisters imagined Christ himself directly speaking to them as they saw and heard Christian Renatus, whose name even suggested he was Christ reborn.

Another example of Christel's enthusiastic style of preaching—including many examples of the new words that Zinzendorf criticized in his letter of reprimand—is found in an address to the children's choir on Holy Innocents' Day, December 28, 1748:

> Now the whole congregation is beginning to speak children's talk, to get a child's sense, to have children's marital hearts, to have children's marital matters in the innermost parts of their hearts with the husband. And we won't accept another cabinet, another marital bed that is not childed [*gekindert*]. You are in the cabinet, in the marital bed, and whoever from the congregation wants to go there has to go like a child; whoever from the choirs wants to go there has to go like a child. Every

soul has to go like a child, an innocent child in swaddling clothes, like a thingy that cannot yet think, cannot yet hear right, cannot yet see right, cannot yet feel right, cannot yet eat right except for porridge.[141]

As children they still had that pure state of mind, according to Christel, that the adults wanted to attain in order to become one with Christ.

> Look, children, you have this blessing at an advantage over all grown-up people, over all grown-up brothers and sisters. And if a child, such a small little sweetheart as you are, does not truly lie in the marital bed with spirit, body, and soul, then one cannot really determine the cause or say why. Because you are predestined, you are bled, you are souled, and you are templed [*gehüttet*]; all your thoughts are marital, all your senses are marital, all you feel is marital, and the older a child becomes the more it needs to turn around and become like it was in its earliest infancy again.[142]

It is possible that Christel tried to imitate Rubusch, who was even more creative in his speech and better at inventing new words. Not many texts by Rubusch survive. The diary of the single brothers only summarizes the contents of his meditations; to my knowledge none of them survive in the Congregational Accounts or in the anthologies of addresses to the single brothers.[143] A few surviving letters in the Unity Archives, however, give insight into Rubusch's style and inventiveness.

> My dear, dear, dear, dear, dearest heart Hasse!
> I love you and so do my dear hearts who all send you their quite affectionate greetings and kisses. Greet and kiss everyone who knows me and who loves me, but especially those who love and feel the side hole, who touch it, be-taste it, behold, be-drop, be-taste, be-watch, bedabble, be-listen, be-lay, be-crawl, be-bed, be-touch, be-eat, and be-drink it. Greet the entire congregation in Urb for me; I love them dearly.[144]

And in a letter to two brothers in Livonia:

> You all know what kind of lover, admirer, and worshipper of the dearest side hole I am and that I am a declared enemy of all that does not go into it or comes out of it. Because everything else is rubbish, is rubbish, is rubbish. Be it as beautiful, as pretty, as necessary as may be, I tell you,

it is rubbish. But what comes out of it [the side hole] are pure delicacies, fat and wholesome meals, graces and blessings that one can eat and drink, yes, that one can eat fried, baked, cooked, souped, spooned, pestled, forked, knived, and plated. Afterwards one will have an easily digestible stomach, veins, heart, taste, and palate. I am always for the best.[145]

It seems likely that Zinzendorf's objections against certain linguistic practices were directed at the experimental style of Rubusch and Christel, which others unquestionably tried to imitate as well.

The language of the 1740s gave expression to the new ideas developing in Moravian communities. In many respects it was the language of playing children. The provocative, playful behavior of the mid-1740s was encouraged by Moravian leaders as an expression of joy at having found true faith in Christ. A true believer, so it was said, was redeemed by the blood of Christ and no longer needed to lead a pious life of abstinence from wordly pleasures in order to achieve salvation. Moravians wanted to be like children, to believe like children, to speak like children, and to act like children. The ideal of childlikeness opened the door to endless experimentation, which soon focused on the side wound, or side hole, of Christ. The side hole was not only a metaphor for the passion and death of Christ, but was seen as the birthplace of the souls of the true, born-again believers, and as the place where the union with Christ could take place. The believers were to mortify sinful desires of the flesh and prepare to wed Christ, their bridegroom and future husband. They also began to believe it was possible to die to sin and to become sinless and pure. Eschatological expectations were rising.

# 5

## SONGS OF THE SIFTING

It will take several years for us to get rid
of these songs, since people learned them
by heart.
—*Zinzendorf at Barby synod, September 10, 1750*

At the celebration of the twenty-fifth anniversary of the founding of Herrnhut on June 17, 1747, an unusual musical competition between Zinzendorf and his son took place in Herrnhaag. After the congregation had sung "various old hymns that previously had been very common in the congregation," Christian Renatus got up and sang, "Lovely Side Hole! dearest Side-Hole! Sweetest Side Hole, made for me." The diary entry continues, "That was the opportunity for a very unusual battle of hymns between father and son, between the cantor and the organist of the church. The ordinary [Zinzendorf] sang old hymns from his riches, and Renatus came in with a verse from the current liking of the church. From all this the difference between the former and the present blessing of the church became quite evident."[1]

## Reactions

As noted above, Moravians were well aware of the continuing changes in their theology, seeing them as a dynamic progression of a divine revelation of grace. The account of the celebration from 1747 is a further confirmation of this. The Moravians considered their hymns, sung at the numerous meetings in their communities, a preeminent expression of their new understanding of the nature of God and of their relationship with him. Not only were these hymns an expression of the Sifting Time; in a way they were the Sifting Time itself.

In this chapter we will analyze the texts of some of the hymns that were sung during the late 1740s. We will find that their imagery was derived from bridal mysticism, as many of the hymns sang about the sensual relationship between the believer and Christ.

Group singing was central to Moravian piety. It reflected the piety of the individual and of the community; it strengthened the fellowship, and it communicated theological ideas among the community. The Pietists in seventeenth- and eighteenth-century Germany promoted singing in conventicles and other small groups. Influenced by mystical traditions, they considered singing an expression of the soul, aroused by the Holy Spirit, and a means for communal communication.[2] Group singing strengthened the group identity as well as the faith of the individual.

While the traditional Lutheran hymns served to impart doctrine and confession, Pietist songs stressed the immediate experience of God and personal spiritual unification with Christ, and left room for ecstatic experiences.[3] Zinzendorf characterized hymns as "melodic expression[s] of our ideas among ourselves and before God our Creator."[4] For him, hymns were not ordinary texts but rather a better expression of divine truths; they were theology on a higher level. Singing for Zinzendorf and the Moravians was a spirit-filled, almost ecstatic matter: "A song is not ordinary but it is sublime speech, when the soul is filled with a more than ordinary, uplifted representation of God and with [other] heavenly, sacramental church matters."[5] Songs stem directly from the Holy Spirit, according to Zinzendorf, whether they are written down or, even more so, they originate spontaneously. Rhyme was of minor importance to him; it simply helped with the memorization and therefore internalization of the songs.

Hymns were also part of the Moravians' communal liturgy, their common ritual or performance. Singing was the center of each religious meeting, and some, such as Holy Communion, consisted solely of continuous singing. Important acts were accompanied by and underlined with singing. For example, reception into the congregation or admission as a communicant member occurred during the singing of an appropriate verse. Songs were frequently the topic of sermons. Bethlehem workers sang hymns as they went to work on the land. Songs were sung at the deathbed to accompany the departing soul into heaven. On special occasions hymns were randomly chosen for the attendants by letting the hymnbook fall open.[6] And in Herrnhaag and Bethlehem the single brothers wrote "blood verses," songs about Jesus's blood and wounds, on each door in their choir house.[7]

Following the uncovering of the crisis of the Sifting Time, the treatment of hymns and hymnbooks illustrates how crucial hymns were thought to be.

In the early 1750s, in the garden of an English Moravian in London, Christian Renatus ceremonially buried all the "things belonging to the previous period," symbolically ending the practices and teachings of the Sifting Time. The hymns, however, he dug up again and threw onto a fire to "solemnly burn them."[8] In February of 1749 the congregation in Herrnhut was told that in the future "no uncorrected" (i.e., unauthorized) hymns were to be sung anymore; instead, only hymns from the fourth supplement were allowed.[9] In December of that same year the workers and the helpers of the Herrnhut single brothers' choir were asked to hand over their "handwritten hymnbooks,"[10] and we know this happened in other congregations as well.[11] A statement by Friedrich von Watteville, then leader of the Moravians in Holland, during an official meeting about the Sifting Time is revealing: "When the first song of this kind was sung in Zeist, I called the laborers to me and I made clear that when such a song was sung again or if only they would tolerate it, I would not be able to work with them anymore and they could take up their staff and leave. Then it was over."[12] Like other leading Moravians, Watteville apparently considered the singing of particular hymns an expression of the Sifting, and believed that by banning the hymns he had ended the Sifting.

Hymnbook of 1749

What were the songs of the Sifting Time? It is sometimes claimed that they were the hymns in the twelfth appendix to the Herrnhut hymnal. This assumption is an example of how previous historians tried to define the Sifting Time by considering anything that was unusual in their eyes to be elements of the crisis.[13] In fact, this appendix was published in 1745, years before the actual crisis took place. The fourth supplement to it was printed during the Sifting Time and contains hymns dating up to November of 1748. But it apparently does not contain hymns that were later considered objectionable; during the very service when the Herrnhut congregation was instructed that it could no longer sing "uncorrected verses," several hymns from the fourth supplement were sung.[14] Among the deleted phrases in the diary of the Theological Seminary in Marienborn are many hymn titles. None of these hymns can be found in the printed hymnals, suggesting that the songs of the Sifting are not those traditionally considered to be Sifting Time hymns.[15]

Until recently, the songs of the Sifting Time were not known from Moravian sources, which contained only descriptions of the characteristics of these songs. Friedrich Christoph Steinhofer, a Lutheran minister closely related to the Moravians, described the lyrics and tunes in a concerned letter to Zinzendorf from March 1749: "Not only the familiar songs about the marital connection with the husband predominate in their singing, but many others [are to be heard] transformed from expressions, songs, and tunes that are derived from carnal merrymaking and secular disgrace and are invented by Satan, which are sung with a ragingly glowing feeling of love; [they are sung] at many and even at the most important occasions."[16]

Steinhofer's description is confirmed by opponents of the Moravians. Volck writes,

> They made various hymns to the tunes of the most shameful, smutty songs and sang them in their religious meetings. Even the coarsest people are annoyed by them. I will only give a few examples. They made hymns to the melody of a dance, called the "Siebensprung," and also to the melody of the smutty song "Allhier auf diesen Platz, da find ich meinen Schatz." Furthermore they sing songs to the tune of another saucy song: "Wenn du mein Schätzel wilt seyn, must du micht lieben allein." Likewise to well-known marches.[17]

Moravian opponents such as Volck, Bothe, and others also printed the texts of almost sixty hymns allegedly sung by the Moravians,[18] but until recently there was no reason to believe these were authentic Moravian songs. However, a few years ago a book was discovered in the object collection of the Unity Archives in Herrnhut. The book measures only 10 × 7.5 cm (4 × 3 in) and is handwritten in a minuscule script. It contains a Latin translation of the Song of Songs with a Latin commentary, various Latin verses from other books of the Bible, quotations from Luther, Augustine, Jerome, and other church fathers, and two sections of hymns. On the last page of the book the notation "49 9 Jul. 23 Aug. 6 Wochen" indicates the period of six weeks during the summer of 1749 when the texts were copied.

The first section of hymns (pp. 65–75) contains ninety-two verses, of which only four are found in printed Moravian hymnals. Another eight are variations on hymns from the hymnal. Sixteen of these verses are also found in anti-Moravian publications, such as Volck's *Entdecktes Geheimnis*, Bothe's *Zuverlässige Beschreibung*, and the journal *Acta Historico-Ecclesiastica*. The 1749 hymnbook thus confirms many of the songs found in the anti-Moravian pamphlets as Moravian and makes it more likely that other songs found in the pamphlets are authentic as well.

Some of the songs in the hymnbook are fragments of verses found in other sources. Sometimes words are left blank, possibly because the copyist could not read the original or because they were written down from memory. In some instances there is only a single line of text belonging neither to the previous nor to the next verse; there are also many abbreviations, and in some cases the text remains illegible.

Apparently, in the late 1740s it was not uncommon for Moravians to possess handwritten hymnbooks like this one that contained hymns not available in print. Bothe writes, "There were all kinds of strangely written verses that the pilgrims [the Moravian leaders] or others of the Cross-and-Blood Congregation brought to Berlin. To those who had them, they were a great blessing and they were so well received that a little boy copied them, for him to make some money."[19] Volck quotes twenty-two hymn verses from a similar hymnbook with tunes in his possession, compiled by the fifteen-year old Philipp Samuel Nonhebel.[20] Later, when the content was no longer considered acceptable, they were ordered to be turned in. Bothe notes, "All the handwritten verses were collected and demanded back in order to deliver them to the fire or to the privy. Thus this foolish pleasure came to an end."[21] Bothe's depiction is consistent with what we know from Moravian sources. When Moravians distanced themselves from their radicalism of the late 1740s, they destroyed anything that could remind them and posterity of these ideas. The 1749 hymnbook was probably given to the Unity Archives at a later date.

As stated above, popular tunes were used for the songs from the Sifting Time. Although it was not unusual for such tunes to be converted to church melodies, the adversaries of the Moravians described those used in the Sifting Time in particularly negative terms.[22] "Only Count Zinzendorf would think of using the tunes of whore songs as sacred hymns," asserted Volck.[23] A handwritten tune book, given to the Unity Archives around 1900, contains not only the usual hymn tunes, but also seventeen additional tunes that correspond to songs we would consider as originating during the Sifting Time. The tune book was originally owned by Catharina Höffly, a musician among the single sisters in Herrnhaag, Herrnhut, and Marienborn.[24] Although many of the tune titles (the first line of the most common hymn it was used for) are crossed out, and even the index of tune titles is replaced with a different one, it is still possible to decipher the tune titles. Some of them correspond to the songs in the manuscript hymnbook; others correspond to texts found in publications by Volck and Bothe. By combining these sources, we not only know the texts of the "forbidden" songs, but their melodies as well.²⁵

Hymns

The 1749 hymnbook disproves the traditional characterization of the Sifting Time as a period in which the blood and wounds of Christ were the center of Moravian piety. Only a very small number of songs in the hymnbook actually deal with the wounds of Christ. There is one hymn of five verses about swimming in the blood that flows from Jesus's wounds.²⁶ Another text is a variation on the "Te Deum Laudamus": "Ihr Wunden, euch loben wir" (O wounds, we adore thee). Although this hymn addresses all the wounds of Christ, it specifically focuses on the wound in his side, the side hole, which it describes as the birthplace of the church and as a place of security and warmth for the congregation.

The side wound as the home of the individual believer is one of the predominant topics in the 1749 manuscript hymnbook. It is compared with the image of the rock from Isaiah 51:1 from which the believers are "hewn"; here in this "cleft of the rock" the "dove," as an image for the individual believer, finds refuge, in accordance with Song of Solomon 2:14. The winds blowing around the cross (*Kreuzluft*) carry the believer into the side wound. The believer becomes a cross-air bird, a bird flying around the cross and aiming for the side wound.²⁷ As discussed above, inside the side wound the believer is comfortable: he is at home, where he has his bed and table. The believer can go to sleep in the side. Going into the side wound or penetrating the side wound is an image of becoming one with Christ. This imagery can also be found in printed Moravian hymnals.

From being a part of the body of Christ, the side hole becomes a *pars pro toto* for Christ—the side hole *is* Christ. In many of the hymns Jesus is addressed as "side hole" in many variations: "little hole" (*Hölchen*), "dearest little side" (*liebstes Seitelein*), "divine side" (*göttliches Seitelein* or *göttliches Seitenhölchen*), or "charming hole" (*charmantes Hölchen*). The side hole is at once Christ as well as the entrance to his body.

The songs from the Sifting Time use themes and imagery of bridal mysticism, in which Christ is the bridegroom and the soul is the bride who is in love with him. Christ is also the husband and the believer the wife. In twenty-five of the ninety-two hymns of the manuscript hymnbook Christ is addressed as *Schätzel* (sweetheart) or even more frequently in the double diminutive *Schätzelein*. The believer refers to himself as *Herzel* (dear heart or sweetheart) but sometimes also as *Schätzel*. A frequent word in the hymns is "charming" (*charmiren, charmant*). The side hole (i.e., Christ) is "charming"; it entices and charms the believer as a lover does.[28]

The believers' infatuation with Jesus is quite serious. The songs mention thumping and jumping of the heart, laughing, and trembling from head to toe. The eyes tear in longing for the husband. The believer claps his hands out of pure excitement.[29] The believer becomes like wax and melts away; in the mystical tradition this is called *liquefactio*.[30] The believer experiences excessive joy, is ravished out of himself and cannot remain in his senses (*abalienatio*).[31] The longing of the believer for Christ is so strong that it hurts. The believer is lovesick: "I am sick with love" (krank bin ich vor Liebespein), which is a direct quote from Song of Songs 2:5. Not only does the believer long for Christ, Christ also longs for the believer: "Bridegroom, my eternal husband, / who cannot do anything without me."[32]

The love between Christ and the believer is expressed in kisses, in reference to the opening verse of the Songs of Songs (1:2): "Let him kiss me with the kisses of his mouth." Thousands of sweet kisses are exchanged in the songs of the 1749 hymnbook.

> Kissing, kissing must be done,
> oh, do not interrupt.
> Now you are alone
> just for me, my darling.[33]

Every part of the body is being kissed: from the smallest hair to the feet ("bis aufs kleinste Härgen und die Füßgen"), from head to toe. The believer purses his lips for Christ to kiss him. They kiss one another so tightly that their mouths are linked to each other. The kisses are sweet and taste of honey and sugar candy (Song of Songs 4:11). These kisses are not devout kisses as a sign of reverence, such as kissing the feet or wounds of Christ. In the songs of the 1749 hymnbook, it is Christ who kisses the believer as a lover kisses his bride, and the believer returns the kisses. Kissing is part of the game of love, *ludus amoris*.[34]

> Play, just play, I want to laugh with tears,
> let me sleep, my darling, you can wake,
> Embrace me while I am resting,
> Kiss me on both of my closed eyes.[35]

The bed in the hymns is the nuptial bed into which Christ will take the believer. This is a common mystical image for the place where the unification of the believer and the divine will occur. It can be found in the Song of Songs: "Behold, thou art fair, my beloved, yea, pleasant: also our bed is green" (1:16). The believer is lying in his bed, waiting and longing for his lover, while watchmen stand guard (Song of Songs 3:7).

> We go to sleep with him,
> because he likes it so much.
> sixty are ordered to keep watch around the bed.
> Sleep well [repeat six times]
> sixty are ordered, etc.[36]

According to Bernard of Clairvaux, sleeping in Christ's embrace illuminates the senses, drives away death, and gives eternal life.[37]

In the words of the songs, Christ holds the believer in his arms and they embrace one another. The embrace is in fact a metaphor for sexual intercourse, the ultimate union of the soul with the divine. The Song of Songs is not very specific about this image, but Bernard of Clairvaux and his successors elaborated upon it.[38] It is the final stage of union between the believer and the divine, a *unio indistinctionis* in which the two are the same.

> when we are lying in each other's arms
> and cuddling up into one another
> so that two darlings become
> one spirit, flesh and bone.[39]

The believer and Christ are joined together and have become one soul.

> Since we've on each other lighted,
> We are Bone out of one Bone,
> Souls into one Soul united;
> That's indeed an Union![40]

What happens during the embrace is best described in the following verse:

> I am lying in his arms
> as his spoiled little darling.
> When he wants to kiss and embrace me,
> I am passively his sweetheart.[41]

During the embrace the believer remains passive, is silent, lies still, and enjoys himself while Christ embraces and kisses him (Song of Songs 1:2). "For us it is: enjoy, enjoy, / and for him: kiss, kiss."[42] The believer is to be as submissive to the divine as a wife is to her husband.[43] The idea of passivity appears in several verses; the believer even refers to himself as being a "slave" and a "love slave." The believer is also "unconscious" like the sleeping bride in the Song of Songs.

> My desperate tears,
> my loving rage
> turned into gentle longing,
> into passive destitution.
> Even if he does not want to kiss me anymore,
> I am his mute sheep,
> I do not desire nor want to know anything,
> I am lying unconscious as if asleep.[44]

This leads to the next metaphor, that of death. The love bed becomes the sickbed in which the believer waits for the lover to kiss him well again. The love of the believer for Christ is so intense that the believer becomes sick, loses his senses (mir vergehn die Sinne mein), and "rejoices himself to death" (mich freuen muß zu Tod). Christ kisses the believer to death, and when they embrace the believer dies in his arms. This is the mystical death, or *mors mystica*, described by Bernard of Clairvaux as an ecstasy when the soul is removed from life's cares. Dying with Christ is a recurrent theme with later mystics.[45] The sickbed becomes a deathbed, which equals Christ's grave. The believer is in the grave with Christ, and when he dies in his arms he becomes pure and free of human sin: he is completely one with the divine.

Consequently, the frequent image of the bed is the place of unification with Christ. The bed stands in the side hole; it is the day bed (*Ruhebett*), the nuptial bed (*Ehebett*), and ultimately the deathbed. The images for the place where the bed stands are interchangeable as well: the side hole is the love chamber as well as the grave of Christ.

> Let us enjoy the sickbed
> let us be ruttishly invigorated at the grave side,
> where we in pains of death
> go for a stroll, as in the woods.[46]

> Brothers and sisters, our day bed
> is our husband's burial place,

where we lay down our body and soul,
sleep well, rest, cover his flesh and bone.[47]

Acts

The songs of the Sifting express mystical ideas in a vivid and graphic way. But do we know what Moravians did during singing? How were these songs used and sung? From various examples we know that the words of the songs were often accompanied and expressed by movements, gestures, or other actions. For example, when during the 1748 single brothers' festival in Herrnhaag the assembled men sang the line "Now thou be kissed by the entire brethren's choir," each man kissed his neighbor, representing Christ.[48] Many of the songs speak of joy, delight, and cheerfulness to be expressed by clapping, so it is reported that each time the worshippers sang a line such as "clap your hands with joy," they actually clapped their hands.[49] According to the anonymous editor of the *Acta historico-ecclesiastica*, they did the same each time the word *Schätzel* (sweetheart) was sung: "When such expressions are sung in their verses, the whole congregation in Herrnhut will clap their hands, as I was recently told by an acquaintance who saw it himself in their church."[50] Volck prints an anonymous letter from a visitor to Herrnhaag who observed the children gesticulating to songs similar to those analyzed here.

> I attended the children's service, where I saw to my amazement that the children were drilled and trained as little comedians. They sang certain songs, and after singing, these small monkeys made their gestures and did their tricks: one moment they were kissing their hands, the next moment they beat their breasts at the words "it's thumping, it's hopping, it's throbbing." When they sang the words "I am lovesick," each child put his head at another one's breast, while making amorous and yearning gestures as if they were going to faint for love. One moment they were all clapping their hands, one moment they were hopping, and the next they were jumping. I had to sigh in my heart about the tricks these children were up to and they had learned from their teachers.[51]

If these songs were merely following old mystical traditions, why did they soon cause so much embarrassment that they had to be collected, destroyed, and buried into oblivion? From the reactions by Steinhofer, Volck, and Bothe quoted above, we can deduce that they viewed the songs as a sign of religious fanaticism. The problem with the songs of the Sifting Time was that they

*Fig. 6   Singet, springet, klopfet in die Hände.* Drawing of playing children in "Stammbüchlein für Elisabeth von Zinzendorf," p. 16. Pen drawing by Friedrich von Watteville, ca. 1755. Unity Archives, Herrnhut, Germany.

were not sung in a traditional worship setting, but actually seem to have been acted out. During 1748 Christian Renatus formed a *Schätzel Gesellschaft* (company of sweethearts) and told the members they had actually reached the highest stage of the *unio* with the bridegroom. On top of this, in December of 1748 he declared the single brothers of Herrnhaag to be "sisters." The scarce reports describing the events of the following months link hymns such as the ones discussed here to the extravagances taking place. The imagery no longer metaphorically referred to Holy Communion; metaphors were now taken literally and carried out.[52] The lying down, the embrace, the kisses—all this was performed by the men and women. The resulting intimate physical contact, combined with a perfectionist belief that they were released from any sin, were the grounds for allusions to "the carnal aberrations" we find within texts on the Sifting Time. Therefore, it is not surprising that the hymns that accompanied the frivolities were soon destroyed and forgotten.

# 6

## THE ACTUAL SIFTING

Till we his Wife shall be.
—*Collection of Hymns*, pt. 3, no. 108

The events of December 6, 1748, are key to understanding the Sifting. The ceremony that day was in many ways the logical consequence of the developments of the previous years, of the teachings by Zinzendorf and by the other leaders, and especially of the events during the preceding months. Had this culmination not taken place, it can be argued, what happened in the 1740s would have been viewed in a different light altogether.

It was on December 6 that Christian Renatus von Zinzendorf declared that the single men in Herrnhaag were no longer to consider themselves men, but from then on would all be "sisters." The following day, Christel and Rubusch went to nearby Marienborn and repeated the ceremony with the single brothers living there. Only a few days earlier the diary of the single brothers in Marienborn noted, "On November 29 the brothers attended the choir day [in Herrnhaag]. A new and blessed period began for the laborers, the helpers, and the *praeparands*."[1] The same was noted in other sources as well, indicating that many participants perceived the events of the fall of 1748 as the start of a new era.[2] On December 4 the church observed the Festival of the Husband (*Mannesfest*). The theme of this festival, first celebrated in 1745, originated in bridal mysticism and celebrated "the marriage of the Lamb with our souls."[3] In 1748 the single brothers in Herrnhaag no longer wished to celebrate the mystical marriage in joyful expectation of what was to come; that year they believed the dividing line between heaven and earth was no longer relevant.

The night before the Festival of the Husband all single brothers received red choir ribbons to be worn the next day instead of their usual green ribbons. During the celebration of Holy Communion on December 4, Christel and the other administering brothers entered the meeting hall wearing red surplices. The suggestion of the corporeal presence of Christ was so real that, as Christel repeatedly spoke in a strong voice the words "The Lord is here!," several members of the congregation actually turned around, expecting to see Christ in the back of the hall.[4] The belief in living at the end of times was real in Herrnhaag, and the expectation of an immediate eschaton was high. This expectation led to the ceremony two days later, when Christel pronounced the single brothers to be sisters.[5] In this chapter we will closely examine the texts that record the ceremony and find that Moravians during the late 1740s believed they could mortify the flesh and become sinless. This implied that men would lose their gender identity and become virginal even before death. As such, they would be able to enjoy the mystical marriage on earth, not only within but also outside of marriage.

The Sources

As far as we know, three primary sources for the ceremony of December 6, 1748, exist, two of them Moravian and one non-Moravian. The first and the shortest reference is found in the private diary of Johann Christoph Becker, a single brother who experienced the ceremony in Marienborn a day after Christel first performed it in Herrnhaag: "December 7 [1748]. After the brothers in Herrnhaag were all confirmed and pronounced as single sisters the day before, we have now experienced this astounding thing here as well this evening. We were given the benediction by the dear Renatus, Rubusch, and Caillet by the laying on of hands. There was Communion and foot washing. I left in the middle of this fever and went to Bethlehem."[6]

The second reference is found in the diary of the single brothers in Marienborn, which survives, unlike the diary of the single brothers in Herrnhaag for the critical years of 1748 and 1749, because an editor, in an attempt to save the diary, blackened the critical passages. Fortunately, the entries for December 6 and 7, 1748, are still legible.

> [Dec.] 6 was again an indescribably blessed day for our choir. At 3 o'clock in the afternoon everyone went over to the choir day [in Herrnhaag]. The side hole declared us all to be sisters, condemned the brotherhood and consecrated us as sisters, and sealed us through our eating and drinking his side hole. In the end we closed with a foot washing, during which dear Christel sang verses by heart.
> 
> Because only a few of us were able to attend yesterday's meeting, the dear hearts Christel and Rubusch, etc. came over here on the 7th. After

a few conferences the meeting started at 9 o'clock for all the communicant brothers, when the side hole bestowed on us the same as what happened in Herrnhaag yesterday."[7]

The third and most detailed source for the ceremonies in Herrnhaag and Marienborn comes from Christian Hart, the former Moravian who published his experiences among the Moravians in Herrnhaag and Zeist after returning to his hometown of Stargard in Pomerania. He extensively described the same gender-changing events:

> This period lasted until the Festival of the Husband in November 1749 [i.e., December 1748] when the two elders of the single brothers, the young Count Christel and Rubusch, yet again came up with something new. They claimed the Savior had made clear to them that the single brothers should no longer be brothers but that he had declared them to be single sisters or maidens. In order to carry out this matter, a meeting was held with the communicant brothers to absolve them, to forgive them all of their sins, however great they were, not only those that had happened but also the ones that were still to happen. The young men's bond and the young men's point were dissolved. The verdict was given that everything from the past, when one spoke about young men's matters (*de cupiditatibus carnis*), was damned. Christel broke a staff with his own hands, pronounced the verdict, and thus they were absolved of their sinful lusts.
> 
> After that [the brass instruments] were blown and [the hymn] was sung: "Glory be to the hour of sentence, glory be to the hour, glory be to the hour, glory be to the hour of sentence!" Then everyone fell down on their knees and the elders first gave the benediction to each other: Rubusch to Christel, Christel to Rubusch. Then these two gave the benediction by the laying on of hands to all the others [and made] everyone into sisters....
> 
> Afterwards the same happened in Zeist, because young Count Christel went there himself and carried it out the same way when I was present. Although he did not perform the ceremony with the staff and the condemnation, as mentioned above, the classes were still organized the same as in Herrnhaag.[8]

The three accounts of these events are strikingly similar and, despite minor inconsistencies, seem to agree about what happened. Hart, though he mistakenly identifies 1749 (rather than 1748) as the year these events took place and the Festival of the husband as taking place in November (rather than December), and though he was not in the Wetterau but in Zeist at the time, seems well informed about the events. He fails to mention the repetition of the ceremony in Marienborn the next day, but notes that Christian Renatus performed a similar gender-changing ceremony in Zeist. This must have happened when Christel and Rubusch passed through Zeist on their way to London in May of 1749.[9]

Brothers as Sisters

In order to understand what it meant for "brothers" to become "sisters," we need to examine Moravian ideas about gender as they were taught by Zinzendorf and other leaders during the 1740s.

As we have seen, Zinzendorf applied the metaphors of bridal mysticism to marriage between husband and wife. In accordance with Zinzendorf's reading of Ephesians 5:22–33, marriage was seen as an image of the bond between Christ and the church. Christ was the heavenly husband and man was the earthly husband; the wife in this metaphor represented the church, and the husband became "vice-Christ." So Zinzendorf and his fellow Moravians saw the uniting of husband and wife as a reflection of the unification of Christ and the church; consequently, sexual intercourse became a liturgical or even a sacramental act.[10] According to mid-eighteenth-century Moravian ideas, a believer could experience union with Christ both during Holy Communion and through sexual intercourse. If comparable to sexual intercourse, then, Communion could be described with terminology normally reserved for sex, and in the late 1740s this is exactly what the Moravians did. Communion became the "embrace" (*Umarmung*) of the husband, where Christ "penetrated" (*durchgehen, durchleiben*) the individual to eventually become one with him or her (*vereinen*).

This bridal imagery was not reserved for married couples or single sisters. Like the medieval mystics, who were typically members of celibate orders, the Moravian single men took to mystical ideas with great enthusiasm. In one of the hymns they sang,

> O dear Lamb, your side wound
> has made me, your dear sinner, your bride.
> Because I was taken from there,
> I am your bride and you are my bridegroom.[11]

*Fig. 7* A Moravian Communion service in 1753. Pen drawing by Friedrich von Watteville in an album for Elisabeth von Zinzendorf. The image shows the characteristic layout of a Moravian *Saal*. Women are placed on the left side of the *Saal*, men on the right-hand side. The laborers sit at the front, facing the congregation. The drawing shows the distribution of the bread, simultaneously on both the sisters' and the brothers' side. A woman is assisting with the distribution on the sisters' side. Wine bottles and chalices are lined up on the table. Unity Archives, Herrnhut, Germany.

Or another verse:

> Day in day out he calls me his "sweetheart,"
> and he names himself my "darling sweetheart."
> Although it is a mystery for dryness [those who are dry of heart],
> I eat it up like sugar.
> I am lying in his arms as his spoiled darling
> and when he wants to kiss and embrace me,
> I passively am his wife.[12]

The brothers considered themselves to be Christ's "sweethearts," "darlings," or "brides." They even let him "embrace" them so that they could be his "wives." In 1748 Christian Renatus and his fellow leader Rubusch began signing their names as "Christelein von Hölgen" and "Joachim von Höhlgen."[13] Like a wife taking the name of her husband, they took the name of their husband, the side hole (i.e., Christ), indicating they were married to him. This union was the highest state of bridal mystical longing for Christ.

The single brothers' bond with the Savior was envisioned as a male-male relationship. How did men reconcile this imagery with their male gender? Was it problematic for male believers to use metaphors taken from bridal mysticism to describe their relationship with Christ?

It has been argued that Moravians solved this dilemma by feminizing Christ.[14] Aaron Fogleman claims that Moravians altered the gender of the Trinity by disempowering God the Father, declaring Christ the Creator, calling the Holy Spirit "Mother," and attributing female characteristics to Jesus. By regendering Jesus as both male and female, both "men and women believers could have a sensuous spiritual relationship with their Savior."[15]

Fogleman's thesis of a Moravian belief in a female Jesus has evoked criticism among scholars. Peter Vogt challenges this view and stresses the emphasis on Jesus's masculinity in Zinzendorf's theology. Although a "certain simultaneousness" of masculine and female elements in Zinzendorf's image of Christ seems to exist, Vogt argues that the female elements of Christ played only a secondary role for Zinzendorf, who maintained, "He is the husband, we all are the husband's wife."[16] Katherine Faull and Craig Atwood assign more importance to the female metaphors in Zinzendorf's Christology and gender ideas. According to Faull, Christ "enacted femaleness" by bleeding, nurturing, and giving birth to the church through his side wound, but, Faull rightfully claims, for Moravians he remained a man. Discussing Zinzendorf's ideas on the gender role of male believers in their relationship with Christ, she introduces the term "temporal masculinity." According to Zinzendorf, men are to act as men and husbands while being aware of the femininity of their souls. They are the brides of Christ.[17] Atwood also disagrees with Fogleman's claim that eighteenth-century Moravians viewed Jesus as female, arguing that they saw him as more of an androgynous figure. Through his side wound Christ had given birth to the church, thus restoring the lost androgyny of the old Adam and becoming the new Adam.[18]

The use of feminine metaphors for Jesus or God was not as unusual or controversial as Fogleman claims. For instance, hymn writers such as Gottfried Arnold and Paul Gerhardt used both male and female attributes for God.[19] Neither was the use of motherly language for God unbiblical: "as a mother comforts her child, I will comfort you" (Isa. 66:13). Zinzendorf referred to Jesus's speaking of himself as a hen who gathered her chicks under her wings (Matt. 23:37; Luke 13:34). So when Zinzendorf used female metaphors for Jesus, he believed he stood on a solid biblical foundation.

Zinzendorf repeatedly spoke metaphorically of Jesus as mother: "He is also a mother for us, though not according to the members of his body." The true miracle for Zinzendorf was that Jesus *as a man* could give birth. According to Zinzendorf, Christ the creator was father; as a human being with body and soul he was brother, bridegroom, and husband. But his corpse, after his soul had departed his body, was the mother who gave birth to the souls of men. As Adam had "supernaturally" given birth when Eve was taken from his rib, Jesus gave birth to all Christian souls from his pierced side wound as a womb.[20] The side wound was the spiritual birthing place of all true Christians, who were born again to a new, eternal life while the mother died in labor: "that is the real and true story of our genesis—a gospel!"[21] A few years later Zinzendorf addressed the topic of the birthing Savior again. During an address on Good Friday 1751 in Herrnhut, he said, "the point is that a man gives birth," which he called "the prophetic miracle."[22]

In my opinion, the feminization of Christ played a role among Moravians, but in a different way than Fogleman suggests. Female metaphors for Christ were used, not in order for male believers to come to terms with their submissive (feminine) role in the union with (the male) Christ, but rather to describe the true miracle of Christ's humanity and death: through his death Christ, as a man, gave birth to the church. So for Moravians Christ was foremost the bridegroom, the man, the husband, the one who wished to penetrate the believers. It was not Christ who was feminized in Moravian theological ideas, but the believers. Zinzendorf solved the question of how men could be brides of Christ by teaching that the souls of all humans, men and women, are female. It is believed that he first publicly introduced this concept at the wedding of his daughter Benigna to Johannes von Watteville in Zeist in 1746, where he said, "All souls are sisters. He knows the secret. He has created all souls, the soul is his wife. He did not make *animos*, not male souls among the human souls, but only *animas*, female souls who are his brides.... So to conceive the human soul as male is the greatest foolishness."[23] Because all souls, whether a man's or a woman's, were female, each soul could unite with Christ and become his wife as a bride unites with a groom. Just as the grammatical gender of the Latin word for soul, *anima*, was female, so too, Zinzendorf held, was the natural gender of the soul.[24]

The idea of all souls being female was by no means new or unique to Zinzendorf and the Moravians. As early as the twelfth century, mystic writers, both male and female, elaborated on this concept, also arguing from the grammatical gender of *anima*. Early eighteenth-century Puritans in New England often characterized the soul as female, allowing men to use bridal metaphors for their union with Christ.[25] For Zinzendorf this concept was not only a metaphor, and some of his followers seem to have considered it an attainable reality, as became clear during the ceremony of December 6, 1748. Masculinity, according to Zinzendorf, was temporal and earthly: "There are no male souls in the world, not in heaven or on earth. Everything about our bodies that is temporarily male will have ended from the moment that the corpse descends into the earth."[26] The moment when the soul would become female was not during life but after death. Masculinity, said Zinzendorf, was a "borrowed situation"; men had undergone a metamorphosis whereby for the time being they had exchanged their original female gender for another one. Men would cease being men only in the afterlife.[27] But during life on earth there was much they could do to come close to this ideal.

Other gender-related ideas factored in as well. Pious groups in the Atlantic world of the eighteenth century associated devout believers not with strength or toughness but rather with femininity and weakness. In order to be saved, both men and women had to be passive, submissive, and contrite—qualities supposed to be feminine.[28] As early as 1735 an outside observer noted that the men in Herrnhut did not appear very masculine: "The men themselves take on rather effeminate manners. As they affect a loving character, they often disguise their male language. They laugh and weep within one breath. Everything with them is supposed to be hearty, lovely, or nice."[29]

Again, submissiveness and passivity were considered female qualities. This similarity with Christ made women "respectful" according to Moravian standards; every man should attempt to become like them. Women had already attained a similarity to Jesus's corpse, while men were still burdened with their masculinity, which was often equated with carnal desires and lustful thoughts.[30] In Moravian speech male gender-specific behavior (*Mannsgebärde*) was generally connected to sin and considered to be the opposite of "virginal" or pure (*jungfräulich*) behavior. Especially the men in the single brothers' houses were encouraged to die to sin, to all sexual longings and lustful thoughts (1 Pet. 2:24). This is what Zinzendorf meant when he said "all differences between the sexes end with a corpse."[31] Consequently, when a believer mortified his sin, "death"—and therefore the moment when all male souls returned to their feminine nature—could already occur during life on earth.

The disappearance of gender differences followed logically from mid-eighteenth-century Moravian teachings. Since a Moravian was to model his or her life in every aspect according to the example Jesus had set during his time on earth, the ultimate goal was to identify with the corpse of Jesus and mortify all earthly sinful thoughts and feelings—in Zinzendorf's words, "to deaden oneself to all undesired thoughts and things by the corpse of Jesus; to let oneself become cold and dead, stone dead, against all lusts and everything that can soil one's soul and body."[32] So if one was to become like Christ in his death, no sinful sexual ("male") thoughts were to cross one's mind; thus, the distinguishing gender characteristics would also disappear.[33]

Again, these ideas were not unique to the Moravians. The image of the virginal men can be traced to the Book of Revelation: "These are they which were not defiled with women; for they are virgins" (Rev. 14:4). The metaphor of Christ as the heavenly bridegroom joining himself to virginal believers (male and female) existed already in the early church. As noted above, Bernard of Clairvaux and other medieval authors employed the metaphor of the soul as bride of Christ. References to the idea of the disappearance of gender differences can be found in thirteenth-century writings, as well as among Zinzendorf's contemporaries. Members of Conrad Beissel's community in Ephrata, Pennsylvania, for example, believed the distinction between the genders was a consequence of the Fall and would ultimately be abolished. Men in Ephrata were taught to curb their male will and become submissive and female.[34]

During the 1740s the mortification of the flesh and the resulting disappearance of gender differences became a recurrent theme among Moravians. It was the topic of a hymn Zinzendorf wrote for Anna Maria Lawatsch on her birthday on November 6, 1743.[35] Brother Johannes preached about this matter in Herrnhaag as early as March 25, 1745: in view of Jesus's chaste and virginal "human members" (*Menschheitsglieder*) one could purify, heal, and sanctify one's own sinful members. By killing off the old "weak and sinful members" one could become chaste and similar to Jesus's holy corpse, "so that the concept of the sexes, with everything depending on that, had almost disappeared."[36]

Although Zinzendorf usually taught that men would lose their masculinity *after* death, he and other leaders also gave their followers reason to believe the differences between the genders had already begun to disappear here on earth. Throughout 1747 Zinzendorf himself gave several sermons about the "disappearance of masculinity" and the merging of the single brothers and single sisters into one choir, thereby setting the stage for the events at the end of the following year.

Zinzendorf presented these ideas during a carefully planned ceremony on May 6, 1747. The single choirs in Herrnhaag had just celebrated their annual choir festivals: the brothers on May 2 and the sisters on May 4. Now Zinzendorf called them both to a love feast in Marienborn, where he explained how during Holy Communion one could have a foretaste of the marriage with Christ. Through the body of Christ during Communion one mortified one's own sinful body so that nothing remained but the soul; thus both sexes became one and the same in spirit. Zinzendorf then invited both single choirs to observe Communion together. This was highly unusual; normally they would have Communion either within their choirs (*Chorabendmahl*) or with the entire congregation (*Gemeinabendmahl*). In order to symbolize the joining of the two choirs, the men and women were not placed on opposite sides of the meeting hall as usual. Instead, the sisters, wearing white festive dresses, were seated in the center of the hall while the men sat around them. It is important to understand the eschatological character of this celebration. During the events of December 1748, eschatological anticipation had turned into an immediate experience in the present, but now the communicants were only having a "foretaste," "in expectation" of what was to come. The last words of the closing hymn were "until we see what we believe."[37]

During the following weeks Zinzendorf spoke about this subject several times in Herrnhaag: when Jesus's corpse mortified human flesh, "nothing would remain but the common soul."[38] In one address he announced that a new era had begun: "although bodily we are still men, we are no longer men in the spirit, because in faith we are all sisters."[39] Later that year Zinzendorf told the brothers and sisters in congregations such as Gnadenfrei in Silesia and Herrnhut that from now on they would form "one choir" and that he wished that the brothers "would forget their manliness and their somewhat rough ways."[40] By teaching that men were essentially women, Zinzendorf enabled Moravian men to envision their intense love for Christ in the same sensual manner as women did. But although he told them that the true nature of a man was that of a woman, and spiritually they had already become similar, he believed they would not physically lose their gender until the end of times: "The brothers can hardly wait until their bodies become like the one who carried him [i.e., the Virgin Mary], when the sign [of the Son of man, Matt. 24:30] appears in the clouds to bring about change for the whole world."[41] But eschatological expectation among Moravians—including Zinzendorf—was building dramatically during 1748 and 1749. We have seen that people actually turned their heads during worship meetings expecting to see Jesus physically present in their midst. And in February of 1749 (only a few days before he wrote the letter of reprimand) Zinzendorf explained to his listeners in London that all that prevented Jesus from physically appearing among Moravians was the continued existence of a few "unfaithful souls" in the church.[42]

The younger generation of his son Christian Renatus, Rubusch, and the other single brothers could no longer wait. During the previous years, they had learned that male gender was an interim condition and that the true state of every believer was indeed female. They had learned that any manly (sinful) gender identity was only temporary and that inside each man a maiden was hiding. They had learned that by mortifying their sins, men were able to become virginal. They had also come to believe that the presence of Christ was something they could already experience on earth; they felt so close to Christ that they thought eternity had already begun on earth. And now they believed that Christ himself had ended their masculinity and declared them to be women. On December 6, 1748, Christian Renatus von Zinzendorf declared all brothers to be sisters. Henceforth they would be the maidens who could lie in the arms of the husband, as they believed the biblical Song of Songs described.

Close Reading

A better understanding of the gender-changing ceremony comes from a close reading of the three sources, in combination with an examination of the ideas expressed by Zinzendorf and Watteville in the months before December of 1748. Becker's diary does not give any explanation for what it meant to be "pronounced as sisters," but the Marienborn diary offers more detail: "The side hole declared us all to be sisters, condemned the brotherhood, and consecrated us as sisters." The original German for the critical phrase translated here as "condemned the brotherhood" is "der Brüderschafft den Stab gebrochen," literally meaning "broke the staff over the brotherhood." This refers to the breaking of the staff by a judge when pronouncing a death sentence. Breaking the staff over the brotherhood thus means a death sentence was pronounced on the male state; the male gender had been eliminated.[43]

The third surviving account of this ceremony, written by Christian Hart, uses almost identical language while providing greater detail.

> In order to carry out this matter a meeting was held with the communicant brothers to absolve them, to forgive them all of their sins, however great they were, not only those that had happened but also the ones that were still to happen. The young men's bond and the young men's point were dissolved. The verdict was given that everything from the past, when one spoke about young men's matters (*de cupiditatibus carnis*), was damned. Christel broke a staff with his own hands, pronounced the sentence, and so they were acquitted of their sinful lusts.[44]

Hart explains that at the beginning of the ceremony absolution was given to all the brothers for whatever sins they had committed in the past as well as for any sins they would commit in the future. By "sins" matters of a sexual nature were understood. Therefore it did not make sense to talk about the "young men's point" (*Jünglingspunkt*) anymore, since these were all matters relating to the state of being a single brother, especially regarding sexual thoughts and desires. Next Christel took a staff, broke it, and threw it on the floor, condemning the past and the need to suppress carnal lust. From then on, manliness with all its *cupiditatibus carnis* (desires of the flesh) had come to an end; the brothers were acquitted of "sinful lusts" and had become pure and virginal. As maidens they could sleep in the arms of Christ; they could be embraced and unite with him. In other words, they had reached the highest state a mystical believer aspired to: union with Christ.

For Christel, declaring the single men to be virginal sisters was the logical conclusion of his father's teachings. With the chaste and dead body of Christ in mind, the believer, likewise, needed to die to sin. If then the human body was entirely "dead" and no (manly) carnal lust remained, the body had lost its masculine characteristics and had become, so to speak, virginal. However, what Christel and Rubusch were doing on December 6, 1748, was not the same as what Zinzendorf and Watteville had previously taught. They turned the teachings around when they first absolved all brothers from all past and future(!) sins and then declared them to have become virgins. Neither pious contemplation nor any dying to sin on the part of the believer was involved; their sins were absolved by their choir leaders, who acted on behalf of Christ.

A central element of the ceremony was the idea that the men had reached a state of perfection. Other texts confirm that the brothers indeed believed this. Addressing the problems of the Sifting Time in 1750, Johannes considered the developments in Herrnhaag a misapprehension of the idea of "blessed sinfulness" (*selige Sünderschaft*), a concept Moravians had been proclaiming for many years: the realization that one's sins are forgiven places a person in an altered, blissful state. Nevertheless, one remains a sinner who will sin again. Johannes accused the brethren in Herrnhaag of having turned this around and made "sins and lusts" acceptable because they no longer mattered. Similarly, Spangenberg attributed the events of the late 1740s to a neglect of the awareness that all humans are sinners and to the mistaken belief that a true child of God does not sin anymore.[45]

Zinzendorf had laid the groundwork for the idea that it was possible for believers to become perfect by becoming more and more "Christlike." During Holy Communion, as explained above, the believer was to surrender to the sanctifying force of Christ. Zinzendorf described mortification as an ongoing process. During Communion Christ stretches his holy dead body over the believers to mortify their bodies "until finally the sinful body would cease completely." Each time the believer subjects himself to the work of Christ's spirit, the process of mortification continues "until it leads to completion."[46]

The idea of perfectionism was expressed by having become virginal or, in Moravian parlance, having become "sisters." Apparently, the men took their new state quite literally. Hart writes that from then on they took Communion as maidens. They would also call one another sister: "for example, instead of 'Brother Neissert' they would call him 'Sister Neissert,' etc."[47] Another source talks about a society of "Sixty Queens" (cf. Song of Songs 6:8), consisting of a group of sixty select men and women in Herrnhaag during 1749 who were to keep a watch by themselves in their rooms.[48] Not much else is known about their activities, but the name of the group suggests it is another example of feminine terminology applied to both men and women.

A later statement by Johannes von Watteville confirms that the men's change of gender was not just a metaphor to describe their blissful state of mind, but at least some men actually believed they had become sisters. Addressing the single brothers in Marienborn in March of 1750, Watteville said it was acceptable to believe metaphorically that they were sisters who sleep in the arms of Christ, but called it an unfounded idea that they were *physically* sisters.[49]

This literal interpretation of religious metaphors sets Moravians apart from other religious groups. Seventeenth-century Puritans in New England, who used very similar eroticized language to describe their longing for God, may not have applied the spiritual metaphors to the sexual relations between husband and wife.[50] Susan Juster cautions against thinking that early modern Pietists really envisioned themselves in a physical relationship with God, even though they may have used sexualized language to describe this relationship. Juster wants us to distinguish passionate language from actual sexual desire.[51] Other historians, such as Richard Rambuss, read sacred eroticism not merely in a metaphorical way but as genuine eroticism, both heterosexual and homosexual.[52] Rambuss discusses a private form of devotion, "closet devotion," that is, devotional prayer and contemplation in one's inner sanctum. For Moravians this was not private devotion but communal devotion. Sexuality was part of the communal discourse, and the sacred eroticism did not remain limited to meditation but was acted out. Moravians during the late 1740s believed they could enact the metaphors used to describe the believer's relationship with Christ. For them, the metaphors became reality.

Let us now turn again to the single brothers' festival of 1749. As we saw in chapter 4, the day concluded with a display of a dying body and a Communion service at a new, presumably empty grave. At this point in the book, this symbolism of this event makes better sense. The display of a "sickly and dying body" was an example for all attending men to die to sin and to become virginal. Then the entire single brothers' choir went to a fresh grave, embodying Zinzendorf's idea that anything "temporarily male will have ended from the moment on that the corpse descends into the grave."[53] During the following Communion service the men united with Christ. Like the events of December 1748, this was a celebration of the state of perfectionism Moravian men had attained.

By acquitting the brothers not only of their past sins but of all sins they were yet to commit, Christel had taken the Lutheran understanding of justification by faith to its extreme consequence. If one's sins will be forgiven eventually, does that not imply that one's current and even future sins will be forgiven? No longer were the Herrnhaag men bound to any biblical commandments. For Moravians, an antinomian phase had begun.

Consequences

On December 6, 1748, by absolving the single men in Herrnhaag from their past and future sins, Christel gave them carte blanche to do anything they wanted. The weeks and months to follow can be considered the height of the Sifting Time. During this time, anything was possible. Central was the antinomian conviction that believers had already reached the stage when their sins were forgiven. What was once labeled as sinful behavior no longer was considered as such. From now on believers could freely act out what they believed to be ways to actually experience and enjoy nuptial union with Christ. It is questionable if Zinzendorf would have intervened had it not come to this phase.

According to this mode of thinking, the sacrament of Communion became irrelevant. It was no longer necessary as a means for each individual to mortify his flesh in order to be purified. The men had discovered a different way to unite with Christ. Indeed, on Good Friday of 1749 fifty-seven single brothers in Herrnhut, under the leadership of Caillet, refused to partake in Holy Communion. In explanation, the diary notes that "they did not lose out on anything anyway."[54]

What exactly happened during this final antinomian phase is difficult to determine, since most of the records were destroyed in order to prevent later generations from gaining an understanding of the true nature of the Sifting. The congregational and single brothers' diaries from Herrnhaag for the years 1748 and 1749 do not survive, only the diary of the single men in nearby

Marienborn. Based on later references in letters or minutes, combined with information from non-Moravian sources, only a fragmentary image can be sketched.

On December 28, 1748, three weeks after the gender-changing ceremony, Christel gave a remarkable address to the children at Herrnhaag. It was the Feast of the Holy Innocents, and the children had a prayer day. Christel spoke fervently to them about the "marital bed," and encouraged them: "Just like when a few children kiss one another, cuddle one another, marry one another, that is how the husband marries us, and that's how it is."[55] He recounted how side-hole devotion had begun among the children and spread to the adults. Now he wanted the children to embrace the idea of the marital bed as enthusiastically as they had taken up the idea of the side hole: "This matter will burst forth among you like a sunrise into the air, sooner among you than among the congregation. It will move from you into the choirs and not from us to you. Just like the side hole truly comes from the children, just like the children brought the side hole into the congregation, that is how the children will truly bring the cabinet and the marital bed even more into the congregation than anything else."[56] Christel hoped that the new piety would be taken up by the children and that the adults would follow.

With the men made into "sisters," the differences between the genders ceased to exist. The strict division of a Moravian congregation into choirs based on gender and marital status thus became obsolete. A redacted section of the Marienborn diary states that "the entire congregation from now on formed only one choir." Therefore, a new organization was needed. On December 15, 1748, Christian Renatus divided the congregation into fifteen new "classes" or "assemblies." These assemblies were to meet every day and to be held "jointly" (*gemeinschaftlich*), men and women together. All references to the word "assembly" in entries in the Marienborn diary during the following weeks were deleted by a later editor, suggesting these assemblies were considered a part of the crisis.[57]

The abolition of "manliness" and the absolution of sins implied freer relations between men and women. Surviving Moravian sources do not say much about the character of the classes and assemblies, but a description of the new classes is found in Hart's account of his experiences with the Moravians. Since Hart at the time was living in Zeist (where Christel performed the gender-changing ceremony in May of 1749), his text describes the situation in this Dutch congregation, although he adds information about Herrnhaag that he had received from a certain "Brother S": "Because the single brothers were sisters now, they were divided into three classes. The first one was the maidens' class; from the maidens' class one was moved up by lot into the brides' class; from the brides' class the wives who sleep in the arms of the King were taken by lot. This was the third class, also called the sweethearts' class [*Schätzelclasse*]. I passed through these three classes myself, or, as they call it, I enjoyed this bliss."[58]

Passing through the classes was thought of as being courted by a lover: beginning as Christ's girlfriend, next becoming his bride, and ultimately finding fulfillment as his wife and beloved. Those at the highest stage were the *Schätzel* (sweethearts). The activities of the *Schätzel* are important for our understanding of the Sifting Time.

## The *Schätzel*

References to the importance of the *Schätzel* turn up in unexpected places. In his memoirs eminent German jurist Johann Jacob Moser did not spend too many words on his short-lived flirtations with Moravianism, but among the few things he did mention were the Sifting Time and the role of the so-called *Schätzel*. According to Moser, these *Schätzel* among the single brothers in Herrnhaag had committed "quite disgraceful things" that had since been "wisely covered up" by the church.[59]

Moravians sometimes called the Sifting Time the "Schätzel Periodus."[60] The letters from Zinzendorf and Anna Nitschmann to Christian Renatus in February of 1749, instructing him to end the abuses they had heard about, suggest that the activities of the *Schätzel* companies were at the heart of the problem. As the first reason for calling Christel away from Herrnhaag to London, Zinzendorf wrote, "Contrary to your promise you have established a *Schätzel* company I do not want to hear or know about." And Anna Nitschmann wrote, "On account of Papa I have to say to you once more that he is completely beside himself about you and the entire *Schätzel* matter. He does not want to write to you a single word anymore until you give up these things completely."[61]

References to the *Schätzel* are frequently found in Moravian sources from June 1748 onward.[62] They usually appear in a context of playfulness, kissing, and celebrations of the "marital" (*ehelich*) union with Christ. In these texts both believer and Jesus are called *Schätzel*, referring to the reciprocity of their alleged loving relationship. A verse in this context is revealing. It is part of a poem written by the single brothers in Ebersdorf for Christian Renatus's birthday on September 19, 1748. In this song about the bridal union of Jesus with the believer, Jesus kisses and penetrates the *Schätzel* in a marital embrace:

> Whoever is a *Schätzel* sings:
> O dear Lord Jesus Christ!
> Kiss, kiss, O kiss me please,
> pass through me nuptially.
> Make me hot through and through
> O hole! O Kyrie Eleison.[63]

The word *Schätzel* appears thirty times in the songs in the 1749 handwritten hymnal. Indeed, most of these songs of the Sifting resemble love songs, and the subject of the love is Jesus, who is called by such names such as "husband," "groom," "man," "side hole," and "darling." The brides, or the *Schätzel*, sing of their affection, amorousness, lovesickness, desire, and raging love for the side hole, who will give them bridal and nuptial joy. The side hole and the *Schätzel* give each other kisses—endless kisses that taste of honey and are as sweet as candy. And in the delight of the side hole's embrace the *Schätzel* and the side hole will become one: "yea deep, real deep therein" (ja tief, recht tief hinein).[64] The poetic language of these hymns reveals an exuberant and extravagant eroticism.

In the previous chapter we found that Moravians in 1748 and 1749 expressed the love between believer and Christ with kisses. The loving relationship between the believer and Christ, from courting to the marriage bed, where Christ eventually will finally embrace and unite with the believer, is described in language derived from bridal mysticism and the Song of Songs. The believer passively enjoys the lovemaking of Christ.

Hart describes a meeting of the *Schätzel* class in Zeist during which participants celebrated the matrimonial union with their husband. In antiphonal singing the leader of the meeting asked the *Schätzel* present several questions, which they answered affirmatively: "Well, good evening, my dear *Schätzel*, do you look forward to the nuptial bed?" After singing the refrain "Oh, I feel, oh, I feel, oh, I don't know what I feel," the men responded by singing, "Yes, we await our husband's bed." Again they sang the refrain, and then the leader asked, "Is he going to give you strong kisses?" The men answered, "Yes, strong kisses he gives us," followed by "Oh, I feel, oh, I feel, oh, I don't know what I feel." Other questions the leader asked included "Are you going to lie in his arms?"; "Are you his dearest *Schätzel*?"; and "Are you his old wives?" Each time the *Schätzel* affirmed the question and sang the chorus: "Oh, I feel, oh, I feel, oh, I don't know what I feel."[65]

Hart's account of what happened after the single brothers in Herrnhaag had been acquitted and become virginal is the most detailed we have found so far. Even though Hart had left the Moravians and the book was intended as a warning against Moravian heresies, his account has generally proven truthful. Thus it is worthwhile to read what he says about the *Schätzel* after the gender-changing event of December 6, 1748:

> Then freedom reigned as never before in Herrnhaag. For example, the *Schätzel* class of the single brothers and the single sisters formed one class now. They held combined love feasts and their own meetings, which the other classes were not allowed to attend. They swarmed out together at night in an unchristian fashion, they boozed, so that it was said among the other brethren, The *Schätzel* ate it and drank it all up, they incurred a debt and now we have to pay for it!
>
> During the love feasts they sat on each other's laps, touching one another and playing together. A certain brother N. was present and told me this. Yea, the sisters even visited the brothers in their beds, as some brothers told me. And that is supposed to be a congregation of Jesus Christ, as they call themselves!
>
> Yea, and what happened among the married people! The married women grabbed single brothers. They found a married woman by the name of Demuth with a single brother named Gutbier behind a screen, while she was completely naked. Another sister caught her thereby and made the case known. The single brother was hastily sent to the congregation at Zeist. There was suspicion and quarreling among the married people, as they did not trust each other.[66]

This might seem to be an example of the usual accusations of sexual deviancies among religious opponents, but there is reason to believe that there is truth to these allegations and that some form of free relations between the sexes indeed existed in Herrnhaag and elsewhere.[67] Johannes von Watteville considered a case of adultery in the Moravian congregation he uncovered at Neusalz in Silesia in May of 1750 to be related to the crisis of the Sifting Time.[68] According to Hart, both single brothers and single sisters engaged in loose behavior, disregarding the strict rules of separating the genders and purposely violating any common rules of conduct. This was the continuation of the anti-Pietist playfulness and silliness that began a few years earlier, with the difference that now it took place not only among the single brothers but among both men and women. Obviously, there is a sexual element to the behavior Hart is describing, but nowhere does he say that actual free sexual intercourse took place.

Even if not as explicit, several paragraphs of Zinzendorf's letter of reprimand deal with similar transgressions: anyone engaged in a conversation on sexual matters was to be dismissed from the church (par. 3). Excluded from Communion for a period of a year was any single brother caught with a woman, be it a single sister, a married woman, or a widow, and so was the woman in question (par. 11); any brother discovered in a locked room with a sister (par. 18); as well as any man kissing a sister or another brother or making obscene gestures (par. 19).[69] Hart's account makes these paragraphs in Zinzendorf's letter of reprimand seem much more comprehensible.

Hart summarizes Moravian teachings and practice between 1748 and 1750 as "*Schätzel*, marriage bed, and cabinet matters."[70] A similar formulation is found in the report of the single brothers' festival of 1748: "cabinet and bed matters with the Lambkin." The cabinet was the room in which married couples had sexual intercourse.[71] After Christel and Rubusch declared all single brothers virginal and free of sin in December of 1748, it was possible for all men to celebrate the marital union with Christ, and they did so with great enthusiasm. Did this enthusiastic behavior perhaps include physical aspects?

Sexual Aspects

To what extent was the crisis of the Sifting Time sexual? Although Cranz categorically denied that "works of the flesh" took place, many other Moravian historians seem to think this possible or even probable.[72] Cranz's history of the Moravian Church was, of course, part of the campaign to publicize the new image of the church during the second half of the eighteenth century, but even Cröger, in his official history of the Moravian Church written during the 1850s, left open the possibility of carnal excesses.[73]

The contemporaries Zinzendorf, Johannes von Watteville, and Friedrich von Watteville all seem to have believed sexual excess was part of the Sifting. At the special conference during the Barby synod of 1750, each of them used the term *fleischlich* (carnal) when discussing the nature of the recent crisis.[74] The words "an unbridled carnal freedom" near the end of Zinzendorf's 1749 letter of reprimand also suggest the crisis was in fact about sexual matters.

Zinzendorf's letter to his son Christian Renatus also appears to confirm the role of sexuality. In this letter Zinzendorf does not contest any of the mystical ideas of how the consumption of the marital union with Christ would also be granted to the single brothers, but he does deny that this was already happening in the present: "the major heresy that we enjoy the marriage with the Savior *already here*."[75]

Johannes von Watteville said something similar in addressing the Sifting Time problems in Herrnhaag and Marienborn in 1750: "I do not regard anyone as a brother who teaches that we already in the present can be truly united with the husband and be in a true union and connection with him; I deem him mad and deluded."[76] In his letters to Christian Renatus written during the same visit, Johannes confirmed that he had spoken to some twenty people who indeed had "fallen into lusts" because of the teaching of the close presence of Christ in the congregation and the marriage with him.[77] He also mentioned the deceitful behavior of some "rogues among the *Schätzel*," and he forewarned Christel that he would be hearing things about certain men he could never have imagined.[78]

Most specific and explicit about the sexual nature of the crisis, however, is a paragraph inserted by Zinzendorf at the end of the published report of his activities during the week he wrote the letter of reprimand. In fact, it is so straightforward that it is astonishing it has not been noticed before. At the end of the account of the seventh week of Zinzendorf's official diary as published in the Congregational Accounts, following the text of an address in which the count spoke about recent imputations against the Moravians, this statement by Zinzendorf is included: "*Nota Ordinarii*: I cannot hold against the world that they speak and think so badly about us, when I consider what ungodly consequences our own people sometimes draw from my addresses— for example that since the souls of the single brothers are sisters, brothers can have physical relations with sisters in a physical way without harm."[79] The note summarizes the nature of the Sifting and confirms the findings of this study: the single men in Herrnhaag and Marienborn had taken Zinzendorf's teachings, specifically about the femininity of all souls, literally and drawn the conclusion they had become so Christlike that they had already mortified all earthly sinful thoughts and feelings. In other words, the men had become "virginal" on earth, and consequently they could have sexual contact with women even outside of marriage. Zinzendorf was so specific about the physical aspect of the events that in his distress he repeated the words "der Hütte nach" (physically).[80] The note also confirms that Zinzendorf, despite his later denials, understood very well what had happened in Herrnhaag.

The situation in Herrnhaag was not the first time Moravians had been confronted with a scandal of a sexual nature. Five years earlier, in September of 1744, the community in Herrnhut was shaken when it became public that Hütschel, a manservant in the Herrnhut inn, had committed adultery with four single women. He and the women were incarcerated in the local jail, and the matter was handed over to the secular authorities. The Zinzendorfs, as lord and lady of the manor, sent Carl Heinrich von Peistel as their authorized agent to Herrnhut to put things right. Peistel's investigation revealed that several people in Herrnhut, to various degrees, were involved in sexual scandals.

As a consequence of his investigations, five families were removed from Herrnhut "because of their indecent and disorderly conduct." In addition, several young married couples were advised to leave, and seventy members from all choirs were disciplined by being excluded from the meetings for the communicant members. The four women who had sex with Hütschel were punished with blows by a rod, administered by two sisters, and were later sent to work as servants on farms in the neighboring village of Berthelsdorf. Finally, the major offender, Hütschel, was forced to join a military unit from Pirna.[81] Interestingly, in the *Apologetische Schlußschrift*, an apologetic work in question-and-answer format published in 1752, Zinzendorf, when asked about how secular authorities were to respond to the "abominable accusations" made against the Moravians, compared the situation in Herrnhaag in 1748/49 with that in Herrnhut in 1744. In doing so, he implied that both situations were of a similar, sexual nature.[82]

Based on the previous, it seems safe to conclude that the Sifting Time to a great extent revolved around sexual excesses. The question now arises whether these excesses took place only between men and women or if they possibly also included same-gender sexual activity. Elsewhere I have weighed the possibilities of same-gender sexual activity during these months, especially among the single men.[83] As we have seen, the liturgical texts used by the single men had a striking sensual quality. Christ as the husband of his church was to have knowledge of (intercourse with) his believers. Images for Communion and sexual intercourse became so intertwined that it cannot be said with any certainty whether the texts refer only to spiritual matters or also to physical acts. During celebrations such as the single brothers' festival of May 1748, the most burning desire of the men, it was said, was to be "physically embraced" by Christ.[84] These desires were fulfilled as elders Christian Renatus and Rubusch performed acts on behalf of the side hole (i.e., Christ). For example, when Christel received a group of men and women into the Moravian congregation at Herrnhaag with a kiss, he told them it was the side hole himself kissing them.[85] And when the single men in Herrnhaag sang to the side hole to bless each one of them, Christel and Rubusch went through the rows and blessed every man present. The report of the event stated, "the side hole presented itself certainly to every brother in the person of our Christelein and Rubusch."[86] It also seems possible that not only the elders but each man in the congregation acted on behalf of the side hole. For example, when the brothers at the single brothers' festival of May 1748 in Herrnhaag sang, "Now thou be kissed," they kissed one another believing they were kissing Christ.[87] And when they sang, "Now thou shall be embraced," they linked arms with

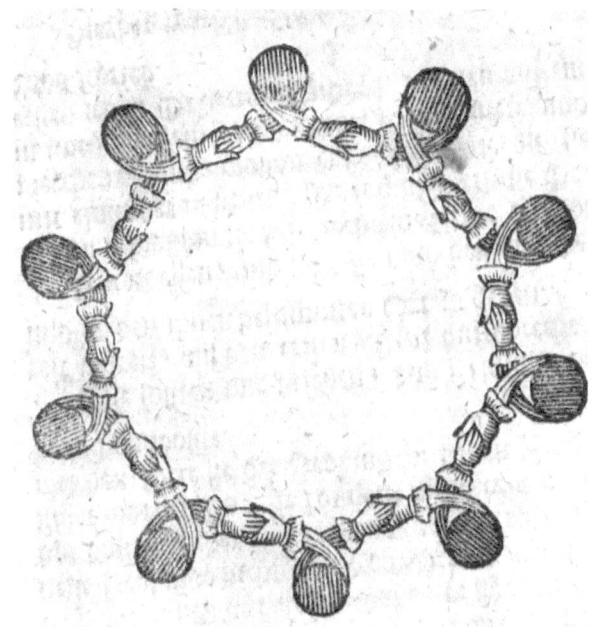

*Fig. 8* Circle of Moravian men with their arms linked together, as seen from above. Copper engraving from Bothe, *Zuverläßige Beschreibung*, 1751/52. Moravian Archives, Bethlehem.

one another. So it was believed possible to pass on a blessing or an act such as a kiss or an embrace from Christ to another person.

Thus, in the late 1740s not only was the Moravian desire for Christ expressed in erotic metaphors, but these metaphors were sometimes taken quite literally. Literal interpretation of the metaphorical teachings of their leaders was typical for the Moravian single men in those years. For example, after singing, contemplating, and speaking about the side wound of Christ as the point through which the believer could gain access to Christ's heart and unify with him, Moravians in Herrnhaag placed a giant side wound made of papier-mâché, complete with streams of red fluid flowing out, in front of the brothers' house, and entered the side wound by physically walking through it.[88] And when they sang about the kisses of Christ, they kissed one another, in the belief that they had kissed Christ and Christ had kissed them. Is it possible that as the men sang that they wanted to go "deep therein" (*tief hinein*) or that they wanted to "nuptially embrace" the side hole, these words were accompanied by actual actions? Is this what Christian Renatus meant when he told the single brothers in Herrnhut in July of 1748 "how being inside the side hole is not to be taken spiritually, but one may and can *realistically* enter it with body and soul"?[89] The marital relationship of the men with their Savior was not only a metaphor but appears to have been actually practiced.

In this context there are two texts that seem to suggest same-gender sexual activity occurred among the men in 1748. The first is a letter written by Christel from Zeist on October 11, 1748, to Matthias Hasse, a thirty-one-year-old single Moravian man who was staying among Moravian circles in Livonia at the time and who was clearly sad and envious that he was missing out on the wonderful things happening at Herrnhaag. Christel attempted to comfort Hasse: "The side hole will most certainly hug and embrace you in Livonia too, so that you may forget Germany. Just take the dearest *Schätzel* by the body, do not compliment him, command him. Kissing, kissing must be done and remain passive, then you will have nothing but wedding days in Livonia. Buntebart may give you one or the other verse. But you have to keep it to yourself. Live well in the hole!"[90]

Christel was suggesting the side hole (Christ) could also make Hasse happy by hugging and embracing him. This could be a metaphor for Communion, but when followed with an explanation of how it might be accomplished, it does not seem to refer to Communion anymore: "Take the dearest *Schätzel* by the body." Who is this *Schätzel*? Is it Christ, or is it one of the initiated single brothers? If it refers to Christ, what does it mean to take Christ "by the body"? And what did Christel mean when he said, "Do not compliment him, command him"? How could one possibly compliment or command Christ? Could this letter be referring instead to an act performed with another single brother with whom physical contact took place? If so, then the omission of compliments makes sense. It was not supposed to be a sexual act between two people but a means of receiving Christ's love by one and passing it on to the other; it was Christ and not the physical partner who should be the center of attention.

There is another interesting aspect to Christel's letter to Hasse. The words "Kissing, kissing must be done" are actually a quote from one of the popular hymns of these years, "Geküßt, geküßt muss sein": "Kissing, kissing must be done, oh, do not interrupt. Now you are alone just for me, my *Schätzel*." Was this perhaps one of the songs to be used during the act Christel was describing in his letter?

The adoration of the side hole, the numerous songs about going inside the side hole, and even actual reenactments of penetrating the side hole all seem to suggest that penetrative sex would fit this metaphor. An entry in the diary of the single brothers in Herrnhut seems to imply that Christian Renatus was talking about penetration: "Christel spoke of the equality between us and our husband, beginning from the moment when a dear heart can believe and feel: 'That moment when the side was cut, I—Hallelujah!—sprang thereout.' That's when the husband frames himself so thoroughly into us that we become side holes and the side hole becomes us, etc."[91] Penetrative sex between men as part of a religious ritual makes sense if the anus is considered to be an image of the side hole. We know that Moravian men compared the vagina to the side hole, but did they also make this comparison with the male anus?

The second text suggesting same-gender sexual activity possibly taking place among certain Moravian men does make this comparison. In his *Zuverläßige Beschreibung*, Bothe does not relate the following incident as proof of same-gender sex (of which he does accuse the Moravians elsewhere in his book)[92] but as an illustration of the utter unreasonableness of Moravian leaders such as Christian Renatus. Bothe had learned of various examples of Moravian depravities from Abraham, a baptized Jew who came to Berlin after leaving the Moravians in the Wetterau. Once an unnamed brother with whom Abraham was arguing had offended him by turning around and showing Abraham his behind. To Abraham's surprise, when he complained to Christian Renatus, elder of the single brothers, about this "unbrotherly" behavior, Christel took sides with the ill-mannered brother and reprimanded Abraham instead: "You did not do that nicely. You disturbed this brother in his blessedness, and you are not a friend of the side hole. If you would love it, then this brother's ass could be a side hole for you too!" Even if Christian Renatus's words cannot be verified, the existence of Abraham can. According to Bothe, Abraham was called "Herz" by the Moravians, and the lists of Herrnhaag include an Abraham Herz, a Jew born in Grossglogau on January 28, 1704, who had lived with the Moravians since 1747 and who matches Bothe's description.[93]

If the story is true, what did Christel mean when he said that one brother's anus could be a side hole for the other? As we have seen above, the side hole was frequently referred to as the place to go into. Would it be too much to speculate that unification with the side hole may have involved—perhaps only in some places and only among certain single brothers—being penetrated by another man who acted on behalf of Christ? If so, then it was not only men and women, but unmarried men as well, who were able to perform the symbolic act of unification between Christ and the church through physical intimacy with one another.

In July of 1748 Christian Renatus had told the single brothers in Herrnhut "how being inside the side hole is not to be taken spiritually, but one may and can realistically enter it with body and soul."[94] It does not seem infeasible that Christel meant this could physically happen among the single men. It is quite possible that single men—most likely a select group of initiates—practiced ritualized same-gender sex, not as an exchange of expressions of romantic love but as a way of bestowing upon each other the love of Christ. In the sexual act the brethren did not experience the affection of their partners; rather, they believed they were enjoying the marriage with Christ.

It seems likely that extramarital sexual activities between men and women and same-gender acts among men lay at the core of the Sifting Time. Initially same-gender rituals seemed to have taken place solely among select initiated men during 1748. But after the ceremony of December 1748 all single men were absolved from any sinfulness and could engage in any act previously considered sinful. From then on, the mystical union with Christ could be celebrated outside the realm of marriage.

Other Groups

As we saw above, the culmination of the Sifting Time consisted of various elements: antinomianism, perfectionism, disregard of Holy Communion, and the belief that union with the divine was possible through sexual intercourse among the pure inside and outside of marriage. These elements were not unheard of among religious groups of the early modern period. Though it was not part of the faith system of most mainstream Protestant denominations, surprisingly many groups practiced ritualized sex. A notorious example was the group around Eva von Buttlar, the Society of Mother Eva. After members were purified and released from their earthly desires and lusts, they had sexual intercourse among each other. They called this "blending" (*Vermischung*), by which the believer "blended" together with the flesh of Christ, as found in the bodies of the fellow believers, who had crucified their human flesh and lusts (Gal. 5:24); they no longer lived themselves, but Christ lived in them (Gal. 2:20).[95]

Another group with ideas about sexuality and sinlessness similar to the Moravians' in 1748 may have been the Philadelphian Society or Sion Congregation at Ronsdorf in the Rhineland, under the leadership of Elias Eller. Nineteenth-century church historian Max Goebel suggested that members of the Ronsdorf community believed that as true Christians they were unable to sin any more. This antinomian belief allegedly resulted in "carnality," when men and women became too intimate with each other during love-feast celebrations.[96] In other areas as well, Goebel saw many parallels between Ronsdorf and the "enthusiasm" at Herrnhut and Herrnhaag, although he was likely not aware of what happened in Moravian communities during the

Sifting. More recent scholarship on the Ronsdorf group seems to give little credence to these imputations of sexual transgressions.[97]

A lesser-known example of antinomianism resulting in promiscuous sex occurred in Upper Silesia during the 1740s. Inspired by the works of Johann Arndt, a revival occurred among a group of twenty Bohemian families who had settled in Zechlau near Tarnowitz under the leadership of carpenter and lay preacher Wenzel Hetzmann. Allegedly, the group came under the influence of two itinerant Moravians from Berlin "who spoke of pure grace from the Lamb." The teaching of free grace resulted in the belief in an imminent end of times, and in October of 1744 Hetzmann's followers began giving away their possessions. Hetzmann and his assistant Kredzeck were taken into custody, but after their return to Zechlau they claimed "they both had done penance, they had both died with Christ and were risen again with him; that Christ and his Spirit had come into their flesh; that they were free from the law and that they were united with Christ so that they did not need the means of grace of the Word and the holy sacraments anymore because they had Christ, the living word and bread, in their flesh." Because they had Christ "in their flesh," they believed they had become immortal. They also believed they were able to pass on the living Christ to anyone who obediently subjugated themselves to them through sexual intercourse. Allegedly, for a period of a year and a half, Hetzmann and Kredzeck had promiscuous sexual relations with ten Bohemian women, claiming to share with them the living flesh and blood of Christ and to bestow on them eternal life.[98]

At the end of the 1730s a sect of about twenty members existed in Bordelum on the North Frisian coast who believed they were without sin and unable to sin. Under the leadership of David Andreas Bähr (1710–43), members claimed to be free of carnal desires and lust, believing sex among the pure was not in any way sinful.[99]

Between 1745 and 1750, followers of Hieronymus and Christian Kohler in Brügglen, Switzerland, were led to believe they could reach perfection and that they were unable to sin once they reached this state.[100] Female members of the sect had sex with the Kohler brothers in the belief they would be sanctified.

Some members of the community in Ephrata, Pennsylvania, may have believed God would not see any sinful acts they committed; however, they adhered to strict celibacy, so their antinomianism probably did not lead to sexual activity.[101]

Another group in Pennsylvania was the so-called New Born in the Oley Valley, followers of Matthias Baumann (d. 1727). Baumann taught the possibility of sinless perfectionism and preached that with one's body a New Born person could not sin before God—"from which they drew dangerous consequences," one chronicler commented.[102] One of Baumann's followers wrote to her relatives in Germany, "Here God has absolved me from all sin—I can sin no more; for which I now praise, and shall ever laud his name."[103] Heinrich Mühlenberg reported to Halle after encountering a surviving member of the New Born in 1747: "They feign having received the new birth through mediate inspiration, apparitions, dreams, and the like. When one is thus regenerated, he fancies himself to be God and Christ himself, and cannot, henceforth, sin no more [sic]."[104] The New Born rejected the Bible and the sacraments as unnecessary means to salvation since they had already attained union with the divine. In his address to the single brothers at Marienborn about the issues of the Sifting, Johannes compared Moravian teachings of perfectionism to the New Born in Pennsylvania, implying that this was what some Moravians believed during the Sifting: "It is a false assumption [to believe] that when one only has the side hole one can do whatever one can think of and be frivolous and free. Otherwise it would end up in the false doctrine of the New Born in Pennsylvania who teach: it only matters to become a child of God and to receive forgiveness of sins; then one can do and sin however one wants. God forbid!"[105]

These ideas were not new within Christianity, and it is apparent that during the first half of the eighteenth century various groups believed in some form of perfectionism and sinlessness, which in some cases manifested itself in promiscuous sex. For a short while, and possibly only among restricted groups, Moravians, thinking they had reached a state of perfection before God, engaged in extramarital sex, which they believed to be a spiritual practice without sin. As many Moravian leaders realized this was a consequence of their teaching and practice of the previous years, the resulting shock was great. They considered this a true crisis or a "Sifting" by Satan.

Spread

Now that we have gained a better understanding of the nature of the crisis, some questions still remain. How widespread was the crisis? Which groups within the church participated? Did the ideas spread to other congregations besides Herrnhaag? And who were the people held responsible? The last question may help us answer some of the other questions. The names mentioned by Zinzendorf, Anna Nitschmann, and Jonas Paulus Weiss include

Joachim Rubusch, John Cook, François Caillet, Johannes Ettwein, Anton Vierorth, and a "Caroline" in Ebersdorf.[106] Rubusch, whom we have encountered several times above, comes off especially badly; Zinzendorf specifically blamed him for having deceived Christel.

John Cook, a former Roman Catholic, is often referred to as an Italian, and was in fact born in Livorno, Italy, on June 22, 1720; his name was presumably anglicized. A sailor, after joining the Moravians in London he sailed on various Moravian ships. He visited Bethlehem in December of 1743, and in the fall of 1746 we find him in Herrnhaag, where on November 26 he was received into the choir of the single brothers. Soon he became one of the helpers. On September 9, 1747, he went to Herrnhut. In the following year Zinzendorf considered sending him to Algiers and Constantinople, but instead Christian Renatus made him the new pastoral head of the single brothers' choir in Herrnhut on August 15, 1748. The reason for this promotion must have been his active support of the ideas of the Sifting Time. During the following months he was one of the instigators of the practices in Herrnhut, but a week before Christmas of 1748 he returned to Herrnhaag, where he died suddenly on February 15, 1749. Later Zinzendorf blamed Cook's Italian temperament for his role in the Sifting Time.[107]

The events considered part of the Sifting seem to have taken place predominantly among the single choirs, both the brothers and the sisters. Anna Nitschmann, in her letter to Christian Renatus, expressed disapproval not only of Christel but also of Anna Johanna Piesch, chief eldress of the single sisters' choir: "I hope you received my last letter to you and Anna Johanna and gathered that I am disturbed to the highest degree about your [*Euer*, plural] behavior."[108] Addressing the problems of the Sifting in Herrnhaag in March of 1750, Johannes von Watteville warned the single sisters against "phantasies and things that absolutely do not suit a true maiden [sister] and choir heart [*Chorherzel*]."[109]

The lists from Ebersdorf in the Unity Archives do not make it possible to identify unequivocally who "Caroline" was.[110] She must have been a single sisters' laborer, however, and the fact that she was from Ebersdorf is significant, since it suggests that the sisters' choir there was involved in the Sifting. Other single sisters' choirs may have participated as well.

To what extent the married people were involved is more difficult to answer. The language surrounding the gender-changing events of December 1748 is ambiguous: whereas some texts say "all brothers," single and married, became sisters, others seem to imply this happened only among the single brothers. Hart gives the example of a married woman, Sister Demuth, committing adultery with a single man, Brother Gutbier, but this could also have been an unrelated event.[111] Among the key figures listed are Johannes Ettwein and Anton Vierorth. Both were married and in charge of the married people's choirs in Herrnhut and Herrnhaag, respectively. In his memoir, written much later in life when he was the leader of the American Moravian Church, Ettwein blamed his youth and inexperience for his getting so involved in the ideas and practices of the Sifting Time. In fact, he was so involved that on February 28, 1749, very soon after the arrival of Zinzendorf's letter of reprimand in Herrnhut, he and his pregnant wife hastily left Herrnhut and walked 290 miles to Herrnhaag. Herrnhut had become, as Ettwein writes in his memoir, "too hot" for him.[112] Vierorth (1697–1761), who had studied theology in Jena and Halle, became a private teacher and chaplain for the Hallart family in Reval and St. Petersburg before joining the Moravians and becoming a minister at Herrnhaag. Besides the fact that Zinzendorf lists him as one of the active participants in the Sifting, little else is known about his role.[113]

The lack of detailed source material makes the geographical distribution of the Sifting Time phenomena difficult to ascertain, but they were clearly not limited to Herrnhaag. Zinzendorf carefully addressed his letter of reprimand to all congregations, indicating he believed the ideas and practices had spread widely. It is safe to say that the intense adoration of the side hole, combined with the bridal mysticism of Moravian marital theology, spread to all Moravian communities, both in Europe and overseas, but whether people in all Moravian communities were involved in extramarital sex based on these convictions is much less certain. Herrnhut seems to have been affected almost as much as Herrnhaag. One of the main whistleblowers, Peistel, came from Herrnhut, and there are many examples of Herrnhut's participation in Sifting Time practices presented throughout this study. In an unpublished history of the first decade of the Moravian congregation at Neusalz, Uttendörfer concludes that Neusalz, together with other Silesian congregations, was very much affected by the spirit of the Sifting Time.[114] After Johannes von Watteville dealt with the situation in Herrnhaag in February and March of 1750, he continued on to Herrnhut and the Silesian communities, where he held meetings and addresses similar to those in Herrnhaag. This is a further indication that the practices of the Sifting Time were occurring in these places as well. Johannes states that while Gnadenberg was fairly unaffected by the Sifting, Gnadenfrei "went quite far during the previous period."[115] To what extent other congregations were involved is harder to determine and requires further research.

We have seen several instances of Moravian leaders intentionally disseminating new insights and teachings from Herrnhaag to other communities. For example, in May of 1747 Zinzendorf began preaching in Herrnhaag and Marienborn about the disappearance of male gender characteristics and the possible blending of the sisters' and brothers' single choirs into one. In October of that year he preached these ideas in the Silesian congregation of Gnadenfrei, and in November he did the same in Herrnhut. After the conclusion of the single brothers' festival of May 2, 1748, Christian Renatus immediately traveled to Herrnhut, where the single men had postponed their festival in anticipation of his arrival. There he introduced the single men to the "single brother's marital religion." In September of the same year he traveled to Zeist with his father before returning to Herrnhaag on November, 12, 1748, for what turned out to be the final phase of the Sifting Time. Ideas were consciously communicated and transferred from one community to the other, by personal visits and by the sending of letters and reports. Did any of the doctrine of the perfection found in Christ as it was taught in Herrnhaag in December of 1748 spread to other congregations as well? According to Hart, Christel performed the gender-changing ceremony in Zeist while he was on his way to London in May of 1749.[116] Between December 1748 and his departure for London in May of 1749 Christel remained in the Wetterau, but other leading brothers, such as Caillet, were sent to other communities during these months.

In Herrnhut Caillet introduced the latest innovations from Herrnhaag, notably that the marital union with Jesus can already be enjoyed in the present; he also started a *Schätzel* company consisting of both men and women. He left Herrnhut, "quietly," for Silesia on April 16, 1749, the day after the unexpected arrival of a new choir leader of the single brothers who was to replace him and end the abuses.[117]

On December 13, 1748, a group of single men left the Wetterau on their way to Pennsylvania. There is no doubt that they were instructed to bring the latest insights to Bethlehem. A group of single brothers sent to Bethlehem earlier in 1748 had caused tensions there. The leading men in Bethlehem were perplexed by the attitude of the newcomers, who wanted to remain a separate group because of their special status as "instructed" (*eingerichtet*) brothers and belittled the other single brothers in Bethlehem for not having progressed far enough in their insights into the mystery of the union with Christ.[118] The group that left the Wetterau in December had experienced the gender-changing ceremony and were in London during the time Zinzendorf wrote the letter of reprimand. Zinzendorf complained to his son that none of them were suitable or inclined to be married, so he sent them off to Pennsylvania as "a society of single sisters" but instructed them to get used to the idea that they would eventually have to marry women.[119] Clearly Zinzendorf, although using terminology similar to that used by his son, did not consider the men to have reached a final state of perfectionism; he wanted them to get married so that they could be "a vice-Christ." In another letter he claimed to have "cured" the men of their misapprehensions.[120]

# 7

## THE AFTERMATH OF THE SIFTING

It is a miracle we are not over and done with.
—*Jonas Paulus Weiss at the General Synod, 1764*

As the full nature of the recent events became evident, Moravian leaders began to address the situation. In previous chapters we saw how Johannes von Watteville visited the European congregations during the first half of 1750 and spoke to the problems in his sermons and his conversations with individual members. Synods were held among leaders to discuss how things could have gone wrong. Surprisingly, the church did not break apart over the crisis. Leaders were able to guide Moravians away from everything they had recently embraced so enthusiastically.

In this chapter we will investigate the fate of individual leaders of the Sifting. Texts from the aftermath of the crisis confirm that there was indeed a widespread antinomian belief among Moravians that had led to sexual transgressions. As a solution for the now-rejected notions of recent years, Moravian leaders guided their followers back to the blood-and-wounds theology of the early 1740s, which seemed to have been all but forgotten during the Sifting.

## Consequences

Reactions in the various congregations to Zinzendorf's letter of reprimand followed immediately. Moravian congregations in Berlin, Neusalz, and Copenhagen expressed their embarrassment and assured him they would follow the new directions.[1] In Herrnhut the arrival of the letter had immediate personal consequences: as we saw above, Ettwein and his wife, who served as married choir helpers, hastily left Herrnhut soon after Zinzendorf's reprimand was read to the congregation. A few weeks later, Caillet, helper of the single brothers' choir, also left after being replaced by Luedecke, who had been sent over from London to deal with the situation. Peistel, returning from his visit with Zinzendorf in London, announced to the Herrnhut congregation that unauthorized hymns were no longer allowed to be sung in the congregational meetings.

Although the shock over the recent events was great within the church, most of the instigators remained in leading positions. Some were told to take time for inner reflection. Ettwein writes in his memoir how, after their arrival in Herrnhaag, he and his wife had to live separately (she with their newborn daughter in Lindheim, he in Herrnhaag) and that he was placed under "discipline" for a year. With the washing of his feet, he writes, the period of discipline was formally ended, and he was called again to actively serve the church.[2] His earlier involvement in the Sifting Time did not stand in the way of his election to bishop in 1784 and his leadership of the American Moravian Church until his death in 1802.

Caillet too spent some time wandering around. He did not leave as suddenly as Ettwein, but when his replacement arrived in Herrnhut he saw the writing on the wall. "He seemed more humble than before," noted the diary. Caillet left on April 16 for Silesia, and showed up in Neusalz in September of 1749 to say goodbye after having received a call to London. According to his memoir he was director of a Moravian children's home in Yorkshire from 1749 until 1751. From then on he no longer held positions of responsibility. In 1751 he was moved to Fulneck, "where he translated the Weeks" (the Congregational Accounts). Copying and translating the "weeks" was often an activity assigned to people in need of some sort of penance or suffering from an illness. The memoir suggests Caillet indeed suffered from a chronic condition. In 1752 he was moved to the Moravian Church in Bedford, "for the sake of his Health," where he continued his translations. The single brothers' synod in London, which he attended in 1752–53, seemed to provide a turning point and reconciliation in his life: "Since the Single Brethren's blessed Synod at which he was and which was a remarkable Time to him, he has lived a very happy, chearful and contented Life in a blest union and Conversation with the Man of Smart." He died only a few years later, on January 3, 1755, in Bedford.[3]

Even Rubusch, undeniably one of the most instrumental instigators of the Sifting, was not completely demoted. After he was called to London together with Christian Renatus in May of 1749, he became pastoral helper (*Pfleger*) at the Theological Seminary when it was moved from Marienborn to Barby later that same year. According to his memoir, in 1750 he was appointed member of the "Generaldiaconats-Collegium," a board overseeing finances of the church, in Zeist. There he married the double widow Catharina Elisabeth Heintschel on June 19, 1750; both moved to Herrnhut, where he became postmaster. In 1770, after Catharina died, he married Mariana Duschesse and became chair of the local board of overseers in Herrnhut. We are much less informed about his inner feelings regarding his role in the Sifting Time than about Ettwein's or Caillet's. His memoir was not written by himself but by someone else from the Herrnhut congregation, shortly after his death on May 5, 1773. It grossly understated his involvement with the Sifting Time: "He resisted the wretched Sifting of the church and of his choir with all his might during these years, but in the end he was swept away by the current."[4]

Johannes von Watteville's role during these years was ambivalent. Before his departure to America in early 1748 he did not seem to be opposed to anything that was going on in the Herrnhaag brothers' choir. He promoted the playfulness among the single brothers, and in Bethlehem he was an active proponent of side-hole devotion. He continued to use side-hole vocabulary in his letters from Bethlehem; at a later date an editor—perhaps Watteville himself—deleted all instances of it. Johannes was smitten with Christian Renatus and a devoted admirer of anything his brother-in-law did. While separated from Christel during his American journey, he was jealous of Rubusch, who remained at Christel's side; even before his departure, he had asked Zinzendorf not to let Rubusch too near Christian Renatus.[5] From America he wrote his brother-in-law the most intimate outpourings in the typical creative language of the late 1740s:

> Just think, my heart's Christelein! Your Johannes is in America and you are in Europe. The two sweethearts, the two intimate sweethearts who sit so closely together in the side hole, are physically so far from each other. Is it true or is it a dream? When I was reading your letter it was as if I were only 20 or 30 miles from you. But in reality I am many hundred miles away. But sweetheart, in the *pleura* [side wound] we are close together and there I can be really closest to you. Closer than any of your other sweethearts. The farther physically, the more sensitive in the hole. Whatever I can say about my self is: I am Johannes the Hole, Johannes in the Hole, Johannes 3/4 Hole, penetrated, permeated, bled through, fleshed through, corpsed through, hallowed through, wedded through, and how can I express this to you powerfully and completely, a creature from Jesus's side, created to be known by him every day, to hang on to his dear corpse and to be an eternal child hanging at his *pleura* and lying in it like a child in his mother's lap; a child that is sided through by him every day and that is in him and he in him. At the same

time a sinner, a maggot, that although blessed is still less satisfied with himself than any other sweetheart. But I am blessed and I am a neat thing. I am flesh and bone of my husband and of my fellow playmates ["Mitgespiel*innen*," feminine form]. You are one of those too, who are so keen on him and who cannot stand it if he does not know them every day and treats them fine maritally. There you have a summary of my theology.[6]

Once he had a better understanding of what had happened in Europe during his absence, Johannes quickly changed his tone. In July of 1749 he wrote Zinzendorf how worried he had been for a long time about the developments in Europe, for which he blamed Rubusch: "I must admit that I consider him an unfortunate instrument used by Satan."[7] The fact that Johannes was away from Herrnhaag and the other congregations when the crisis blew up turned out to be fortunate for him. When he returned to Europe in the fall of 1749 he was able to transform into the reformer who would cleanse the church of its previous transgressions.

However, many in the church remembered Watteville's earlier position. Some years later, when Zinzendorf anxiously asked his servant, Johann Nitschmann, if his wife Erdmuth had adhered to Sifting Time ideas, Nitschmann was able to reassure the count that she had not. Nitschmann, however, could not resist adding that Johannes, on the contrary, had been "quite involved with those principles."[8] Johannes Petsch, whose attempts to become part of Christel's inner circle failed because of his alleged "pietistic disposition," had witnessed events in Herrnhaag from close up, and in a letter to Zinzendorf in 1752 he left no doubt about Johannes's lack of credibility as "reformer": "No one else but Johannes is the man who delivered Christel into the hands of those disastrous men who maltreated and abused his youth. Johannes is the man who established Rubusch, Gammern, Andresen, and men of equal fanaticism in the pulpit of the congregation and on the laborers' bench of the single brothers' choirs. Johannes is the man who suppressed all well-intended and sufficiently early opposition by his own authority and under the neat but specious pretext of humbling the pietistically self-righteous seminarians and adherents of Johann Nitschmann." Having laid the foundation for the crisis, Johannes became, Petsch continues, the one to lead the church out of the mess: "When he finally noticed that his own minions during his absence in America wanted to become superior to him, he believed he had the opportunity to initiate a reformation and to execute it himself. A reformation of this trouble of which he laid the foundations himself. A reformation that could not have any legitimacy with me or anyone else who knew about its first origin and the first characteristics of this monstrous system, because the reformer was guilty to the highest degree and still he wanted to wash his hands of it."[9] According to Petsch, Johannes conveniently put all the blame on Rubusch as the one who seduced Christel. Not surprisingly, Zinzendorf did not appreciate Petsch's letter.

## Christian Renatus

The greatest casualty of the Sifting may well have been its main culprit, Christian Renatus.[10] Formerly the widely respected leader of the single brothers, he now experienced a major downfall when the full extent of the new teachings became clear. From his birth Christian Renatus had led a sheltered life. The only time he lived outside the seclusion of a Moravian community was when he went to school in Jena between 1737 and 1739, and even there he was surrounded by pious teachers who were followers of his father. Throughout his life he was the object of almost unreserved affection and adoration from members of the church, who called him Christel, Christelchen, Christelein, or Christulus. The (somewhat loose) translation of his name—Christ Reborn—suggested to his strongest supporters that he should be considered the reincarnation of Christ. This is why at the celebration of Christel's birthday in Herrnhut in 1749, for lack of a portrait of the young count, a painting of Christ's nativity was displayed instead.[11]

Christian Renatus enjoyed a privileged position within the church. At the early age of sixteen he became coelder of the single brothers throughout the church, and when the chief elder, Johannes von Watteville, left for America at the beginning of 1748, Christel took his place. He was nineteen when he was ordained a deacon of the Moravian Church; only seven months later, in January of 1748, he became a presbyter.

Christel advocated his father's beliefs and concepts without inhibition. He also unreservedly adopted Rubusch's ideas and promoted them enthusiastically. As Zinzendorf's son he gained high influence over the single brothers and the other choirs. The combination of Zinzendorf's marital theology and the side-wound devotion of the single brothers became for Christel a subject of endless experimentation.[12] A contributing factor was the renunciation of pietistic anxiety and morality. Sexuality was no longer considered sinful; on the contrary, it was transformed into a holy, sacramental act. Any objections and warnings that might have been expressed against the activities of Christel, Rubusch, and their inner circle were dismissed as the worrying of old Pietists.

*Fig. 9* Portrait of Christian Renatus von Zinzendorf (1727–1752). Oil on canvas, artist unidentified. Unity Archives, Herrnhut, Germany, GS 047.

Christel did not see the end coming; and when it came, it hit him all the harder. Jannasch called his downfall "the catastrophe of his life."[13] A poem he wrote shortly after he received the reprimand from London in February of 1749 reveals his inner feelings. He should have kept his marital relationship with Christ a secret, he says, and not carelessly shared it with too many others. Now he compares his frankness to being unfaithful to his husband:

> One thing, oh dearest heart,
> I think it has happened
> that we made a mistake
> and were too loud about
> the most secret things.
> That will cause trouble for us.

Fearing negative consequences when any "dog and pig" got hold of the matter, he prayed everyone involved could keep quiet: "Seal each mouth" so that "Perhaps damage can be avoided. / But if it has already happened: / Temper justice with mercy."[14]

It was only after his arrival in London that he began to distance himself gradually from the earlier teachings. On May 23, 1749, Christel saw his father, who, after an initial harsh reception, made him his right-hand man. In August of 1750 the two of them, along with Johannes and others, visited Herrnhaag for the first time since Christel had been called away the year before. It was during this visit, according to Jannasch, that he realized that he and his confidants had let their sensual desires (*sinnliche Triebe*) run free instead of truly worshiping the Savior.[15] In September Christel attended the Barby synod, where leaders of the church discussed the Sifting.

Absolution in Herrnhut

Following the synod, Christel visited Herrnhut with his father in October of 1750. He had not been there since May and June of 1748, when he initiated the single brothers of Herrnhut into the new insights of the Herrnhaag brothers. Now he had to shamefully admit that he had come to see matters differently. It was also time for absolution; several single brothers who had been excluded from certain choir activities were fully readmitted. Ironically, it was Christel, who had played such an instrumental role in promoting the ideas and practices of the Sifting, who absolved the men.[16]

Zinzendorf addressed the single sisters in Herrnhut and gave them absolution as well.[17] As an outward sign of their renewal, he changed the color of their choir ribbons, which indicated to which choir a sister belonged: widows wore white, married women blue, and single sisters—like the single brothers—green. During a special ceremony on November 24, the sisters received new pink choir ribbons.[18] A private diary describes the ceremony: "At this time (as far as I can remember) it occurred that the single sisters who used to have green ribbons received red ones [i.e., pink]. After the ceremony was over the sisters stayed behind [in the hall]. As the bell rang and the remaining part of the congregation entered for the service it was a special sight to see them sitting as if they were newborn."[19]

The change in choir ribbons was a visible symbol of forgiveness and marked the beginning of a new era. Although no written reference to a similar ceremony for the single brothers exists, they seem to have changed their choir ribbons as well. Having worn green ribbons at festive occasions up to 1748—most likely around their shirt collars—they wore red ribbons in 1749 and 1750. Soon thereafter, the single brothers no longer wore choir ribbons, which became exclusively an element of female dress culture. This change may be an indicator of changing gender norms.

The memoirs of individual Moravians contain many references to the Sifting Time.[20] The extensive memoir of Johann Daniel Gottwalt, written in 1800 when the author was seventy-four years old, is helpful and may represent the experiences of many who were involved. Gottwalt speaks of how his "innate depravity," which had lain dormant since he joined the church, manifested itself again, leading him to engage in "true sins," by which he likely means sexual acts.

> And as the Sifting Time during this time and during the following year 1749 took hold in Herrnhut more and more, I as well was carried away by it in many ways. I strayed from my childlike connection with the Savior and lapsed into many difficult things, causing me much pain and grief.
>
> My innate depravity, which had revealed itself strongly already by many seductions and bad examples in the world before I joined the church, had lain dormant ever since I was within the church. Now it awoke all the more violently and I lapsed into many things and deviations and true sins, causing me unspeakable pain and fear. I could not forgive myself for having grieved my dear Savior so much, who until then had shown me so much grace and mercy.

Gottwalt describes his conduct during 1748 and 1749 as a manifestation of sinful desires that he was otherwise able to suppress. He also speaks about the forgiveness and assurance he experienced after the crisis was over: "But I cried unto him incessantly with a thousand sinner's tears to forgive me and to not let my preciously purchased soul fall into sin and to take me under his care. He did not keep me crying for long because he knew it came from the heart. From then on he showed his forgiveness graciously in my heart. I became cheerful again and entered into my childlike connection with him again as previously, and he was my one and only."[21] The next year, 1750, would be a year of absolution and closure. On New Year's Eve both Johannes von Watteville and Zinzendorf announced the end of the Sifting.[22]

Christel remained mostly in Herrnhut until, on August 2, 1751, he traveled with his brother-in-law, Johannes, to London. There he appeared to be affected by depression, which hard work could not hide. At the end of February of 1752 he fell ill with tuberculosis (*Schwindsucht*). Over the next few months the illness progressed, and on May 28, 1752, Christian Renatus von Zinzendorf died. He was twenty-four years old.

## Return to Blood-and-Wounds Theology

While Johannes von Watteville was visiting the congregations during 1750 he addressed the problems related to the Sifting. As discussed above, the best example of his method and procedure is his address to the single brethren at Marienborn on March 4, 1750. He carefully touched upon various elements of the Sifting: Christ as the bridegroom, physical intercourse, the teachings regarding the side hole, evangelical freedom and antinomian sinlessness, as well as the idea that all men not only have female souls but are physically female already. In each case Johannes directed the brethren toward the blood, the wounds, and the passion of Christ: "The side hole, the wounds of Jesus, the blood of the Lamb, all this is the ground, the source and foundation of all our blessedness!"[23] Johannes returned to the image of Christ on the cross and shifted the focus away from the side wound as the one important wound of Christ and the place of new birth. He had to be careful not to supplant the sense of liberation the brethren had found through grace with the Pietist legalism they had so passionately disassociated themselves from. He told them they had taken their anti-pietistic exuberance too far when they let "pranks, tomfoolery, and foolishness" pass for evangelical freedom. Johannes had to strike a balance between antinomianism and legalism. He vehemently denied that the men had physically already become sisters and stressed that the male body was still very well capable of sin.

In his address, he frequently used terms from the first half of the 1740s, before Moravian piety began to focus on the side wound of Jesus, such as "cross," "blood," "wounds," "passion," "Lamb," and its diminutive, "Lambkin." "The entire bloody Savior, his passion, and all his wounds belong together," Johannes said. "If the Savior had not suffered so much for us from his body and soul, had he not sweated so much, had he not been martyred, had he not been nailed, had he stayed away from his passion, we would not have a side hole from which life, blood, and water flowed and the new birth from the *pleura* would not have come about."[24] Johannes carefully guided the brethren from their exclusive focus on the side wound to a devotion of the entire tortured body of Christ. On New Year's Eve, during a review of the past year in Herrnhut, he remarked that "the most important event [of 1750] was the final and complete victory of the doctrine of God's passion and bloody wounds throughout all our congregations after the previous time of sifting."[25]

Spangenberg, who had kept his distance from most of the characteristics of the Sifting, expressed similar opinions.[26] He had returned from Pennsylvania together with the Wattevilles, arriving in London in November of 1749.

During the first months of 1750 he traveled through the congregations on the Continent, and in May he attended the Provincial Synod in Gnadenberg. The minutes paraphrase his remarks about the Sifting Time: "Neglecting the sinners' point has contributed much to our diversion. One has forgotten that there is a root of evil within the nature even of a child of God and that without the Savior and his wounds we cannot live, just like a fish without water. If the previous circumstances lead us to remember this eternally and that we remain sinners, then this has great benefit for us. He hopes so from the bottom of his heart."[27] And many years later he reflected on the Sifting Time: "We did not always have the passion of God in mind and in our hearts. Had we not lost sight of the Savior's life, passion, and death, we would not have been caught up in the Sifting we still have to be ashamed of."[28]

As Johannes and Spangenberg urged, in order to turn away from the teachings and practices of the Sifting Time, Moravians returned to their earlier devotion of the passion of Christ, including its focus on his blood and wounds. This shift found expression even in art. Paintings that did not fit the renewed concentration on Christ's suffering were replaced with new ones. In 1751 Johann Valentin Haidt painted two large paintings for the sisters' house in Herrnhut; they still exist in the Unity Archives in Herrnhut.[29] One, the *Covenant of Sisters*, is an allegorical depiction of the first eighteen sisters who founded the single sisters' choir in 1731. The other, *The Twenty-Four Sisters' Choirs*, shows a multitude of single women from all nations around the resurrected Christ. Both concentrate on the entire tortured body of Christ and not only on his side wound, in contrast to the similar paintings, dating from the late 1740s, that they replaced. According to a description from 1748 of one of the earlier paintings, "Near the organ an illuminated painting depicted the twenty-four sisters' choirs from different places and nations, led by their dear eldresses, singing and playing [their musical instruments] for the side hole, shining from the clouds."[30] Both the 1748 painting and the one that replaced it depict the symbolic twenty-four different sisters' choirs and representatives from various places and nations. The difference is in the way Christ is represented: whereas the 1751 painting shows Christ full length, the 1748 painting showed just the side hole. Only one Moravian painting survives that shows a shining side hole: *Zinzendorf as the Teacher of the Nations*, also attributed to Haidt.

Returning to beliefs from earlier years is a conservative, if not reactionary, development. In the long run, by restoring the piety of the first half of the 1740s, the Moravian Church lost much of the dynamic creativity it had possessed during the first decades of its existence. No longer were inventive

*Fig. 10  Zinzendorf as the Teacher of the Nations.* Oil on canvas by John Valentine Haidt, before 1750. Unity Archives, Herrnhut, Germany, GS 583.

renewals in texts and imagery welcome, as the church carefully guarded against a return of anything recalling the time of Sifting. In doing so, it sowed the seeds of a conservatism that became predominant after Zinzendorf's death.

It should be clear that Moravian blood-and-wounds devotion cannot be considered typical of the Sifting Time. On the contrary, Johannes and other Moravian leaders considered the abandonment of the earlier blood-and-wounds theology the cause of the excesses of the Sifting Time, and a return to it the remedy for everything that had gone wrong.

The Sifting Time left Moravians with a sense of embarrassment. Had they not firmly believed they were the Savior's own people? They now realized that they were far from infallible themselves. Although some members left the church disillusioned, most stayed, and in the years after 1750 Zinzendorf and the other leaders succeeded in keeping the church together. But his successors knew that the lasting survival of the church was possible only if a complete change of direction took place. They were able to accomplish this in the years after 1760.

# 8

## THE POST-ZINZENDORF ERA

I will die and everything will stay and
remain and become even better.
—*Zinzendorf, at the synod in
Berthelsdorf, June 21, 1756*

Immediately after Zinzendorf's death in May of 1760, a process of rapid transformation began, much more fundamental and profound than that a decade earlier. The Moravians became a mainstream Protestant denomination, with its own customs and practices but theologically hardly any different from the Lutherans. As we will argue in this chapter, the changes of the second phase are intricately connected with the Sifting Time as well. The Moravians' effort to distance themselves from anything related to radical religion led to the more conservative, noncontroversial Moravian Church of the second half of the eighteenth century. Even the swiftness of the adaptations was related to the Sifting Time.

When Count Zinzendorf died in Herrnhut on May 9, 1760, he left the church he had founded, built, and held under firm control until his death without immediate leadership.[1] Anna Nitschmann, Zinzendorf's second wife, longtime companion, and coleader, died only twelve days later, on May 21. Within less than two weeks the Moravian Unity had lost its two undisputed leaders. Since Zinzendorf had left no direct male descendants, his son-in-law, Johannes von Watteville, considered himself the obvious future leader. However, other church leaders hardly gave him a chance to claim power. Without delay they established a collegial form of leadership in which power was shared among a group of men. One was Spangenberg, who had successfully built the Moravian Church in America and was called back from Pennsylvania as soon as his replacement had arrived in Bethlehem. On May 30, two weeks after Zinzendorf's funeral, a new board, the Ratskonferenz, was formed in Herrnhut. Consisting of twenty brethren under the chairmanship of Johannes von Watteville, it declared itself the interim administration of the Unity until a General Synod could be convened. Women were not invited to this initial meeting.[2]

Surprisingly, this new administrative body, although officially serving only as interim board, quickly set a new direction. Even before a large General Synod met in 1764, directional decisions were made in many areas. Instead of holding on to the heritage of their recently departed leader, Zinzendorf's successors lost no time in dismantling important aspects of his legacy. As I will demonstrate, the changes were a reaction to the crisis of the Sifting Time.

The minutes of the interim board document only formal parts of the conversation. A good additional source for how changes were planned and implemented is the correspondence between the new board and the leaders in Bethlehem;[3] because of the great distance between Herrnhut and Bethlehem, many considerations and concerns were necessarily communicated in writing. In the years following Zinzendorf's death the church reformed itself regarding the position of women, theology and worship, sexuality and marriage, and leadership style. Even the General Economy of Bethlehem, a form of communalism that was easily associated with radical religion, was dismantled.

Although the transition of the Moravian Church after 1760 is a crucial phase in the history of the Moravian movement, it has surprisingly not been a subject of much discussion in Moravian historiography. For example, in his 1967 *History of the Moravian Church* Kenneth Hamilton simply calls the last four decades of the eighteenth century "years of readjustment" during which the church, to many people's surprise, managed to survive thanks to the skillful leadership of men like Spangenberg.[4] He does not describe, however, the reasons why the church needed to be "readjusted." For Hamilton and many other Anglo-American Moravian historians, Zinzendorf was a well-intended but eccentric mystic whose theology was characterized by repulsive excesses. The era of reorientation after his death therefore seemed a welcome return to sanity. Others, such as German historian Gerhard Meyer, are much more negative about the post-Zinzendorf era: "Spangenberg succeeded in removing anything ingenious from the Moravian Church in order to obtain the recognition of the Lutheran churches," Meyer claims, blaming Spangenberg's timidity and weakness for the loss of so many valuable elements of the Zinzendorf era.[5] American scholar Craig Atwood attributes the changes during the Spangenberg era to a lack of charisma on the part of the new leaders.[6]

In the following we will find that in the years after 1760, Moravians made every effort to free themselves from any possible association with radical religion. Many eighteenth-century Protestants considered mysticism a dangerous form of Christianity and mystics to be enthusiasts. Moravians were intent on reinventing the public image of the Moravian Church. By stressing their pre-Reformation origins, they presented themselves as a denomination as old and respected as, if not older than, other Protestant churches.

Women

When the Ratskonferenz met for the first time on May 30, 1760, three issues were on the agenda: the future organization and leadership of the Moravian Church, access to the archives, and the role of women within the church.[7] The last was one of the most contentious issues within the church, admitting no delay. For the next decades the position of women would occupy the synods. And although major changes were implemented in the years immediately following Zinzendorf's death, the issue would never be satisfactorily resolved, from the position of either the men or the women, during the rest of the century.

Moravian women had long enjoyed positions of authority: they were leaders of the women's choirs, they participated at all administrative levels of the church, they were ordained, preached, and served at Communion. Even though their role was mostly restricted to settings with only women present, they played a much more active role than in many other contemporary religious groups. Traditionally the active participation of women was limited based on the biblical command for women to remain silent (1 Cor. 14:34), but Zinzendorf believed this text applied only to the specific situation in the Christian congregation at Corinth. Based on his reading of the role of women in the apostolic church, he gave them a much more active role in the Moravian Church. From an early age, Anna Nitschmann enjoyed a leadership position and played an almost prophetic role.

Other nonconformist religious groups of the time, such as Quakers, early Pietists, Methodists, and Baptists, also allowed women greater roles within their movements than in established religion. But in most of these groups, after being influential at the beginning, women became marginalized.[8] We see a similar tendency among Moravians.

The count frequently had to explain and defend his ideas on the role of women within the Moravian Church.[9] Resistance to those ideas came into the open immediately after the great leader had passed. Anna Johanna Piesch, one of the women leaders, describes in her memoir how she had a premonition of the coming change when both Zinzendorf and Anna Nitschmann died: "My anxious thoughts and premonitions did unfortunately come true in considerable measure, and to my inexpressible pain, I had to witness that these dear people were almost completely forgotten, especially the dear Mama [Anna Nitschmann]."[10] When the Ratskonferenz met for the first time on May 30, 1760, they did not invite any women, wanting to discuss the future participation of women among themselves before they allowed women to participate in subsequent meetings.

In the eighteenth century women with strong positions and prophetic voices were generally associated with fanatical religion.[11] Anton Rhode, Lutheran minister in Grosshennersdorf near Herrnhut, paraphrased French philosopher Pierre Bayle in discussing Anna Nitschmann's role as "prophetess": "with all fanatical sects you will find that there is always a woman involved as the main figure."[12] In the years after 1760 Moravians tried hard to lose the stigma of fanaticism. With women playing such a prominent role in the church, Moravians could easily be taken for enthusiasts.[13]

The debate regarding women was predominantly about their authority within the church and the visibility of their participation in the life of the church. It involved the issues of the ordination and consecration to church offices; liturgical participation at Holy Communion; their role at confirmations, consecrations, and ordinations; and their participation in the leadership of the church on both local and Unity levels. The role of women within their own choirs and in the pastoral care of women was not discussed, nor did the question arise whether they were allowed to give meditations in any of the discussions. As far as we can see, the female choir leaders of the single sisters' and the widows' choirs continued to address their choirs with meditations.

Zinzendorf's justification for ordaining women as *diaconissae* and *presbyterae* was based on the practices of the early church. His successors continued to refer to the early church, but only as it suited them. Although they carried on ordaining women as deaconesses because it was "an apostolic practice," they excluded women from the order of presbyter as early as 1762 on the grounds that "the ordination of women as presbyters is without precedent in the apostolic church and ceases therefore from now on."[14] In 1789 the General Synod introduced further restrictions on female ordination. Regarding women, the term "ordination" was to be replaced with "consecration." In order to further distinguish between the ordination of men and the consecration of women as deacons, these acts were no longer to be performed at the same service. Thus, the consecration of a woman would no longer appear unnecessarily "solemn," and it was made clear that both rites were not seen in any way as equal.[15] Although the consecration of deaconesses continued for several decades after Zinzendorf's death, it ceased before the end of the eighteenth century; the last deaconess was consecrated in 1790.

The reason women's ordinations (or "consecrations") continued for so long was that the responsibilities of deaconesses were mainly internally within the choirs. Most likely the public was unaware of these ordinations. More concern was caused by the public participation of women in the liturgy of the church. During Zinzendorf's lifetime women assisted during Holy Communion and at confirmations, consecrations, and ordinations. The Book of Ceremonies describes how at Communion services a deaconess handed the bread from a basket to the presbyter, who then broke it in two and gave it to the communicant sisters. To emphasize the importance of this practice, an engraving included in the 1757 Book of Ceremonies depicts the assistance of women at the distribution of the bread on the sisters' side.[16] Apparently, as claimed at the 1764 General Synod, the church had suffered "consequences and reproaches" because of the active role of women during Holy Communion.[17] As early as March of 1761 the interim administration ruled that women were no longer to participate in the distribution of the wine. The General Synod of 1764 discussed the assistance of women at Communion extensively. Because of the opposition of the sisters, however, synod was unable to disallow women from assisting at Communion, and reluctantly gave its consent for women to assist "when necessary."[18] Synod proceeded similarly with the question whether women could continue to assist at ordinations and confirmations. During the ordinations of women, a sister—most likely one of the female presbyters or "church eldresses"—was to assist the bishop during the ceremony. When female candidates were admitted to Holy Communion, they were to be confirmed by a sister.[19]

Most discussion during the years after Zinzendorf's death dealt with the issue of women's involvement in the administration of the church. This discussion was prompted not only by concern about the perception of the Moravian Church by outsiders, but also and possibly predominantly by internal resistance among men within the church to female leaders. During a committee meeting at the 1764 General Synod the term *Schwestern-Regiment* was used, a variation on the negatively connoted German term *Weiberregiment* (petticoat government), with the general word for women (*Weiber*) replaced by the more Moravian term *Schwestern* (sisters). A *Schwestern-Regiment* was thus an undesirable situation where women ruled the church, something many Moravian men had great fears about.[20]

It was generally agreed that the strict separation of genders within the church and within the choir system made it necessary for women to continue having charge of the pastoral care of their own gender. On the local level, female choir leaders and the wives of the minister, the warden, and other local officials continued to be included as members of the elders' conferences of each congregation. But compared to earlier years their roles were limited. Synod resolved that single sisters could no longer be in charge of the various Moravian girls' schools but that in the future a married couple should be placed at the head of the schools.[21] Furthermore, each widows' choir and each single sisters' choir was placed under a male curator who administered their secular affairs.[22]

More controversial than the discussion about local involvement of women was the issue of including women in the administration of the church on a regional or Unity-wide level. The 1764 synod determined that women were not official members of the new Unity administration but appointed a number of women as assistants of the Directorate, whom the Unity elders could call on in case they needed advice. Minutes from the 1760s confirm that women were sometimes present during the deliberations, but the 1769 General Synod reduced the assistance of women to the lower-ranking Helpers' Department. The 1789 synod was the last to discuss the position of women in the leadership of the overall church. The great number of women present (fifty-five, to sixty-four men) caused great concern to many men. It was held in Herrnhut, and members of the Herrnhut congregation commented on the large number of women represented at the highest authority of the church. This time the women resisted any attempts to exclude them from synod. The lot, however, did not approve of any of the proposed compromises. In the end, synod decided to leave it up to the Unity Elders' Conference to determine which and how many women were to be invited at each future synod.

The determination and swiftness of the brethren to restrict the roles of women within the church became evident even before the first official synod after Zinzendorf's death. The following example, taken from correspondence between the interim administration in Herrnhut and the elders in Bethlehem, illustrates their ingenuity in reaching their goal. As Bethlehem was the center of Moravian activity in America, the Elders' Conference in Bethlehem was not only in charge of its local congregation but also supervised the work in other Moravian congregations in America as well as the missions among the Native Americans and in the Caribbeans. The interim administration, wanting to remove this responsibility from the (mixed) Bethlehem elders, installed a new board, the Ökonomatskonferenz, consisting only of men, as the supervising board of all ecclesiastical affairs within the American Moravian Church. Women continued to be members of the local Elders' Conference, but they were not permitted to serve on the new board. The brethren in Herrnhut were thus able to set new rules and exclude the sisters from the leadership of the Moravian Church in America. Surprisingly, they did not ask the lot for approval for this fundamental decision.[23]

Theology and Worship

Other areas where major changes were introduced after Zinzendorf's death were the theology of the church and, as a consequence of changing theological ideas, Moravian liturgy and hymnody. Soon after Zinzendorf's death we can detect a gradual but determined departure from controversial aspects of his theology. Zinzendorf was not a systematic theologian; he never wrote an overview of his thoughts. As an experiential theologian he discussed his beliefs in countless addresses and sermons, whose subject matter was often determined by the happenings of the day. Therefore, if the theology of the church was to be readjusted, access to Zinzendorf's works had to be controlled.

In the spring of 1761 the interim administration discussed a new edition of Zinzendorf's works. Although Zinzendorf himself had undertaken a revision of several of his collections of sermons, a more fundamental reworking seemed necessary.[24] The count's successors did not deem a mere revision and correction of Zinzendorf's discourses sufficient, nor did they think it appropriate to amend "the writings of a dead man of God."[25] They proposed to compile a selection of texts and extracts, similar to an earlier edition of various texts by Zinzendorf in English, the so-called *Maxims*.[26] At the end of the following year Spangenberg was able to inform the leaders in Bethlehem that progress had been made. Gottfried Clemens, editor of the earlier revisions of Zinzendorf's works, had collected suitable published and unpublished discourses by Zinzendorf, to be printed in the order of the books of the Bible. The following comment by Spangenberg in a letter to Bethlehem is telling: "It is the intention not to insert anything purely problematic that would only lead to new controversies."[27] Clemens was not alone in his work; a committee of several brethren read the texts before they were printed. By the time the General Synod met in 1764, the first volume had already been published; a second volume had been approved and was ready for print.[28] Nothing was changed in the texts, it was reported to synod; they "only had left out what seemed not suitable for the public."²⁹ Omitting anything controversial meant critics would soon be unable to find anything in Zinzendorf's works to criticize. To Spangenberg this seemed a much more effective method than responding to the anti-Moravian publications.³⁰ Zinzendorf was being reinvented by selecting only those texts that seemed fit for a new era and by omitting what did not fit the new identity of the church.

Another way of controlling the reception of Zinzendorf's theology within the church was to read his discourses during the evening services of the congregations. Needless to say, only an approved selection of texts was read. In a letter to Bethlehem Spangenberg described how in Herrnhut Zinzendorf's discourses were read with the congregation almost daily, and encouraged the Bethlehem elders to do the same.³¹

As a result of the changing understanding of the church about its teachings, and especially about the form in which theological ideas were expressed, hymns and liturgies also came under close scrutiny. The interim administration reminded itself always to distinguish, when something was to be printed, between publications for internal use and publications intended "for the world." A third appendix to the so-called London Hymnal that was already at the press was hastily withdrawn within a month of Zinzendorf's death. The hymns in the planned appendix must have contained such Zinzendorfian language that they were not deemed suitable for use within the church.³² A revision of the *Kleine Brüdergesangbuch* (1754), containing a selection from previous Moravian hymnals in a more convenient size, was completed in March of 1761. The previous edition had been out of print for many years. For the time being, the interim administration was able to fill the need with this new edition.³³

Not surprisingly, the liturgy book also caused concern. Moravians liked to think of their liturgies as statements of their confession. During a discussion among the interim administration in February of 1761 it was evident that the liturgy book in its current form could not be considered a "liber confessionis." A revision that left much out and replaced it with new material seemed necessary.³⁴ In a letter to Bethlehem Spangenberg wrote, "We are considering printing a new edition of the liturgy book. However, one finds many expressions and phrases in the book that are incomprehensible to many brothers and sisters. And one cannot really explain these either." Spangenberg invited the Bethlehem brethren to send him their comments and suggestions regarding the liturgies so that they could be incorporated in a revised liturgy book.³⁵

Eventually, work on a new hymnbook and a new liturgy book turned out to be lengthy undertakings. A first selection of eleven revised liturgies was published in 1770; other liturgies followed in subsequent years.³⁶ Christian Gregor, not only a talented composer but a skilled poet, selected, edited, reworked, and rewrote hundreds of hymns from the Zinzendorf era. They were published in 1778.

Sexuality

Central to Zinzendorf's theology were his ideas on sexuality and marriage. Alterations of the church's theology regarding marriage were made after his death in a more subtle and less explicit manner than in other areas. At the end of the eighteenth century not many of his original ideas regarding sexuality and marriage remained intact, although the forms by which new couples were instructed (*eingerichtet*) in marital matters remained basically unchanged.

In the 1780s Watteville and Spangenberg wrote down instructions for the helpers of the various choirs. Faull calls this formulation part of a process of codification of earlier oral practices. It also served to introduce and consolidate new ideas within the church regarding many aspects of life. The instructions for the helpers of the married choirs, the minister and his wife in most congregations, reveal the changed theological ideas regarding marriage.[37] They also indicate that the outward forms, the procedure and method to instruct newlywed couples in sexual matters, remained largely unchanged. The helpers were to educate the newlyweds on the spiritual aspects of their union and to instruct them on how to have sexual intercourse. The preferred method of intercourse remained sitting up on a bench. Before and after their first intercourse the couple had in-depth pastoral conversations with their choir helpers, who encouraged them to have sex about once a week. Outwardly, this was very similar to the practice of the 1740s and 1750s, but there were major differences.

The 1785 instructions leave out important aspects of Zinzendorf's marital theology. They do not mention a crucial point for Zinzendorf, avoiding carnal lust during intercourse. Since lust was considered sinful, Moravians during the first decades of the century thought that by having lustless sex they would be able to have sinless sex. This concept was missing completely from the 1785 instructions. Sexual intercourse was no longer part of the communal discourse but had to be done "in quiet, unnoticed by others, alone and undisturbed." The instructions also seem to stress that the goal of marriage was merely to produce children, and the purpose of sexual relations was to sustain the "tender love" between the couple. The 1785 instructions still used the metaphor of the husband representing Christ and the wife as the church, but no longer stated that the couple could experience the union with Christ during sexual intercourse. Instead, the metaphor now served as a model for the loving care of the husband for his wife and obedience of the wife to her husband. These changes fit general developments within the church after Zinzendorf's death: while the established outward forms and traditions were retained, many fundamental aspects of Zinzendorf's theology were abandoned.[38]

Publications

One important way of promoting the new course of the church was by means of publications. After 1760 the church tried to silence critics with a range of new, positive publications on Moravian history, mission work, and theology. Although most publications of the latter half of the eighteenth century were primarily aimed at the outside public, they also served to consolidate the newly reinvented image of the church among its members. As Jonathan Yonan points out, the Moravian Church after Zinzendorf's death chose to defend itself not in the form of apologetic publications, but rather with "impartial" ones, which were thought to show the truth and persuade church opponents.[39]

The new series of publications was a departure from the public silence Zinzendorf had imposed during his final years. After several apologetic works were published during the early 1750s, no new ones came out, and Moravian publications mainly served internal purposes: daily watchwords (*Losungen*), Zinzendorf's revised sermons, and liturgical materials. The only general overview of the history, organization, and liturgical customs and practices of the church intended to enlighten the general public was the *Book of Ceremonies* (1757), published in different editions in German and in French, with a series of sixteen copper engravings.[40] But now that Zinzendorf had passed away, the interim administration concluded that "the reasons for this silence had ceased."[41]

The first major project was, in fact, an idea Zinzendorf had already considered. David Cranz, author of the *Book of Ceremonies* and former secretary to the count, reminded the interim administration of Zinzendorf's plan to let him go to Greenland to study Moravian work there,[42] and they agreed to the plan. His voluminous study, with exhaustive descriptions of geography and history of the island and a factual description of the Moravian mission, was printed in 1765, reprinted in 1770, and soon translated into Dutch, English, and Swedish. It received good reviews and helped change public opinion of the Moravians.

The same synod that approved the publication of Cranz's book on Greenland dealt with several other book projects as well. Although the lot declined a Moravian translation of the Bible, other publications were considered: a history of the Caribbean (the lot rejected Cranz as proposed author and Georg Oldendorp was chosen instead), an exposition of Moravian doctrine, a biography of Count Zinzendorf, and a description of the organization of the Moravian Church in combination with its history.[43]

Cranz soon took on the last project and wrote the "Idea Constitutionis Fratrum" together with an extensive history of the Moravian Church. The original idea was to publish both parts together, with the history being the introduction to the "Idea Constitutionis." The "Idea Constitutionis" was presented to the General Synod of 1769 but was never voted upon. It remained in manuscript, perhaps because at its completion it was already superseded by the organizational changes instituted by synod. The history portion was printed in 1771.[44]

It took some time to determine who would write the exposition of Moravian doctrine and the biography of Zinzendorf. Georg Waiblinger had written a first draft of the doctrine (*Idea Fidei Fratrum*), but the General Synod of 1769 did not approve it for publication.[45] The next synod, in 1775, entrusted Spangenberg with writing the *Idea Fidei Fratrum*. Completed within a few years, it placed the Moravian Church explicitly on the foundation of the (Lutheran) Augsburg Confession and stressed commonalities with the other churches of the Reformation. Much of Zinzendorf's theology and language was lost.[46]

The biography of Count Zinzendorf was intended not only to refute the many attacks on his personality and character, but to present a revised image of the count, suited for the new self-perception of the church. Several authors were considered, including the Frankfurt publicist and politician Friedrich Carl von Moser, but Spangenberg wanted to undertake this significant task himself.[47] Within weeks of his arrival in Herrnhut from Pennsylvania, he took control of the project. His statement at the meeting of the interim administration of January 5, 1763, applies to the biography as well as to the other publications of the church: in such a work, Spangenberg said, "one wants to say nothing but the truth, but certainly not the whole truth."[48] After many years of selecting material, writing, revising, and cutting chapters, he brought out the biography between 1772 and 1775, containing a respectable total of 2,258 octavo pages.[49] Upon completion, Spangenberg, wanting to prevent any contradictions between his book and the sources, not only destroyed earlier versions of his work as well as his research notes, but also burned many of the original sources he had used to write his book. Spangenberg's biographer, Gerhard Reichel, recognized the Zinzendorf biography as a successful attempt to depose Zinzendorf and to minimize his influence while keeping up the appearance of Zinzendorf's continued authority.[50]

Zinzendorf's successors shaped the future by controlling the past. They did this not only by means of publications but through the newly founded Unity Archives.[51] Anything that did not fit the new public image of the Moravian Church or that would contradict publications such as Spangenberg's Zinzendorf biography was to be eliminated and destroyed. The transformation of the church was comprehensive and covered most aspects of the church.

Leadership

Perhaps the most contentious issue after Zinzendorf's death was who would succeed him. The new direction of the church would depend upon the choice.[52] From the standpoint of the Zinzendorf family it seemed obvious that Johannes von Watteville, married to Zinzendorf's oldest daughter Benigna, would take over the leadership.

During the 1740s Johannes, or Johann Michael Langguth as he was called then, had worked his way up in the Moravian Church. Ever since Zinzendorf's return from America he had belonged to the inner circle around the count. He was ordained a coepiscopus in 1743, and the next year he was appointed "vice-elder of all congregations" (immediately under Christ the chief elder). That same year he was adopted by Zinzendorf's longtime friend Friedrich von Watteville, paving the way for his becoming a nobleman. From 1745 on he could officially bear the title *Freiherr* (baron). Undoubtedly, all this was done in preparation for his marriage to Zinzendorf's oldest daughter, Benigna, which took place on June 20, 1746, during a synod in Zeist in the Netherlands. Already part of Zinzendorf's staff, he had now become a member of the Zinzendorf family. When the oldest and only surviving male heir of the Zinzendorf family, Christian Renatus, died in 1752, Johannes stood first in line to become head of the family. Although the question of succession was never openly discussed at synods or conferences, it is clear that Johannes was generally expected to become Zinzendorf's successor.[53] During the final years of Zinzendorf's life he had become, next to Anna Nitschmann, Zinzendorf's closest confidant and coworker. In the attendance lists of synods and other meetings, his name always came second, immediately after Zinzendorf's. And when Zinzendorf and Anna Nitschmann passed away, Johannes communicated the death of both "disciples" to all the churches.[54] Not surprisingly, he presided at the first meeting of the interim board, the Ratskonferenz.[55] But Johannes was not made the new leader of the Moravian Church.

As part of the post-1760 transformation of the Moravian Church, the church departed from Zinzendorf's autocratic leadership style. Instead of following a single leader, the church chose a collegial form of government. Between synods the general oversight of the church in internal and external matters would rest with a board of nine men, the Unity Directorate (after 1769 called the Unity Elders' Conference). The sisters, as mentioned above, were invited to join only when their assistance was needed. This form of administration ensured the participation of more brethren in the discussion process on a more equal basis than in the past, and because the members of the board could offset one another, no individual could become too strong within the church. There had been boards (conferences) in prior years, but Zinzendorf naturally dominated most discussions and did not always feel bound by the decisions they made.

The collegial style of government was to become characteristic of the Moravian Church. On all levels, worldwide (the Unity), regional (provincial), and congregational, collegial boards were henceforth to have oversight. In addition to his position as lord of the Berthelsdorf manor and his rank as imperial count, Zinzendorf had based his authority on his position as "disciple" of Christ, the title he used from 1751 on rather than "apostle" or "prophet" as some leaders of sectarian groups called themselves. This title was not as innocent as Spangenberg later wanted his readers to believe. Zinzendorf was not merely someone who tried to follow Jesus "like a disciple," but rather "the disciple whom Jesus loved" (see, e.g., John 21:7).[56] Zinzendorf claimed to be in direct communication with Jesus, whose plans for the Moravians were revealed through him. The minutes of the first meeting of the Ratskonferenz after Zinzendorf's death document the concern that Zinzendorf's role as intermediary between the church and Christ had now ceased and that from then on Christ would deal with the Moravians more directly.[57] Although the General Synod was the highest human authority in the church, the church did not want to be governed by majority votes. To ensure that decisions in the post-Zinzendorf era would not be based solely on human insight, the 1764 synod renewed its adherence to the lot as a means to let Christ rule his church.[58] The Moravian Church considered itself a theocracy, which it defined as "the immediate rule of the Savior in the church."[59]

By the time the 1764 synod convened, the new collegial style had been firmly established among the interim administration, and Johannes had already learned to share authority over the church with his colleagues. A statement about the new constitution issued by the interim administration in 1762 indicates that fears existed within the church that "the family of the deceased Papa would arrogate something in church matters" and that members of the family would claim positions for which they were not equipped nor called by Christ.[60] According to the statement, the new theocratic constitution of the church would ensure that no one from the family could claim an office without a call to that office. The claim of the Zinzendorf family, headed by Johannes, to succeed the late count as leader of the Moravian Church was rejected. In the past Christ had ruled the church through the intermediation of Disciple Zinzendorf, but from now on the church placed itself under the direct rule of Christ. Furthermore, the church took over all debts Zinzendorf had incurred on behalf of the church, which after his death had passed to the family. In return the Zinzendorf family gave up all claims to exclusive power within the church.[61] During subsequent years, this debt proved to be a heavy burden on the church, and the church's financial situation became one of the main concerns of Zinzendorf's successors;[62] not until 1801 was it finally paid off.

A personal letter from Heinrich XXXI, Count Reuss ("Ignatius"), in Zeist reveals Johannes's difficulties in adjusting to the new situation. With unusual frankness Ignatius wrote about tensions among members of the interim administration:

> We do not hear or see very much of Johannes. He is going through the mill. The plan of the interim administration is "we," and they strongly object to his usual word "I." Regarding the management of affairs it has got to the point that he is not allowed to make a resolution [by himself] but the conference has to do it. That is good but sometimes human nature interferes and we old ones sometimes go too far. You know what I mean and you know Leonhard [Dober]. . . . But please do not mention anywhere what I have written about Johannes. Dear Johannes is sickly and suffers from all kinds of odd attacks.[63]

At the 1764 synod Johannes still enjoyed much support among the delegates. During the election for president of synod he received the highest number of votes. It looked as if the collegial form of administration as instituted during the previous years might be overruled by synod and Johannes would be put into the position he so much desired. But in a surprise move it was decided to put the matter to the lot, which decided synod was to be presided by a committee of four, including Johannes. We can only suspect that the idea of Johannes presiding at synod by himself reminded some delegates too much of the synods during the Zinzendorf era. By turning to the lot they prevented this from happening. This course of events also implied the church would no longer be ruled by majority vote alone.

The shift from Zinzendorf's leadership style to a collegial form of administration, along with attempts to limit the influence of the Zinzendorf family over the church, were fundamental changes. One may wonder why they were brought about by the men who had been Zinzendorf's closest collaborators. During the previous years, most of these men, despite their love and great admiration for the count, had at times experienced deep humiliation because of him. A postscript to the summary declaration about the new constitution, issued by the interim administration in 1762, is telling. It acknowledges that Zinzendorf ruled "as a dictator" and that men who were appointed to high positions were never really able to exercise their offices.[64] Even if the word *Dictator* was perhaps not used with its modern negative connotation, the frustration is evident. As long as Zinzendorf was alive, they did not question their subordinate positions; now that he had passed away, they believed their time had come.

### Aftermath of the Sifting Time

However, frustration with Zinzendorf's autocratic leadership style is not sufficient to explain the complete change of course after his death. Zinzendorf's successors were sensitive to public opinion. The transformation of the church served to appease the public and to ensure survival of the church. At the same time, after the Sifting Time had shown the dangers of the radical elements in Moravian theology, they were no longer willing to defend such teachings. In the years leading up to the General Synod of 1764 Johann Friedrich Köber negotiated with various governments about the future of the Moravian communities in their territories. In order to be assured of the support of the authorities in these areas, it was necessary to prove the orthodoxy of the Moravians and to avoid any semblance of fanaticism. Köber asserted that Moravians were loyal subjects and tried to remove any concerns that Moravians were following the directives of any other leader or seeking excessive privileges.[65] But the thoroughness and swiftness with which the transformation was executed in so many areas can only be explained if a deep discontent with Zinzendorf already existed prior to his death. This discontent, I would like to argue, was related to Zinzendorf's reaction to the Sifting Time.

In previous chapters we saw how Zinzendorf responded to the crisis of late 1748 and early 1749. Apart from a short-lived initial forcefulness, the count appeared surprisingly aloof. In his letter of reprimand to all the congregations he threatened to leave the Moravian Church and found a new community if his followers did not obey and end the abuses. But in his letter to Christian Renatus his harshness has already softened. During the subsequent months Zinzendorf remained practically inactive, showing a remarkable lack of leadership. He made some personnel changes in Herrnhaag, Herrnhut, and elsewhere, but he did not address the theological aspects of the Sifting Time in his discourses or in any of the conferences he held. He seemed in no haste to go out and visit the congregations that were involved with the practices of the Sifting Time. Zinzendorf left it to Johannes to deal with the situation after he and Benigna returned from Pennsylvania in November of 1749. Only at the synod in Barby in September of 1750 did he finally speak extensively about the crisis.

Zinzendorf also did not distance himself from his teachings that had given rise to many of the problematic ideas and practices.[66] He laid the blame for the Sifting not on his theology but on what others had made of it. At the 1750 synod Zinzendorf strongly defended the playfulness of the 1740s.[67] Whereas Johannes, Spangenberg, and other leaders urged the members to return to the doctrine of Christ's suffering and death, Zinzendorf continued to teach many of the ideas that had led to the events of the late 1740s. During the last decade of his life, Zinzendorf held fast to these ideas, even defending them at great length, and when he published revised versions of earlier published volumes of sermons he did not change or omit the critical passages.

Several of the apologetic works published by the Moravians in the early 1750s were directly instigated by Zinzendorf and can be considered his writings. In three major publications edited by Spangenberg Zinzendorf defended his theology and the Moravian Church.[68] Shortly after Spangenberg returned from Pennsylvania—more or less against his will and highly frustrated with the recent developments within the church—Zinzendorf asked him to defend the Moravians in writing. This was a clever move to appease Spangenberg's dissatisfaction and tie Spangenberg to him again. By including Spangenberg in the defense of his theology, Zinzendorf turned his greatest internal critic into his closest accomplice.

Peter Vogt notes that Spangenberg's apologetics were written in the first place for people who were close to the Moravians, friends and members who were alarmed by the great number of attacks against the Moravians and needed to be reassured these attacks were unfounded.[69] An additional reason for the apologetics seems to have been to give clarification about the teaching of the church in times of uncertainty. With the uncovering of the abuses of the Sifting the church was condemning things that were previously taught as the highest truths. The apologetics therefore served to make clear which ideas were still valid and to reaffirm the doctrine of the church. In no way did Spangenberg's apologetic writings of the early 1750s defend the problems of the Sifting Time; what was defended were ideas that eventually led to the Sifting Time.

During the 1750s many of the principles that had led to the Sifting Time were being defended and upheld in the official apologetics as well as in the revised editions of Zinzendorf's works. For example, the doctrine of the femininity of souls was an essential part of the teachings of the Sifting Time. It was first publicly announced at the synod in Zeist in 1746, and the text of Zinzendorf's address was printed in the *Zeister Reden*. The revised edition of the *Zeister Reden* from 1758 made minor changes in the paragraph in question but left the general idea unchanged. Beyreuther, comparing the revised edition of Zinzendorf's *Homilies on the Litany of the Wounds* from 1759 with the original edition from 1747, concluded that the two editions are "not fundamentally" different.[70] Nor did Zinzendorf distance himself from his ideas on gender. For example, in December of 1759, a few months before his death, he restated his principle that all male characteristics will disappear when the soul "marries" Jesus.[71]

By defending his theology Zinzendorf wanted to prove that even though abuses had taken place, the core of his theology was sound and others had misunderstood and abused his teaching. However, it became increasingly clear within the church that the Sifting was a consequence of many of the ideas taught in earlier years. The crisis of the Sifting had proven the dangers of the radical elements of Moravian theology of the 1740s. But Zinzendorf, despite an initial shock, did not draw many conclusions about his own contribution to the crisis and defended his theology with full force. For the time being, the other leaders were silenced, but as soon as he was dead, they were ready to change the course of the church and abandoned what had led to the crisis and continued to alarm the public.

When the first general synod after Zinzendorf's death ended on August 27, 1764, the new direction of the church and the new leadership style were firmly set. Many of the principles that had led to the Sifting, as well as anything else in Moravian theology that was considered controversial to the public, were abandoned. Theologically, as Zinzendorf's successors claimed, the only differences between the Moravians and the Lutheran churches were in outward forms such as liturgy, organization, and customs. The thoroughness of the changes was a belated result of the Sifting. Zinzendorf's successors were committed to proving to the public that Moravians had distanced themselves from the radical theology that had led to the Sifting Time. While Zinzendorf was alive such a change of direction would have been impossible.

# 9

## WHAT WAS THE SIFTING TIME?

To write a coherent history of the enthusiastic course the Moravians and their leader took, with its singular manifestations, plainly placed in the context of its entire development, may just as well not be possible anymore.
—*Johannes Plitt, ca. 1840*

Christian Renatus von Zinzendorf, one of the main personalities of the Sifting Time, used an interesting metaphor while looking back on the events of the previous years and on his personal role in the crisis. During a meditation for the single brothers in Herrnhut on August 16, 1750, on his first visit there since the summer of 1748, he compared himself to "an eagle, soaring up high into the air, but who in the end, as he wanted to fly over the cross, hit the cross and found his way back."[1] With this image obviously borrowed from the Icarus myth, Christel described his own development in relation to the extravagancies of the recent past: as the eagle rises up into the air he comes close to his goal in heaven, perhaps too close, ignoring the fact that the church on earth remains a church under the cross. And so the bird falls down to earth. The cheerful cross-air bird had become a wounded eagle.

The flight of the soaring eagle symbolizes the development of the 1740s. Moravians believed they were witnessing a continuous progression of divine revelation. Themes rapidly succeeded each other as the central focus of Moravian devotion—the sacrificial Lamb of God, the blood and wounds of Christ, the playful cross-air bird, the side hole, Jesus as the husband of the soul, the marital chamber—eventually leading to the removal of the ability to sin.

Central to Moravian theology was the teaching on marriage. Moravians were far removed from the idea that romantic love should be the basis for marriage. Moravian marriages were arranged by the church; the families of the couple usually had no say at all, especially if the parents were not members of the church. Marriage was a communal affair, completely controlled by the church. At the same time, it was a sacred affair. Based on their reading of Ephesians 5, Moravians considered marriage a reflection of the union of Christ (husband) with the church (wife). The mystery of the union of Christ with his believers could be experienced and enjoyed during sexual intercourse. According to Zinzendorf, echoing bridal mystical teachings of earlier mystics, when husband and wife have intercourse, they enact the final marriage of Christ and his bride. Human intercourse, according to these ideas, is an anticipation of the unification of Christ and the believer that will take place in heaven. Therefore, Moravians called heterosexual marital sex a sacramental act. Not marriage itself, but rather the act of intercourse within marriage, was believed to be a sacrament. Whereas many of Zinzendorf's radical Pietist contemporaries rejected marriage because they considered sex to be sinful by definition, Zinzendorf thought he had removed sin from intercourse by teaching people to have sex without lust.

Marital sex played an important role in the life of Moravian communities: couples were encouraged to have sex on a regular basis, and church elders evaluated the sexual experience with them. For many, the Moravian attitude toward sex must have been liberating, and Moravian ideas and practices regarding sexuality must have contributed to their success. For others, these same ideas were highly controversial and provoked opposition to the Moravians. Not all radical Pietists, of course, were convinced by Zinzendorf's concept of sex without sin. Halle Pietists, like most Lutheran theologians, were perhaps unclear on marriage, but they were clear on their rejection of the sacred nature of marriage.[2] The threat to Moravian marriage, however, did not come from outside but from within. Zinzendorf's marital theology (as his *Ehereligion* has come to be known in English) was part of a larger constellation of ideas. During the crisis of the late 1740s it became obvious that these teachings had led to the assumption that the union with Christ could also be experienced during extramarital sex, thus undermining the exclusive position of marriage.

The Sifting Time, as the crisis came to be called, was a culmination of various elements in Moravian theology and practice—Zinzendorf's marital theology, side-hole devotion, bridal mysticism, the ideal of the childlike nature of a true believer, eschatological expectation—all of which culminated in antinomianism and perfectionism. None of these elements by themselves would have been considered objectionable had they not resulted in extramarital sexual practices, or as Zinzendorf put it, "the major heresy that we enjoy the marriage with the Savior already here."[3] What troubled Moravian leaders during 1749 and 1750 was not the blood-and-wounds devotion; on the contrary, that was seen as its cure. Nor would the sidehole devotion have been considered dangerous had it not been associated with the crisis.

What took place during the late 1740s was a literal though creative interpretation of bridal mysticism, combined with the antinomian belief that Christ had already forgiven man not only of past sins, but also, and this is crucial, of all future sins. In early December of 1748 Christian Renatus von Zinzendorf and other leaders of the single brethren performed ceremonies proclaiming that the single brethren were to be considered virginal and pure, without sin, and that whatever they did could no longer be considered sinful. During the eighteenth century a traditional and simplified understanding of sin was often connected to ideas about carnal lust and sexuality. The absolution proclaimed by Christian Renatus has to be seen in the context of sexuality. From then on every act, especially every sexual act, was no longer considered sinful. Whereas Zinzendorf taught married couples to have sex without sin by removing lust from the sexual act, Christian Renatus removed sin from sex by declaring men to be without the ability to sin. But while Zinzendorf elevated the status of marriage as the exclusive place to physically enjoy the union with Christ, Christel transgressed the marital bounds and reduced the preeminence of heterosexual marriage. Although Moravian leaders and archivists were determined to destroy any textual evidence, the few remaining sources suggest that this absolution resulted in sexual freedom. Single people, just like married couples before them, now participated in the physical unification of Christ and the believer without the guilt of sexual transgression hanging over them. When news of this licentiousness reached Moravian leaders in London, they stepped in to end the situation.

The crisis touched upon core elements of Moravian theology: marriage, sexuality, and the union with Christ. This was a crisis about marriage and about Zinzendorf's marital theology. Zinzendorf's teachings on sexuality had led to sexual excess and licentiousness, exactly as his opponents had predicted. To their dismay, because of the prospect of extramarital sex based on antinomian beliefs of perfectionism, Moravians now found themselves in the company of radical groups such as the Pennsylvania New Born, the Ronsdorf

Sect, and, worst of all, the Society of Mother Eva. And so it became a crisis about marriage.

As the Sifting Time revealed shortcomings of Moravian doctrine, Moravians engaged in a process of change. The undesired effects of the Sifting Time gave many of them second thoughts about the teachings and identity of the church. After Zinzendorf's death they were willing to abandon anything that connected them to radical religion: the strong position of women within the church, bridal mysticism, the sacramental nature of marital sex, and even the communal household that existed in their settlements in Pennsylvania. In the end, the Sifting reaffirmed that the spiritual relationship with Christ could only be celebrated and experienced within marriage and not outside. In the ensuing process of change, the character of Moravian marriage changed as well. By the 1780s, Moravians, who had previously caused a stir among Protestants with their teachings about the exalted sacramental role of marital sex, adapted to a more widely accepted concept of marriage; Ephesians 5:22–23 was now read as a model for the loving care of the husband for his wife and obedience of the wife to her husband. Sexual intercourse was not a means to experience the union with Christ but only a symbol of the bond of Christ and the church, intended to maintain the tenderness between husband and wife.[4]

The Moravians were able to change from a radical-Pietist movement to an accepted evangelical denomination. To a certain extent, their willingness to change was the result of outside pressure. In order to gain recognition from local governments, they had to abandon their enthusiastic past. At the same time, Moravians were willing to transform because the deficiencies of their teachings had already become apparent to them during the Sifting Time. Consequently, they may have been willing to abandon radical elements of their theology more quickly than if the crisis had not occurred. Although they institutionalized some of their peculiarities, such as the use of the lot, the Moravians now became a well-respected church.

The Moravians were not the only radical-Pietist group undergoing change during this time. W. R. Ward argues that during the second half of the eighteenth century the evangelical movement, which previously had drawn from a wide variety of ideas, fell apart, making room for a new form of evangelicalism that did not include the radical mystical elements of earlier years.[5] Moravians were successful in distancing themselves from fanaticism and gaining respect within the Protestant world. This transformation from dangerous fanatics to well-respected pious Christians may best be illustrated by the following characterizations by outsiders.

In 1759, shortly before Zinzendorf's death, Johann Gottlieb Töllner, professor of theology and philosophy at Frankfurt an der Oder, described the Moravians as the worst fanatics of his time. According to Töllner, fanatics base their religion on inner feelings rather than on the outer word of God and pretend to have immediate divine revelations. He characterized Moravian beliefs as "a mixture of fallacies and fanaticisms without compare."[6] Fifteen years later, John Newton, best known as author of the hymn "Amazing Grace," related in a letter to a friend how Moravians had dropped their "wildnesses" and "extravagancies": "from the time of the Count's death, they have been gradually emerging into the light, & relinquishing these peculiarities which they could not justify."[7] Another decade and a half later, in 1789, the Pennsylvania physician, writer, and leader of the American Enlightenment Benjamin Rush characterized the Moravians as "a numerous and respectable body of Christians in Pennsylvania."[8] Many other examples of positive characterizations of the Moravians could be added.

The transformation during the second half of the eighteenth century and the rejection of radical elements of their piety made Moravians more acceptable to those theologians who were calling for a "more reasonable religion" and a middle way between the extremes of enthusiasm and freethinking, between an exclusive reliance on faith and one on reason. These "enlightened" thinkers believed the essentials of the Christian faith could be confirmed by the study of nature. They hoped that concentrating on the essential truths of religion, and abandoning enthusiasm and superstition, could cause Christianity to be united again. As Moravians renounced enthusiastic notions and based their theology fully on biblical exegesis, they came more in line with the "reasonable religion" of the time. But where the religious Enlightenment emphasized practice and morality, Moravians underlined the importance of the inner experience of God. To many enlightened Protestants, of course, this emphasis on religious experience was dangerously subjective.[9]

Our definition of the Sifting Time is a narrow one, based as it is on how those who were immediately involved defined it. But even contemporaries seem to have reached a broader definition. As the Moravian Church began to distance itself from anything resembling enthusiasm and fanaticism, more elements of the piety of the 1740s began to be associated with the Sifting Time. Within a few years, side-hole language became suspect because it was perceived as being connected to the crisis. For example, in 1765 David Nitschmann ordered the destruction of the 1748 and 1749 diaries of the Nazareth single brothers. Fortunately, they still survive, and aside from side-hole vocabulary they contain nothing connected to what is defined here as the actual crisis.[10]

The negative term "Sifting Time" came to play a positive role in the historical narrative. By pointing out the errors and transgressions of an earlier era, one could simultaneously argue that God had saved the Moravians; the church had turned around and lessons were learned. The further away the observer stood from the Sifting Time, the broader his definition of the crisis came to be. By the twentieth century the term was used almost indiscriminately, without a clear definition but with the understanding that it encompassed a wide range of unconventional Moravian ideas and practices. Of course, many things considered to be aspects of the Sifting Time by modern authors would not have caused alarm among contemporaries; they would not have caused Zinzendorf to write his letter of reprimand or Moravian archivists to destroy textual evidence.

Early in the morning of November 8, 1756, several months after his wife's death, Zinzendorf was reading through Erdmuth's papers. In some of the letters from the late 1740s he came upon odd terms he did not understand: "Michels Weiber" and "Geißbeckel." When he asked his secretary for clarification, Johann Nitschmann explained the words were terminology from the Sifting Time. Nitschmann noted in his diary that the count "had to laugh about them." Nowhere else in the surviving records do these terms appear, and their meanings remain obscure.[11]

This study has only partially lifted the veil that covered the Sifting Time. Eighteenth-century Moravian archivists succeeded in destroying most of the textual material from this period, and what survives allows only a limited view of what occurred. Questions remain, not only about the details of the Sifting but, more importantly, for future consideration.

What does the way Moravians distanced themselves from the Sifting Time imply for how they viewed gender roles? One may argue that the ideas promulgated by the Zinzendorfs were not widely accepted within the church. The great fluidity of gender roles that existed during Zinzendorf's lifetime disappeared in the years thereafter. In the end, Moravian men refused to take on female gender roles as they had done previously, and were no longer willing to concede (male) roles of authority and power to the women within the church. Was this a confirmation of traditional gender roles, or rather an adaptation to changing gender roles?[12]

We have identified the ideas that came to the fore during the 1740s and specifically during the Sifting Time around 1749. It remains to be investigated where these ideas came from and how Moravian thought related to that of other radical Pietists. It appears that the ideas Moravians preached attracted many people within and outside of Europe; Moravians were very much a part of eighteenth-century religion and cannot be dismissed as an isolated group. But the Moravian change of course after 1760 may also suggest that eighteenth-century religion was changing. We explained this new course as a belated reaction to the Sifting Time and as an appeasement of the expectations of the governments of the territories where the Moravians were active. Further investigation is needed to determine if these changes were indeed a progressive adaptation to the changing religious environment of the second half of the eighteenth century. More than in the past, we must differentiate between the Moravian Church before and after Zinzendorf's death. Apparently the changes of the post-Zinzendorf era went further than has previously been realized. Hence, this is also a study about change within a religious movement and about how Moravians changed from a radical, controversial religious group to a more mainstream, conventional denomination.

# 10

## THE SOURCES

The history of the Sifting Time is not to
be destroyed but has to be preserved as
proof of the miraculous help by the Savior
to his people.
—*Interim constitution 1762*

Recently appointed Moravian archivist Christlieb Suter was familiarizing himself with the records in the Unity Archives in Barby in the summer of 1802 when he came upon a sealed bundle of documents compiled by his predecessors almost forty years earlier. The matter greatly aroused his curiosity. According to the label the bundle's contents included a selection of documents relating to the Sifting Time, but he did not dare break the seal and open the packet himself. Instead, Suter sent the packet to his superiors, the Unity Elders' Conference (UEC) in Berthelsdorf near Herrnhut. The brethren of the UEC opened the packet, read the contents, and—with great disgust—threw everything onto the fire.[1] This is how the last remaining documents that could have shed light on the nature and character of the Sifting Time were forever lost. The lack of records from the Sifting Time is a serious problem for the study of this phase of Moravian history. Moravian archival collections are usually uncommonly rich in materials and dense in textual records, but documents from the Sifting Time are rare.

In this final chapter I would like to examine the records that were used for this study. The records are very much part of the narrative of the Sifting Time. Moravian leaders wanted to control the historical narrative about their church. They did so by controlling what went into the archives and what was left out. After the scandal of the late 1740s became known, those involved immediately began to erase the documentary record. Moravian leadership of the 1760s decided to "revise" the contents of the archives and discard anything that could cast an unfavorable light on the church. Although some were of the opinion that at least a selection of Sifting Time records needed to be preserved, the action by Suter and the Unity leaders of 1802 foiled this plan. What kind of records, then, are available to study the crisis of the late 1740s?

## Destruction of Records

In recent years archivists have called attention to the processes that form records, "the creative act or authoring intent or functional context behind the record."[2] Archival records are created with intent and are preserved—or sometimes destroyed—with a purpose. Archivists therefore question the traditional idea of archives as an impartial collection of documents able to give the historian objective insight into the past. Hilary Jenkinson, the influential early twentieth-century British theorist of archival thought, considered impartiality a primary feature of archives and authenticity a secondary feature. For Jenkinson archives were "free from the suspicion of prejudice in regard to the interests in which we now use them: they are also . . . equally free from the suspicion of having been tampered with in those interests."[3] Archivists, however, have come to understand archives as a subjective collection of records compiled for specific reasons. The process of archiving is no longer considered "invisible," as Tom Nesmith, Eric Ketelaar, and others argue, but is now studied as a determining factor in "forming society's memory" through the decision on what goes into the archives, how documents are organized and described, and what documents are excluded.[4] Ketelaar introduced the term "archivalization": the conscious or unconscious choice to archive something. This concept is important when studying Moravian archival collections. Archivists are not neutral custodians, but are active in shaping the collective memory.[5]

Among the issues on the agenda of Zinzendorf's successors requiring immediate attention was control over the archives.[6] Moravians believed that Zinzendorf had received direct instructions from Christ and that he had recorded these revelations in his so-called green books.[7] It was therefore necessary to establish control over these documents, which, in their opinion, laid out the future direction of the church. Control over the archives also meant control over sensitive personal information about members and congregational leaders, as well as control over the past and over how the history of the Moravians was going to be written in the subsequent years. In the historical works produced by Moravians during the decades after Zinzendorf's death they reinvented themselves as a more conventional religious group, downplaying their enthusiastic and radical-Pietist past. Zinzendorf's successors quite rightly understood that the archives were not about the past at all, but about the future.

The General Synod of 1764, the first directive synod after Zinzendorf's death, resolved to establish the Unity Archives as a central repository for all the records of the worldwide Unity.[8] Because of the relative political stability of the Dutch Republic, the Moravian community of Zeist was chosen as the location for this institution. The care of the archives was entrusted to a committee of five brethren, but before these men began their work, another committee, the Revisionscollegium, consisting of five trustworthy brethren, was to select all sensitive material, such as forthright and frank personal letters of a pastoral nature, correspondence of female leaders, diaries and correspondence of Christian Renatus and other key figures of the Sifting Time, as well as the diaries of Count Zinzendorf himself. Interestingly, when they found "a bundle of pieces and letters relating to the Sifting period," the revisers showed a remarkable sense of historical awareness and decided not to destroy these records but to preserve them for a future historian of the church, "because that time constitutes its own period in the Brethren's history that cannot be denied."[9] The committee decided to seal these papers and leave it up to the UEC to deal with them. Unfortunately, forty years later the archivist as well as the members of the UEC lacked the historical foresight of the revision committee and burned the papers without hesitation.

The destruction of material regarding the Sifting Time had begun many years earlier. As we saw above, in the early 1750s Christian Renatus, together with several other men, burned papers relating to the crisis as a symbolic act whereby they distanced themselves from the events of the previous years. The hymn texts that were buried, however, were dug up and burned, apparently because they were considered so incriminating that they could not even be left in the earth. Fortunately, a songbook with hymns from the Sifting was discovered at the Unity Archives in Herrnhut.

Even though Moravians destroyed a great number of records deemed unworthy to be preserved in their archives, on the whole they can be considered good record keepers. Moravians' care for archiving and recording their activities is connected to their Pietist background. Like other Pietists, they were less interested in the correct dogmatic formulation of their theology than in true and authentic experience of their faith. Personal experiences with the divine were recorded in narratives: addresses and discourses, biographies (the *Lebensläufe*), and diaries. Moravians considered these texts part of the continuous history of the true children of God, beginning with the founding of the church in the first century and continuing until their own time.[10] The archives were intended as the continuation of the Bible, documenting the history of the children of God, and the source for later generations to learn that the eighteenth-century Moravians were "God's people." Therefore, the question of what was to be included in the archives and what was not was given serious consideration.

Diaries

In order to document the daily course of events in their communities, Moravians kept communal diaries. Each unit that considered itself a community kept such a diary: the congregations, the choirs within the congregations, mission stations, schools, and also groups of men and women traveling together. The diary of the Herrnhut congregation began in 1727, and when other Moravian communities were founded, they were encouraged to keep such a diary too. From 1741 on every Moravian congregation was instructed to keep a communal diary and to record the important events of each day.[11] These diaries contain entries about religious meetings, important visitors, the arrival and departure of traveling Moravians, the construction of communal buildings, special religious experiences, and some of the resolutions of the leaders of the congregation. These occurrences were considered to be part of the life of the congregation, part of their service to God, and therefore part of the liturgy. The diaries include few facts about daily life—although they are sometimes misinterpreted in this regard—but they contain what Germans call *Heilsgeschichte* (*historia salutis*, God's salvific activity in history). When an event or a reference was included in the diary, it was emphasized and obtained an elevated status. By recording selected events of the day in their communal diaries, Moravians made them part of the sacred history of the congregation.

The diaries of the single brothers, who were at the center of the events of the Sifting Time, are important source materials. The Herrnhaag single brothers' diary exists for the years leading up to 1747, but the entries for the critical years of 1748 and 1749 do not survive, except for a copy of the months of August and September of 1749.[12] Reinhard Schlözer, one of the leaders among the single brothers, took the 1749 volume—which possibly also contained the year 1748—with him when he left Herrnhaag in 1750. According to nineteenth-century Unity Archivist Ludwig von Schweinitz, as of 1792 the diary was in the archives of the Moravian community of Gracehill in Ireland, where Schlözer had his last post, but when Schweinitz inquired about it in 1848 he was told it had been destroyed.[13]

A parallel diary of the seminary in Marienborn for those years still survives, however. Because of its close proximity to Herrnhaag, the single brothers in the Marienborn seminary were very much part of the developments in Herrnhaag. Although the Marienborn diary is written for the most part in a fairly factual style, it contains essential information for this study. A later editor sanitized the diary and protected it from destruction by crossing out individual words or entire passages throughout. What makes this diary such a crucial text is that in doing so, he indicated at the same time that these passages were considered controversial. In that way, the diary helps us know what contemporary Moravians labeled as part of the crisis of the 1740s, and thus to understand the nature of the crisis of the 1740s. The deleted passages are mostly still readable; a century ago Herrnhut church administrator and historian Otto Uttendörfer deciphered most of the deleted words and scribbled the original text in the margins.[14]

The 1748 diary of the single brothers in Herrnhut, kept by Christian Gregor, survived in the archives of the Herrnhut congregation until the end of World War II, when passing Russian troops set fire to a great number of buildings in Herrnhut, including the *Gemeinhaus* on the town square, which contained the archives of the Herrnhut congregation. Fortunately, a century earlier Schweinitz had made transcriptions from the single brothers' diary, which he kept in his collections of notes on the Sifting Time. Although he did not copy the diary in its entirety, his transcriptions are an invaluable source for the theology of the single brothers during that critical year.[15]

Even if the single brothers' choirs in the various congregations were at the center of the Sifting Time, other groups were involved as well. It would be especially interesting to see what occurred among the single sisters. Unfortunately, there are no extant diaries of the single sisters in Herrnhaag or Herrnhut. One can only speculate why these diaries did not survive.

Of special significance is the official diary of Zinzendorf and his staff. It was known under different names: *Gemeindiarium* (church diary, 1747–48), *Gemeinhausdiarium* (church house diary, 1749), *Diarium der Hütten* (diary of the tents or diary of the tabernacle, 1750–53), or *Jüngerhausdiarium* (diary of the house of the disciple, 1754–60). The last has more or less become the official designation in German publications. A standard English title does not seem to exist; in this study we used the eighteenth-century name "Congregational Accounts."

During Zinzendorf's lifetime the Congregational Accounts contained the official proceedings of Zinzendorf and his household, as well as reports received by Zinzendorf from the various congregations and mission stations, the texts of new hymns, and memoirs of deceased members. After Zinzendorf's death the Congregational Accounts developed into a regular news publication of the church (*Gemeinnachrichten*). Most older Moravian congregations owned or still own their copies; many of them ended up in Moravian collections in Herrnhut, Winston-Salem, Bethlehem, and London. The Congregational Accounts were bound and preserved in their entirety and contain references that might otherwise have been destroyed because of their Sifting Time content. However, the volumes from before 1819 were only distributed in manuscript form, which is not very conducive to access.[16] The tightly written volumes still contain many unknown texts.

A useful source for Moravian theology and practice during the 1740s is descriptions of the festivals as found in the diaries. During these years the festivals increased in frequency and became central elements of life in a Moravian community. Christian holidays, commemorations of events in the short history of the young Moravian movement, as well as leaders' birthdays were occasions to stage elaborate celebrations. The festivals, which have obvious parallels to the festive culture of European courts,[17] consisted of many elements, including music, images, three-dimensional displays, sermons, new hymn texts, special dress, illuminations, decorations with garlands, and triumphal arches and other temporary structures. The single brothers' house in Herrnhaag was the center of this festive culture, but similar events took place in other Moravian communities as well, including the woods of Pennsylvania. The celebrations were purposefully planned and prepared. They served as a stage to experiment with new ideas, promote and visualize Moravian theology, strengthen the group coherence and group identity of the community, and establish a spiritual hierarchy within the church. The diary descriptions illustrate how new ideas were introduced and how the theology of the community developed and evolved. In the older literature these festivals are sometimes considered illustrations of the decadence of the Sifting Time, when Moravians supposedly preferred to celebrate rather than work.[18] Although individual celebrations are mentioned in some studies, no systematic study of the festive culture of Moravians during the mid-eighteenth century exists.

Discourses and Addresses

Important sources for our study are the many discourses and addresses by Zinzendorf, Johannes von Watteville, Christian Renatus, and others.[19]

Discourses were held for the entire congregation or for individual groups (the choirs). Zinzendorf was a charismatic preacher who tirelessly gave one or more discourses each day. Most times he did not prepare a full text or even an outline but spoke extemporaneously. In order to preserve his speeches, Zinzendorf, like many other religious leaders,[20] had specially trained men take down his words as he spoke them, and he corrected and approved the texts himself before they were distributed in print or in handwritten form.[21] Many of Zinzendorf's addresses were published, but many more were distributed in the handwritten Congregational Accounts (*Gemeinnachrichten*), mainly for use within the church. It is sometimes claimed that the handwritten texts do not add much to the texts that were published in print, but this is not entirely correct.[22] It appears that Zinzendorf's more unconventional ideas about, for example, the disappearance of the differences between the sexes, playfulness, and marriage are to be found in the handwritten addresses rather than the printed ones. Some of these ideas were considered special revelations, to be shared only within the church and not with outsiders, who would have little understanding of them. Since much of the scholarship on Zinzendorf's theology is based on printed texts, therefore, many important aspects of his theology have not received sufficient attention.

Despite the abundance of surviving texts, Moravian preaching has not been the subject of extensive study, as Peter Zimmerling rightfully observes.[23] Moravians distinguished between sermons (*Predigten*) and discourses, addresses, and homilies (*Reden*). Sermons, for Zinzendorf, were intended to teach the basic principles of the gospel, primarily for a general (non-Moravian) audience, while discourses were "heart-to-heart conversations."[24] A sermon was meant to preach atonement to those who did not know or who had not experienced it, while a discourse spoke about the experience of atonement to those who had felt it in their hearts.

Consistent with eighteenth-century rules of rhetoric and homiletics, it seems likely that the form of a sermon differed from that of a discourse. Moravians also distinguished between sermons and discourses, depending on the place where they were given. When Moravians had access to publicly acknowledged preaching places, such as in Marienborn and Barby and also in England, they would give sermons there, whereas the discourses in their more informal halls (*Säle*) in Herrnhut or Herrnhaag were not referred to as sermons until much later. Because of the lack of in-depth studies on the form of Moravian preaching, these can only be preliminary remarks. The content, style, and development of Moravian preaching represent largely unexplored territory.

From the extant discourses we can learn which elements of the teachings and practice of previous years Moravian leaders rejected, and thus gain insight into the nature of the Sifting Time. Many discourses by Zinzendorf, both printed and unprinted, were used. Due to their abundance, a systematic study of all his discourses was impossible. Discourses by others are scarcer, though some by the count's son-in-law, Johannes von Watteville, can be found in the Congregational Accounts or in special collections. Important for this study are those from 1750 in which he addressed the abuses of the previous years. Christian Renatus's addresses were evidently popular, but few are extant. From those few we know, however, that he had an inspiring, charismatic style. Joachim Rubusch also gave regular addresses. Some are included in the diary of the seminary at Marienborn, and Uttendörfer quotes some as well in his study of the seminary.[25] The diary of the single brothers in Herrnhaag gives short summaries of the topics of meditations by Rubusch and others.

Synods

From 1736 on Moravians regularly held synods. Once a year, or sometimes even more frequently, the main representatives from the many regions of Moravian activity would gather. A variety of matters would be discussed, undertakings would be evaluated, and plans would be made for future projects. Often ordinations took place and workers were dispatched into new fields of work. During Zinzendorf's lifetime he dominated these gatherings: the minutes testify to hour-long monologues by the count, sometimes cautiously interrupted by a question or an objection by one of the brethren of sufficient prominence. Under Zinzendorf synods were not democratic events where decisions were made by majority vote. Only after his death were they given a more representative character, with delegates from each region. But even when votes were cast, in many cases approval by the lot was needed.

In the context of this study, a number of synods are significant. During a "provincial" (regional) synod for Silesia held at Gnadenberg in May of 1750, Johannes von Watteville addressed the transgressions of the previous years. Neither Zinzendorf nor Christian Renatus was present, but later that year, at a synod in Barby and especially during a special committee meeting on September 26, the first in-depth discussion among Moravian leaders about the Sifting Time took place. The almost verbatim minutes of these synods contain relevant information about the nature of the Sifting Time.[26]

## Anti-Moravian Writings

Writings by the opponents of the Moravians are another useful source for understanding the nature of the Sifting Time. The excesses of the late 1740s were a welcome topic for anyone desiring to cast the Moravians in a negative light. During Zinzendorf's lifetime hundreds of pamphlets attacking or defending the Moravians were printed.[27] Because of their obvious bias, such polemical works have previously been discounted by most scholars. For example, in their study of Herrnhaag and the Sifting Time, Erbe and the other members of the Moravian history study group make only passing remarks about "spiteful" authors such as Volck and Frey, not considering their works an adequate source on the 1740s.[28] On the other hand, as early as 1886 Göttingen church historian Albrecht Ritschl called upon historians to include the works of the opponents in their study of the Moravian Church. But Ritschl's appeal fell on deaf ears, as most historians continued to treat the claims made by the anti-Moravian pamphleteers with disbelief.[29]

The works by eighteenth-century anti-Moravian authors may be far from impartial, but Moravian sources are biased as well, especially considering that Moravians sifted through their archival repositories and removed any material that would shed an unfavorable light on their church. Surprisingly, however, some of the claims of the anti-Moravian writers can often be substantiated by Moravian sources. For ex-ample, the handwritten hymnbook from 1749 discovered in the Unity Archives is a Moravian source for many songs and verses that had been known only from anti-Moravian texts.

Furthermore, the opponents were often well informed about the internal affairs of the Moravian congregations. Most of the polemical writings used for this study were not written by theologians attacking Zinzendorf and his followers for their theology; rather, they were the works of disillusioned former members who wished to reveal what they considered the wickedness and untrustworthiness of the Moravians: the titles of their works often contain words like *entdecken* (to reveal) or *Geheimnis* (secret). They could draw on their own experiences and sometimes still had contacts within the church to keep them apprised of the latest developments. Some of their pamphlets are thus valuable source material.

### Alexander Volck

An important polemicist against the Moravians was Alexander Volck, town clerk and notary in Büdingen, the town neighboring Herrnhaag. Volck's relationship with the Moravians was complicated and changeable. Within a decade he turned from one of their earliest supporters and a leading member of the Moravian group in Büdingen into one of their fiercest public opponents.

From his correspondence with the Moravians we learn that Volck was born in the Erzgebirge region of southern Saxony, probably in Annaberg.[30] Both he and his wife, Anna Margaretha Sophia, applied for membership in the Moravian Church as early as 1739. In 1750 Volck explained what initially attracted him to the Moravians: their apostolic Christianity, their religious fervor, and their tasteful worship services.[31] However, initial problems arose in 1740 when Volck accused the leader of the Büdingen group, David Stöhr, of "unbrotherly falseness."[32] As a consequence of his disloyalty, Volck was excluded from the congregation, but, after repenting, he was readmitted at the end of that same year. From then on the Volcks faithfully attended the Moravian meetings in Büdingen as well as in Herrnhaag. Volck seems to have been a dedicated member; he even wrote poetry in Moravian style.[33] Their son, Nicolaus Christoph, who worked in Johann Christoph Stöhr's print shop, repeatedly applied for church membership between 1741 and 1744. After Anna Margaretha Volck died in the summer of 1743, Alexander asked the Moravians for help in finding a new wife. Although an initial marriage attempt failed, Volck married Juliane (last name not known), with whom he had another son in the summer of 1745.[34] The fact that this son, Christian David, was named after the founder of Herrnhut, and that David Nitschmann served as the child's godfather, indicates that Alexander Volck was by now fully integrated into Moravian circles. It is unclear what happened exactly, but when his relationship with the Moravians turned sour, things became ugly.

Between 1748 and 1751 he published *Entdecktes Geheimnis der Bosheit der Herrnhuter* (Revealed secret of the malice of the Herrnhuters) in seven *entrevues* (interviews) or parts; the text is in the form of a conversation or interview between two fictional characters. The work was popular, and the individual parts were reprinted several times. The first part was even reprinted in Philadelphia in 1749. A Dutch translation was printed in Amsterdam, but the English translation Volck mentions in part 6 never appeared.[35] According to Johann Friedrich Köber, Zinzendorf's legal counsel in Dresden, Volck's revelations about the Moravians caused quite a stir and complicated Köber's negotiations with the Saxon government. Köber hoped the book would be confiscated by the censor in Dresden, but he realized that would not happen without the Moravians taking Volck to court.[36]

Volck was well informed about what was going on at Herrnhaag and Marienborn. His years of active involvement with the Moravians had given him extensive insight, and he also seemed to have been kept apprised by residents of Herrnhaag, even after he officially severed ties with the Moravians. The accuracy of Volck's allegations against the Moravians is confirmed, for example, in a letter by Friedrich Christoph Steinhofer, a Lutheran minister with close ties to the Moravians. Steinhofer reported to Zinzendorf that the individuals referred to in Volck's book had admitted in private that in fact "things were four times worse" than the book described.[37]

*Heinrich Joachim Bothe*

Like Volck, Heinrich Joachim Bothe was a former Moravian who turned against them. Less biographical information is available on him than on Volck. Most of what we know about him is found in his book, *Zuverläßige Beschreibung des Herrenhutischen Ehe-Geheimnisses* (Reliable description of the Moravian marriage secret), published in two volumes in Berlin in 1751 and 1752. Bothe, a follower of the radical Pietist Johann Conrad Dippel, heard about Herrnhut for the first time in 1736, when he had recently returned to Berlin from St. Petersburg. In December of that same year he visited Herrnhut and was deeply impressed with what he heard there, so different from Dippel's theology: Christ had redeemed the world by his incarnation, passion, and death, and anyone who believed this would be saved. It was not until 1742 that Bothe fully joined the Moravians. The following year he served as Zinzendorf's tailor, and soon thereafter was assigned responsibilities with the Moravians in Berlin. He first became a small group leader, then an assistant preacher, and finally "general servant and overseer" (*General-Diener und Aufseher*). He also served as distributor of Moravian publications shipped to him from Marienborn. The membership lists in the Unity Archives confirm that Bothe was also the leader of the group of married men.[38] An undated evaluation of the members of the Berlin congregation gives the following assessment: "Bothe is a group leader and servant. He is diligent and faithful in doing what he is told. However, he is not a sinner,[39] and because he is a quick-tempered person one has to fear he may play a nasty trick. His wife is a wicked woman but not without feeling. She attends our services and is often deeply touched. In their marriage they are very opposed to each other. He is a tailor."[40] And a "nasty trick" he played indeed. According to Bothe's preface, reading the sixth part of Volck's *Entdecktes Geheimnis* opened his eyes about the Moravians and made him realize he was not a "dumb ox" (*dummer Ochse*) but a rational person. In addition to Zinzendorf's authoritarian manner, the final provocation for Bothe appears to have been the Moravian teaching and practice regarding marriage. In several places in the book Bothe mentions that he was not made privy to the inner details of the marital theology, although he was a married man himself. The assessment of the Bothes above confirms that Moravians did not think them worthy candidates to be initiated into the secrets of Moravian marital theology. Did he perhaps regard this exclusion as a sign of rejection? In any case, he recounts that he was disillusioned by the change in piety he observed among Moravians over time: from simply preaching salvation through Christ, they began to express their theology in unusual and provoking terms. This disillusionment must have occurred during the late 1740s and may even have been related to the end of the Sifting Time, when many Moravians had to distance themselves from what they had earlier embraced with great enthusiasm.

Bothe's book recounts many internal matters and scandals in order to reveal the "falseness" of the Moravians. Although the text is permeated with anti-Moravian spite, many of his descriptions can be verified from Moravian sources. He had read Volck's work and refers to it in various places, but can be considered an independent source. He offers information similar to that given by Volck, but sometimes provides additional details and reports many things not mentioned by Volck.

*Christian Hart*

Equally informative though less vicious than Bothe or Volck is Christian Hart's account of his time with the Moravians. Hart, a mason born near Stargard in Pomerania, was living in Stettin when he became acquainted with a group of local Moravians. He joined them on September 12, 1744, and in 1746 he left for Herrnhaag, where he was officially received into the church. In July of 1748 he was transferred to Zeist in the Netherlands, where construction of the Moravian buildings was well under way and where his mason's skills were very much in demand. According to his own words, Hart began to consider leaving Zeist in 1749 "when the evil had very much increased." He kept a notebook of all the "useless prattle and sinful things" he witnessed.[41] He waited until the last few days of 1750 before finally saying farewell to the Moravians and returning to his hometown of Stargard. Andreas Petrus Hecker, deacon at the Marienkirche in Stargard, published Hart's account in the form of an interview in the following year.

Hart can be considered an eyewitness to the developments related to the Sifting as they occurred in Zeist. Like Bothe, he took part in the things he describes. He also relates events happening in Herrnhaag during the years he was already residing in Zeist, based on what others told him.[42] Comparison of his information with Moravian sources shows Hart to be a reliable source.

## Andreas Frey

Andreas Frey's pamphlet about the years he lived among the Moravians in Marienborn and Herrnhaag is instructive as a critical eyewitness account of the years leading up to the Sifting Time. Based on information he gives in his pamphlet, Frey was born around 1685. He lived in Falkner Swamp, northwest of Philadelphia, and was one of the early followers of Conrad Beissel, the founder of the community at Ephrata. In 1728 Frey convinced people in Falkner Swamp to be baptized by Beissel.[43] Later he belonged to the Associated Brethren of Skippack. This group of Philadelphians believed true Christians could be found among all denominations and rejected the division of Christianity into different "sects" (denominations).[44] When Spangenberg came to Pennsylvania in 1736 he lived in the house of Christoph Wiegner, the place where the Skippack Brethren met. Consequently, many members of the Skippack group, including Frey, became interested in the ideas of the Moravians.

A Moravian source describes Frey as "Reformed, Swiss, Pennsylvanian, Mennonite, Behmenist, Evangelical," reflecting the different stages of his religious development.[45] If this information is correct, we may assume that Frey was of Swiss descent;[46] immigrated to Pennsylvania; was originally Reformed; became a Mennonite; was a follower, as we saw, of Conrad Beissel (who was influenced by the mystic Jacob Böhme); and finally became "evangelical," that is, Moravian. In a letter sent from Marienborn to Margarethe Merkel, a fellow member of the Skippack group, Frey repudiated her accusations of having lost his Philadelphian ideals and fallen into "sectarianism." The wording of his letter is an interesting Moravian version of the Philadelphian ideal: he writes that all souls renewed by the "dear blood of the slain Lamb" are "true members of the body of Jesus Christ."[47] At that time, Frey still believed that the Moravians were such Christians.

Frey met Zinzendorf when the count visited Pennsylvania in 1742, and he attended Zinzendorf's Pennsylvania synods during the first half of that year. He then joined the Moravians in Bethlehem and became elder of the single brothers, although he continued to live in Falkner Swamp, not wishing to live in Bethlehem, where living space was limited.[48] He accompanied Zinzendorf on his return to Europe in January of 1743, visited Moravian congregations in London, Amsterdam, Heerendijk, and Herrnhut, and attended a synod held by Zinzendorf in Silesia that same year.

Frey lived in the Wetterau, but when he objected to the cramped quarters of the single brothers' house he was allowed to live in a summer house on the grounds of the Marienborn manor, soon named "Andreasburg" after him. Later he had a room in the Lichtenburg in Herrnhaag. He described himself as a "Pensylvanian Hermit . . . in the Garden-Lodge." He kept a different appearance from the other Moravians by not shaving his (Mennonite) beard. Although he lived alone and was somewhat older than most other single men, he was a member of the single brothers' choir and saw how the men engaged in frivolous play during 1746 and 1747. This shocked him to the core and confirmed for him that Moravians were not the true Christians he initially thought them to be. He was finally able to return to Pennsylvania in 1747, where he documented his experiences in a letter, first published by Christoph Saur in Germantown and later in Germany. An English translation was printed in 1753.[49]

When Frey's discontent became apparent, Zinzendorf, knowing Frey had witnessed things he did not want to come out in the open, feared he would publish accounts of his experiences. It is interesting to note that Zinzendorf expected Frey to reveal "the truth."[50] Later, after Frey's account had been printed in Germantown, the brethren in Bethlehem asked a group of newly arrived men from Europe how accurate it was: "They laughed about Frey's writing and said that in reality things were ten times worse, but that they considered these things to be nice [hübsch]."[51] Moravians were genuinely worried about Frey's publication. The helpers' conference in Bethlehem held a special meeting about it in November of 1748. Although some things in it were not entirely correct, the Bethlehem helpers reluctantly admitted that many things were indeed true.[52]

# NOTES

## PROLOGUE

1. Diary single brothers Bethlehem, November 16, 1748, BethSB 1, MAB. The line is from hymn 2157, v. 10, written by Zinzendorf for the birthday of his son, Christian Renatus, on September 19, 1745.
2. Christian Thomas Benzien was born in 1715 in Reval (Tallinn, Estonia) and died in Gnadenthal, Pennsylvania, in 1757.
3. Acrelius, "Visit," 418–19. Israel Acrelius (1714–1800) served as Lutheran minister in the Swedish church in Wilmington, Delaware, from 1749 to 1756, when he returned to Sweden.

## ACKNOWLEDGMENTS

1. Also see Benham, *Memoirs of James Hutton*, 563; Erbe, *Herrnhaag*, 58–59.

## INTRODUCTION

1. D'Emilio and Freedman, *Intimate Matters*, vii; Wiesner-Hanks, *Christianity and Sexuality*; Bloch, "Changing Conceptions"; Godbeer, *Sexual Revolution*; Godbeer, *Overflowing of Friendship*; Parsons, *Reformation Marriage*.
2. For a discussion of sexuality within (mostly German) Pietism, see Gestrich, "Ehe, Familie, Kinder im Pietismus," 498–521; Temme, *Krise der Leiblichkeit*; Breul and Soboth, "'Der Herr wird seine Herrlichkeit'"; Breul, "Ehe und Sexualität"; Breul, "Marriage and Marriage-Criticism"; Gleixner, "Zwischen göttlicher und weltlicher Ordnung"; Roeber, *Hopes for Better Spouses*.
3. Roeber, *Hopes for Better Spouses*.
4. Temme, *Krise der Leiblichkeit*, 452–53.
5. Võsa, "Johann Georg Gichtels Verhältnis." On Beissel and Ephrata see Bach, *Voices of the Turtledoves*; Vogt, "Ehereligion: The Moravian Theory."
6. Breul, "Gottfried Arnold."
7. Temme, *Krise der Leiblichkeit*.
8. Scholarly study of Zinzendorf's ideas on marriage dates back at least a century: G. Reichel, *Zinzendorfs Frömmigkeit*, 171–92; Jannasch, "Erdmuthe Dorothea," 76–84; Tanner, *Die Ehe im Pietismus*; E. Beyreuther, "Ehe-Religion"; G. Beyreuther, "Sexualtheorien"; Atwood, "Sleeping in the Arms of Christ"; Atwood, *Community of the Cross*, 87–95; Breul, "Ehe und Sexualität"; Breul, "Marriage and Marriage-Criticism"; Vogt, "Ehereligion"; Vogt, "Zinzendorf's 'Seventeen Points'"; Faull, "Married Choir Instructions"; Peucker, "In the Blue Cabinet." On Zinzendorf's ideas on sexuality in the context of his contemporaries, see Roeber, *Hopes for Better Spouses*, chap. 5.
9. G. Reichel, *Zinzendorfs Frömmigkeit*, 185–86; Jannasch, "Erdmuthe Dorothea," 77, 81–82; Renkewitz, *Hochmann von Hochenau*, 389. Breul sees some parallels with Jane Leade's ideas. He

argues that Zinzendorf's marital theology was influenced by Philadelphian ideas but that Zinzendorf independently developed his ideas further ("Ehe und Sexualität," 412).

10. Hochmann von Hochenau, *Glaubens-Bekänntniß* (1702), printed in Renkewitz, *Hochmann von Hochenau*, 407–12. Hochmann was a proponent of the possibility of divorce for secular marriages. Interestingly, he did not think church consecrations of marriages were necessary at all. He only recommended them for Christian believers so as not to give offense.

11. Moravian couples were instructed to have intercourse while sitting up and staying as motionless as possible; only a "slow movement" based on a six-quarter time signature was allowed. See Peucker, "In the Blue Cabinet," 24–26.

12. "The Moravian teaching on the marriage relationship assumed massive importance not only because it obviously draws upon elements of Lutheran pietism but also because it just as clearly broke the boundaries of that tradition." Roeber, *Hopes for Better Spouses*, 148.

13. For an overview of recent publications, see the bibliography of publications in English from 2000 to 2010 in *Journal of Moravian History*, no. 9 (2010). The German journal *Unitas Fratrum* publishes regular bibliographic overviews of new publications in Moravian studies. The yearbook *Pietismus und Neuzeit* offers a detailed overview of recent titles on international Pietism and Evangelicalism.

14. Also see Atwood, "Interpreting and Misinterpreting," 175.

15. Atwood, "Zinzendorf's 1749 Reprimand," 66.

16. Atwood, "Interpreting and Misinterpreting," 182.

17. For example, Fogleman, *Jesus Is Female*, passim.

18. The recent four-volume German standard work *Geschichte des Pietismus* (1993–2004) gives priority to the nonseparatist form of Pietism, but radical Pietism seems to have been the original form of Pietism (Shantz, *Introduction to German Pietism*, 151); also see Wallmann, "Kirchlicher und radikaler Pietismus."

19. Schneider, "Der radikale Pietismus im 18. Jahrhundert," 108. On radical Pietism also see the edited volume Breul, Meier, and Vogel, *Der radikale Pietismus*, with several essays regarding the terminology; Schneider, "Der radikale Pietismus in der neueren Forschung"; Ward, *Early Evangelicalism*; Shantz, *Introduction to German Pietism*.

20. Schneider, "Philadelphische Brüder." The relationship with the Halle Pietists is further discussed in chap. 1.

21. Schneider, "Der radikale Pietismus im 17. Jahrhundert," 406; Schneider, "Understanding the Church"; Wallmann, *Der Pietismus*, 101–2.

22. Shantz, *Introduction to German Pietism*, 158.

23. Ibid., 155. Other models are the spiritualist-alchemist model, the millennialist model, and the conventicle model.

24. Dietrich Meyer calls the Moravians a "bridge" between radical and ecclesiastical Pietism (D. Meyer, "Die Herrnhuter Brüdergemeine als Brücke").

25. Shantz, *Introduction to German Pietism*, 203.

26. Bach, *Voices of the Turtledoves*; Marcus Meier, *Origin of the Schwarzenau Brethren* (Philadelphia: Brethren Encyclopedia, 2008); Temme, *Krise der Leiblichkeit*.

27. See the bibliography.

CHAPTER 1

1. Address by Zinzendorf at the celebration in Herrnhaag of the founding of Herrnhut on June 17, 1747, quoted in Hahn and Reichel, *Zinzendorf*, 65.

2. On Gersdorf's library (including bibliographic references), see Schulz, "Viel Anschein." Schulz analyzes a recently discovered inventory of her library, which was accessible to Zinzendorf while growing up.

NOTES TO PAGES 12–17   189

3. A new biography of Zinzendorf is highly desired. Weinlick, *Count Zinzendorf*, dates from 1956. The Zinzendorf biography by Beyreuther is also outdated. For shorter overviews, see Schneider, "Nikolaus Ludwig von Zinzendorf"; Schneider, "Philadelphische Brüder"; D. Meyer, *Zinzendorf und die Herrnhuter Brüdergemeine*; Freeman, *Ecumenical Theology of the Heart*; Vogt, "Nicholas Ludwig von Zinzendorf"; Atwood, *Community of the Cross*; Ward, *Early Evangelicalism*, chap. 6. For Zinzendorf's full name and title, see Spangenberg, *Leben Zinzendorf*, preface, [3].

4. On the Philadelphian movement, see Hans Schneider, "Philadelphier," in *Religion in Geschichte und Gegenwart: Handwörterbuch für Theologie und Religionswissenschaft*, 4th ed., vol. 6 (Tübingen: Mohr Siebeck, 2003), 1266; Schneider, "Der radikale Pietismus im 17. Jahrhundert," 405–6; Durnbaugh, "Jane Ward Leade." On the Philadelphian aspects of Moravianism, see Schneider, "Philadelphische Brüder." Also see Vogt, "'Philadelphia.'"

5. Bernet, "Stadt Gottes"; Bernet, *Gebaute Apokalypse*.

6. Schneider, "Der radikale Pietismus im 17. Jahrhundert," 398–406.

7. Schneider, "Philadelphische Brüder," 19–21.

8. Schneider, "Nikolaus Ludwig von Zinzendorf als Gestalt," 15; Renkewitz, *Hochmann von Hochenau*, 382–89.

9. On Erdmuth Dorothea, see Jannasch, "Erdmuthe Dorothea"; Geiger, *Erdmuth Dorothea*.

10. The current Czech name of the village of Söhle (in Moravian texts often spelled "Sehlen") is Žilina near Nový Jičín. On Christian David, see Sterik, *Mährische Exulanten*.

11. Müller, *Geschichte der Böhmischen Brüder*, 3:371n109.

12. Sterik, "Die böhmische Emigranten."

13. Weigelt, "Zinzendorf und die Schwenckfelder."

14. Studies of the early years of Herrnhut: Müller, *Geschichte der Böhmischen Brüder*, 3:368–76; G. Reichel, *Die Anfänge Herrnhuts*; D. Meyer, "Zinzendorf und Herrnhut," 20–34; Wollstadt, *Geordnetes Dienen*; Sterik, *Mährische Exulanten*. Sterik's recent book analyzes the memoirs (*Lebensläufe*) written by the immigrants from Moravia about their background and reasons for settling in Herrnhut.

15. Printed in Hahn and Reichel, *Zinzendorf*, 75–80. English translation in Peter C. Erb, *Pietists: Selected Writings* (New York: Paulist Press, 1983), 325–30. See pars. 15 and 2.

16. For example, Ward, "Renewed Unity"; Atwood, *Community of the Cross*, 21–25. Also see Noller, "Die Rezeption."

17. Müller, *Geschichte der Böhmischen Brüder*; Crews, *Faith, Love, Hope*; Atwood, *Theology of the Czech Brethren*.

18. Atwood, "Use of the 'Ancient Unity.'"

19. Schneider, "Philadelphische Brüder," 15.

20. Arnold, *Die erste Liebe*; Uttendörfer, *Zinzendorf und die Mystik*, 5–6, 41–42; Wollstadt, *Geordnetes Dienen*, 43–48; Peucker, "Ideal of Primitive Christianity."

21. See Sterik, "Böhmische Emigranten" and *Mährische Exulanten*.

22. According to Zinzendorf's account of the events of 1727 on August 10, 1749, quoted in Hahn and Reichel, *Zinzendorf*, 110.

23. Spangenberg, *Leben Zinzendorf*, 435; diary Herrnhut [August 1727], quoted in Hahn and Reichel, *Zinzendorf*, 104.

24. G. Reichel, *Die Anfänge Herrnhuts*.

25. Bahlcke, "Religiöse Kommunikation." On the introduction of the office of acolyte, see Vogt, "Geschichte und Aktualität des Akoluthenamts." On the reception of hymns of the Unity of the Brethren in Herrnhut, see D. Meyer, "Rezeption des Liedguts."

26. "Wir beruffen uns aber auf kein Böhmisches *Glaubens-Bekenntniß*, sondern nur auf Mährische *Disciplin* und Zucht." Minutes of special conference at Zeist synod, May 24, 1746, 16 (emphasis added).

27. Synod in Hirschberg, 1743, quoted by Schneider, "Philadelphische Brüder," 12.

28. On Pietism, see *Geschichte des Pietismus*; Ward, *Early Evangelicalsm*; Shantz, *Introduction to German Pietism*.
29. "Vom Pietismo sind wir directe das *oppositum*." Minutes of synod in Marienborn, July 26, 1745, 14th session, 457.
30. See Meyer and Peucker, *Graf ohne Grenzen*, 165–167. The claim goes back to Spangenberg, *Leben Zinzendorf*, 5.
31. D. Meyer, "Zinzendorf und Herrnhut," 30–34; Becker, *Zinzendorf und sein Christentum*, 178–211; Geiger, "Zinzendorfs Stellung." Also see Wagner, *Zinzendorf-Muhlenberg Encounter*.
32. Schneider, "Die 'zürnenden Mutterkinder.'" The older literature is mostly written from a Moravian perspective.
33. See minutes of winter synod in Marienborn, December 6, 1740, 4th session, 24, R.2.A.4, UA. For a comparison between the mission enterprises of Herrnhut and Halle, see Lehmann, "Punktuelle globale Präsenz."
34. Also see Atwood, "Hallensians Are Pietists."
35. "Der Pietisten Plan ist ein gantz eigener Plan, der unsern gantz entgegen ist; das merken sie auch. Die Hauptsachen sind, keine Manchetten tragen, kein Poudre in der Päruque haben, sonst aber sich gantz ordentlich kleiden, nicht tanzen, nicht spielen, nichts von Taback halten, von den *Theologis irregenitis* übel sprechen und dergleichen mehr." Minutes of winter synod in Marienborn, December 6, 1740, 4th session, 24–25, R.2.A.4, UA.
36. Address by Zinzendorf at a synod in Herrnhaag, May 12, 1747, quoted in Hahn and Reichel, *Zinzendorf*, 122.
37. Congregational Accounts, November 11, 1752. I am grateful to Rüdiger Kröger for this reference.
38. General overviews of Moravian missions in English are outdated. Most studies of Moravian missions concentrate on a particular area. An excellent study of Moravian missionary work in the Caribbean in its Atlantic context is Sensbach, *Rebecca's Revival*.
39. Breul, "Theological Tenets."
40. Schneider, "Der radikale Pietismus im 18. Jahrhundert," 130–33.
41. Uttendörfer, "Aus Zinzendorfs Alltagsleben," 85–100; Shantz, *Introduction to German Pietism*, 159–62.
42. The word "choir" (German *Chor*) derives from the Greek word *choros*, meaning group or band. These choirs had nothing to do with musical choirs. German uses different grammatical genders for a singing choir (*der Chor*) and for a pastoral choir (*das Chor*).
43. There are studies of individual choirs, such as the sisters' choir, the choir of the older girls, and the widows' choir. Katherine Faull is preparing a study on the pastoral instructions of the choirs.
44. On the ribbons, see Peucker, "Pink, White, and Blue."
45. During the first twenty years in Bethlehem, when no private households existed, there were also separate choir houses for the married men and the married women.
46. Atwood, *Community of the Cross*, 188–94.
47. Zinzendorf, *Zeister Reden*, 207.
48. For recent literature on Zinzendorf's marital theology, see chap. 1.
49. Diary single brothers Herrnhut, February 20, 1744. In September he inquired if the brothers were sleeping that way (ibid., September 21, 1744).
50. Address by Zinzendorf at dedication of the dormitory of the single brothers, Herrnhut, November 1, 1745, Hs 33, UA.
51. The number of laborers is from January 1747, and the number of brothers is from 1746. Carstensen, *Stadtplanung im Pietismus*, 119.
52. On Anna Nitschmann, see Martin, "Anna Nitschmann."

53. In addition, there were over one hundred members of the pilgrim congregation (including missionaries on furlough or waiting to go on mission), as well as thirty children and forty servants. R.27.292.33, UA.
54. Hahn and Reichel, *Zinzendorf*, 149–61; D. Meyer, "Moravian Church as a Theocracy."
55. Report of single brothers' festival, Herrnhaag, May 4, 1748 (longer version); Congregational Accounts, September 16, 1749, quoted in Hahn and Reichel, *Zinzendorf*, 158. Also see Rhode, *Schlüssel zu Herrnhut*, 522n; Volck, *Das entdeckte Geheimnis*, 6:739.
56. On the lot, see Sommer, "Gambling with God: Revelation, Reason, and the Use of the Lot," chap. 4 in *Serving Two Masters*.
57. Diary single brothers Herrnhaag, April 16, 1745.
58. "Zum Schluß dieses Seegen-Tages früh gegen 4 Uhr als den 25ten war noch ein allgemeiner Abendseegen und dann gingen wir am Sabbath der Empfängniß unsers Mannes noch etliche Stunden schlafen." Diary single brothers Herrnhaag, March 24, 1747.
59. Vogt, "'Everywhere at Home.'"
60. Diary single brothers Herrnhaag, April 11, 1746.
61. Sensbach, *Rebecca's Revival*, 178–91; Peucker, "Aus allen Nationen."
62. Erben, *Harmony of the Spirits*, 236–41.
63. Bynum, *Wonderful Blood*, 14.
64. On blood devotion, see Pugh, "Brief History of the Blood"; Bynum, "Blood of Christ," Bynum, *Wonderful Blood*. On Moravian blood-and-wounds devotion, see Atwood, *Community of the Cross*, 95–112; Atwood, "Understanding Zinzendorf's Blood and Wounds Theology." Also see Wheeler, "'Der schönste Schmuck.'"
65. Andreas Grassmann to Zinzendorf, Herrnhut, May 4, 1742, quoted in Erbe, *Herrnhaag*, 165–69.
66. The original text: *Herrnhuter Gesangbuch*, pt. 2, no. 1949. English translation: *Collection of Hymns*, no. 398.
67. On the Litany of the Wounds, see Erbe, "Herrnhaag," 82–83; Faull, "Faith and Imagination"; Atwood, "Zinzendorf's Litany of the Wounds"; Atwood, *Community of the Cross*, 203–8. Minutes of helpers' conference, Bethlehem, December 20, 1744, BethCong 79, MAB.
68. Bettermann, *Theologie und Sprache*.
69. Atwood, *Community of the Cross*, 101.
70. "I Believe too, throughout all Days / A holy Christendom there was, / Th' Assembly of Believers pure, / A Church, which is and shall endure." *Collection of Hymns*, pt. 3, no. 1, art. 7; Zinzendorf, *Ein und zwanzig Discurse*, 307. The address was about the seventh article of the Augsburg Confession. Also see Atwood, *Community of the Cross*, 96; Peucker, "Zinzendorf's Plan," 62–63.
71. For an in-depth overview of mystical traditions in Christianity, see McGinn, *Presence of God*, definition at 1:xvii.
72. Schneider, "Johann Arndt und die Mystik"; Ward, *Early Evangelicalism*, 7–10.
73. Johannes Wallmann argues that Pietism did not so much appreciate and adopt Bernard of Clairvaux's bridal mysticism (as opposed to Albrecht Ritschl), but that orthodox Lutheranism was especially interested in bridal mysticism (Wallmann, "Bernhard von Clairvaux"). Also see Ward, *Early Evangelicalism*; McGinn, *Presence of God*, 3:168–216.
74. For an overview of the discussion, see Philipp, "Zinzendorf und die Christusmystik"; Renkewitz, *Im Gespräch*, 96–98; D. Meyer, "Christus mein ander Ich."
75. Ward, *Early Evangelicalism*, 109.
76. D. Meyer, introduction to Meyer and Sträter, *Zur Rezeption mystischer Traditionen*, xi; D. Meyer, "Cognitio Dei experimentalis," 238–40. Framing the discussion about mysticism in terms of heretical versus orthodox, as the authors of some of the essays in this volume do, is not helpful.

77. On Zinzendorf's view of history, see Uttendörfer, *Zinzendorfs Weltbetrachtung*, 117–55; Peucker, "Zinzendorf's Plan."

78. Martin Dober's description, 1747, R.6.A.a.10.3, UA. Also see Erbe, *Herrnhaag*, 126–27; Hahn and Reichel, *Zinzendorf*, 162–64.

79. [Hecker], *Gespräch*, 45–51.

80. Diary single brothers Herrnhaag, March 26, 1747; Congregational Accounts, March 26, 1747; also see Uttendörfer, "Zinzendorf und die Entwicklung," pt. 3, 23.

81. Zinzendorf, *Homilien über die Wundenlitanei*, 83.

82. Diary single brothers Bethlehem, May 5, 1748, BethSB, no. 1, MAB.

83. Diary single brothers Marienborn, November 29, 1748.

84. "(24) Bis gegen 1750 sind 4 Haupt-Periodi anzumerken, wovon der erste seinen Anfang nimmt den 1. January 1742 und in der Mitte ein wenig pausirt. Es ist aber von 41 an ja nicht in gleiche epochas abzutheilen. Es wird sich selbst zeigen, so bald eine neue angeht. 1741 Mensem Mars. (25) Bis hieher haben wir das Geheymnis des Kaufmanns vorgestellt, der die Perle fand. Die folgenden Periodi werden 1. das Senf-Korn, bis in den 2ten Periodum 2 gegen die Mitte des Netzes, und gegen das Ende wird sich die Sauerteigs-Art offenbahren. Mensem Martii 1741." "General-Reguln" 1744, Spangenberg Papers, MAB.

85. Frey, *True and Authentic Account*, 58–59, 64.

86. "Johannes: Wir sind in unsern Chören manche Periodos duchpassirt. Eine Zeitlang war eine geszliche Führung, darauf folgte eine wirklich leichtsinnige Zeit. Nun sind sie wieder mehr aufs Sünder-Pünctgen gekommen." Minutes of single brothers' synod, 8th session, December 29, 1752.

87. Ward, "Renewed Unity," 115.

CHAPTER 2

1. Also see G. Meyer, "Die Epoche der Wetterau"; Faull, "Faith and Imagination"; Atwood, "Interpreting and Misinterpreting."

2. Cranz, *Alte und neue Brüder-Historie*, 489, 502–8.

3. Spangenberg, *Leben Zinzendorf*, 1629–30.

4. See the letter from Johannes Petsch to Zinzendorf, August 2, 1752, in which he describes Schrautenbach as "a former satirist mocking the so-called cross-air birdies who became a cross-air donkey and cross-air calf himself."

5. Schrautenbach, *Der Graf von Zinzendorf*, 364–65. About Schrautenbach, see the introduction by Gerhard Meyer to the modern reprint of his Zinzendorf biography (Hildesheim: Georg Olms, 1972).

6. J. Plitt's "Denkwürdigkeiten" (as the work is usually referred to) was never printed, but handwritten copies were produced for the Unity Archives and for use at the various seminaries of the church in Europe and America. The Moravian Archives in Bethlehem hold a copy. Plitt differs from his predecessors in that he did not intend to write history for apologetic purposes. Also see G. Meyer, "Die Epoche der Wetterau," 41–51.

7. Quoted in Cranz, *Alte und neue Brüder-Historie*, 501.

8. Cranz, *Alte und neue Brüder-Historie*, 509. See also ibid., 501–2; "Interimsverfassung" [1762], SynConf 52, MAB.

9. Cröger, *Geschichte der erneuerten Brüderkirche*, 2:74–83, 2:162–69, 2:182.

10. Ibid., introduction to vol. 2.

11. Atwood, "Interpreting and Misinterpreting," 177.

12. Ibid.

13. Cranz, *Alte und neue Brüder-Historie*, 505–8; Spangenberg, *Leben Zinzendorf*, 1628–32.

14. Schrautenbach, *Der Graf von Zinzendorf*, 366.

15. J. Plitt, "Denkwürdigkeiten," par. 246.
16. H. Plitt, *Zinzendorfs Theologie*, 2:ix, 1:xviii. On Hermann Plitt, see Aleksander Radler, "Die theologischen Implikationen der Zinzendorfdeutung Hermann Plitts," *UF*, no. 10 (1981): 68–85.
17. Pfister, *Die Frömmigkeit des Grafen Zinzendorf*, 89–90. On Pfister, see Albrecht Grozinger in *Biographisch-Bibliographisches Kirchenlexikon* (Nordhausen: Traugott Bautz, 1995), s.v. "Pfister, Oskar."
18. G. Reichel, *Zinzendorfs Frömmigkeit*, esp. 69–112. One of the chapters in Reichel's book is entitled "Zur positiven Erklärung und Würdigung der Sichtungszeit" (The positive explanation and assessment of the Sifting Time).
19. Atwood, "Use of the 'Ancient Unity'"; Peucker, "Beyond Beeswax Candles."
20. John Holmes, *History of the Protestant Church of the United Brethren*, 2 vols. (London, 1825–30), 398–401.
21. L. Reichel, "Early History," 179–82. Reichel acknowledged that Cammerhoff had brought this "sentimental nonsense" to Bethlehem. However, "with his death all vestiges of these delusions ceased at once."
22. Levering, *History of Bethlehem*, 186–88. F. F. Hagen passed an even sharper judgment on Cammerhoff, who supposedly infested the American Moravian Church with the Herrnhaag fanaticism, "and it so completely enervated the Church that it has not, to this day, recovered its pristine zeal and power." Hagen, *Unitas Fratrum in Extremis*, 7.
23. J. Hamilton, *History of the Church*, 116–25, 194–95. In 1895 he had published "History of the Unitas Fratrum" as part of the American Church History Series. In 1967 Hamilton's son, Kenneth G. Hamilton, published an edited version of his father's work that he had brought up to date through the year 1957: *History of the Moravian Church*.
24. It may be noted that Hamilton seems to imply—unintentionally—that the church already lost this original piety after August 13, 1727. J. Hamilton, "History of the Unitas Fratrum," 457; J. Hamilton, *History of the Church*, 124.
25. Hutton, *History*, 271–82.
26. Sessler, *Communal Pietism*, 11–12.
27. Ibid., 156–60.
28. Ibid., 164–77.
29. Ibid., 162.
30. In Neisser, *History of the Beginnings*, 131.
31. Gollin, *Moravians in Two Worlds*, 11–14, 20, 91–93. The assumption that Moravians neglected their work and spent unnecessary money on festivals during the Sifting Time can be found in the work of nineteenth-century authors such as J. Plitt ("Denkwürdigkeiten," par. 246), Burkhardt ("Zinzendorf und die Brüdergemeine," 560), and L. Reichel ("Early History," 181–82).
32. Hamilton and Hamilton, *History of the Moravian Church*, 105.
33. Burkhardt, *Entstehung und geschichtliche Entwicklung*, 1:75–76. This positive view is missing from his earlier "Zinzendorf und die Brüdergemeine."
34. Kölbing, "Zur Charakteristik," 254–56, 260. Jannasch, "Christian Renatus"; Uttendörfer, "Zinzendorf und die Entwicklung."
35. Bettermann, *Theologie und Sprache*. Kenneth Hamilton based his more positive assessment of the 1740s (see above) on Bettermann's study.
36. Ibid., 209.
37. Ibid., 4.
38. Renkewitz, "Luther und Zinzendorf"; see also Renkewitz, *Im Gespräch*; Eberhard, *Kreuzes-Theologie*.
39. Gösta Hök, *Zinzendorfs Begriff der Religion* (Leipzig: Harrassowitz, 1948); Leiv Aalen, *Die Theologie des jungen Zinzendorf* (Berlin: Lutherisches Verlagshaus, 1966); Pierre Deghaye,

*La doctrine ésotérique de Zinzendorf (1700–1760)* (Paris: Klincksieck, 1969). About this discussion, see Bouman-Komen, *Bruderliebe*, 27–43.

40. Some American Moravians trying to separate Zinzendorf from the "true" Moravian Church (like Gapp, see above) argue that he was not a Moravian but a Lutheran. In this argumentation, Lutheranism is not a criterion of sound theology as it was for some German historians, but merely a sign of otherness.

41. G. Meyer, "Einführung in die Sichtungszeit," vi; E. Beyreuther, *Zinzendorf und die Christenheit*, 229.

42. E. Beyreuther, *Zinzendorf und die Christenheit*, 229, 238–52.

43. "Der Graf hat sie eingeleitet und abgebrochen, sie kam durch ihn und endete durch ihn, sie ist sein Werk gewesen." E. Beyreuther, *Zinzendorf und die Christenheit*, 238.

44. Erbe, "Herrnhaag." On Herrnhaag as *lieu de mémoire*, see M. Gill, "Die Zeit der Brüdergemeine."

45. Erbe, *Herrnhaag*.

46. Ibid., 159.

47. Ibid., 145. The members of the study group read the 1740s in terms of an organic view of history.

48. D. Meyer, "Zinzendorf and Herrnhut," 50–51.

49. Fogleman, *Jesus Is Female*, 73.

50. Ward, *Early Evangelicalism*, 110. Also see Ward, *Protestant Evangelical Awakening*, 156.

51. Atwood, "Zinzendorf's 1749 Reprimand," 61.

CHAPTER 3

1. The original German letter is edited and printed in Peucker, "'Blut' auf unsre grünen Bändchen,'" 81–88. Atwood translated the letter into English; see "Zinzendorf's 1749 Reprimand," 67–74. An earlier (partial) edition is in Hahn and Reichel, *Zinzendorf*, 172–76. Zinzendorf wrote other letters of reprimand (*Strafbriefe*) to all the congregations—for example, a letter he wrote on September 16, 1752, about transgressions regarding marital matters and the separation of the sexes, PP Zdf 58, MAB.

2. "Gott im Himmel, seit ihr verrück[t] in Köpfen oder wie ist es?" Anna Nitschmann to Christian Renatus, [February 10, 1749].

3. Although Great Britain used the old calendar until 1752, Moravians mostly dated their records according to the new style. The dates here are all new style.

4. Minutes of special conference during Barby synod, September 26, 1750, 135v. In 1756 Zinzendorf mentioned he received the first account of the "Sifting" from Jonas Paulus Weiss, diary Johann Nitschmann, November 6, 1756.

5. Peistel, "Lebenslauf," *Nachrichten aus der Brüder-Gemeine* (1837): 838.

6. "Das entdeckte Geh[eimnis] der Bosh[eit] der H[errn]H[uter], diese infame Charteque, hat viel Schaden gethan. H.[ennicke] hat sie auch gelesen und sagte: sie meritirte verbrannt zu werden. Dazu komt noch des Superintendent Hofmanns von Wittenberg ganz neuer Tractat von den Grund Irrthümern, die er uns in der Lehre von der Dreyeinigkeit Schuld giebt und eine ganz neue Zeitung aus Hannover, daß in dasige Landen alle Gemeinschriften und Privatversamlungen bey hoher Straffe verboten werden." Johann Friedrich Köber to Zinzendorf, Dresden, January 19, 1749, R.5.A.10.d.41, UA. In Köber's next letter, dated February 8, 1749 (no. 42), he repeated his concerns and stressed it was a miracle that Hennicke, given the hostile sentiment in the city, remained "amicable and kindhearted."

7. Carl Gottlob Hofmann, *Gegründete Anzeige derer Herrnhuthischen Grund-Irrthümer in der Lehre von der heiligen Dreyeinigkeit und von Christo* (Wittenberg and Zerbst, 1749).

8. "Wilste noch mehr solche Kirchenhistorien gedruckt haben, wie die, darinnen dein Nahmen so fleissig stehet, die izt in Dreßden herumgeht und vielleicht die Gemeine um ihre Aufnahme bringet? Ich habe mich neulich geschämt, wie Graf Hennike gesagt hat: das Buch solte durch den Hencker verbrannt werden, denn es ist ja bei weitem so unwahr nicht, als es scheinet. Kämen wir dem Lamm so reine als der Menschen Augen vor!" Zinzendorf to Christian Renatus, London, February 10, 1749.

9. On the 1749 act by the British Parliament, see Podmore, *Moravian Church in England*, chap. 8. Recognition in England was expected to have favorable results in other parts of Europe as well.

10. Zinzendorf to Christian Renatus, February 10, 1749.

11. See the letter by Arvid Gradin, who pursued conversations with the archbishop in Stockholm: Gradin to Zinzendorf, Stockholm, December 13, 1748, R.19.F.a.1.36.

12. Volck, *Das entdeckte Geheimnis*, pt. 6, Vorrede, pars. 6–9.

13. "Nun allerliebstes Christelgen, ich kann dir nicht steiff seyn, ob du gleich sehr grosse Fehler gemacht hast." Zinzendorf to Christian Renatus, February 10, 1749.

14. "Nachmittags nach 6 Uhr kam unser liebes Herz Christel in Bloomsbury an und wurde von den Brüdern mit vielen Freuden, von seinem Papa aber etwas rauh und wie Eleazar von Mose Levit. 10,16 empfangen." Congregational Accounts, May 23, 1749 (n.s.). Traveling with Christian Renatus were Joachim Rubusch, Heinrich XXXI, Count Reuss, Nicolaus von Watteville, Br. Buntebart, Br. Seidel, Gottlob Königsdörfer, Johann Christian Wohn, Ole Bakker, Zacharias George Caries, Br. Singer, Jacob Hirschel, and the married brother Jacob Kohn.

15. Zinzendorf to Johannes von Watteville, London, March 16, 1749, R.20.C.23.b.120, UA.

16. Diary Herrnhut, March 12, 1749, in Congregational Accounts 1749, suppl. 6; March 23 and 31, 1749.

17. Johannes von Watteville to Zinzendorf, Bethlehem, July 31, 1749.

18. See his memoir, R.22.180.2, UA.

19. Contemporary translation in Frey, *True and Authentic Account*, 19. Volck also described him as short (*Entdecktes Geheimnis*, 2:62).

20. Diary Herrnhut, April 15 and 16, 1749.

21. "Und habe weder von nahen noch fernen die allergeringste Idee von den Sachen gehabt, die in meinem Briefe stehen. Den hab ich blos nach meiner gewöhnlichen Art geschrieben, daß wenn ich eine Sache höre, ich mir 24 Möglichkeiten dazu vorstelle.... Ich habe nicht eine Silbe gewußt von den Entrevenuen [Volck's book] und von allen in der Welt grassirenden Ideen von unsern Principiis, bis ich in einem Briefe von Köbern gelesen um den Monat Mai oder Juni." Address by Zinzendorf, in minutes of special conference during Barby synod, September 26, 1750, 135v.

22. This becomes clear from the "nota" Zinzendorf added to the Congregational Accounts covering the week of February 9–15, 1749. See chap. 7.

23. Address by Johannes von Watteville, in minutes of Provincial Synod in Gnadenberg, May 12, 1750, 23.

24. Watteville's letters from America: R.20.C.36.g; R.21.A.183.e.II; R.14.A.33, UA.

25. Cranz notes that Watteville was sent out to all congregations "to speak with every member." *Alte und neue Brüder-Historie*, 508.

26. H. Reichel, "Ende der Brüdergemeine Herrnhaag," 52.

27. Congregational Accounts, April 19, 1749.

28. Schneider, "Christoph Friedrich Brauer."

29. Copies of the printed edicts dated February 12 and March 6, 1750, in the library of MAB, Malin 687.

30. Johannes von Watteville's address to the single brothers in Marienborn, March 4, 1750. Also see his letters from Herrnhaag from February and March of 1750 to Zinzendorf and to

Christian Renatus. His letters to Zinzendorf depict the situation regarding the "occurring extravagances in doctrine and practice" (R.20.C.36.g.254) much more favorably than in what he writes to Christel.

31. See Watteville's letter about his visitations in Silesia: Johannes von Watteville to Zinzendorf, Neusalz, May 7, 1750, R.7.A.5.14, UA.

32. Minutes of Barby synod, vol. 1, 138v, 141v, R.2.A.28.A, UA. At the earlier conferences in London during the fall of 1749 the term "sifting" was used repeatedly for various difficult circumstances, but nowhere does it appear to have been used for the recent crisis.

33. Schneider, "Der radikale Pietismus im 18. Jahrhundert," 119; Schneider, "Zu den Begriffen 'Sichtung.'" A text in Zinzendorf, *Naturelle Reflexionen*, 312, suggests that the term "persecutions" is used when they come from the outside, whereas "siftings" come from inside.

34. Quoted by Schneider, "Zu den Begriffen 'Sichtung,'" 216.

35. Spangenberg, *Leben Zinzendorf*, index s.v. "Sichtungen."

36. See Schneider, "Zu den Begriffen 'Sichtung,'" 217.

37. Conference at Bloomsbury, October 3, 1749, 48, R.2.A.26.7, UA.

38. Minutes of "Ratstag," London, 7th session, September 5, 1753, 400–20, R.2.A.33.B.1, UA.

39. Cröger, *Geschichte der erneuerten Brüderkirche*, 3:149–57.

40. "Wir müssen es indeß gestehen: Satanas habe unser begehrt, aber unsers Lammes Schweiß ließ es nicht zu. Dem Lamm sey Preiß." Minutes of Provincial Synod, Gnadenberg, May 12, 1750, 23.

41. "Johannes listed among the main events [of the past year] the final and complete victory of the doctrine of God's passion and bloody wounds in all our congregations after the previous Sifting Time" (Unter den Hauptmomentis erwähnte Johannes den endlich totalen Sieg der Lehre von Gottes Marter und blutigen Wunden in allen unsern Gemeinen nach der vorigen Sichtungszeit). Diary Herrnhut, December 31, 1750 (copy by L. von Schweinitz), R.24.B.79, UA. New Year's address by Zinzendorf, Congregational Accounts, December 31, 1750; also Cranz, *Alte und neue Brüder-Historie*, 501–2.

42. "Schätzelperiodus," in memoir Cornelis van Laer (1705–74), Moravian congregation at Zeist, PA II, R.7.8, Utrechts Archief; "Seitenhöhlchenszeit," Unity archivist Christlieb Suter in a records disposal list from 1803, R.4.E.9.2, UA; "der leichtsinnige Periodus," David Nitschmann on a document folder, R.3.A.8.13.b, UA; "lustige Zeit" in Reuter's *Rissbüchlein*, quoted by Carstensen, *Stadtplanung im Pietismus*, 384.

43. Erbe, *Herrnhaag*, 8.

44. For example, Cröger, *Geschichte der erneuerten Brüderkirche*, 2:162–69; H. Plitt, *Zinzendorfs Theologie*, vol. 2; Hahn and Reichel, *Zinzendorf*, 162–63.

45. Spangenberg considers 1745 as the beginning of the Sifting: *Leben Zinzendorf*, 1628. The following authors consider 1746 as the beginning: Cranz, *Alte und neue Brüder-Historie*, 502; Burkhardt, *Die Brüdergemeine*, 1:72–73; Levering, *History of Bethlehem*, 186–88.

46. Gollin, *Moravians in Two Worlds*, 11n; Kinkel, *Our Dear Mother the Spirit*, 31.

47. Gollin, *Moravians in Two Worlds*, 11n; Fogleman, "'Jesus ist weiblich,'" 171n5.

48. J. Plitt, "Denkwürdigkeiten," par. 246.

49. J. Reichel, *Dichtungstheorie*, 13–28.

50. Gollin, *Moravians in Two Worlds*, 11n.

51. For example, in an address on March 2, 1757, Congregational Accounts; also printed in Zinzendorf, *Auszüge über die vier Evangelisten*, 1176.

52. Johannes: "Aber das erste was ich im ledigen Brüder Chor, als einen Anfang des schlimmen Periodi angemerkt habe, das war Anno 44, da ich in Marienborn war. Da waren etliche leichtsinnige Leute auf dem Herrnhaag um Christeln herum, die seine Unschuld misbrauchten." Single brothers' synod, 13th session, January 15, 1753, 289.

53. The verse was "Denn wir sind errettet aus aller Fährlichkeit" from Heinrich Bonn's "O wir armen Sünder," *Herrnhuter Gesangbuch*, no. 105, v. 5.

CHAPTER 4

1. "Mit heutiger Post wurde ein ernstliches Schreiben des Ordinarii wegen einiger eingerißenen Unordentlichkeiten in alle Hauptgemeinen expedirt." Congregational Accounts, February 11, 1749.
2. The letter has been published in German and English. See bibliography.
3. Minutes of special conference during Barby synod, 1750, 140v. Also see Spangenberg, *Declaration*, 100; Zinzendorf to Mag. Friedrich Christoph Steinhofer, London, March 24, 1749, R.20.C.31.c.141, UA.
4. Minutes of special conference during Barby synod, 1750, 142r.
5. On the white surplice, see Erbe, *Herrnhaag*, 189–95; Adelaide L. Fries, *Customs and Practices of the Moravian Church*, rev. ed. (Winston-Salem: Board of Christian Education and Evangelism, 1973), 34–36.
6. Report of single brothers' festival, Herrnhaag, May 2, 1748 (longer version).
7. Zinzendorf in Congregational Accounts, September 8, 1748, quoted in Erbe, *Herrnhaag*, 189, also 191; letter of reprimand, par. 10; Spangenberg, *Declaration*, 49.
8. "Something came over us with the holy surplices. With this dress our souls have a premonition of the future marriage with the side hole" (Es ist was in uns gefahren / Mit den heiligen Talaaren, / Bey der Tracht ahnt unsern Seelgen / Künfftge Ehe mit dem Höhlgen). Poem by Christian Renatus for Zinzendorf, Erdmuth Dorothea, and Anna Nitschmann [1748], R.20.E.36.7, UA.
9. Christel was buried wearing a surplice and with a laurel wreath on his head, perhaps in preparation for the heavenly marriage with Christ. Congregational Accounts, May 31, 1752.
10. "It is nothing unusual that young people in the world also adorn themselves like that and that young men wear white during parades [*Einzügen*] and other solemnities. The only difference is that we do it in the sense of a burial shroud [*Grabkittel*] that our dear Lamb was wearing as it appeared to his [disciple] John." Report of single brothers' festival, Herrnhaag, 1748 (shorter version).
11. Zinzendorf, in Congregational Accounts, September 8, 1748, quoted in Erbe, *Herrnhaag*, 189.
12. There is evidence Moravians wore surplices when having sexual intercourse. The sexual act was understood as an earthly representation of the heavenly unification of the soul with Christ. See Peucker, "In the Blue Cabinet," 23n64, 27.
13. On this day they celebrated the Feast of the Husband (*Mannesfest*). Diary single brothers Marienborn, December 4, 1748. Also see minutes of special conference during single brothers' synod in London, January 12, 1753, 348.
14. Volck, *Das entdeckte Geheimnis*, 4:500, 509.
15. In an address on March 2, 1757, Congregational Accounts; also printed in Zinzendorf, *Auszüge über die vier Evangelisten*, 1176.
16. "Thereafter some had a truly blessed and jolly love feast because of our dear Caillet's arrival in the congregation six years ago today" (Nach allen hatten einige ein recht selig und lustigs Liebesmahl wegen unsers lieben Caillets Ankunft zur Gemeine heute vor 6 Jahren). The redactor was not consistent, however, and left the word *lustig* in other entries such as November 2 and 9, 1748.
17. Minutes of special conference during Barby synod, 1750, 162r–v.
18. See Erbe, "Das Leben ein Spiel," *Herrnhaag*, chap. 18; Bettermann, *Theologie und Sprache*, 110–21.
19. Arnold, *Historie und Beschreibung*, 58.
20. To this day, Matthew 11:25 forms a central element of the Moravian Easter morning litany. On the Order of Fools (*Närrchenorden*), see Erbe, *Herrnhaag*, 58–63; D. Meyer, "Zinzendorf und Herrnhut," 49; Vogt, "'Headless and Un-erudite,'" 116. Zinzendorf also

used the English term "simpleton" (English poem on Christian Renatus, ca. 1750, PP Zdf 68, MAB).

21. Cranz, *Alte und neue Brüder-Historie*, 506. Zinzendorf had left the Wetterau on March 29, 1746; Johannes and Christel left for Zeist on May 6.

22. For example, Friedrich Oswald Geller to Johann Nitschmann, Marienborn, July 29, 1746. See below.

23. His memoir in *Nachrichten aus der Brüdergemeine* 44 (1862): 81–88. On Rubusch, also see Uttendörfer, "Zinzendorf und die Entwicklung," pt. 4, 29–33.

24. *Herrnhuter Gesangbuch*, no. 2251; contemporary English translation in *Collection of Hymns*, pt. 3, no. 110. On February 24, 1746, a hymn, "Was singen Creuzluft Vögelein," was "revised and nicely changed." This may well have been an earlier version of "Was macht ein Creuzluftvögelein" that was mentioned in the diary for the first time on March 19. Also see Erbe, *Herrnhaag*, 88–94. The differences between a Moravian "cross-air bird" and a Pietist were discussed at the synod in Herrnhaag in 1747.

25. *Herrnhuter Gesangbuch*, nos. 2204, 2218, 2224, 2226, 2229, 2231, 2245, 2246, 2255, 2263, 2270, 2275, 2277, 2280, 2282, 2284, 2288, 2289, 2292, 2293, 2294, 2301, 2305, 2309, 2312, 2313, 2318, 2319, 2328, 2336. The image of the *Creuzluftvögelein* originated in a song written by Christian Renatus in June 1744 (no. 2166). Zinzendorf used the image in a song written for Christian Renatus's birthday on September 19, 1745: "ein Creuz-luft-vögelein, kränkelnd vor liebes-pein nach Jesu Seiten-schrein," no. 2157.

26. Friedrich Oswald Geller to Johann Nitschmann, Marienborn, July 29, 1746.

27. Also see Bettermann, *Theologie und Sprache*, 55.

28. [Hecker], *Gespräch*, 38–39: "Und wenn man siehet in ihr (der Brüder) Haus, die Pietisterey ist raus."

29. Contemporary translation in Frey, *True and Authentic Account*, 17.

30. [Hecker], *Gespräch*, 19. On these cards, see Fogleman, *Jesus Is Female*, 80–82; Atwood, "Little Side Holes." Fogleman claims Moravians used these cards in the sexual instructions for married couples. Atwood believes the cards were teaching tools for children.

31. "Ich habe öffters gesehen, daß die verehlichten Brüder sich mit den ledgen Schwestern so familiar gemacht, daß sie einander aus einem Winkel in andern getrieben, gekitzelt, ja gar so lang als die Schwestern gewesen, haben sie sich lassen von Brüdern in die Erde hinlegen, wie es noch am vergangenen Freytag in der Mangelstube geschehen ist. Ich habe selbst gehört, daß die ledigen Schwestern erstaunlich raisoniret und gesagt: die Brüder sind viel ärger als die Buben auf der Gaße. Ich habe schon etliche mahl eine gewisse ledige Schwester abends angetroffen, daß sie hat auf einen gewißen Bruder aufgepaßt, bis er gekommen, um sich mit ins Spielen einzulaßen." Geller to Nitschmann, Marienborn, July 29, 1746.

32. Minutes of special conference during Barby synod, 1750, 151v, 145v.

33. Volck, *Das entdeckte Geheimnis*, 2:60–62.

34. Ibid., 2:85.

35. "Jeremias" (Risler?) to Br. Carstens in Lübeck, St. Petersburg, September 29, 1749, in *Acta Historico-Ecclesiastica oder gesammlete Nachrichten von den neuesten Kirchen-Geschichten* 13 (1750): 1053–55.

36. This hymn is "Seine heisse Schätzelküsse"; see chap. 6.

37. Volck, *Das entdeckte Geheimnis*, 4:479.

38. Contemporary translation in Frey, *True and Authentic Account*, 16–17.

39. Spangenberg related this at the special conference during the Barby synod in 1750: Minutes, 143v.

40. Diary single brothers Herrnhaag, December 22, 1746.

41. Zinzendorf, introduction to *Gemeinreden*, vol. 2.

42. The sermon was circulated in the handwritten Congregational Accounts (suppl. 13, 1747).

43. Circular letter by Zinzendorf with a postscript by Johannes to all congregations, January 12, 1747, R.3.A.8.11, UA; also PP Zdf 20, MAB. Also see Uttendörfer, "Zinzendorf und die Entwicklung," pt. 4, 21–25.

44. For example, Meyer claims Zinzendorf's ideal of childlikeness and playfulness was a reaction against the Enlightenment: "Die Herrnhaager Frömmigkeit war ein leidenschaftlicher Protest gegen einen rationalen Kopfglauben ohne Herz." D. Meyer, "Zinzendorf und Herrnhut," 80, also 49. On Zinzendorf and the Enlightenment, see Faull, "Faith and Imagination."

45. Minutes of Provincial Synod in Gnadenberg, 1750, 33.

46. Cammerhoff to Zinzendorf, May 22–24, 1747, PP CJF 2, MAB.

47. Atwood, *Community of the Cross*, 72. Also see Vogt, "'Headless and Un-erudite,'" 114–15; G. Meyer, "Die Epoche der Wetterau," 15; G. Meyer, "Einführung in die Sichtungszeit," viii–xi. Address by Zinzendorf on the ideal of childlikeness, August 1747, in *Homilien über die Wundenlitanei*, 389–99.

48. "Singet, springet, klöpfet in die Hände." The booklet was made by Friedrich von Watteville and is held in the *Stammbuchsammlung* of the Unity Archives.

49. Volck, *Das entdeckte Geheimnis*, 4:508. For the full quote, see chap. 5.

50. *Acta Historico-Ecclesiastica* 13 (1750): 959. See chap. 5 for more examples.

51. Address by Zinzendorf to single brothers in Marienborn about play, January 8, 1747, in Congregational Accounts, 1747, suppl. 13.

52. Frey, *True and Authentic Account*, 19n.

53. Arnold, *Historie und Beschreibung*, 57–61.

54. Greven, *Protestant Temperament*, 63.

55. Vogt, "'Headless and Un-erudite.'" Also see Uttendörfer, "Zinzendorf und die Entwicklung," pt. 3, 5–11; Faull, "Faith and Imagination," 30.

56. Arnold, *Historie und Beschreibung*, 57–61.

57. "1) Die Brüder welche ihren Kopf ums Seitenhöhlgen laßen könnten, solten nach ihrem Herzen handeln und in Br. Rubusch Stube gehen, die 2) die wohl ihr Pläzgen im Seitenhöhlgen wußten, aber doch noch drum verlegen waren, gingen in Br. Gammerns Stube, die 3) die ihr Plätzgen noch nicht so ganz drinnen hätten blieben auf dem Saal. Die mittelste Claße war die stärckeste." Diary single brothers Herrnhaag, January 8, 1747.

58. "[W]o lauter unköpfligte Leute darauf waren; theils hatten [sie] ihre Köpfe untern Armen, theils in der Dasche [Tasche] und untern Füssen." Diary single brothers Herrnhaag, September 25, 1747.

59. "Abends hielt Christelein abermals den Abendmahlsbrüdern eine allerliebste Viertelstunde und redete unter andern davon, wie es der Heiland gerne sähe, wenn wir mit Seinem Seitenhöhlchen recht menschlich craß und ohne Kopf und Verstand umgingen und unsre Hütte participire davon wirklich." Diary single brothers Herrnhut, July 29, 1748.

60. The daily watchwords, or *Losungen*, were Bible texts, chosen for each day and printed in a new edition for every year.

61. Hart's report is quoted in [Hecker], *Gespräch*, 26–27. The congregational and choir diaries often give an indication of the topic of the addresses held each day. Zinzendorf's discourses were published in the Congregational Accounts.

62. "Ueber die Biebel haben die Pilger manchmal gelacht und kurtzweil damit getrieben." Bothe, *Zuverläßige Beschreibung*, 1:14.

63. Rhode, *Schlüssel zu Herrnhut*, 390–1.

64. Volck, *Das entdeckte Geheimnis*, 5:547. Lewis Bayly, *The Practice of Piety, directing a Christian, how to walk, that he may please God* (1613), was translated into German: *Praxis Pietatis: Das ist Übung der Gottseligkeit* (1st ed. 1628). See Jan van de Kamp, "Die Einführung der christlichen Disziplinierung des Alltags in die deutsche evangelische Erbauungsliteratur durch Lewis Baylys Praxis Pietatis (1628)," *Pietismus und Neuzeit* 37 (2011): 11–19.

65. Frey, *True and Authentic Account*, 19–20. Frey is quoting Caillet, who, in the original German, supposedly said, "denn die Biebel wäre ein solcher Quarck, daß man möchte darüber ausspeyen" (quoted in Volck, *Das entdeckte Geheimnis*, 4:396).
66. Schneider, "Understanding the Church," 26–28.
67. Sheehan, *Enlightenment Bible*, 64–85.
68. Ibid., 110.
69. *Collection of Hymns*, pt. 3, no. 398; Zinzendorf, *Homilien über die Wundenlitanei*, 140–51.
70. Zinzendorf, *Homilien über die Wundenlitanei*, 149–51. Also see Kaiser, *Zinzendorfs Schriftverständnis*.
71. Diary Herrnhut, January 29, 1749.
72. Bettermann, *Theologie und Sprache*, passim; Vogt, "'Honor to the Side'"; Vogt, "Gloria Pleurae!"; Atwood, "Understanding Zinzendorf's Blood and Wounds Theology"; Atwood, *Community of the Cross*, chap. 7.
73. Point 1 and point 17 of the letter of reprimand, respectively.
74. Address by Zinzendorf to Bethlehem congregation, n.d. (1749 or later), PP Zdf 24, MAB.
75. Private conference about the title of "Papa," Barby, September 1, 1750, R.2.A.28.A.1, 56; minutes of special conference during Barby synod, September 26, 1750, 151v. About the idea of the side wound as the birthplace of souls, see Bettermann, *Theologie und Sprache*, 82–88. Vogt, "'Honor to the Side,'" 94.
76. Vogt, "'Honor to the Side,'" 91, 99.
77. See above.
78. Diary single brothers Herrnhaag, April 8, 1746.
79. "Die Lehre dieses Jahrs ist das Seitenhöhlgen gewesen." Zinzendorf during the night watch service on New Year's Eve, December 31, 1747, in Congregational Accounts.
80. Description of the celebration in the Congregational Accounts and in the diary of the single brothers in Herrnhaag, March 31, 1747. There are some differences between the two descriptions. Also see Schellinger's hymn in *Herrnhuter Gesangbuch*, no. 1883.
81. Diary single brothers Herrnhaag, September 19, 1747.
82. Diary Herrnhaag congregation, September 20, 1747.
83. See the line in the *Te Sponsam* liturgy: "'Cause in the Rock-hole sits the Dove, / And that Lion her Guard doth prove" (*Collection of Hymns*, pt. 3, no. 95; *Herrnhuter Gesangbuch*, no. 1882, v. 12). More on this symbolism and on the display in Marienborn (including a drawing) in Peucker, "Kreuzbilder und Wundenmalerei," 148–49.
84. Vogt, "'Honor to the Side,'" 98–103.
85. Ibid., 102–3.
86. Ibid., 96.
87. "Br. Rubusch held the meetings about the right way of being a sinner and that no man can be [a right sinner] than by the wounds and by the delight in the wounds" (Br. Rubusch hilt die Haußviertelstunde und eingerichtete [Viertelstunde] von dem rechten Sündersein und daß es kein Mensche sein kann, als ders durch die Wunden geworden und durch deßelben Genuß in den Wunden, etc.). Diary single brothers Herrnhaag, June 27, 1746.
88. Frey, *True and Authentic Account*, 19.
89. Diary single brothers Herrnhaag, June 15, 1746.
90. Also see Erbe, "Herrnhaag," 44.
91. Also see Bynum, *Wonderful Blood*, 14: "The body parts of Christ and the saints represented in devotional images and reliquaries are synecdoches for the whole person—indeed, for the glorified person."
92. The report of this day exists in two versions: a longer, more detailed version and a shorter, edited version that was published in the Congregational Accounts (see bibliography).

The editor was probably Zinzendorf, who tried to tone down the enthusiast language and theology. Other descriptions are found in [Hecker], *Gespräch*, 47–50, and Volck, *Das entdeckte Geheimnis*, 4:435–46. The account published by Hecker is surprisingly accurate, including details not found in the Moravian report.

93. Erbe, *Herrnhaag*, 133, 145.

94. Written by Johannes von Watteville. *Herrnhuter Gesangbuch*, no. 2307; *Collection of Hymns*, pt. 3, no. 52.

95. "Der vielfältige Heiland / von dem man sang weiland, / ist mit allen seinen Wunden / im Höhlgen verschwunden." The text of this hymn is not found in the *Herrnhuter Gesangbuch* or in the *Collection of Hymns*. Unlike the English translations of other hymns in this section, this is my translation.

96. Diary single brothers Herrnhaag, March 26, 1747.

97. "Der ganze blutige Heiland mit allen seinen Wunden und unser ganzer Chorplan und Erfahrung werde im Seitenhöhlchen als in einem *compendio* zusammengebracht." Diary single brothers Herrnhut, August 5, 1748. Similarly, Zinzendorf stated in the introduction to the *Gemeinreden*, "The holy side of Jesus is a central point from where one can deduct everything spiritual" (n.p.). Also see *Herrnhuter Gesangbuch*, no. 2343, v. 1: "Among us people of the cross, the side hole often passes for the entire Lamb" (Bey uns creutz-leutelein / gilt oft der seiten-schrein / fürs ganze Lämmelein).

98. Johannes von Watteville's address to the single brothers in Marienborn, March 4, 1750.

99. "[D]aß sie diese letzter [die Seiten-Wunde Christi] vor die Gebärmutter der Gläubigen ausgeben, und derselben Oefnung als eine Abbildung [d]es weiblichen Geburtsgliedes ansehen, und aus dem Grunde in den Unterleib zu versetzen gesucht, und mit dem Ausdruck der Lende benant." S. J. Baumgarten, *Theologische Bedencken*, 6. Sammlung, 2nd ed. (Halle, 1753), 788–89. Zinzendorf was obviously referring to the first edition from 1748. On Baumgarten, see Sorkin, *Religious Enlightenment*, chap. 3.

100. Bothe describes how for many young, "but also many older," Moravians the image of the side wound ("a mere painted bloody thing"), in combination with the teaching of the similarity of the female gender with the corpse of the Savior, caused many "disgusting imaginations" (*Zuverläßige Beschreibung*, 1:17–18).

101. Zinzendorf spoke about how both male and female genitalia were sanctified through the incarnation: "Die Schwestern haben das klare und unwiedersprechliche Bild von der heiligen Seite Jesu, die ihm am Creuz geöffnet worden, da er unsre Seelen herausgeboren hat" (Congregational Accounts, May 14, 1748). The idea was already expressed in a hymn from 1744 (*Herrnhuter Gesangbuch*, no. 1944). Zinzendorf never abandoned his belief that women bore the "image" of Christ on their bodies; see, e.g., address by Zinzendorf to single sisters in Herrnhut, December 29, 1759, PP Zdf 106, no. 12, MAB.

102. "Alle Küsse, die ich meiner Gemeine geben werde, die sollst du tausendfach kriegen; alle Umarmungen, die sollen auf dich concentrirt seyn. Ich will mit einer jeden Schwester in specie ausreden. Ich will ein jedes in mein Ehetempel, ins Höhlchen hinein nehmen und will es so küssen, so umarmen, so embrassiren, und ich will einer jeden ledigen Schwester ihr Hüttchen und Seelgen in mein Hüttchen und Seelchen hineinnehmen und ich will mich so mit ihnen einlassen, als es noch nie gewesen." Address by Christian Renatus to single sisters in Herrnhaag, May 4, 1748. The copy in the Unity Archives (Hs. 49) was edited and corrected by Zinzendorf. For example, he changed the word *Ehetempel* (marital temple) into *Chyram* (from the Greek χειρας, cleft, fissure, slit).

103. "Ach Seitenhöhlgen, umfasse ein jedes Selgen, umfange dies Chor in diesem Augenblick, und mache es in diesem Moment wie Elisa. Wir wollen das Kind sein, lege dich über einen jeden ledigen Bruder gestreckt, auf ein jedes Glied eines jeden ledigen Bruders, fahre in das ganze Geäder des ledigen Brüderchores hinein und durchwalle, durchfahre, durchleibe und

durchseele dieses ganze Chor so entsetzlich, so unbeschreiblich und doch so bräutgamsehelich, als wirs noch nie empfungen, als wirs nie göttlicher empfinden werden, wenn wir dich auch einmal leiblich sehen werden." Report of single brothers' festival, Herrnhaag, 1748.

104. The image of Elisha had appeared already in the Litany of Wounds (1744): "O ye five holy Wounds, / Do unto us as Elishah did unto the Child!" Zinzendorf, *Homilien über die Wundenlitanei*, 282–84. Also see Atwood, *Community of the Cross*, 167, 206–7. Marsha Keith Schuchard points out that Kabbalists as well as Scottish and Jacobite masons used the image of Elisha lying on top of the widow's son in their rituals. Schuchard, *Why Mrs. Blake Cried*, 43–44, 352n32.

Zinzendorf connected the image with Song of Songs 8:6 and explained it as a prayer to be "glued" together with Christ and unified with him. McGinn, "Mysticism and Sexuality." For an overview of sexual metaphors used in other religions, see Götz, "Sex and Mysticism." McGinn speaks about the "lived erotic paradox" in Christian mysticism: Christian mystics used highly sexual language to describe the ineffable, while at the same time avoiding any sexual activity (51). This paradox does not apply to Moravians during the mid-eighteenth century: Moravians did not abstain from sex, but they incorporated bridal mysticism into their ideas of human sexuality.

105. *Collection of Hymns*, pt. 3, no. 398. German: "O ihr heiligen fünf Wunden, / Machts wie Elisa, wir wollen daß kind seyn." *Herrnhuter Gesangbuch*, no. 1949.

106. Hessel-Robinson, "Erotic Mysticism"; Long, *Eucharistic Theology*; Winship, "Behold the Bridegroom Cometh!"; Godbeer, *Sexual Revolution*, chap. 2.

107. Diary single brothers Herrnhut, October 7, 1745.

108. "Abends hatten wir eine sehr geseegnete Arbeiter-Conferentz und Rubusch redete vieles von der ehlichen Umgang des Lammes." Ibid., February 18, 1746. "Das der Heyland mit den Abendmahls-Brüdern dahin arbeitete, wie er sie zu rechten verliebten Herzel im Heyland machen könnte, und daß einen rechten Abendmahls-Bruder sein müste wie ein Mann (und das viel mehr) gegen seine Frau." Ibid., May 9, 1746.

109. "Wir könnten jetzt nicht nur unsere Finger in seine Nägel und unsre Hand in seine Seite legen, sondern würden so gar von ihm erkannt und von seinen Schweiß und Leichnams-Dunst durchgangen und kämen in die allernächste und wesentliche Vereinigung mit seiner Person." Diary single brothers Herrnhaag, April 14, 1747.

110. Hessel-Robinson, "Erotic Mysticism," 97. Also see Godbeer, *Sexual Revolution*, 79.

111. Although the original was destroyed by fire in 1945, a nineteenth-century (partial) copy survives. See chap. 10.

112. "In the evening, after everything else, our dear heart Renatus held a separate quarter hour for the communicant brothers because we had not had a congregational Communion in a long time. He hoped that each brother, despite the deprivation of the sacramental joy of the flesh and blood of our dear Lamb, we could still eat and drink his fill from his [the Lamb's] side hole" (Abends nach allem hielt unser allerliebstes Herzel Renatus allen Abendmahlsbrüdern eine aparte Abendmahlsviertelstunde, weil wir lange kein Gemeinabendmahl gehabt und wünschte dabei herzlich, daß ein jeder Bruder bei Entbehrung des sacramentlichen Genusses des Fleisches und Blutes unsers Lämmlein dennoch täglich, stündlich und momentlich sich möge satt essen und trinken aus seinem Seitenhöhlchen). Diary single brothers Herrnhut, May 31, 1748.

113. Schneider, "Understanding the Church," 28.

114. "Afterwards Br. Rubusch spoke about the marriage with our husband, not only during Communion but also daily, yea, every hour we get something to live on" (Nach derselben [sprach] der Br. Rubusch von Verehligung mit unserm Manne und das nicht nur bey Abendmahlen, sondern so täglich, ja stündlich so was zu zehren zu krigen). Diary single brothers Herrnhaag, June 6, 1746. "During the congregational quarter hour Br. Johannes spoke about the necessity of the daily joy of His flesh and blood for each active new creature" (In der Ge-

meinviertelstunde redete Br. Johannes bey Gelegenheit des heutigen Wort des Heylands von der Nothwendigkeit des täglichen Genußes seines Fleisches und Blutes bey einem jeden lebendigen neuen Creatürlein"). Ibid., June 6, 1747.

115. "Nach derselben hielt [Christel] den Abendmahlsbrüdern eine aparte Viertelstunde und redete von dem zärtlichen und einfältigen realen Umgang mit dem allerliebsten Seitenhöhlchen, wie man das im Seitenhöhlchen drinne sein nicht geistlich zu verstehen habe, sondern realiter mit Leib und Seele hineinfahren dürfe und könne." Diary single brothers Herrnhut, July 28, 1748.

116. "Unsre Hütte werde so wesentlich eingeseelt, eingeleibt und eingegeistet von unsers Mannes Seele, Leib und Geist, daß es in der vollendeten Gemeine kaum vollkommener und ganzer sein könne." Ibid., July 29, 1748.

117. The following day, Christian Renatus "spoke of the equality between us and our husband, beginning from the moment when a dear heart can believe and feel: 'That moment when the side was cut, I—Hallelujah!—sprang thereout.' That's when the husband frames himself so thoroughly into us that we become side holes and the side hole becomes us, etc." (redete von der Egalität zwischen uns und unserm Mann, die von der Zeit angehet, da ein Herzel das glauben und fühlen kann: 'Momentlich, da der Stich geschah, da fuhr ich raus, Halleluja!' Da cörpert sich der Mann so wesentlich in uns nein, daß wir zu Seiten und das Seitelein zu uns wird, etc.). Ibid., July 30, 1748. The last line is a quote from *Herrnhuter Gesangbuch*, no. 2336; *Collection of Hymns*, pt. 3, no. 159.

118. "After all that, the communicant brothers had a separate quarter hour during which Christel wished that because they had so few [celebrations of] choir Communion, the Savior as their husband might replace it with his daily embraces and his manly presence so that each day and moment could have its own meal from the side hole" (Nach allem hatten wieder die Abendmahlsbrüder eine aparte Viertelstunde, worin ihnen Christel wünschte, daß weil sie so wenig Chorabendmahl hatten, sie sichs möchten vom Heiland ihrem Mann, mit seinen täglichen Umarmungen mit seiner mannhaften Nähe ersetzen lassen, so daß jeder Tag und Augenblick seine eigene Mahlzeit aus dem Seitenhöhlchen haben möge). Diary single brothers Herrnhaag, July 31, 1748.

119. "The side hole will inflame and infect our bodies so much that every vein will be pervaded and infected by his man's blood so that we may contaminate one another, with eyes full of man's eyes and with hearts full of marital joy from the Side Hole" (Das Seitenhölchen inflammire und infiscire unsre Hütte so, daß jedes Aederchen von seinem Mann-Geblüte durchzogen und infisciret würde, daß wir einander damit anstecken könnten, mit Augen voll Manns-Augen, mit Herzen voll Ehegenusses aus dem Seitenhöhlchen). Ibid., July 29, 1748.

120. "Das sind die Hüttenseligkeiten, die besonders in diesem 1748ten Jahre im ledigen Brüderchore angehen, die das Seitenhöhlchen unsern Hüttchen auch will zu genießen geben." Ibid. This seems to be a different understanding than the "inner, spiritual form of Communion" that radical Pietists like Hochmann von Hochenau promoted instead of the traditional celebrations of Communion in the "secular" churches. See Schneider, "Der radikale Pietismus im 18. Jahrhundert," 126.

121. "Nachdem wir diesen wichtigen Tag mit verschiedenen seligen Gelegenheiten, mit einer schönen Illumination ~~das kränkelnde und sterbende Hüttlein vorstellend, worauf das ganze Chor an das xxxx fertigte Grab fuhr xxxx xxxx überaus selige~~ obzwar kleines Abendmahl vor einige Arbeiter beschloßen." Diary single brothers Marienborn, May 2, 1749.

122. Diary Paedagogium in Peilau, September 20, 1749.

123. On Zinzendorf's ideas about the Sabbath, see Vogt, "Zinzendorf's Theology of the Sabbath."

124. "During the Bible study Rubusch told us that our choir would soon be transformed into a swarm of bees [circling] around the dead corpse of Jesus because everything already began to come to life" ([Rubusch] hilt uns eine Bibelstunde, das unser Chor bald in einen Bienenschwarm

um die todte Leiche Jesu werde verwandelt werden, weil schon alles lebendig an zu werden fing [anfing zu werden]). Diary single brothers Herrnhaag, April 15, 1746.

125. "[Johannes] hilt allen Chören eine Viertelstunde. Unsre war die letzte aber recht safftig und schmackhafftig von der Leiche und deßen Dunst, Tufft und Creuzes-Luft, Wunden und Närbgen." Diary single brothers Herrnhaag, November 27, 1746.

126. Congregational Accounts, March 31, 1747.

127. "Durch seine wahre Effluvia und Ausdünstungen, durch die Luft aus dem Stein Ritz würden alle fleischliche Lüste und falsche Regungen und Ausdünstungen in uns ausgetrocknet. Besonders aber geschehe das, wenn sich unser Mann mit seinem todtkalten Leichnam Glied vor Glied über uns breite, bey der heiligen Communion in uns eingehe und aus dem noch übrigen Viertel Erdschwamm den Gift nach und nach vollends heraus ziehe und unsere Hütten seiner Leiche ähnlich mache." Address by Zinzendorf during *Singstunde* on Good Friday, March 31, 1747, in Congregational Accounts.

128. These lines were sung separately, but in the hymnal they only appear as part of longer hymns: *Herrnhuter Gesangbuch*, nos. 2255, 2283, and 2335. A more extensive version is to be found in the Congregational Accounts of August 13, 1748. The English translation is in *Collection of Hymns*, pt. 3, no. 126.

129. *Collection of Hymns*, pt. 2, no. 398.

130. Communion was sometimes called "the unification with the Savior's corpse" (die Vereinigung mit des Heilandes Leichnam). Address by Zinzendorf to single brothers in London, February 1, 1749, PP Zdf 95, MAB; Breul, "Ehe und Sexualität," 411.

131. Addresses by Zinzendorf, September 21 and December 13, 1747, respectively, in Congregational Accounts.

132. Matt. 27:60; Mk. 15:46; Lk. 23:53.

133. For examples, see the hymn texts in chap. 5.

134. "One cannot sin, one is dead. The members, which are on earth, are dead. The sinful members are deadened. One cannot sin because the old man was buried into Christlikeness, into a Christlike nature that is incompatible with sinning" (Man kan nicht sündigen, man ist tod. Die Glieder, die auf Erden sind, die sind tod. Die Sündenglieder sind gesterbt. Man kan nicht sündigen, denn der alte Mensch ist begraben in die Jesushaftigkeit, in die Jesushafte Natur, mit der ist das Sündethun incompatible). Address by Zinzendorf at single brothers' festival, Herrnhut, May 10, 1748, PP Zdf 94, MAB.

135. Diary single brothers Herrnhaag, September 27, 1749. Johannes wrote to Christel about Heithausen: "The period after your departure, when Heithausen was apostle and head, was an especially unblessed time" (Herrnhaag, March 3, 1750).

136. Zinzendorf in introduction to the *Zugaben* (supplements) to the hymnal, quoted in Hahn and Reichel, *Zinzendorf*, 170–71.

137. See James Hutton, quoted in Benham, *Memoirs of James Hutton*, 563. Also see Erbe, *Herrnhaag*, 58–59.

138. Interestingly, the word *Seitenhöhlchen* is crossed out in the copy at the Bethlehem archives. Later that year, Zinzendorf complained to Bethlehem: "Dear Brothers and Sisters. I read so much about the *Seitenhölchen*. Don't you know my letter to the congregations from February 10, 1749 and the warning I gave regarding such expressions?" Letter by Zinzendorf to Bethlehem congregation, n.d. (1749 or later), PP Zdf 24, MAB. Was it possibly Johannes von Watteville, who continued to use the term in his letters to Europe, who did not see the point in prohibiting the use of the word *Seitenhöhlchen*?

139. Minutes of special conference during single brothers' synod in London, January 12, 1753, 349.

140. "Er wird an dem heutigen Tag ein jedes Seelgen unter ihnen so durchleiben, durchseelen und durchgeistern, als es noch nie geschehen. Er sagt heute zu seinem Jungfernchor: Ich weiß, daß du mich lieb hast, ich habe was gutes an dir gefunden. Ich habe die Zärtlichkeit, die

du gegen mich hast, das ganze Jahr durchgefühlet. Ich habe mit den Seitenhölgens-Seeligkeiten, die ich in die Gemeine habe fliessen lassen, recht in dein Chor können eindringen. Du hast alles aufgefangen, ja auch ein Tröpflein kleine hat das Chor so seelig, so manneshafftig gemacht, wie mans jetzt sieht." Address by Christian Renatus to single sisters in Herrnhaag, May 4, 1748.

141. "So fängt jetzt die ganze Gemeine an, Kindersprache zu reden, Kindergefühl zu kriegen, Kinder-Eheherzel zu haben, Kinderehelichkeiten im Innersten ihres Herzens mit dem Manne zu haben. Und ein ander Cabinet, ein ander Ehebett, das nicht gekindert ist, lassen wir nicht passiren. Ihr seid im Cabinet, im Ehebett, und wer von der Gemeine hinein will, müß als Kind hinein, wer von den Chören hinein will, muß als ein Kind hinein, ein jedes Seelchen muß als ein Kindlein, als ein unschuldiges Kindelein in den Windeln, als ein Dingel, das noch nicht denken kann, noch nicht recht hören, noch nicht recht sehen, noch nicht recht fühlen, noch nicht recht essen kann als Brei, und das zur Not." Address by Christian Renatus to the children in Herrnhaag, December 28, 1748. The cabinet was the room where couples had sex.

142. "Seht ihr Kinder, die Gnade habt ihr vor allen großen Leuten, vor allen großen Gemeingeschwister zum Voraus. Und wenn ein Kind, ein solch klein Schätzelein wie Ihr seid, nicht im Ehebett wahrhaftig liegt mit Geist, Leib und Seele, so kann man die Ursach gewiß nicht beschreiben und auch nicht sagen. Denn ihr seid dazu predestinirt, ihr seid dazu geblütet, ihr seid dazu geseelet und seid dazu gehüttet, und alle eure Gedanken sind ehelich, alle eure Sinne ehelich, all euer Gefühl ist ehelich, und je größer ein Kindel wird, je mehr hats nötig wieder umzudrehen und zu werden, wie es in der allerkleinsten Kindheit war." Ibid.

143. Uttendörfer quotes discourses by Rubusch from September 17, 20, and 23, 1747, from R.8.33.f in "Zinzendorf und die Entwicklung," pt. 4, 31–33.

144. "Mein liebes, liebes, liebes, allerliebstes Herzel Hasse! Ich habe dich lieb und meine Herzel, die dich alle recht zärtlich grüßen und küßen lassen, grüsse und küße ja alles von mir, das mich kennt und lieb hat, doch besonders das, was Seitenhöhlgen lieb hat und befuhrt, befühlt, beschmeckt, betrieft, bekuckt, behorcht, beliegt, bekriecht, bebettet, betistet, be-ißt und betrinckt. Grüße ja die ganze Urbsche Gemeine von mir, ich hab sie lieb." Rubusch to Matthias Hasse, Lindheim, June 22, 1747, R.21.A.62.95, UA.

145. "Ihr wißt, was ich vor Liebhaber, Verehrer und Anbeter des allerliebstes Seitenhöhlgens bin und gewiß mit euch ein abgesagter Feind von allem, was nicht daheraus und dahinein geht. Denn alles andere ist Stuß, ist Stuß, ist Stuß. Es mag auch so schön, so hübsch, so nothwendig seyn, wie es will, so sage ich, es ist Stuß. Aber was daheraus kommt, sind lauter Delicatessen, fette, feiste Mahlzeiten, Gnaden und Seeligkeiten, die man eßen und trinken kan, ja die man gebraten, gebacken, gekocht, gesuppt, gelöffelt, gestößelt, gegabelt, gemeßert, und getellert haben kan, nach dem man einen guten verdaulichen Magen, Ader, Herz, Geschmack und Gout hat. Ich bin immer vor das Beste." Rubusch to Buntebart und Matthias Hasse, Herrnhaag, October 27, 1747, R.21.A.62.96, UA.

CHAPTER 5

1. Congregational Accounts, June 17, 1747. One copy in the Bethlehem archives mistakenly has "Liebesstreit" instead of "Liederstreit." For the hymn Christian Renatus sang, see *Collection of Hymns*, pt. 3, no. 58; original in *Herrnhuter Gesangbuch*, no. 2281.

2. See Bunners, "Musik"; Bunners, "Gesangbuch."

3. Bunners, "Pietismus und kirchliches Lied," 230.

4. Zinzendorf at the dedication of the new English Moravian hymnbook, September 2, 1754, in Congregational Accounts.

5. "Ein Lied ist keine ordinaire, sondern eine erhabene Rede, da die Seele mit einer mehr als ordinairen und aufgeschwungenen Repraesentation Gottes oder der himmlischen, sacramentlichen und Kirchen-Materien erfüllt ist." Ibid.

6. For example, the day before the departure of Brother Kaschke from Bethlehem to Surinam, Nathanael Seidel randomly picked hymns for each brother present at his farewell love feast (diary single brothers Bethlehem, March 22, 1745). This is a Moravian variation on the Pietist custom of bibliomancy.

7. The blood verses represent the actual blood as it was put on the doorframes by the Israelites in Egypt (Exod. 12); also see Ezekiel 45:18–20. Nathanael Seidel picked the verses a few days later. Diary single brothers Bethlehem, July 3 and 9, 1745. For a similar example in Herrnhaag, see Cröger, *Geschichte der erneuerten Brüderkirche*, 2:181n.

8. Zinzendorf asked, "Was bedeutet aber das, was in Christels Diario vom Begraben steht? So ein Begräbniß ist auch hier in London in Thakers Garten gewesen." Johann Gottlob Königsdörfer answered: "Der Sinn dabey war, daß alle vorige Sachen, die zu dem Periodo gehörten, begraben seyn solten, und es wurden auch die geschriebne Lieder auf eine Art begraben, die aber wieder herausgenommen und danach solenniter verbrant wurden." Minutes of special conference during single brothers' synod in London, January 12, 1753, 350.

9. Diary Herrnhut, February 22, 1749. Before hymns were published, Zinzendorf edited them.

10. Diary single brothers Herrnhut, December 15, 1749.

11. Bothe, *Zuverlässige Beschreibung*, 1:19. Also see 2:55.

12. Minutes of special conference during Barby synod, September 26, 1750, 144r.

13. J. Reichel, *Dichtungstheorie und Sprache*, 15–18; Weinlick, *Count Zinzendorf*, 200.

14. See above.

15. The titles are "Ich lebe frey und ungebunden" (June 8, 1748); "Ach Eh-Manns Einsamkeit" (November 16, 1748); the tune "Schweigt, Schweigt" (December 22, 1748); "Ehre dem rothen Mund" (December 31, 1748); "Ach dieser G——ist zu geheim, b——unser Ehbett——Gebein" (April 16, 1749, few words illegible); and "Salve, Salve, Ihre Wüsteneyen" (May 8 and June 1 and 21, 1749). Diary Theological Seminary in Marienborn.

16. "Im Singen praevaliren eben nicht nur ins ganze die bekante Verse von der ehelichen Connexion mit dem Manne, sondern noch viel andere, welche von denen in der fleischlichen Lustbarkeit und Schanden der Welt gewohnten und vom Satan aufgebrachten Red-Arten, Liedgen und Melodien, auf unser Objectum transformirt und mit einer Verliebtheit, welche rasend glüht (so ist der Ausdruck selbst in einem Psalm) bey mancherley, auch den wichtigsten Gelegenheiten gebraucht werden." Mag. Friedrich Christoph Steinhofer to Zinzendorf, Stuttgart, March 14, 1749, R.20.C.31.c.140, UA. Friedrich Christoph Steinhofer (1706–1761), a Lutheran minister, was in close contact with the Moravians between 1731 and 1748.

17. Volck, *Das entdeckte Geheimnis*, 5:535–36.

18. Ibid., 5:538–41, 6:696–704; Bothe, *Zuverlässige Beschreibung*, 2:47–55; *Acta Historico-Ecclesiastica* 13 (1750): 959–62. Fourteen hymn verses are printed here, quoted from a letter by an unnamed single man in Herrnhaag to his sister, dated July 21, 1748.

19. Bothe, *Zuverlässige Beschreibung*, 1:18.

20. Volck, *Das entdeckte Geheimnis*, 6:694–704. Philipp Samuel Nonhebel (1733–1800) was the son of Johann Jacob Nonhebel and Angelica Elisabeth, née Roha, who married Daniel Adolph von Ravenstein in 1746 after her first husband died. Philipp Samuel died in Neudietendorf.

21. Bothe, *Zuverlässige Beschreibung*, 1:19. Also see 2:55.

22. On the criticism of contemporaries regarding Pietist hymn tunes, see McMullen, "Melodien geistlicher Lieder." Spangenberg defended the use of secular tunes in *Declaration*, 33–34.

23. Volck, *Das entdeckte Geheimnis*, 5:537.

24. Anna Catharina Höffly was born in Bern on October 28, 1709, and died in Herrnhut on March 26, 1774. She joined the Moravians in 1741 and taught music to the single sisters in Herrnhut and Herrnhaag. See her *Lebenslauf*, R.22.61.38, UA, also in Congregational Accounts

1774, suppl. 9, I.7. The tune book is among the tune books in the library of the UA, NB. IV.R.1.51.51, H.4. A tune book contains the musical arrangement and title of each tune.

25. A selection of these hymns with their tunes has been published in Peucker, "Songs of the Sifting," 73–87.

26. McGinn traces the image of the divine flowing within the Trinity to David of Augsburg: "This dynamic picture . . . was to have a long history in German mysticism." McGinn, *Presence of God*, 3:116.

27. On the image of the bird (*Kreuzluftvögelein*) in Moravian poetry, see Dohm, *Poetische Alchimie*, 341–346. Also see Erbe, *Herrnhaag*, 88–94.

28. See Zedler, *Grosses vollständiges Universal-Lexicon*, s.v. "charmiren."

29. Compare the seventh stanza of Philipp Nicolai's "Wie schön leuchtet der Morgenstern": "Er wird mich noch zu seinem Preiß aufnehmen in das Paradeis; des klopf ich in die Hände."

30. "Liedbüchlein," no. 22: "Dran kennen wir uns gleich: man wird wie Wachs so weich." For examples of melting (*liquifactio*) in the works of medieval mystics, see McGinn, *Presence of God*, vol. 3; see index under symbols, mystical.

31. Petry, *Late Medieval Mysticism*, 47.

32. "Bräutgam, mein ewger Mann, der ohne mich nichts mehr tun kann." "Liedbüchlein," no. 13.

33. "Geküßt, geküßt muss seyn, ach rede mir nichts drein. Jetzt bistu ganz allein / für mich, mein Schätzelein." Ibid., no. 5.

34. McGinn, *Presence of God*, 3:222–44, esp. 235–37. On the idea of the game of love in Moravian poetry, see Dohm, *Poetische Alchimie*, 350–51.

35. "Spiel nur, spiel, ich wil mit Thränen lachen, laß mich schlafen, du, mein Schatz, kanst wachen. Embrassir mich weil ich ruh, küß mir meine Äuglein zu." "Liedbüchlein," no. 30.

36. "So gehen wir mit ihm schlafen, weils ihm so wohlgefellt. 60 sind schon eine Waff um Bettelein bestellt. / Schlaft wohl, [6x] / 60 sind schon etc." Ibid., no. 65.

37. McGinn, *Presence of God*, 2:205–6.

38. Ibid., 205.

39. "[W]enn wir uns in Armen liegen / und so ineinander schmiegen, dass ein Geist, Fleisch und Gebein / wird aus uns, 2 Schätzelein." "Liedbüchlein," no. 26.

40. "Seit wir uns zusammen funden, so sind wir Bein von einem Bein, ja, Seel zu einem Seel verbunden. Ach, das mag eine Nähe seyn!" Ibid., no. 79. *Herrnhuter Gesangbuch*, no. 2342; *Collection of Hymns*, pt. 3, no. 148.

41. "Ich liege Ihm in seinen Armen / als sein verwehntes Lieblinglein. Will er mich küssen und umarmen, bin ich passiv sein Herzelein." "Liedbüchlein," no. 51.

42. "Bey uns heißts: genießt, genießt, / und bey ihm: geküßt, geküßt." Ibid., no. 31.

43. Also see Bloch, "Changing Conceptions," 19–20.

44. "Meine desparate Thränen, meine Liebesraserey, ist verkehrt in zartes sehnen, in passive Armuthey. Wil er mich auch nicht mehr küssen, ich bin sein verstummtes Schaaf, mag nichts wollen und nichts wissen, lieg ohnmächtig da im Schlaf." "Liedbüchlein," no. 54.

45. McGinn, *Presence of God*, 2:205–6. On mystical death in Bonaventure, see ibid., 3:110. On Porete, who distinguished three kinds of death, see ibid., 257–61. On *mors mystica* with Meister Eckhart, see ibid., 4:157, 179–81. On mystical death in Zinzendorf's works, see Dohm, *Poetische Alchimie*, 354–55.

46. "Daß wir uns am Krankenbett ergötzen, uns am brünstigsten am Grabe letzen / da wir in des Todes Wehn / wie im Wald spatzieren gehn." "Liedbüchlein," no. 71.

47. "Geschwister, unser Ruhebett / ist unsers Mannes Grabes Stätt, da legt sich Leib und Seel nein / schlaft wol, ruht, deckt sein Fleisch und Bein." Ibid., no. 72.

48. "Geküsset seist du allerseits vom ganzen Jünglingschore." Report of single brothers' festival, Herrnhaag, May 2, 1748 (longer version).

49. Bothe, *Zuverlässige Beschreibung*, 2:55.

50. *Acta Historico-Ecclesiastica* 13 (1750): 959. The following line from a hymn states that clapping is a *"Schätzel*-like" thing: "Klopfet, klopfet in die Händ, schätzelhaftig, ohne End."

51. Volck, *Das entdeckte Geheimnis*, 4:508.

52. On the idea of the permanent consumation of communion among Moravians, see Dohm, *Poetische Alchimie*, 357; and on the literal interpretation of biblical metaphors, ibid., 349.

CHAPTER 6

1. "Den 29ten [November 1748] gingen die Brr. zum Chor-Tage. Es ging ein neuer seliger———[crossed out, illegible] Periodus an vor die Arbeiter, Gehülfen und Praeparanten." Diary single brothers Marienborn. The *praeparands* were being prepared for an office within the choir.

2. David Schneider also mentions a "new period" in his Lebenslauf. This memoir burned with the congregational archives of Herrnhut in 1945 but is quoted by Uttendörfer, *Zinzendorf und die Mystik*, 280–81. Christian Hart mentions the new period as well: [Hecker], *Gespräch*, 50–51 (also see below).

3. Diary Herrnhaag, December 4, 1745. This festival can be documented until 1749.

4. As reported by Brother Andresen at a special conference during the single brothers' synod in London, January 12, 1753, 348: "During Communion on the Feast of the Husband at Herrnhaag there was a very special and blessed feeling. Our late Christel said with a strong voice and a profound feeling: The Lord is here! Which he repeated several times. It was as if the Savior had actually entered the hall. Several brethren and sisters turned around to see him" (Am Mannesfest anno 48 war beym Abendmahl aufm Herrnhaag ein ganz apartes und sehr seliges Gefühl. Unser seliger Christel sagte mit einer starken Stimme und einem durchdringenden Gefühl: Der Herr ist da! Und das wiederholte er etliche mal. Da war es auch nichts anders, als wenn der Heiland sichtbarlich in den Saal gekommen wäre und die Geschwister haben sich auch wirklich nach Ihn umgesehen). Also see diary single brothers Marienborn. On the red surplices, see above.

5. The meaning of this gender-changing event has only recently been recognized. Plitt was aware of Christian Hart's account and mentions it in his chapter on the Sifting Time (J. Plitt, "Denkwürdigkeiten," par. 246). Uttendörfer mentions it in his study on Zinzendorf and mysticism ("according to the latest absurd teaching all souls were sisters and therefore no difference [between the sexes] existed any longer") but failed to grasp the significance of the ceremony (*Zinzendorf und die Mystik*, 285). Fogleman refers to the Becker diary (*Jesus Is Female*, 89).

6. "Den 7. Dez. Nachdem Tags vorher die Brr. in Hhaag mit einem erstaunlichen Gefühl alle zu led. Schww. angenommen und declarirt worden, so haben wir diesen Abend diese erstaunliche Sache auch erfahren und sind von dem th. Ren. [inserted: "Rubusch und Caillet"] dazu eingesegnet worden mit Handauflegung. Es war Abd. Mhl und Fußwaschen; ich gieng mitten aus dem Fieber heraus und nach Bethlehem." Diary Johann Christoph Becker (1719–1789) (R.21.A.196, UA), December 7, 1748. "Bethlehem" is the name of one of the meeting halls in Marienborn. Becker's memoir is included in Congregational Accounts, 1789, suppl. 9.

7. "Den 6ten [December 1748] war wieder ein aussprechlich seliger Tag vor unser Chor. Nachmittags um 3 Uhr ging alles zum Chortag. ~~Das Seitenhöhlgen hat uns alle vor Schwestern declarirt, der Brüderschafft den Stab gebrochen und uns zu Schwestern eingeseegnet, und mit dem Essen und Trinken seines Seitenhöhlgens gesiegelt und zuletzt mit dem Fußwaschen beschlossen,~~ wobey Christelein Verse aus dem Herzen sang. Weil aber sehr wenige von unserm Hause haben bey der gestrigen Gelegenheit seyn können, so kamen die lieben Herzen Christel und Rubusch, etc. den 7ten hieher, und nach verschiedene Conferenzen gingen die Gelegenheiten an um 9 Uhr vor alle Abendmahlsbrüder, da das Seitenhöhlgen uns dasselbe wiederfahren lassen, was gestern aufm Herrnhaag geschehen." Diary single brothers Marienborn.

8. "Dieser Periodus ist fortgegangen bis 1749 [sic; 1748] im November als am Feste des Mannes oder Mannes-Feste, da die zwey Aeltesten der ledigen Brüder, der junge Herr Graf Christel und Rubusch, wiederum auf was neues kamen. Sie gaben vor, der Heiland hätte ihnen klar gemacht, daß die ledigen Brüder nicht mehr solten Brüder seyn, sondern er hätte sie zu ledigen Schwestern oder zu Jungfrauen declariret. Diese Sache einzurichten, wurde zu Herrenhaag erst eine Gelegenheit gemacht mit den Abendmahls-Brüdern, sie zu absolviren, ihnen alle ihre Sünden zu vergeben, sie seyen so groß, wie sie wolten, nicht allein, die geschehen, sondern auch, die noch geschehen würden. Der Jünglings-Bund und Jünglings-Punct wurde aufgehoben. Das Urtheil wurde gesprochen, alles alte, da man von Jüngling-Materien (*de cupiditatibus carnis*) geredet, für verflucht gehalten, und von Christel mit eigener Hand ein Stab gebrochen, das Urtheil gesprochen, so wären sie nun frey gesprochen von den sündlichen Lüsten. Darauf wurde geblasen und gesungen: Ehre der Urtheils-Stund, Ehre sey der Stund, Ehre sey der Stund, Ehre der Urtheils-Stund. Darauf fielen sie alle auf die Knie, die beyden Aeltesten segneten sich zuerst ein, Rubusch den Christel, Christel den Rubusch: diese beyde darauf alle übrige durch Hand-Auflegen, einen jeden zu Schwestern.... Es ist aber nachher auch in Zeyst auf eben den Fuß gekommen, denn der junge Herr Graf Christel ist selbst dahin gekommen und hat es auch so eingerichtet, wobey ich selbst gewesen. Er machte zwar die Ceremonie nicht mit dem Stabe und Verfluchen, wie vorhin gemeldet worden, aber die Classen wurden so eingerichtet wie in Herrenhaag." [Hecker], *Gespräch*, 50–52.

9. The Zeist single brothers' diary for 1749 does not mention the event. The diary is stripped of most of the typical language and style of the late 1740s and is most likely a later, revised replacement.

10. Marriage was not a sacrament for Zinzendorf (as in the Catholic tradition) but sexual intercourse was: "Marriage cannot be called a sacrament, but unification is a sacrament." Zinzendorf, *Haupt-Schlüssel*, 201.

11. "Lämmlein dein Seitelein, hat mich dein Sünderlein, gemacht zu deiner Braut, weil ich daraus erbaut, bin ich daß Bräutel dein, und du der Bräutgam mein." "Liedbüchlein," no. 83; and in *Acta Historico-Ecclesiastica* 13 (1750): 959–62.

12. "Tagtäglich nennt er mich sein Schätzel, sich selbst nennt er mein Schätzelein, ists gleich der Trockenheit ein Rätzel, mir geht es wie Zucker ein, ich liege ihm in seinen Armen als ein verwehntes Lieblinglein, wenn er will küssen und umarmen, bin ich paßiv sein Weibelein." *Acta Historico-Ecclesiastica* 13 (1750): 959–62; and in diary single brothers Herrnhut, June 22, 1748.

13. Two surviving letters by Christian Renatus and one by Rubusch bear this signature: Christian Renatus to Heinrich XXVIII Count Reuss, Heerendijk, September 30, 1748, R.20.B.18.a.30; Christian Renatus to Matthias Hasse, Zeist, October 11, 1748, R.21.A.62.121; Rubusch to Matthias Hasse, Herrnhaag, June 14, 1748, R.21.A.62.97, UA. Johannes von Watteville appears to have imitated this in a letter from America to Christian Renatus: "Was ich Dir aber nun von mir sagen kan, so bin ich Johannes vom Höhlgen, Johannes im Höhlgen, Johannes 3/4 Höhlgen," Long Island, September 17, 1748, R.21.A.183.e.II.409.b (see the extensive quotation from this letter in chap. 8).

14. Fogleman, *Jesus Is Female*, 74–86. In *The Protestant Temperament* Philip Greven links the concept of men being brides of Christ with confused gender identity among early modern American evangelicals, resulting in sexual frustration (124–40).

15. Fogleman, *Jesus Is Female*, 80.

16. Zinzendorf in Spangenberg, *Apologetische Schlußschrift*, 600, quoted in Vogt, "'Er ist Mann,'" 209.

17. Faull, "Christ's Other Self"; Faull, "Temporal Men."

18. Atwood, "'He Has Carried You My Members'"; Atwood, "Union of Masculine and Feminine." The Görlitz mystic Jacob Böhme (1575–1624) taught that Adam combined male and female qualities before the Fall. Because of his desire for the mortal woman Eve, Adam had lost this androgyny.

19. For example, "[Du] brauchst Vaterrecht, und zeigest Muttertreu," in "So führst du doch recht selig" by Gottfried Arnold; "Er deckt uns zu mit seiner Hand, wie eine Mutter tut" in "Es ist fürwahr nicht Menschenkunst" by Paul Gerhardt. Also see Roeber, *Hopes for Better Spouses*, 177. Mack calls the feminized Christ "actually a traditional element of Christian culture" (*Heart Religion*, 19).

20. "Er sey aber auch Mutter zu uns, nicht qua ... Gliedern seines Leibes." Address by Zinzendorf, January 14, 1748, in Congregational Accounts.

21. "Das ist die wirkliche und wahrhafte Geschichte unsrer Geneseos, ein Evangelium!," address by Zinzendorf to the married people, May 14, 1748, Congregational Accounts, suppl. 23. Zinzendorf also applied the image of the "woman in travail" in John 16:21 to Jesus.

22. Address by Zinzendorf, April 9, 1751, in Herrnhut, R.6.A.b.18, UA. This is what Faull calls "permeable masculinity that can enact femininity" ("Temporal Men," 57). The idea of the birthing Savior among Moravians can be found as early as 1746, when Rubusch, at a love feast for the birthday of Brother Gneuss, spoke about "the pregnancy of the Savior and what he would like to give birth to." Diary single brothers Herrnhaag, October 24, 1746. The medieval origins of the idea of Jesus as mother are discussed by Bynum, *Jesus as Mother*. The Society of Mother Eve believed in a birthing God through their leader, Eva von Buttlar (Temme, *Krise der Leiblichkeit*, 300–1). Faull, based on the work of Richard Godbeer, points out that Moravians, like others in early modern times, did not attach specific gender roles exclusively to one gender or the other (Faull, "Masculinity").

23. Zinzendorf, *Zeister Reden*, 208. Also see Zinzendorf's address on brethren as vice-Christs, in Congregational Accounts, 1747, suppl. 82 (not 83 as in Hahn and Reichel), quoted in Hahn and Reichel, *Zinzendorf*, 302. In 1752 he defended this concept again in Spangenberg, *Apologetische Schlußschrift*, 197–98, 598–603.

24. Atwood, "Sleeping in the Arms of Christ," 36; Atwood, *Community of the Cross*, 93; D. Meyer, *Der Christozentrismus*, 51; Faull, "Temporal Men," 64. Also see Ritschl, *Der Pietismus*, 2:369; G. Reichel, *Zinzendorfs Frömmigkeit*, 128–29.

25. Bynum, *Jesus as Mother*, 138; Matter, *Voice of My Beloved*, 141; McGinn, *Presence of God*, 3:169; McGinn, "Mysticism and Sexuality," 50; Godbeer, *Sexual Revolution*, 78–80.

26. Zinzendorf, *Zeister Reden*, 208.

27. Zinzendorf, *Gemeinreden*, 130; Zinzendorf, *Ein und zwanzig Discurse*, 152. Similar ideas are found in the works of Gottfried Arnold (*Geheimnis der göttlichen Sophia* [1700]), who believed in the restitution of an androgynous human being (*Mann-Weib*) after the old man had decayed in the grave (see Temme, *Krise der Leiblichkeit*, 321–23). Conrad Beissel taught that the genders would ultimately be united as men became "virginal" by annihilating their selves (see Bach, *Voices of the Turtledoves*, 45–46).

28. Greven, *Protestant Temperament*, 124–25; Lawrence, *One Family Under God*, 110–11. Lawrence, who is interested in the Methodists, refers to relevant studies about Baptists, early Methodists in the American South, and southern evangelicals with similar findings.

29. [Demelius], *Vollständige Nachricht*, 92.

30. On Zinzendorf's gender ideas, also see Smaby, "Gender Prescriptions"; Atwood, "Union of Masculine and Feminine"; Faull, "Masculinity"; Faull, "Temporal Men"; Vogt, "'Er ist Mann.'"

31. "Und weil bey einer Leiche der Geschlechts-Unterschied aufhöre." Address by Zinzendorf in Herrnhaag, December 13, 1747, Congregational Accounts.

32. Zinzendorf, *Zeister Reden*, 210.

33. In 1752 Zinzendorf restated this concept; see Spangenberg, *Apologetische Schlußschrift*, 600.

34. Clark, "Celibate Bridegroom," 17–18; Hunter, "The Virgin, the Bride"; Bynum, *Resurrection*, 216; Bach, *Voices of the Turtledoves*, 45–46, 54–56. Hochmann von Hochenau used the term "virginal marriages" (Renkewitz, *Hochmann von Hochenau*, 409–12).

35. *Herrnhuter Gesangbuch*, no. 1944, vv. 1, 4. For Zinzendorf, the theme of the "virginal men" can be traced to 1722. See Bouman-Komen, *Bruderliebe*, 239. I am grateful to Craig Atwood for this reference.

36. "The real effect of all of Jesus's members on all our human members caused a holy respect for ourselves that the concept of the sexes with everything depending on that had almost disappeared. But then we remembered that we are still stuck in such bodies that need much work before they look similar to the holy body of the husband" (Der reelle Einfluß aller Jesusglieder auf alle unsere menschlichen Glieder würkete einen heiligen Respect gegen und vor uns selbsten, dass uns darüber fast die Idee der Geschlechter mit allem, was daran hangt, verschwunden war, aber wir besannen uns wieder, dass wir noch in solchen Hütten steckten, daran noch manches gethan werden müste, biß sie dem heiligen Leichnam des Mannes ähnlich säheten). Diary Herrnhaag, March 25, 1745.

37. The events are described in the Congregational Accounts and in the diary of the single brothers in Herrnhaag. Zinzendorf's addresses during this month are included in Zinzendorf, *Homilien über die Wundenlitanei*.

38. "Weil die Hütte durch den Leichnam Jesu dabey getödtet und aus aller, auch sonst rechtmäßigen Activität gesetzt wäre, so bleibe nichts übrig als die gemeinschaftliche Seele." Congregational Accounts, May 6, 1747.

39. "Nachdem nun die ganz neue Oeconomie angegangen ist, da wir erstlich zwar leiblicher Weise noch Männer sind, aber nicht mehr im Geist, denn im Glauben sind wir alle Schwestern" (May 20, 1747). Zinzendorf, *Homilien über die Wundenlitanei*, 83.

40. Address by Zinzendorf to the single brothers in Gnadenfrei, October 1, 1747 (R.4.C.III.7.b, UA; also in Congregational Accounts 1747, suppl. 82); diary single brothers Herrnhut, November 19, 1747; Congregational Accounts, November 19, 1747. See Peucker, "'Blut' auf unsre grünen Bändchen,'" 72.

41. "Die Brüder könnten's kaum erwarten, bis sie auch dem Leibe ähnlich würden, der Ihn [Jesus] getragen [Maria], wenn das Zeichen in den Wolken erscheinen würde, das über die ganze Welt eine Alteration bringen werde." Congregational Accounts, May 20, 1748.

42. Congregational Accounts, February 5, 1749. Also see Volck, *Das entdeckte Geheimnis*, 6:761.

43. Grimm and Grimm, *Deutsches Wörterbuch*, s.v. "Stab"; Zedler, *Grosses vollständiges Universal-Lexicon*, s.v. "Stab (Gerichts-)" and "Stab zerbrechen."

44. [Hecker], *Gespräch*, 50–52. For the original German, see above, n8.

45. "The brothers should not take it [the concept of blessed sinfulness] too far and think that if sin is something good, I will like it and love lusts," quoted in diary single brothers Herrnhaag, March 10, 1750. "Br. Spangenberg reminded that neglecting the issue of sinfulness contributed to getting sidetracked. One has forgotten that even in the nature of a child of God still grounds for evil exist." Minutes of Provincial Synod in Gnadenberg, May 12, 1750, 32–33. About the concept of "blessed sinfulness," see Uttendörfer, "Der arme Sünder," chap. 12 in *Zinzendorfs religiöse Grundgedanken*.

46. "Such a touch of our sinful body occurs during Communion mainly to mortify the sinful body, to extract the poison and to drip in balsam from the wounds until finally the sinful body would cease completely" (Doch geschehe eine solche Berührung unsres sündigen Hütteleins im Abendmahl vornehmlich zur Mortification des sündlichen Leibes, um uns wieder einmal Gift auszuziehen und Wundenbalsam einzuträufeln, bis endlich einmal der sündliche Leib gar aufhöre). The effect of Christ's touch was interrupted when the Communion service was over, but "[a]fter a few days or weeks one comes again and unites with the Savior again and this continues until the spirit of Christ becomes so much that it will finally lead to completion and the Savior will keep us [with him] some day" (In wenig Tagen oder Wochen aber komme man wieder und mache sich wieder in den Heiland hinein und das gehe so fort, bis des Spiritus Christi so viel werde, daß es endlich zur Vollendung hinaus komme und uns der Heiland

einmal zurück behalte). Address by Zinzendorf in Herrnhaag, December 13, 1747, in Congregational Accounts. A few years earlier, in a conversation with Wesley in 1741, Zinzendorf rejected the concept of inherent perfection in the life of a believer, i.e., perfection apart from Christ (see Vogt, "No Inherent Perfection").

47. [Hecker], Gespräch, 52.

48. "It was mentioned that during that period in the year 1749 a number of sixty brothers and sisters formed a separate society and were called the Sixty Queens. They had to keep watch among themselves, where each member had to keep watch alone in a cabinet for several hours." Minutes of special conference during single brothers' synod in London, January 12, 1753, 347.

49. "If I would exaggerate the point of us being sisterly souls, of having to consider the Savior, who bought us on the cross, as our only true husband, and if I would, for example, construe that to mean that brothers are no longer brothers but rather sisters, *also physically, as if they did no longer have brotherly [male] bodies*—that would be an unfounded idea" (Wenn ich aber die Sache, daß wir schwesterliche Seelen sind, daß wir den Heiland, der uns am Creuz erkauft hat, als unseren einigen wahren Mann anzusehen haben, zu weit treiben und es z.E. so verstehen wolte, als wären die Brüder nun keine Brüder mehr sondern Schwestern, *auch der Hütte nach, sie hätten keine brüderliche Hütten mehr,* so wäre das eine ungegründete Idee) (emphasis added). Address by Johannes von Watteville to single brothers in Marienborn, March 4, 1750. Also see Spangenberg, *Declaration*, 62.

50. "Puritan sexuality was not its spiritualization of the erotic but its eroticization of the spiritual." Godbeer, *Sexual Revolution*, 55.

51. Juster, "Eros and Desire," 204.

52. Rambuss, *Closet Devotions*. Also see Lochrie, "Mystical Acts."

53. See above.

54. "Es sey ihnen doch nichts abgegangen." Diary Herrnhut, April 4, 1749.

55. "So wie sich ein paar Kinder mit einander küssen, mit einander herzen, mit einander ehelichen, so ehelicht sich der Mann mit uns und nicht anders." Address by Christian Renatus to the children in Herrnhaag, December 28, 1748.

56. "Und unter Euch bricht diese Materie wie die Morgenröte in die Höhe, unter Euch eher, als in der ganzen Gemeine. Von Euch rückt sie in die Chöre und nicht von uns zu Euch. So wie's Seitenhöhlchen speciell wahrhaftig von Kindern herkommt, so wie die Kinder das Seitenhöhlchen in die Gemeine gebracht, so bringen die Kinder das Cabinet und Ehebett auch wahrhaftig noch viel mehr in die Gemeine als alle andere." Ibid.

57. "The communicant brothers and sisters went to Herrnhaag, where, because the entire congregation was only one choir, our dear heart Christel notified them that from now on they would have common classes or assemblies to be held every day." Diary single brothers Marienborn, December 15, 1748. Already at the single brothers' festival on May 4, 1748, Christel had prayed, "may the side hole make one choir out of the entire congregation." Festival report, R.4.C.III.7.b, UA.

58. [Hecker], *Gespräch*, 52–53. The class of the "wives who sleep in the arms of the King" seems to be a combined reference to Song of Songs 1 and 1 Kings 1:2. Although the Marienborn diary does not distinguish between classes and assemblies, it is possible there were three classes, divided over a larger number (fifteen?) of assemblies.

59. Moser, *Lebensgeschichte*, 93. I am grateful to Peter Vogt for this reference.

60. Diary Johann Nitschmann, November 8, 1756; memoir Cornelis van Laer, EBG Zeist, PA II, R.7.8.

61. Zinzendorf: "Du hast gegen alle dein Versprechen eine Schäzelgesellschafft aufgerichtet, von der ich nichts hören und wißen will." Anna Nitschmann: "Nun solt ich dir nochmahlen von Papas wegen sagen, daß sie [i.e., Zinzendorf] gantz aus einander über dir und der gantzen Schätzelsache wären. Sie wollen dir kein Wort selber mehr schreiben, biß du die Dinge gantz bleiben läßt." Both letters are dated London, February 10, 1749. It seems likely that Zinzen-

dorf's mention of "private societies" in his letter of reprimand (par. 8) referred to the activities of the *Schätzel*.

62. The earliest datable reference is found in the Herrnhut single brothers' diary of June 22, 1748, when the "new" hymn "Tagtäglich nennt er mich ein Schätzel" was introduced by Christian Renatus (see Peucker, "Songs of the Sifting," 86–87).

63. "Wer nun ein Schätzel ist, der singt: Herr Jesu Christ! Küß, küß, ach küße mich, durchgeh mich ehelich. Mache mich durch und durch heiß, Höhlgen! ach Kyrie eleis." R.20.E.36.2, UA.

64. For example, in "Charmantes Höhlchen mein," see Peucker, "Songs of the Sifting," 75–76.

65. [Hecker], *Gespräch*, 22. For the tune of the hymn "Ach, ich fühl," see Peucker, "Songs of the Sifting," 74.

66. [Hecker], *Gespräch*, 53–54.

67. For allegations of sexual misconduct among religious groups see, for example, Lawrence, *One Family Under God*, 99.

68. Uttendörfer, "Neusalz," 90–91.

69. Peucker, "'Blut' auf unsre grünen Bändchen,'" 81–88; English translation in Atwood, "Zinzendorf's 1749 Reprimand," 67–74.

70. "Schätzel-, Ehebetts- und Cabinetssachen" ([Hecker], *Gespräch*, 55).

71. "[D]ie Cabinett- und Bett-Materien mit dem Lämmlein." On the cabinet, see Peucker, "In the Blue Cabinet."

72. Cranz, *Alte und neue Brüder-Historie*, 564. Schrautenbach also denies "immoralities" had occurred (*Graf von Zinzendorf*, 364). German historians from around 1900 believed sexual acts were part of the Sifting: Burkhardt, *Die Brüdergemeine*, 1:74; Jannasch, "Christian Renatus," pt. 2, 80; Uttendörfer, "Zinzendorf und die Entwicklung," pt. 4, 48. Later historians, like Erbe, opposed this idea again: *Herrnhaag*, 144. Also see Weinlick, *Count Zinzendorf*, 200; E. Beyreuther, *Zinzendorf und die Christenheit*, 249.

73. Cröger, *Geschichte der erneuerten Brüderkirche*, 2:74, 84, 162.

74. Zinzendorf: "the false clergy began to aim at carnality" (150r); Johannes: "In the beginning I did not suspect carnality" (ibid.); Friedrich von Watteville: "It was close to made perfect by the flesh" (cf. Gal. 3:3) (152r). Minutes of special conference during Barby synod, September 1750.

75. "Die grobe Irrlehre, das wir des Heilands Ehe *schon hier* haben." Zinzendorf to Christian Renatus, February 10, 1749 (emphasis added).

76. Address by Johannes von Watteville to single brothers in Marienborn, March 4, 1750.

77. "I have a lot of work in your single [brethren's] choir. . . . But really, dear heart, more damage occurred in this choir during the previous time than I imagined. I have already spoken to about twenty people who, because of all the professed 'presence' and 'matrimony,' have fallen into lusts" (In deinem ledigen Chore habe ich jetzo allerhand Arbeiten. . . . Aber würklich, liebes Hertz, im Chor ist mehr in vorigen Zeiten geschehen, als ichs vermuthet habe und ich habe schon ein 20 Leute gesehen und gesprochen, die bey aller vorgegebenen Nähe und Ehlichkeit in die L. [Lüste] gerathen sind). Johannes von Watteville to Christian Renatus, [Herrnhaag, March 3, 1750]. Uttendörfer also reads "L" in this letter as an abbreviation for "Lüste" ("Theologisches Seminar," pt. 4, 48).

78. Johannes von Watteville to Christian Renatus, March 17, 1750.

79. "*Nota Ordinarii:* Wenn ich aber auch bedencke, was manchmal von unsern eignen Leuten vor gottlose Consequentien aus meinen Reden gezogen werden, z.E. weil die Geister der ledigen Brüder Schwestern sind, so können Brüder der Hütte nach mit Schwestern der Hütte nach Umgang suchen und unschädlich haben, so darf ichs der Welt nicht übel nehmen, daß sie so roß- und maulmäßig denckt und redt." Congregational Accounts, February 15, 1749.

80. The word *Hütte* means literally *hut*: "according to the hut." The Luther translation of the New Testament uses this term for "body." The King James Version translates with "tabernacle."

81. The scandal is described in the diary of the Herrnhut congregation, September–October 1744, R.6.A.b.17, UA; with additional information in Ludwig von Schweinitz's copy of that diary, R.24.B.79.

82. Spangenberg, *Apologetische Schlußschrift*, question 838, 335–37. David Cranz refers to this passage in an explicatory note when discussing the Sifting Time. However, because the passage in the *Apologetische Schlußschrift* does not state precisely what was happening in Herrnhut in 1744, it served as a cryptic reference, only comprehensible to insiders (Cranz, *Alte und neue Brüder-Historie*, 502).

83. Peucker, "Inspired by Flames of Love," 59–64.

84. "[H]eute unser ganzes Chor leibhaftig umfangen wird." Report of single brothers' festival, Herrnhaag, 1748.

85. Address by Christian Renatus to the congregation in Herrnhaag, March 10, 1748.

86. "Es war nicht anders, als stünde das Seitenhöhlgen vor einem jeden Bruder leibhaftig, und es präsentirte sich gewiß vor einem jeden Bruder in der Person unsers Christeleins und Rubuschens." Report of single brothers' festival, Herrnhaag, 1748.

87. "Ein jedes küßte seinen Nachbar in der Person des Seitenhöhlgens." That is, while kissing the person next to him, each one believed he was kissing the side hole.

88. Report of single brothers' festival, Herrnhaag, 1748. Also see Hart's description in [Hecker], *Gespräch*, 47.

89. "[W]ie man das im Seitenhöhlchen drinne sein nicht geistlich zu verstehen habe, sondern *realiter* mit Leib und Seele hineinfahren dürfe und könne." Diary single brothers Herrnhut July 28, 1748 (emphasis added).

90. "Das Seitenhölgen wird dich gewiß in Liefland so druken und umarmen, daß du Deutschland vergessen wirst. Nim nur das allerliebste Schätzel beim Leibe, mache keine Complimenten mit ihm, befehl ihn. Geküßt, geküßt muß seyn und hallte dich passiv hin, so wirstu lauter Hochzeittage in Liefland haben. Dir darf Buntebart schon manchmahl ein und das andre Versel geben. Du musst aber vor dich alleine behallten. Lebe wohl im Hölgen. Dein treues Herzelein, Christelein von Hölgen." Christian Renatus to Matthias Hasse, Zeist, October 11, 1748, R.21.A.62.121, UA.

91. Diary single brothers Herrnhut, July 30, 1748 (see chap. 4, n117).

92. According to Bothe, Moravian leaders in Berlin saw reason to disband a prayer group because "various filthy things, yea, even man-with-man scandals," had taken place. Bothe, *Zuverläßige Beschreibung*, 1:41.

93. Ibid., 1:112. Herz, a bricklayer, joined the Moravians on August 19, 1747, and was received into the church in January 1748. His first communion was on March 25, 1748. R.27.294.64, UA. Another instance where it seems that Moravians compared the anus with the side hole appears in the trial of Moravian teacher Michael Jacob Bagewitz; see Peucker, "Inspired by Flames of Love," 62.

94. Diary single brothers Herrnhut, July 28, 1748 (see chap. 4, n115).

95. On the Society of Mother Eva, see Temme, *Krise der Leiblichkeit*; Temme, "From Jakob Böhme via Jane Leade to Eva von Buttlar."

96. Goebel quotes Johann Heinrich Jung-Stilling in this context. Goebel, *Geschichte des christlichen Lebens*, 538–39.

97. Goeters, "Der reformierte Pietismus," 411–19; Bernet, *Gebaute Apokalypse*, 271–99. According to Burkhardt it could not be "proven with certainty" that in Herrnhaag similar sexual things had happened as in Ronsdorf (Burkhardt, *Die Brüdergemeine*, 1:74).

98. "Extract eines Schreibens vom 5. September 1747," in [Thierbach], *Diarium Herrnhutianum*, vol. 2, pt. 1, 92–98. A report on "the fanatical Bohemians in Tarnowitz" existed in the Unity Archives until it was destroyed by Sutor in 1803; see Peucker, "Selection and Destruction," 206.

99. Temme, *Krise der Leiblichkeit*, 425–26.

100. Abraham Kyburz, *Das entdekte Geheimniss der Bosheit in der Brüggler Secte* (Zürich, 1753); Temme, *Krise der Leiblichkeit*, 426–27.

101. Bach, *Voices of the Turtledoves*, 42–43.

102. Rupp, *History*, 417. Also see Bach, *Voices of the Turtledoves*, 12; Schutt, *Peoples of the River Valleys*, 74.

103. Rupp, *History*, 419.

104. Ibid.

105. "Wen man nur das Seitenhöhlgen hat, so kan man thun was einem einfällt, so kan man leichtsinnig und ungebunden seyn, das ist eine Unwahrheit.... [S]onst liefe es auf den Irrthum der Neugebohrnen in Pensylvanien hinaus, welche lehren: es komme nur darauf an, daß man ein Kind Gottes werde und einmal Vergebung der Sünden kriegte, darnach könne man thun und sündigen, wie man wolle, da behüte uns Gott vor!" Address by Johannes von Watteville to single brothers at Marienborn, March 4, 1750.

106. Zinzendorf to Mag. Friedrich Christoph Steinhofer, London, March 24, 1749, R.20.C.31.c.141, UA; Zinzendorf to Johannes von Watteville, London, March 16, 1749, R.20.C.23.b.120, UA; minutes of special conference during Barby synod, 1750, 138v, 147v; Anna Nitschmann to Christian Renatus, February 10, 1749.

107. Levering, *History of Bethlehem*, 167–70; John W. Jordan, "Moravian Immigration to Pennsylvania, 1734–1767," *TMHS* 5, no. 2 (1896): 61. The death year in Jordan's article is incorrect. Cook was the author of "The Burthen'd Pilgrim Released and His Journey to the New Jerusalem" (ms.), which also contains his self-portrait (MSS 13, MAB). Under this he wrote in English, "My Style is simple, & my native Place / Is Itali, but yet my Home is Grace." Cook is mentioned in the congregational diary of Bethlehem and in the single brothers' diary of Herrnhaag. During his visit to Bethlehem he submitted a request to be received into the congregation (n.d., Beth-Cong 268, MAB). The plans for Constantinople and Algiers as well as the discussion about Cook's role in the Sifting Time are mentioned in the minutes of the synods at Krausche (1748), and Barby (1750). I am grateful to Rüdiger Kröger for sharing his research on Cook with me.

108. Anna Nitschmann to Christian Renatus, February 10, 1749. The letter she refers to was not found.

109. "Phantasien und Dingen, die absolut nicht einer wahren Jungfer und Chorherzel geziemen." Address by Johannes von Watteville to single sisters in Herrnhaag, April 2, 1750, Bethlehem Single Sisters, no. 121, MAB.

110. A possible identification is Caroline Augusta Hertel from Castell, later married Hayn. She joined the Moravians in 1733. However, the few dated catalogs from the critical year 1748 (January 1 and March) do not list her. An overview of 1748 mentions she was sent to Herrnhut during that year (R.27.38–39, R.27.294.9 and 45, UA).

111. See above.

112. Memoir Johannes Ettwein, Ettwein Papers, no. 107, MAB.

113. On Vierorth, see Kröger, Mai, and Nippe, *Das Unitätsarchiv*, 49.

114. Uttendörfer, "Neusalz," 86–90.

115. Johannes von Watteville to Zinzendorf, Neusalz, May 7, 1750, R.7.A.5.14, UA.

116. [Hecker], *Gespräch*, 52. See also above.

117. Diary Herrnhut, April 16, 1749. He soon returned to the Moravian Church and went to England, where he was head of a boarding school in Yorkshire and translated the Congregational Accounts. He moved to Fulneck in 1751 and to Bedford in 1752, where he died in 1755. See his memoir, R.22.180.2, UA.

118. Diary single brothers Bethlehem, June 25, 1748, and later, BethSB, no. 1, MAB. Johannes had just left Bethlehem for the Caribbean at the time of their arrival. When he returned, he was able to work things out with them, having a better understanding of their piety. Also see minutes of special conference during Barby synod, 1750, 143–44.

119. Zinzendorf to Christian Renatus, February 10, 1749; address by Zinzendorf to the single brothers on their departure to Pennsylvania, February 15, 1749, Hs. 17, UA (also in Congregational Accounts).

120. Zinzendorf to Mag. Friedrich Christoph Steinhofer, London, March 24, 1749, R.20.C.31.c.141, UA.

CHAPTER 7

1. Diary Herrnhut, March 23 and 31, 1749. The diary for March 1–22 is missing.
2. Memoir Ettwein, Ettwein Papers, nos. 107 and 108, MAB.
3. Caillet's memoir is included in the diary of the Bedford congregation, R.13.D.5.a, UA. "Man of Smart" is a literal translation of the German *Schmerzensmann*, Man of sorrows (Is. 53).
4. Rubusch's memoir, *Nachrichten aus der Brüder-Gemeine* (1862): 81–88.
5. Johannes von Watteville to Zinzendorf, [England], May 3, 1748, R.21.A.183.e.II.408, UA.
6. "Aber dencke einmal an, Herzens Christelein! Dein Johannes ist in America und Du bist in Europa. Die zwey Herzel, die zwey intime Herzel, die im Seitenhöhlgen so nahe beisammen sizen, sind dem Leibe nach so weit von einander. Ists wahr oder ists ein Traum? Wie ich Deine Briefel las, so wars mir nicht anders als wäre ich nur ein 20, 30 Meilen von Dir. Aber ich bin wircklich soviel 100 Meilen weg. Aber Herzel, in der Pleura sind wir dichte beisammen und da kan ich Dir wircklich aufs nächste nahe seyn. Näher als alle deine andre Herzel seyn. Je weiter leiblich, je empfindlicher im Höhlgen. Was ich Dir aber nun von mir sagen kan, so bin ich Johannes vom Höhlgen, Johannes im Höhlgen, Johannes 3/4 Höhlgen, durchgangen, durchfleischet, durchblutet, durchleichelt, durchheiligt, durchehlicht, und wie soll ich Dirs kräftig und ganz genug ausdrücken, ein Geschöpfgen aus Jesu Seite, geschaffen, von Ihm täglich erkannt zu seyn, an seinem Leichlein zu hangen und ein ewiges Kind zu seyn, das an seiner Pleura hangt und drinnen liegt wie ein Kind in der Mutter Schoos, das alle Tage von Ihm durchseitigt wird und in Ihm drinne und er in Ihm ist. Dabey ein Sünderlein, eine Made, das bei aller seiner Seeligkeit doch immer weniger mit sich zufrieden ist als alle andere Herzel. Aber ich bin seelig, ich bin ein niedliches Dingel. Ich bin Fleisch und Bein vom Manne und meinen Mitgespielinnen, davon Du auch eine bist, die auch so erpicht auf Ihn sind, und es nicht ausstehen können, wenn Er sie nicht alle Tage erkennt und ihnen ehelich schöne thut. Da hast Du meine Religion kurz beisammen." Johannes von Watteville to Christian Renatus, copy, Long Island, September 17, 1748, R.21.A.183.e.II.409.b, UA.
7. "I must admit that I consider him an unfortunate instrument used by Satan, as he was not able to ruin the true blood-and-wounds and side-hole theology by law and moral or methodical lectures, to make [this theology] suspect and at least to hold up the progression of grace by excessive, carnal, and fantastical expressions. It was intended to be a new church period of which Rubusch was the author and apostle" (Ich muß bekennen, daß ich ihn vor das unglückliche Instrument halte, deßen sich Satanas bedienet hat, da er die wahre Blut und Wunden und Seitenhöhlgens Theologie nicht durchs Gesetz und moralische und methodische Vorträge ruiniren können, auf einer andern Seite durch übertriebene, fleischliche, phantastische Ausdrücke, dieselbe verdächtig und wenigstens einen Stop in den Gnadengang zu machen. Es soll ein neuer Gemeinpereiodus [sic] seyn, davon Ruhbusch der Autor und Apostel ist). Johannes von Watteville to Zinzendorf, Bethlehem, July 31, 1749, R.14.A.33.16, UA.
8. Diary Johann Nitschmann, November 8, 1756.
9. Petsch to Zinzendorf, Heerendijk, August 2, 1752, 48–52.
10. On Christian Renatus's biography, see Jannasch, "Christian Renatus."
11. Nelson, *John Valentine Haidt*, 69.
12. On one occasion Zinzendorf claimed his son's inclination for the side wound of Christ was a consequence of his being conceived on December 21 of 1726, as the patron of this day was

St. Thomas, the disciple who longed to touch the wounds of Christ. Diary single brothers' synod in Ingatestone Hall, R.2.A.32.b, p. 19.

13. Jannasch, "Christian Renatus," pt. 2, 71.

14. Stanza 22:

> Noch eins, ach treustes Herz, ich glaub es ist geschehen
> das man es schön versehen, daß man zu laut gewest,
> mit den geheimsten Sachen, das wird uns Händel machen
> und träfs uns nur allein, so möchte es noch seyn.

Stanza 24:

> Kans seyn so das selbst zu, versiegle jedes Munde
> Schließ ein ins Herzens Grunde, lenk wieder ein ins Gleiß
> Vielleicht ist noch in Zeiten, der Schaden zu vermeiden
> Ist's aber schon geschehn, laß Gnad vor Recht ergehn.

Poem by Christian Renatus, February 1749, R.20.E.35.122. Also see Jannasch, "Christian Renatus," pt. 2, 77–78.

15. Jannasch, "Christian Renatus," pt. 2, 80–81.

16. Diary single brothers Herrnhut, October 23, 1750.

17. "Now your disciplesses and messengers of the Savior will consecrate you by which everything old will be removed ('That our Mind the Lamb's Resemble and his Corpse our Body's Temple'). May you now receive the benediction of absolution." Address by Zinzendorf in Congregational Accounts, October 25, 1750.

18. Congregational Accounts, November 24, 1750. This was Anna Nitschmann's birthday. In other congregations the green ribbons were replaced with pink ribbons at different dates: London, November 24, 1749; Bethlehem, May 4, 1750; Zeist, January 12, 1752. On the choir ribbons, see Peucker, "Pink, White and Blue."

19. Diary Johann Daniel Gottwalt; Zinzendorf's address in Herrnhut, October 25, 1750, in Congregational Accounts. Also see November 24, 1750, in Congregational Accounts.

20. An interesting study is the (unpublished) thesis by Markus Gill, "Zeit der Brüdergemeine auf dem Herrnhaag."

21. Diary Johann Daniel Gottwalt.

22. Diary Herrnhut, December 31, 1750 (copy by Ludwig von Schweinitz), R.24.B.79, UA; Congregational Accounts, December 31, 1750. Also Cranz, *Alte und neue Brüder-Historie*, 501–2.

23. "Das Seitenhöhlgen, die Wunden Jesu, das Blut des Lämmleins ist allemal der Grund, die Quelle und das Fundament aller unserer Seeligkeit." Address by Johannes von Watteville to single brothers in Marienborn, March 4, 1750.

24. "Der ganze blutige Heiland und seine Marter, alle seine Wunden gehören zusammen und hätte der Heiland nicht erst so viel für uns an Leib und Seele gelitten, hätte Er nicht so geschwizt, wäre Er nicht so gemartert worden, wäre Er nicht angenagelt worden, hätte Er sein Leiden bleiben laßen, so hätten wir auch kein Seitenhöhlgen, daraus uns das Leben, das Blut und Waßer herausgefloßen ist, so wäre die neue Geburt aus der Pleura nicht zustande gekommen." Ibid.

25. Diary Herrnhut, December 31, 1750 (copy by Ludwig von Schweinitz), R.24.B.79, UA.

26. In a letter written in Bethlehem on September 30, 1748, to Zinzendorf, Johannes wrote he could not describe Spangenberg as "a jolly and cheerful cross-air birdie" (R.14.A.33.3, UA).

27. Minutes of Provincial Synod in Gnadenberg, 32–33.

28. "[U]ns die Marter Gottes nicht immer vor Augen und im Herzen war. Wäre des Heilands Leben, Leiden und Sterben uns nicht aus den Augen gekommen, wir würden in die

Sichtungen nicht geraten sein, deren wir uns noch zu schämen haben." Spangenberg, "Dankbare Erinnerung," 1784, par. 30, quoted by G. Reichel, *August Gottlieb Spangenberg*, 219–220n1.

29. Peucker, "Drei Gemälde."

30. Congregational Accounts, May 9, 1748.

CHAPTER 8

1. On the events around Zinzendorf's death, see Dietrich Meyer, "Zu Zinzendorfs Tod am 9. Mai 1760," *UF* 63/64 (2008): 233–44.

2. See minutes of Ratskonferenz. About the years immediately after Zinzendorf's death and about the 1764 General Synod, see Cröger, *Geschichte der erneuerten Brüderkirche*, 3:1–40. Also see G. Reichel, "Die Ära Spangenbergs," chap. 13 in *August Gottlieb Spangenberg*; D. Meyer, *Zinzendorf und die Herrnhuter Brüdergemeine*, 63–93.

3. I am grateful to Beverly Smaby for drawing my attention to this correspondence.

4. Hamilton and Hamilton, *History of the Moravian Church*, 163–75.

5. G. Meyer, introduction to *Leben des Herrn Nicolaus Ludwig Grafen und Herrn von Zinzendorf und Pottendorf*, by August Gottlieb Spangenberg (Hildesheim: Georg Olms, 1971), vi–vii.

6. Atwood, *Community of the Cross*, 224. Katherine Carté Engel discusses the effects of Zinzendorf's death ("a watershed event for the Unity") regarding Bethlehem and the end of the General Economy (*Religion and Profit*, chap. 6). Also see D. Meyer, "Zinzendorf und Herrnhut," 57–64; Mettele, *Weltbürgertum*, 76–82.

7. About the changes regarding the position of women, see Smaby, "No One Should Lust for Power"; Smaby, "Gender Prescriptions"; Smaby, "Only Brothers Should Be Accepted"; Peucker, "'Gegen ein Regiment von Schwestern.'"

8. Paul Wesley Chilcote, *John Wesley and the Women Preachers of Early Methodism* (Metuchen, N.J.: Scarecrow Press, 1991); Mack, *Heart Religion*; Curtis W. Freeman, ed., *A Company of Women Preachers: Baptist Prophetesses in Seventeenth-Century England* (Waco: Baylor University Press, 2011). Also see Strom, "Problems and Promises," 551–52; Shantz, *Introduction to German Pietism*, chap. 7.

9. Uttendörfer, *Zinzendorf und die Frauen*, has a broad selection of quotations by Zinzendorf. Also see Smaby, "Gender Prescriptions."

10. Quoted in Smaby, "Only Brothers Should Be Accepted," 159.

11. Shantz, *Introduction to German Pietism*, 158, 200–3. Also see, for example, Ruth Albrecht, *Johanna Eleonora Petersen: Theologische Schriftstellerin des frühen Pietismus* (Göttingen: Vandenhoeck & Ruprecht, 2005), 145–55; Claudia Wustmann, *Die begeisterten Mägde: Mitteldeutsche Prophetinnen im Radikalpietismus am Ende des 17. Jahrhunderts* (Leipzig: Kirchhof & Franke, 2008); Fogleman, *Jesus Is Female*, 73–104.

12. Rhode, *Schlüssel zu Herrnhut*, 450–51. Rhode probably meant Bayle's assessment of Antoinette Bourignon; see Baar, "Conflicting Discourses on Female Dissent."

13. About Moravians as enthusiasts, see Exalto and Karels, *Waakzame wachters*, chap. 12; Knox, *Enthusiasm*, 413–16.

14. Interim constitution [1762], SynConf 52, MAB. According to Arnold, there were both *diaconissas* and *presbyterae* in the early church who were ordained, performing baptisms and "probably" Communion (*Die erste Liebe*, 1:209–15). A few decades earlier, Arnold's *Erste Liebe* served as a model for the Moravian Church in many respects. See Peucker, "Ideal of Primitive Christianity."

15. "It was proposed to not let the consecration of deaconesses take place during the same worship meeting as when brothers are ordained as deacons, because otherwise the former consecration could be mistaken for an ordination. Someone argued, however, that this rite was very

different from an ordination; the consecration of deaconesses could easily become too solemn if it had to be treated as something separate." Minutes of General Synod in Herrnhut, 1789, R.2.B.48, p. 494, UA.

16. [Cranz], *Kurze, zuverläßige Nachricht*, 40, plate 9.
17. Committee report on the future role of women during the General Synod of 1764.
18. Minutes of General Synod in Marienborn, 1764, 1347–48, 1394.
19. See results (*Verlass*) of General Synod in Marienborn, 1764.
20. Committee report on the future role of women during the General Synod of 1764. About the term *Weiberregiment* see also Zedler, *Grosses vollständiges Universal-Lexicon*, s.v. "Weiber-Regiment."
21. Minutes of General Synod in Marienborn, 1764, 1395–98; Smaby, "No One Should Lust for Power," 163.
22. Minutes of General Synod in Marienborn, 1764, 1351–52, 1388–89; Smaby, "No One Should Lust for Power," 163; Peucker, "'Gegen ein Regiment von Schwestern,'" 65–66.
23. "We thought that for this intended conference only brethren should be taken whose office and gifts are fitting." Letter of the *Enge Konferenz* (interim administration) in Herrnhut, January 29, 1763, Provincial Helpers' Conference, no. 1, MAB.
24. During Zinzendorf's lifetime revised versions were published of the Berlin Discourses (original 1738, revised 1758), the Pennsylvania Discourses (1744/1760), the Zeist Discourses (1747/1759), and the Homilies on the Litany of Wounds (1747/1759).
25. "[I]n eines heimgegangenen Mannes Gottes Schriften etwas zu ändern, ist nicht schicklich." Minutes of interim administration, Herrnhut, April 1, 1761.
26. Zinzendorf, *Maxims*.
27. Spangenberg to Bethlehem Elders' Conference, Herrnhut, December 16, 1762.
28. N. L. von Zinzendorf, *Auszüge aus des Seligen Ordinarii der Evangelischen Brüder-Kirche sowol ungedruckten als gedruckten Reden über biblische Texte, nach Ordnung der Bücher heiliger Schrift gefertigt und herausgegeben von Gottfried Clemens*, 3 vols. (Barby, 1763, 1764, 1765). The volumes on the New Testament followed: *Auszüge . . . über die Evangelisten*, vols. 1–4, ed. Gottfried Clemens (Barby, 1766, 1767, 1769, 1773), vols. 5–6, ed. Jakob Christoph Duvernoy (Barby, 1781, 1792).
29. "Regarding the publication of the extracts we have carefully seen to it that nothing in the original text was changed or replaced with something else; however, we have left out what seemed not suitable for the public, and nothing else was included than what can lead to true edification." Minutes of General Synod in Marienborn, 1764, 74–75.
30. Ibid., 901–2.
31. Spangenberg to Bethlehem Elders' Conference, Herrnhut, January 4, 1763.
32. Minutes of interim administration, Herrnhut, June 10, 1760. The title of the second appendix is *Anhang der übrigen Brüder-Lieder seit 1749. Zweyter Anhang bis 1754* (n.p., n.d.).
33. *Das Kleine Brüder-Gesang-Buch, in einer Harmonischen Samlung von kurzen Liedern, Versen, Gebeten und Seufzern bestehend. Zweyte Auflage* (Barby, 1761). Also see Müller, *Hymnologisches Handbuch*, 41–42. A comparison of the content of the two editions might show if and to what extent the wording of the hymns was changed.
34. Minutes of interim administration, Herrnhut, February 6, 1761.
35. Spangenberg to Bethlehem Elders' Conference, Herrnhut, December 16, 1762.
36. *Liturgische Gesänge der Brüdergemeinen, aufs neue revidirt* (Barby, 1770), foreword; *Litaneyen für die Chöre in den Brüdergemeinen* (Barby, 1773).
37. These choir instructions have been analyzed by Katherine Faull. See Faull, "Married Choir Instructions." On the practice of Moravian sexuality and a comparison of the Zinzendorf era and later years, see Peucker, "In the Blue Cabinet."
38. Also see Faull, "Temporal Men," 75.
39. Yonan, "Evangelicalism and Enlightenment," chap. 3.

40. [Cranz], *Kurze, zuverläßige Nachricht*, usually called *Zeremonienbüchlein*. The text is most likely written by Cranz, but Spangenberg (and also D. Meyer, *Bibliographisches Handbuch*, 107) lists it among Zinzendorf's works. Finze-Michaelsen, "'Die Sache des Heilands,'" 88–89.

41. Minutes of interim administration, Herrnhut, April 19, 1761.

42. Ibid., February 2, 1761. For Zinzendorf's suggestion, see minutes of conference in Herrnhut, February 6, 1760, R.2.A.43.a, UA. On Cranz, see Finze-Michaelsen, "'Die Sache des Heilands.'"

43. Minutes of General Synod in Marienborn, 1764, 1353–59, 1768–69.

44. See Finze-Michaelsen, "'Die Sache des Heilands,'" 103–4. The manuscript was presented at the 1769 synod, but its consideration was postponed; minutes of General Synod in Marienborn, 1769, 175–76. The manuscript of the "Idea Constitutionis Fratrum": R.28.7, UA. Cranz, *Alte und neue Brüder-Historie*.

45. Minutes of General Synod in Marienborn, 1769, 175, 268, 273–75. Waiblinger's manuscript (incomplete): R.28.6, UA.

46. August Gottlieb Spangenberg, *Idea Fidei Fratrum oder kurzer Begrif der Christlichen Lehre in den evangelischen Brüdergemeinen* (Barby, 1779). Translations were published in Danish (1781), Dutch (1782), French (1782), Swedish (1782), and English (1784). Also see G. Reichel, *August Gottlieb Spangenberg*, 223–34; Atwood, "Apologizing for the Moravians"; Seibert, "A. G. Spangenberg und die Idea Fidei Fratrum." On Spangenberg's writing style, see G. Reichel, *August Gottlieb Spangenberg*, 211–13.

47. See the letter by Moser, dated Frankfurt, December 19, 1762, among the correspondence between Moser and his friend Köber, R.21.A.107, UA.

48. "[I]n der man zwar auch nichts als Wahrheit, aber doch nicht die ganze Wahrheit sagt." Minutes of interim administration, Herrnhut, January 5, 1763.

49. About Spangenberg's Zinzendorf biography, see Kröger, "Spangenberg als Biograph Zinzendorfs"; G. Reichel, *August Gottlieb Spangenberg*, 215–22; Hahn, "Das Bild Zinzendorfs," 258–60.

50. G. Reichel, *August Gottlieb Spangenberg*, 222.

51. On the selection process for records, see chap. 10.

52. About this discussion, see Cröger, *Geschichte der erneuerten Brüderkirche*, 3:4–7. Also see D. Meyer, "Zinzendorf und Herrnhut," 57.

53. This was also the case outside the church; e.g., Töllner, *Kurzgefaßte Christliche Kirchengeschichte*, 637.

54. See the copies of his letters in the Bethlehem Archives: BethCong 463.

55. On Johannes von Watteville, see Böttner, "Johannes von Watteville."

56. A Moravian-produced engraved portrait of Zinzendorf identifies him as "A Disciple whom Jesus loveth, Joh. xxi." This portrait was the frontispiece of Zinzendorf, *Maxims*. A historical table of important people in church history from ca. 1780 states that Zinzendorf was "recognized, identified, loved, and honored" as Jesus's beloved disciple (no. 625, Moravian Historical Society, Nazareth, Pa.). I am indebted to Scott Gordon for bringing this document to my attention. Traditional Moravian historiography tried to de-emphasize the implications of the title of disciple (e.g., Spangenberg, *Leben Zinzendorf*, 1884). Also see T. Gill, "Hoheit und Torheit."

57. Heinrich Reuss said during this meeting, "Now we have to hope with confidence that our dear Lord will deal with us more directly, because the former way of directing us mediately through his dear Disciple now ceases" (Nun müssen wir zuversichtlich hoffen, daß unser liebe Herr künftig noch immediater mit uns handeln werde, da der bisherige Weg uns mediate durch seinen lieben Jünger zu belehren, aufhöre). Minutes of interim administration, May 30, 1760.

58. Sommer, *Serving Two Masters*, 86–109.

59. "[D]as unmittelbare Regiment des Heilands in der Gemeine." Minutes of General Synod in Marienborn, 1764, 551.

60. "Es haben manche gefürchtet, daß die Familie des seeligen Papas sich in Gemein-Sachen etwas herausnehmen möchte, das nicht durch des Heilandes Gnadenwahl auf jede Person der Familie gelegt sey." Interim constitution [1762], SynConf 52, MAB.

61. Cröger, *Geschichte der erneuerten Brüderkirche*, 3:6; D. Meyer, "Zinzendorf und Herrnhut," 59.

62. G. Reichel, *August Gottlieb Spangenberg*, 209.

63. "Von Johannes hört und sieht man nicht viel. Er hat eine eigene Schule. Der Plan der Engen Conferenz ist *wir* und da arbeiten sie stark auf das ihm so gewöhnliches Wörtlein *ich*. Das extendirt sich denn auf die Besorgung der Affairen, daß er nicht mehr eine Resolution geben darf, sondern die Conferenz muß es thun, das ist in sich schön, aber die Menschlichkeit mengt sich denn doch vieleicht nein, und wir Alten gehen denn ein bisgen zu weit. Du verstehst mich und du kenst Leonhard." In a postscript: "Was ich von Johannes geschrieben und dergleichen, da läst du nirgends nichts einfließen. Der gute Johannes ist auch äußerlich kränklich und krigt allerley wunderbare Zufälle." Heinrich XXXI. Reuss (Ignatius) to Nathanael Seidel, Zeist, September 28, 1762, PP SNath 6, MAB.

64. Postscript to the interim constitution [1762], SynConf 52, MAB. About Spangenberg's humiliation, see G. Reichel, *August Gottlieb Spangenberg*, 186–187.

65. About these negotiations see the minutes of the 1764 General Synod, esp. 1000–1001.

66. Also see Uttendörfer, "Zinzendorf und die Entwicklung," pt. 3, 47.

67. "Despite all these troubles I have not the least remorse about [the Order of Fools and the playfulness]. What we did back then, I would immediately do it again" (Denn darüber hab ich unter allen Troublen nicht die geringste Reue, und was wir damals gethan, thäte ich heute gleich wieder). Address by Zinzendorf, in minutes of special conference during Barby synod, September 26, 1750, 162v.

68. *Declaration* (1751), *Darlegung* (1751), and *Apologetische Schluß-Schrift* (1752). On Spangenberg's apologetical writings, see Vogt, "Spangenberg als Apologet"; G. Reichel, *August Gottlieb Spangenberg*, 182–85. Spangenberg had written an earlier apologetical work, *Siegfrieds Bescheidene Beleuchtung*, although it was published under Zinzendorf's name. See Spangenberg's personal notebook from 1743, in Spangenberg Papers, PP SpAG 2, MAB.

69. Vogt, "Spangenberg als Apologet," 87.

70. E. Beyreuther, "Einführung in die Vierunddreißig Homilien," xxviii.

71. In an address to the single sisters in Herrnhut on December 29, 1759, various discourses by Zinzendorf to the single sisters, PP Zdf 106, MAB.

CHAPTER 9

1. "Christelein hielt uns Viertelstunde, da er ein sehr schönes und weitläufiges Glaubensbekenntniß ablegte von vorigen Zeiten, im Vergleich mit einem Adler, der sich weit und breit in der Luft herum schwung, zuletzt aber, da er übers Kreuz hinüber wollte, am Kreuz anstieß und dann wieder seinen Weg zurückfand." Diary single brothers Herrnhut, August 16, 1750. Atwood ("Interpreting and Misinterpreting," 175) also uses the Icarus metaphor when discussing the Sifting Time.

2. Roeber, *Hopes for Better Spouses*.

3. "Die grobe Irrlehre, das wir des Heilands Ehe schon hier haben." Zinzendorf to Christian Renatus, February 10, 1749.

4. The 1785 instructions for the married choir helpers call intercourse a "liturgical act" rather than a sacramental act. Faull, "Married Choir Instructions," 106.

5. Ward, *Early Evangelicalism*.
6. Töllner, *Kurzgefaßte Christliche Kirchengeschichte*, 631.
7. Cambridge University Library, papers of John Thornton, letter from John Newman, 1775. I am grateful to Katherine Carté Engel for this reference.
8. Rush, *Account of the Manners*, 49.
9. Rosenblatt, "Christian Enlightenment"; Sorkin, *Religious Enlightenment*; Campbell, *Religion of the Heart*, 16–17; Sheehan, *Enlightenment Bible*; also see Sheehan, "Enlightenment, Religion."
10. Peucker, "Selection and Destruction," 186.
11. "Michels Weiber" (Michael's wives) could be an allusion to Revelation 8. The meaning of the "Geißbeckel" is even more unclear. Is it perhaps a diminutive of *Geißbock*, or male goat?
12. Godbeer draws a parallel between the submissive (feminine) role of men within the socio-political order of traditional societies towards authority and submission to God (*Sexual Revolution*, 79–80). Within such a societal order the imagery of mystical marriage has a place but may not work well when notions of class change. A similar change took place within the Moravian Church, which moved from a strictly hierarchically organized church under Count Zinzendorf to a collegial form of organization under his successors.

CHAPTER 10

1. Peucker, "Selection and Destruction."
2. Cook, "What Is Past Is Prologue," 48.
3. Jenkinson, *Manual of Archive Administration*, 12–13.
4. Nesmith, "Seeing Archives," 27 (with many bibliographic references).
5. Ketelaar, "Tacit Narratives."
6. Minutes of interim administration, May 30, 1760.
7. Peucker, "Was geschah mit Zinzendorfs 'Grünen Büchern'?"
8. Kröger, Mai, and Nippe, *Das Unitätsarchiv*.
9. "[W]eil die damalige Zeit doch einen eigenen Periodum in der Brüderhistorie ausmacht, der nie diffitiret werden kann." Report of archives revision committee, Zeist, July 26, 1765, R.4.E.24.a, UA. Also see Peucker, "Selection and Destruction."
10. On Moravian record keeping see Peucker, "Herrnhuter Archive"; Peucker, "Pietism and the Archive." Gisela Mettele calls Moravian theology of the eighteenth century a "narrative theology," developed by the writing, hearing, and sharing of reports, biographies, conversion accounts, and diaries. Mettele, *Weltbürgertum*, 153; Mettele, "Erudition vs. Experience."
11. Minutes of synod at Marienborn, 26th session, December 20, 1740, R.2.A.4, UA. The Inspired also kept "diaries," containing the addresses of their prophets. Noth suggests the term "diary" was chosen after the Inspired heard about the Moravian diaries (*Ekstatischer Pietismus*, 150n210, 152).
12. For reference numbers of the individual documents, see the listing in the bibliography.
13. See Ludwig von Schweinitz's marginal note in his transcription of J. Plitt, "Denkwürdigkeiten," par. 246 (UA, bd. 4, p. 520); Schweinitz's report as Unity archivist to General Synod, 1848. In 2001 I inquired with Edna Cooper in Gracehill, who confirmed that this diary was not extant in the Gracehill archives.
14. He studied the diary for his research on the history of the Theological Seminary. See, particularly, Uttendörfer, "Zinzendorf und die Entwicklung," pt. 4, 30. The earliest entry with words (*lustig*, jolly) crossed out is from April 5, 1748.
15. Schweinitz's transcriptions were kept in the Unity Archives in a different building in Herrnhut than the congregational records. The Unity Archives survived the fire of Herrnhut practically unscathed.

16. After 1819 some parts were still distributed as manuscripts. Starting in 1849, they were printed in their entirety under the title *Nachrichten aus der Brüdergemeine*. On the Congregational Accounts, see Mettele, *Weltbürgertum*; Mettele, "Die Zirkulation von Wissen"; Beachy, "Manuscript Missions."

17. For example, Barbara Becker-Cantarino et al., eds., "Pomp, Power, and Politics: Essays on German and Scandinavian Court Culture and Their Contexts," special issue, *Daphnis: Zeitschrift für Mittlere Deutsche Literatur und Kultur der Frühen Neuzeit (1400–1750)* 32, no. 1/2 (2003); J. R. Mulryne et al., eds., *Europa Triumphans: Court and Civic Festivals in Early Modern Europe* (Burlington, Vt.: Ashgate, 2004).

18. For example, Johannes Plitt, E. W. Cröger, Guido Burkhardt, Levin Theodore Reichel, Joseph Mortimer Levering, Joseph E. Hutton, and Gillian Lindt Gollin; see chap. 2.

19. Addresses by women also survive. About Moravian preaching within the context of eighteenth-century preaching in general, see Eijnatten, "Reading Audiences."

20. Schneider, "Geheimer Brief-Wechsel," 214; Noth, *Ekstatischer Pietismus*, 145–53.

21. Uttendörfer, "Aus Zinzendorfs Alltagsleben," 59–62; Schrautenbach, *Der Graf von Zinzendorf*, 65, 70–73. David Cranz was one of the stenographers; see Finze-Michaelsen, "'Die Sache des Heilands,'" 79–82.

22. Erich Beyreuther and Gerhard Meyer state this in their introduction to the reprint of Zinzendorf's works. Zimmerling seems to agree with this assessment. Zimmerling, *Ein Leben für die Kirche*, 19n7.

23. Zimmerling, *Ein Leben für die Kirche*, 17. Also see Uttendörfer, *Zinzendorfs Gedanken*, 17–25. Zimmerling downplays the distinction Zinzendorf made between a *Predigt* and a *Rede*.

24. Zinzendorf, 1749, quoted by Uttendörfer, *Zinzendorfs Gedanken*, 18.

25. Uttendörfer, "Zinzendorf und die Entwicklung," pt. 4, 31–33.

26. The original minutes of the synods are preserved in UA. MAB has some contemporary copies. Transcriptions exist in both UA and MAB.

27. See the overview D. Meyer, *Bibliographisches Handbuch*; also see D. Meyer, "Zinzendorf und Herrnhut," 50. On methods and patterns in the controversy regarding Pietism, see Gierl, *Pietismus und Aufklärung*. Also see Zedler, *Grosses vollständiges Universal-Lexikon*, s.v. "Theologische Streitigkeiten."

28. Erbe, *Herrnhaag*, 131, 138.

29. Ritschl, *Der Pietismus*, 2:196 and 377n2. Cröger, *Geschichte der erneuerten Brüderkirche*, 2:170; Burkhardt, "Zinzendorf und die Brüdergemeine," 560; Levering, *History of Bethlehem*, 188n3. Uttendörfer, on the other hand, believed Volck's claims were "essentially correct" ("Zinzendorf und die Entwicklung," pt. 3, 36). In more recent years, historians have included anti-Moravian publications in their examinations: Fogleman, *Jesus Is Female*; Exalto and Karels, *Waakzame wachters*, chap. 11, discussing the polemics in the Netherlands; Roeber, *Hopes for Better Spouses*.

30. Letters received from Alexander Volck and his family, UA, R.19.B.h.3.13–30. On Volck, also see Gembicki, "Der Herrnhaag"; Miller, "Alexander Volck."

31. Volck, *Unumstößliche Vertheidigung*, 36–38.

32. "[U]nbrüderlicher Falschheit." Johann David Stöhr (1702–74), brother of the Büdingen printer Johann Christoph Stöhr, became a minister of the Moravian Church.

33. An example of his poetry in a letter to Brother and Sister Stöhr [early 1743], R.19.B.h.3.9. His poem on Zinzendorf's return from Pennsylvania was printed: *Gedancken uber [sic] die Wiederkunfft Johanan, des theuren Knechtes unsers Lammes und seiner in Jesu verbundenen Reisefährden*, d. [blank space] April 1743, copy in MAB, library Cb 156 (3). The diary of Herrnhaag notes on April 22, 1743, "In Büdingen a *carmen* on Johanan's return was published, written by town clerk Volck, who commissioned it to be printed."

34. The marriage was not registered in the Herrnhaag/Marienborn church register; it probably took place in Büdingen. Juliana died, eighty-eight years old, in Sachsenhausen in 1788.

Maria Belli-Gontard, *Auszüge der Frag- und Anzeigungs-Nachrichten (des Intelligenzblattes)*, vol. 6 (Frankfurt am Main, 1850), 130.

35. For the various editions, see D. Meyer, *Bibliographisches Handbuch*, 411–15. Volck mentions the English translation (*Das entdeckte Geheimnis*, 5:617).

36. See Köber's correspondence, R.5.A.10.d, R.6.D.I.a.1.a.114, UA. Also see diary Herrnhut, April 21, 1749. In 1751 Carl Heinrich von Peistel sued Volck about a "defamatory letter," R.8.30.a.13, UA.

37. "While those persons in Herrnhaag whom this publication concerns the most admitted in private that things were four times worse in reality than is indicated in this *specilegium*" (indem diejenige Personen in Herrnhaag, welche diese Schrift am nächsten interessirt, *intra parietes* gern zugestunden, es seye [neben den eingemischten Calumnien] viermal mehr wircklich vorgegangen als in diesem *Spicilegio* angezeigt worden). Mag. Friedrich Christoph Steinhofer to Zinzendorf, Stuttgart, March 14, 1749, R.20.C.31.c.140, UA.

38. Catalogs Berlin, 1744–49, R.27.7.3–15, UA. The lists of the Berlin congregation at the Unity Archives are incomplete, and the records of the Berlin congregation were lost during World War II.

39. A "sinner" is a person who realizes her or his deficiency in the light of God's redeeming love.

40. R.27.7.11, UA.

41. [Hecker], *Gespräch*, 34. On Hart see Leeuwenberg, "Zu Hause im Seitenhöhlgen," 145–49n6; Peucker, "'Blut' auf unsre grünen Bändchen,'" 46n29.

42. Hart mentions a "Brother S." [Hecker], *Gespräch*, 52.

43. *The Brethren in Colonial America: A Source Book*, ed. Donald F. Durnbaugh (Elgin, Ill.: Brethren Press, 1967), 79–81.

44. On the Brethren of Skippack, see Durnbaugh, "Brethren and Moravians," 54–55. On Frey, ibid., 61–64.

45. "Frey, Andreas: Reformiert, Schweitz, Pensylvanien, Taüffer, Böhmist, Evangelisch. Trustee vom Synodo, Pilgergemeine und Eremit bey Marienborn auf der Andreas-Burg"; "Catalogus der Knecht und Mägde des Lammes," minutes of synod at Marienborn 1744, R.2.A.10.1.a, p. 31, UA.

46. Various online genealogical resources indicate "Altheim" (Altenheim) in Alsace as Frey's place of birth. The Freys were probably Swiss Mennonites who emigrated to Alsace before continuing on to Pennsylvania.

47. Andreas Frey to Margaretha Merckel, Marienborn, August 24, 1745, BethCong 315, MAB.

48. On Frey's involvement with the Bethlehem congregation, see *The Bethlehem Diary*, vol. 1, 1742–1744, ed. Kenneth G. Hamilton (Bethlehem: Moravian Archives, 1971).

49. See bibliography.

50. Zinzendorf: "He cannot do damage in Pennsylvania, but in Europe he might bring to light some pretty truths." Minutes of synod in Herrnhaag, session 20, June 9, 1747, 897–99, R.2.A.23.a, UA.

51. Spangenberg mentioned this during the special conference about the Sifting Time, Barby, September 26, 1750, 143v. The men who arrived in Bethlehem on June 25, 1748, had left Herrnhaag on February 7, 1748 (G. Reichel, *August Gottlieb Spangenberg*, 179).

52. "There is some truth to the stories he includes but also much wrong, and with many details one can immediately tell they are false. For example, he claims to have heard in a conference that carnal lusts were a true balsam for the heart." Minutes of helpers' conference, Bethlehem, November 8/19, 1748, BethCong 86, MAB.

# BIBLIOGRAPHY

PRIMARY SOURCES

The most important primary sources are listed here. Less frequently cited sources are referenced in full in the footnotes.

*Addresses*

Watteville, Johannes von. Address to the single brothers in Marienborn, March 4, 1750, in collection of sermons by Watteville, 1743–67, MS in library of Unity Archives (NB. III.R.4.53.e, also in Hs 51.b).
Zinzendorf, Christian Renatus von. Address to the congregation in Herrnhaag, March 10, 1748 (BethSB 194, MAB).
———. Address to the single sisters in Herrnhaag on their choir festival, May 4, 1748 (Hs 49, UA). The text contains editorial changes by N. L. von Zinzendorf that are included in the Congregational Accounts; an (incomplete) copy of this text (without Zinzendorf's edits) exists in MAB (BethSB 194).
———. Address to the children in Herrnhaag, December 28, 1748, copy by Hark (ThS A.36.i, UA), 66–70.
Zinzendorf, Nikolaus Ludwig von. Address to the single brothers in Marienborn about play, January 8, 1747, in Congregational Accounts, 1747, suppl. 13.
———. Address to the single brothers in Gnadenfrei, October 1, 1747 (R.4.C.III.7.b, UA; also in Congregational Accounts, 1747, suppl. 82).

*Diaries*

Congregational Accounts (German *Gemeinnachrichten* or *Jüngerhausdiarium*). General diary of Zinzendorf and his staff. Official periodical of the church, beginning in 1747. Copies available in most Moravian archives.
Diary of Johann Christoph Becker (1719–1789) (R.21.A.196, UA).
Diary of Johann Daniel Gottwalt (b. 1726), 1741–88 (R.7.E.a.2, UA).
Diary of Johann Nitschmann (1712–1783), 1756–61 (R.21.A.115.b, UA).
Diary of the Herrnhaag congregation, 1744–48 (R.8.33.d–g, UA).
Diary of the Herrnhut congregation, 1749 (R.6.A.b.17, UA).
Diary of the single brothers in Bethlehem, 1742–62 (BethSB 1, MAB).
Diary of the single brothers in Herrnhaag, 1742 (R.8.39.b); 1745 (R.4.C.III.5); 1746–47 (R.8.39.c); August–September 1749 (R.4.C.III.5); 1750 (R.8.39.d); 1751 (R.4.C.III.5, UA).
Diary of the single brothers in Herrnhut, 1744–49. Original lost in 1945, but partial copies by Unity Archivist Ludwig von Schweinitz exist in the Unity Archives (R.24.B.79.II).
Diary of the single brothers (Theological Seminary) in Marienborn, 1748–50 (R.4.B.V.b.2, UA).

Diary of the single brothers in Zeist, 1749 (EBG Zeist, broederkoor, inv. nr. 81).
Diary of the Moravian Paedagogium in Peilau, Silesia, 1749 (R.4.B.IV.2.d, UA).

*Letters*

Geller, Friedrich Oswald. To Johann Nitschmann, Marienborn, July 29, 1746 (R.21.A.114.b.159.a, UA). Nitschmann, Anna. To Christian Renatus, [London, February 10 (new style), 1749] (R.3.A.8.13.b.2); copy in MAB (PP Zdf 23.4).
Members of the interim administration in Herrnhut to the elders in Bethlehem, 1760–64 (PHC 1, MAB).
Petsch, Johannes. To Zinzendorf, Heerendijk, August 2, 1752, copy by Ludwig von Schweinitz (R.21.A.123, UA). Original destroyed by Unity archivist Christlieb Suter in 1802. Copy made by assistant archivist Gottlob Martin Schneider between 1791 and 1795; given to Unity archivist Ludwig von Schweinitz in 1836 and included in one of Schweinitz's collections of transcripts.
Watteville, Johannes von. To Christian Renatus, January–April 1750 (R.20.C.36.g, UA); Oct.–Dec. 1750 (R.6.A.a.46.1.2–5, UA).
———. To Zinzendorf, 1748–49 (R.14.A.33, UA); February–April 1750 (R.20.C.36.g, UA).
Zinzendorf, Nikolaus Ludwig von. Circular letter of reprimand to all the congregations and missions, London, February 10, 1749. Draft in Zinzendorf's hand (R.3.A.8.13.1, UA); fair copy in unknown hand with revisions by Zinzendorf (R.3.A.8.13.2, UA); fair copy in unknown hand with small changes by Zinzendorf that were not incorporated in the final copy (R.3.A.8.13.3, UA); final copy in unknown hand (R.3.A.8.13.4, UA); fair copy for "America," with additional changes by Zinzendorf (R.3.A.8.13.5, UA); fair copy for the Dutch congregations (R.20.C.24.208, UA); fair copy with underlining in red by Zinzendorf (R.24.B.45, UA: Johannes Plitts Notizsammlung zur Sichtungszeit); fair copy for Bethlehem and the other American congregations (Zinzendorf Papers, no. 22, MAB). Text-critical edition of the German text in Peucker, "Blut' auf unsre grünen Bändchen," 81–88; edition of the German text with English translation in Atwood, "Zinzendorf's 1749 Reprimand," 67–74.
———. To Christian Renatus Zinzendorf, London, February 10 (new style), 1749 (R.3.A.8.13.b.1, UA); copy in MA (PP Zdf 23.3); printed in Peucker, "Blut' auf unsre grünen Bändchen," 88–91.

*Minutes*

Synod in Marienborn, July 11–27, 1745 (R.2.A.15.1, UA).
Synod in Zeist, May 12–June 15, 1746 (R.2.A.19, UA; also SynConf 28, MAB).
Synod in Herrnhaag, May 12–June 14, 1747 (R.2.A.23, UA).
Provincial Synod in Gnadenberg, May 12–13, 1750 (SynConf 33, MAB).
Special conference about the events of the previous years during Synod in Barby, September 26, 1750 (R.2.A.28.A.1, 135–64).
Single brothers' synod in Ingatestone Hall and London, Dec. 19, 1752–Jan. 15, 1753 (R.2.A.32.b, UA). Also copies in Moravian Archives of Zeist (broederkoor, inv. nr. 124) and Bethlehem (SynConf 38), but without the special conference.
Interim administration (Ratskonferenz, Enge Konferenz), 1760–64 (R.6.A.b.44, UA; on microfilm at MAB; excerpts from the years 1760–62 at MAB, SynConf 42).
General Synod in Marienborn, July 1–August 27, 1764: minutes (R.2.B.44.1.c, UA), results (*Verlass*) (copies in most Moravian archives), committee report on the role of women (R.2.B.44.4.a.5, UA).
General Synod in Marienborn, July 1–September 17, 1764 (R.2.B.45.1).

*Other*

Chorale book of Moravian tunes. Compiled by Anna Catharina Höffly. MS, ca. 1750 (NB. IV.R.1.51.51, H.4, UA).
"Liedbüchlein 1749." Songbook (MS, 1749, UA).
Plitt, Johannes. "Geschichte der Brüder-Unität alter und neuer Zeit." 4 vols., 1828–41 (MSS 2, MAB). Copy was made for the Theological Seminary in Bethlehem. The original and a copy from the Theological Seminary at Gnadenfeld/Herrnhut are in the Unity archives. Sometimes referred to as the "Denkwürdigkeiten aus der Alten und Erneuerten Brüdergeschichte."
Reports of Single Brothers' Festivals in Herrnhaag, 1746 (R.4.C.III.7.a.5.c, UA); 1747 (EBG Zeist, broederkoor, no. 129); 1748 (longer version R.4.C.III.7.b, R.24.B.78.XI, UA; shorter, edited version in JHD).

*Printed Sources*

Acrelius, Israel. "A Visit by the Rev. Provost Israel Acrelius to the American Cloister at Bethlehem." In *A History of New Sweden or, The Settlements on the River Delaware*, edited by William M. Reynolds, 402–44. Philadelphia: Historical Society of Pennsylvania, 1874.
*Acta Historico-Ecclesiastica oder gesammlete Nachrichten von den neuesten Kirchen-Geschichten* 13 (1750): 959–62.
Arnold, Gottfried. *Die erste Liebe der Gemeinen Jesu Christi, das ist Wahre Abbildung der ersten Christen....* Frankfurt am Main: Zu finden in Gottlieb Friedeburgs Buchhandlung, 1696.
———. *Historie und Beschreibung der mystischen Theologie oder geheimen Gottes Gelehrtheit, wie auch derer alten und neuen Mysticorum.* Frankfurt: Thomas Fritsche, 1703.
Bothe, Heinrich Joachim. *Zuverläßige Beschreibung des nunmehro ganz entdeckten Herrenhutischen Ehe-Geheimnisses, nebst dessen 17 Grund-Artickeln, wornach sie in demselben unterrichtet und eingerichtet werden, mit mehreren merkwürdigen, die Lehre, Lebens-Art und Absichten der so genanten Mährischen Brüder-Gemeine betreffenden Umständen.* 2 vols. Berlin, 1751–52.
Brotherly Union and Agreement of Herrnhut (Brüderlicher Verein und Willkür), 1727. In Hahn and Reichel, *Zinzendorf*, 75–80.
*A Collection of Hymns, with Several Translations from the Hymn-Book of the Moravian Brethren.* Pt. 2. London: James Hutton, 1746. *A Collection of Hymns: Consisting Chiefly of Translations from the German Hymn-Book of the Moravian Brethren.* Pt. 3. London: James Hutton, 1748. This is the English Moravian hymnbook, containing many translations from German Moravian hymns but also original texts.
Cranz, David. *Alte und neue Brüder-Historie oder kurz gefaßte Geschichte der Evangelischen Brüder-Unität in den ältern Zeiten und insonderheit in dem gegenwärtigen Jahrhundert.* 2nd ed. Barby: Christian Friedrich Laux, 1772. English translation: *The Ancient and Modern History of the Brethren....* Translated by Benjamin La Trobe. London, 1780.
[———.] *Kurze, zuverlässige Nachricht von der unter dem Namen der Böhmische Mährischen Brüder bekanten, Kirche Unitas Fratrum Herkommen, Lehr Begrif, äussern und innern Kirchen Verfassung und Gebräuchen.* N.p., 1757. Known as *Zeremonienbüchlein* or *Book of Ceremonies.*
[Demelius, C. F.] *Vollständige So wohl Historisch und Theologische Nachricht von der Herrenhuthischen Brüderschafft....* Frankfurt and Leipzig: Auf Kosten des Autoris, 1735.
Frey, Andreas. *Seine Declaration, oder Erklärung, auf welche Weise, und wie er unter die sogenante Herrnhuter Gemeine gekommen, und warum er wieder davon abgegangen. Nebst der Beweg-Ursache, warum ers publicirt.* Germantown: Christoph Saur, 1748. Text included

in Volck, *Das entdeckte Geheimnis*, 373–476. Translated as Frey, *True and Authentic Account*.

———. *A True and Authentic Account of Andrew Frey: Containing the Occasion of His Coming Among the Herrnhuters or Moravians, translated from the German*. London: J. Robinson, 1753.

*Das Gesang-Buch der Gemeine in Herrnhuth. Daselbst zu finden im Waysen-Hause*. 1735. The hymnbook was reprinted in 1737 and 1741. Between 1737 and 1745 twelve appendices (*Anhänge*) were published, followed by four supplements (*Zugaben*), 1746–48. Cited as *Herrnhuter Gesangbuch*.

*Geschichte des Pietismus*. 4 vols. Göttingen: Vandenhoeck & Ruprecht, 1993–2004.

Grimm, Jacob, and Wilhelm Grimm. *Deutsches Wörterbuch*. 33 vols. Leipzig, 1854–1971.

[Hecker, A. P.] *Gespräch eines Ev.-Luth. Predigers mit einem, der über 6 Jahr sich zu der Gemeine der sogenanten Mährischen Brüder gehalten*. . . . Berlin: Buchhandlung der Berlinischen Real-Schule, [1751].

Moser, Johann Jacob. *Lebensgeschichte, von ihm selbst beschrieben*. 3rd ed. Frankfurt, 1777.

Rhode, August Anton. *Schlüssel zu Herrnhut, oder Entdecktes Lehrgebäude der Herrnhuter*. . . . Berlin and Potsdam: Christian Friedrich Voß, 1755.

Rush, Benjamin. *An Account of the Manners of the German Inhabitants of Pennsylvania, written 1789*. Philadelphia: Samuel P. Town, 1875.

Schrautenbach, Ludwig Carl von. *Der Graf von Zinzendorf und die Brüdergemeine seiner Zeit*. Edited by F. W. Kölbing. Gnadau: H. L. Menz, 1851.

*Some Other Hymns and Poems: Consisting Chiefly of Translations from the German*. London, 1752.

Spangenberg, August Gottlieb. *Darlegung richtiger Antworten auf mehr als dreyhundert Beschuldigungen gegen den Ordinarium Fratrum, nebst verschiedenen wichtigen Beylagen*. Leipzig: Marchesche Buchhandlung, 1751.

———. *Declaration über die zeither gegen uns ausgegangene Beschuldigungen, sonderlich die Person unsers Ordinarii betreffend*. . . . Leipzig: Marchesche Buchhandlung, 1751.

———. *Leben des Herrn Nicolaus Ludwig Grafen und Herrn von Zinzendorf und Pottendorf*. 8 parts. [Barby]: zu finden in den Brüder-Gemeinen, [1772]–75.

———. *Schluß-Schrift, Worinn über tausend Beschuldigungen gegen die Brüder-Gemeinen und Ihren zeitherigen Ordinarium nach der Wahrheit beantwortet werden*. Leipzig: Marchesche Buchhandlung, 1752. Cited as *Apologetische Schlußschrift*.

[Thierbach, J. F.] *Diarium Herrnhutianum, das ist: Gewissenhaffte Erzehlung alles dessen, was einem Evangelischen Lehrer in einigen Jahren mit den Herrnhuthisch gesinnten Seelen begegnet*. . . . 2 vols. Erfurt, 1748–49.

Töllner, Johann Gottlieb, ed. *Kurzgefaßte Christliche Kirchengeschichte, aus dem Lateinischen ins Deutsche übersezt, mit einigen Anmerkungen versehen, und bis auf die gegenwärtige Zeiten fortgeführt*. By Johann Alphonsus Turretin. Königsberg: Hartung, 1759.

Volck, Alexander. *Das entdeckte Geheimnis der Bosheit der Herrnhutischen Secte zu Errettung vieler unschuldigen Seelen, zur Warnung der mit Vorurtheilen eingenommenen Gutmeyner, und zur Offenbahrung der Verirreten und Verwirrten Verführer*. . . . 7 parts (*entrevues*). Frankfurt: Heinrich Ludwig Brönner, 1748–51.

———. *Unumstößliche Vertheidigung der Glaubwürdigkeit des entdeckten Geheimniß der Boßheit der Herrnhutischen Secte*. . . . Frankfurt and Leipzig: Heinrich Ludwig Brönner, 1750.

Zedler, Johann Heinrich. *Grosses vollständiges Universal-Lexicon aller Wissenschafften und Künste*. Leipzig and Halle: J. H. Zedler, 1731–54.

Zinzendorf, Nikolaus Ludwig von. *Auszüge aus des Seligen Ordinarii . . . Reden über die vier Evangelisten*. Edited by Gottfried Clemens. 4 vols. Barby, 1766–73.

———. *Der Oeffentlichen Gemein-Reden im Jahr 1747*. Vol. 1, Zu finden in den Brüder-Gemeinen, 1748; vol. 2, Zu finden in den Brüder-Gemeinen, 1749. Cited as *Gemeinreden*.

———. *Die an den Synodum der Brüder in Zeyst vom 11. May bis den 21. Junii 1746 gehaltene Reden, nebst noch einigen andern zu gleicher Zeit in Holland geschehenen Vorträgen*. Zu finden in den Brüder-Gemeinen, [1747]. Cited as *Zeister Reden*.

———. *Ein und zwanzig Discurse über die Augspurgische Confession, gehalten vom 15. Dec. 1747 bis zum 3. Mart. 1748 denen Seminariis Theologicis Fratrum*. . . . [1748.]

———. *Haupt-Schlüssel zum herrnhutischen Ehe-Sacrament, das ist: Des Hrn. Grafen von Zinzendorf an das Ehe-Chor gehaltenen Reden*. Edited by [Johann Gottlob Seidel]. Frankfurt, 1755.

———. *Maxims, Theological Ideas and Sentences out of the Present Ordinary of the Brethren's Churches, his Dissertations and Discourses from the Year 1738 till 1747*. Edited by John Gambold. London, 1751.

———. *Περι εαυτου, das ist Naturelle Reflexiones über allerhand Materien*. . . . N.p., [1747–48]. Cited as *Naturelle Reflexionen*.

———. *Vier und Dreyßig Homiliae über die Wunden-Litaney der Brüder, gehalten auf dem Herrnhaag in den Sommer-Monathen 1747 von dem Ordinario Fratrum*. Zu finden in den Brüder-Gemeinen, [1747]. Cited as *Homilien über die Wundenlitanei*.

## SECONDARY SOURCES

Atwood, Craig D. "Apologizing for the Moravians: Spangenberg's *Idea Fidei Fratrum*." *JMH*, no. 8 (2010): 53–88.

———. *Community of the Cross: Moravian Piety in Colonial Bethlehem*. University Park: Pennsylvania State University Press, 2004.

———. "Deep in the Side of Jesus: The Persistence of Zinzendorfian Piety in Colonial America." In Gillespie and Beachy, *Pious Pursuits*, 50–64.

———. "'The Hallensians Are Pietists; Aren't You a Hallensian?' Mühlenberg's Conflict with the Moravians in America." *JMH* 12, no. 1 (2012): 47–92.

———. "'He Has Carried You My Members': The Full Humanity of Christ and the Blessing of the Physical Body in Zinzendorfian Piety." In *Alter Adam und Neue Kreatur: Pietismus und Anthropogie; Beiträge zum II. Internationalen Kongress für Pietismusforschung 2005*, edited by Udo Sträter et al., 197–207. Halle: Franckesche Stiftungen, 2009.

———. "Interpreting and Misinterpreting the Sichtungszeit." In Brecht and Peucker, *Neue Aspekte der Zinzendorf-Forschung*, 174–87.

———. "Little Side Holes: Moravian Devotional Cards of the Mid-eighteenth Century." *JMH*, no. 6 (2009): 61–75.

———. "The Mother of God's People: The Adoration of the Holy Spirit in the Eighteenth-Century Brüdergemeine." *Church History: Studies in Christianity and Culture* 68 (1999): 886–909.

———. "Sleeping in the Arms of Christ: Sanctifying Sexuality in the Eighteenth-Century Moravian Church." *Journal of the History of Sexuality* 8 (1997): 25–51.

———. *The Theology of the Czech Brethren from Hus to Comenius*. University Park: Pennsylvania State University Press, 2009.

———. "Understanding Zinzendorf's Blood and Wounds Theology." *JMH*, no. 1 (2006): 31–47.

———. "The Union of Masculine and Feminine in Zinzendorfian Piety." In Faull, *Masculinity, Senses, Spirit*, 11–37.

———. "The Use of the 'Ancient Unity' in the Historiography of the Moravian Church." *JMH* 13, no. 2 (2013): 109–57.
———. "Zinzendorf's Litany of the Wounds of the Husband." *Lutheran Quarterly* 11 (1997): 189–214.
———. "Zinzendorf's 1749 Reprimand to the *Brüdergemeine*." *TMHS* 29 (1996): 59–84.
Baar, Mirjam de. "Conflicting Discourses on Female Dissent in the Early Modern Period: The Case of Antoinette Bourignon (1616–1680)." *L'Atelier du Centre de recherches historiques: Revue électronique du CRH* 4 (2009).
Bach, Jeff. *Voices of the Turtledoves: The Sacred World of Ephrata*. University Park: Pennsylvania State University Press, 2003.
Bahlcke, Joachim. "Religiöse Kommunikation im Dreieck Berlin—Lissa—Herrnhut: Zinzendorf, die Erneuerte Brüder-Unität und das Verhältnis zur polinischen Unitas Fratrum in der ersten Hälfte des 18. Jahrhunderts." *UF*, no. 67/68 (2012): 31–49.
Beachy, Robert. "Manuscript Missions in the Age of the Moravian Community in the Atlantic World." In Gillespie and Beachy, *Pious Pursuits*, 33–49.
Becker, Bernhard. *Zinzendorf und sein Christentum im Verhältnis zum kirchlichen und religiösen Leben seiner Zeit*. 2nd ed. Leipzig: Friedrich Jansa, 1900. [1st ed.: *Zinzendorf im Verhältnis zu Philosophie und Kirchentum seiner Zeit*, 1886.]
Benham, Daniel. *Memoirs of James Hutton: Comprising the Annals of His Life and Connection with the United Brethren*. London: Hamilton, Adams, 1856.
Bernet, Claus. *"Gebaute Apokalypse": Die Utopie des Himmlischen Jerusalem in der Frühen Neuzeit*. Mainz: Zabern, 2007.
———. "Die Stadt Gottes in der Wetterau: Die Geschichte Herrnhaags als ein utopischer Siedlungsversuch im Umfeld des radikalen Pietismus." *UF*, no. 59/60 (2007): 135–72.
Bettermann, Wilhelm. *Theologie und Sprache bei Zinzendorf*. Gotha: L. Klotz, 1935.
Beyreuther, Erich. "Ehe-Religion und Eschaton bei Zinzendorf." In *Studien zur Theologie Zinzendorfs: Gesammelte Aufsätze*, 35–73. Neukirchen-Vluyn: Buchhandlung des Erziehungsvereins, 1962.
———. "Einführung in die Vierunddreißig Homilien über die Wunden-Litanei (1747) und in die Zeister Synodalreden (1746)." In *Reden während der Sichtungszeit in der Wetterau und in Holland*, by Nikolaus Ludwig von Zinzendorf, xxvi–xxxvii. Nikolaus Ludwig von Zinzendorf Hauptschriften 3. Hildesheim: Olms, 1963.
———. *Zinzendorf und die Christenheit, 1732–1760*. Marburg an der Lahn: Francke-Buchhandlung, 1961.
Beyreuther, Gottfried. "Sexualtheorien im Pietismus." Diss., Ludwig-Maximilians-Universität München, 1963.
Bloch, Ruth H. "Changing Conceptions of Sexuality and Romance in Eighteenth-Century America." *William and Mary Quarterly*, 3rd ser., 60 (2003): 13–42.
Böttner, Renate. "Johannes von Watteville." In *Lebensbilder aus der Brüdergemeine*, edited by Dietrich Meyer, 77–87. Herrnhut: Herrnhuter Verlag, 2007.
Bouman-Komen, Truus. *Bruderliebe und Feindeshass: Eine Untersuchung von frühen Zinzendorftexten (1713–1727) in ihrem kirchengeschichtlichen Kontext*. Hildesheim: Olms, 2009.
Brecht, Martin, and Paul Peucker. *Neue Aspekte der Zinzendorf-Forschung*. Arbeiten zur Geschichte des Pietismus 47. Göttingen: Vandenhoeck & Ruprecht, 2006.
Breul, Wolfgang. "Ehe und Sexualität im radikalen Pietismus." In Breul, Meier, and Vogel, *Der radikale Pietismus*, 403–18.
———. "Gottfried Arnold und das eheliche und unverehelichte Leben." In *Alter Adam und Neue Kreatur: Pietismus und Anthropologie; Beiträge zum II. Internationalen Kongress für Pietismusforschung 2005*, edited by Udo Sträter et al., 357–69. Tübingen: Max Niemeyer, 2009.

———. "Marriage and Marriage-Criticism in Pietism: Philipp Jakob Spener, Gottfried Arnold, and Nikolaus Ludwig von Zinzendorf." In *Pietism and Community in Europe and North America, 1650–1850*, edited by Jonathan Strom, 37–53. Brill's Series in Church History 45. Leiden: Brill, 2010.

———. "Theological Tenets and Motives of Mission: August Hermann Francke, Nikolaus Ludwig von Zinzendorf." In *Migration and Religion: Christian Transatlantic Missions, Islamic Migration to Germany*, edited by Barbara Becker-Cantarino, 41–60. Chloe, Beihefte zum Daphnis 46. Amsterdam: Rodopi, 2012.

Breul, Wolfgang, Marcus Meier, and Lothar Vogel. *Der radikale Pietismus: Perspektiven der Forschung*. Göttingen: Vandenhoeck & Ruprecht, 2010.

Breul, Wolfgang, and Christian Soboth, eds. *"Der Herr wird seine Herrlichkeit an uns offenbahren": Liebe, Ehe und Sexualität im Pietismus*. Halle: Verlag der Franckeschen Stiftungen, 2012.

Bunners, Christian. "Gesangbuch." In *Glaubenswelt und Lebenswelten*, edited by Hartmut Lehmann, vol. 4 of *Geschichte des Pietismus*, 121–42. Göttingen: Vandenhoeck & Ruprecht, 2004.

———. "Musik." In Lehmann, *Glaubenswelt und Lebenswelten*, 430–55.

———. "Pietismus und kirchliches Lied im 17. und frühen 18. Jahrhundert. Zu einigen Forschungsfragen." In *Musikkonzepte—Konzepte der Musikwissenschaft: Bericht über den Internationalen Kongress der Gesellschaft für Musikforschung Halle (Saale) 1998*, edited by Kathrin Eberl and Wolfgang Ruf, 226–32. Kassel: Bärenreiter, 2000.

Burkhardt, Guido. *Entstehung und geschichtliche Entwicklung der Brüdergemeine mit besonderer Berücksichtigung des Deutschen Zweiges der Unität*. Vol. 1 of *Die Brüdergemeine*. Gnadau: Unitäts-Buchhandlung, 1893.

———. "Zinzendorf und die Brüdergemeine." In *Real-Enzyclopädie für protestantische Theologie und Kirche*, 508–92. Gotha: Rudolf Besser, 1864; also published separately: *Zinzendorf und die Brüdergemeine*. Gotha: Rudolf Besser, 1866.

Bynum, Caroline Walker. "The Blood of Christ in the Later Middle Ages." *Church History* 71 (2002): 685–714.

———. *Jesus as Mother: Studies in the Spirituality of the High Middle Ages*. Berkeley: University of California Press, 1984.

———. *The Resurrection of the Body in Western Christianity, 200–1336*. New York: Columbia University Press, 1995.

———. *Wonderful Blood: Theology and Practice in Late Medieval Northern Germany and Beyond*. Philadelphia: University of Pennsylvania Press, 2007.

Campbell, Ted A. *The Religion of the Heart: A Study of European Religious Life in the Seventeenth and Eighteenth Centuries*. Eugene, Ore.: Wipf and Stock, 2000.

Carstensen, Ulrike. *Stadtplanung im Pietismus: Herrnhaag in der Wetterau und die frühe Architektur der Herrnhuter Brüdergemeine*. Herrnhut: Herrnhuter Verlag, 2009.

Clark, Elizabeth A. "The Celibate Bridegroom and His Virginal Brides: Metaphor and the Marriage of Jesus in Early Christian Ascetic Exegesis." *Church History* 77 (2008): 1–25.

Cook, Terry. "What Is Past Is Prologue: A History of Archival Ideas Since 1898, and the Future Paradigm Shift." *Archivaria* 43 (1997): 17–63.

Crews, C. Daniel. *Faith, Love, Hope: A History of the Unitas Fratrum*. Winston-Salem, N.C.: Moravian Archives, 2008.

Cröger, E. W. *Geschichte der erneuerten Brüderkirche*. 3 vols. Gnadau: Unitätsbuchhandlung, 1851–54.

d'Emilio, John, and Estelle B. Freedman. *Intimate Matters: A History of Sexuality in America*. 2nd ed. Chicago: University of Chicago Press, 1997.

Dohm, Burkhard. *Poetische Alchimie: Öffnung zur Sinnlichkeit in der Hohelied- und Bibeldichtung von der protestantischen Barockmystik bis zum Pietismus.* Tübingen: Max Niemeyer Verlag, 2000.
Durnbaugh, Donald F. "Brethren and Moravians in Colonial America." *UF*, no. 25 (1989): 51–68.
———. "Jane Ward Leade (1624–1704) and the Philadelphians." In *The Pietist Theologians: An Introduction to Theology in the Seventeenth and Eighteenth Centuries*, edited by Carter Lindberg, 128–46. Malden, Mass.: Blackwell, 2005.
Eberhard, Samuel. *Kreuzes-Theologie: Das reformatorische Anliegen in Zinzendorfs Verkündigung.* Munich: Chr. Kaiser Verlag, 1937.
Eijnatten, Joris van. "Reaching Audiences: Sermons and Oratory in Europe." In *Cambridge History of Christianity*, vol. 7, *Enlightenment, Reawakening and Revolution 1660–1815*, edited by Stewart J. Brown and Timothy Tackett, 128–46. Cambridge: Cambridge University Press, 2008.
Engel, Katherine Carté. *Religion and Profit: Moravians in Early America.* Philadelphia: University of Pennsylvania Press, 2009.
Erbe, Hans-Walter. *Herrnhaag: Eine religiöse Kommunität im 18. Jahrhundert.* Hamburg: Wittig, 1988.
———. "Herrnhaag: Tiefpunkt oder Höhepunkt der Brüdergeschichte?" *UF*, no. 26 (1989): 37–51.
Erben, Patrick M. *A Harmony of the Spirits: Translation and the Language of Community in Early Pennsylvania.* Chapel Hill: University of North Carolina Press, 2012.
Exalto, John, and Jan-Kees Karels. *Waakzame wachters en kleine vossen: Gereformeerden en herrnhutters in de Nederlanden, 1734–1754.* Heerenveen: Groen, 2001.
Faull, Katherine M. "Christ's Other Self: Gender, the Body, and Religion in the Eighteenth-Century Moravian Church." *Covenant Quarterly* 62, no. 2 (2004): 28–41.
———. "Faith and Imagination: Nikolaus Ludwig von Zinzendorf's Anti-Enlightenment Philosophy of Self." In "Anthropology and the German Enlightenment: Perspectives on Humanity," edited by Katherine M. Faull, special issue, *Bucknell Review* 38, no. 2 (1995): 23–56.
———. "Girl Talk: The Role of the 'Speakings' in the Pastoral Care of the Older Girls' Choir." *JMH*, no. 6 (2009): 77–99.
———. "The Married Choir Instructions (1785)." *JMH*, no. 10 (2011): 69–110.
———, ed. *Masculinity, Senses, Spirit.* Lewisburg: Bucknell University Press, 2011.
———. "Masculinity in the Eighteenth-Century Moravian Mission Field: Contact and Negotiation." *JMH* 13, no. 1 (2013): 27–53.
———. "Temporal Men and the Eternal Bridegroom: Moravian Masculinity in the Eighteenth Century." In Faull, *Masculinity, Senses, Spirit*, 55–79.
Finze-Michaelsen, Holger. "'Die Sache des Heilands': David Cranz (1723–1777), sein Leben und seine Schriften." *UF*, no. 41 (1997): 75–108.
Fogleman, Aaron Spencer. *Jesus Is Female: Moravians and the Challenge of Radical Religion in Early America.* Philadelphia: University of Pennsylvania Press, 2007.
———. "Jesus Is Female: The Moravian Challenge in the German Communities of British North America." *William and Mary Quarterly*, 3rd ser., 40 (2003): 295–332.
———. "'Jesus ist weiblich': Die herrnhutische Herausforderung in den Deutschen Gemeinden Nordamerikas im 18. Jahrhundert." *Historische Anthropologie* 9, no. 2 (2001): 167–194.
Föller, Oskar. *Pietismus und Enthusiasmus: Streit unter Verwandten; Geschichtliche Aspekte der Einordnung und Beurteilung enthusiastisch-charismatischer Frömmigkeit.* Wuppertal: R. Brockhaus, 1998.
Freeman, Arthur J. *An Ecumenical Theology of the Heart: The Theology of Count Nicholas Ludwig von Zinzendorf.* Bethlehem: Moravian Church, 1998.

Geiger, Erika. *Erdmuth Dorothea, Countess Von Zinzendorf: Noble Servant*. Translated by Julie Tomberlin Weber. Winston-Salem, N.C.: John F. Blair, 2006.

———. "Zinzendorfs Ehen und sein Eheverständnis." In Meyer and Peucker, *Graf ohne Grenzen*, 43–51.

———. "Zinzendorfs Stellung zum Halleschen Bußkampf und zum Bekehrungserlebnis." *UF*, no. 49/50 (2002): 13–22.

Gembicki, Dieter. "Der Herrnhaag (1738–1750): Skandal für Zeitgenossen, Ort der Erinnerung für Herrnhuter/Moravians." *Büdinger Geschichtsblätter: Historisches Nachrichtenblatt für den ehemaligen Kreis Büdingen* 22 (2011): 253–66.

Gestrich, Andreas. "Ehe, Familie, Kinder im Pietismus: Der 'gezähmte Teufel.'" In *Geschichte des Pietismus*, vol. 4, *Glaubenswelt und Lebenswelten*, edited by Hartmut Lehmann, 498–521. Göttingen: Vandenhoeck & Ruprecht, 2004.

Gierl, Martin. *Pietismus und Aufklärung: Theologische Polemik und die Kommunikationsreform der Wissenschaft am Ende des 17. Jahrhunderts*. Göttingen: Vandenhoeck & Ruprecht, 1997.

Gill, Markus. "Die Zeit der Brüdergemeine auf dem Herrnhaag in der Wahrnehmung späterer Generationen." Thesis, Predigerseminar Herrnhut, 2000.

Gill, Theo. "Hoheit und Torheit: Zinzendorfs Titel." *UF*, no. 49/50 (2002): 1–11.

Gillespie, Michele, and Robert Beachy, eds. *Pious Pursuits: German Moravians in the Atlantic World*. European Expansion and Global Interaction 7. New York: Berghahn, 2007.

Gleixner, Ulrike. "Zwischen göttlicher und weltlicher Ordnung: Die Ehe im lutherischen Pietismus." *PuN* 28 (2002): 147–84.

Godbeer, Richard. *The Overflowing of Friendship: Love Between Men and the Creation of the American Republic*. Baltimore: Johns Hopkins University Press, 2009.

———. *Sexual Revolution in Early America*. Baltimore: Johns Hopkins University Press, 2002.

Goebel, Max. *Geschichte des christlichen Lebens in der rheinisch-westphälischen evangelischen Kirche*. Vol. 3, *Die niederrheinische reformirte Kirche und der Separatismus in Wittgenstein und am Niederrhein im achtzehnten Jahrhundert*. Koblenz: Karl Bädeker, 1860.

Goeters, Johann Friedrich Gerhard. "Der reformierte Pietismus in Bremen und am Niederrhein im 18. Jahrhundert." In *Geschichte des Pietismus*, vol. 2, *Der Pietismus im achtzehnten Jahrhundert*, edited by Martin Brecht and Klaus Deppermann, 372–427. Göttingen: Vandenhoeck & Ruprecht, 1995.

Gollin, Gillian Lindt. *Moravians in Two Worlds: A Study of Changing Communities*. New York: Columbia University Press, 1967.

Götz, Ignacio L. "Sex and Mysticism." *Cross Currents* 54, no. 3 (2004): 7–22.

Greven, Philip. *The Protestant Temperament: Patterns of Child-Rearing, Religious Experience, and the Self in Early America*. Chicago: University of Chicago Press, 1988.

Hagen, F. F. *Unitas Fratrum in Extremis, or Thoughts on the Past and Present Condition of the Moravian Church in America, Respectfully Submitted to the Provincial Synod of 1893 at Bethlehem, Pa*. Bethlehem: Moravian Publication Office, 1893.

Hahn, Hans-Christoph. "Das Bild Zinzendorfs nach seinem Tode." In Brecht and Peucker, *Neue Aspekte der Zinzendorf-Forschung*, 256–71.

Hahn, Hans-Christoph, and Hellmut Reichel, eds. *Zinzendorf und die Herrnhuter Brüder: Quellen zur Geschichte der Brüder-Unität von 1722 bis 1760*. Hamburg: Friedrich Wittig, 1977.

Hamilton, J. Taylor. *A History of the Church Known as the Moravian Church, or the Unitas Fratrum, or the Unity of the Brethren, During the Eighteenth and Nineteenth Centuries*. Bethlehem: Times, 1900.

———. "A History of the Unitas Fratrum or Moravian Church, in the United States of America." In *A History of the Reformed Church, Dutch, the Reformed Church, German*, *and the Moravian Church in the United States*, by E. T. Corwin, J. H. Dubbs, and J. T. Hamilton, 425–508. American Church History Series 8. New York: Christian Literature, 1895.

Hamilton, J. Taylor, and Kenneth G. Hamilton. *History of the Moravian Church: The Renewed Unitas Fratrum, 1722–1957*. Bethlehem, Pa.: Moravian Church, 1967.

Hessel-Robinson, Timothy. "Erotic Mysticism in Puritan Eucharistic Spirituality." *Studies in Spirituality* 19 (2009): 98–112.

Hunter, David G. "The Virgin, the Bride, and the Church: Reading Psalm 45 in Ambrose, Jerome, and Augustine." *Church History* 69 (2000): 281–303.

Hutton, Joseph E. *A History of the Moravian Church*. London: Moravian Publication Office, 1909.

Jannasch, Wilhelm. "Christian Renatus Graf von Zinzendorf." Pt. 1, ZBG 2, no. 2 (1908): 45–80; pt. 2, ZBG 3, no. 1 (1909): 62–93.

———. "Erdmuthe Dorothea, Gräfin von Zinzendorf, geborene Gräfin Reuss zu Plauen. Ihre Leben als Beitrag zur Geschichte des Pietismus under Brüdergemeine dargestellt." ZBG (1914).

Jenkinson, Hilary. *A Manual of Archive Administration Including the Problems of War Archives and Archive Making*. Oxford: Clarendon Press, 1922.

Juster, Susan. "Eros and Desire in Early Modern Spirituality." *William and Mary Quarterly*, 3rd ser., 60 (2003): 203–6.

Kaiser, Tobias. *Zinzendorfs Schriftverständnis in seinem theologiegeschichtlichen Kontext*. Herrnhut: Herrnhuter Verlag, 2013.

Ketelaar, Eric. "Tacit Narratives: The Meanings of Archives." *Archival Science* 1 (2001): 131–41.

Kinkel, Gary Steven. *Our Dear Mother the Spirit: An Investigation of Count Zinzendorf's Theology and Practice*. Lanham, Md.: University Press of America, 1990.

Knox, R. A. *Enthusiasm: A Chapter in the History of Religion, with Special Reference to the XVII and XVIII Centuries*. Oxford: Clarendon Press, 1950.

Kölbing, Paul. "Zur Charakteristik der Theologie Zinzendorfs." *Zeitschrift für Theologie und Kirche* 10 (1900): 245–83.

Kröger, Rüdiger. "Spangenberg als Biograph Zinzendorfs: Die Entstehungsgeschichte von Spangenbergs Leben Zinzendorfs." *UF*, no. 61/62 (2009): 59–73.

Kröger, Rüdiger, Claudia Mai, and Olaf Nippe. *Das Unitätsarchiv: Aus der Geschichte von Archiv, Bibliothek und Beständen*. Herrnhut: Comenius-Buchhandlung, 2014.

Lawrence, Anna M. *One Family Under God: Love, Belonging, and Authority in Early Transatlantic Methodism*. Philadelphia: University of Pennsylvania Press, 2011.

Leeuwenberg, H. "'Zu Hause im Seitenhöhlgen.' De 'Sichtungszeit' in Zeist." In *De Zeister Broedergemeente 1746–1996*, edited by Aart de Groot and Paul Peucker, 144–49. Zutphen: Walburg Pers, 1996.

Lehmann, Hartmut. "Punktuelle globale Präsenz: Die Missionsaktivitäten von Halle und Herrnhut im Vergleich." In *Etappen der Globalisierung in christentumsgeschichtlicher Perspektive / Phases of Globalization in the History of Christianity*, edited by Klaus Koschorke, 183–93. Wiesbaden: Harrassowitz, 2012.

Lempa, Heikki, and Paul Peucker, eds. *Self, Community, World: Moravian Education in a Transatlantic World*. Bethlehem: Lehigh University Press, 2010.

Levering, Joseph Mortimer. *A History of Bethlehem, Pennsylvania, 1741–1892: With Some Account of Its Founders and Their Early Activity in America*. Bethlehem, Pa.: Times, 1903.

Lochrie, Karma. "Mystical Acts, Queer Tendencies." In *Constructing Medieval Sexuality*, edited by Karma Lochrie, Peggy McCracken, and James A. Schultz, 180–200. Minneapolis: University of Minnesota Press, 1997.

Long, Kimberly Bracken. *The Eucharistic Theology of the American Holy Fairs*. Louisville, Ky.: Westminster John Knox Press, 2011.
Mack, Phyllis. *Heart Religion in the British Enlightenment: Gender and Emotion in Early Methodism*. Cambridge: Cambridge University Press, 2008.
Martin, Lucinda. "Anna Nitschmann (1715–1760): Priesterin, Generalältestin, Jüngerin der weltweiten Brüdergemeine." In *Frauen, Gestalten, Diakonie*, edited by Adelheid M. von Hauff, 393–409. Stuttgart: Kohlhammer, 2007.
Matter, E. Ann. *The Voice of My Beloved: The Song of Songs in Western Medieval Christianity*. Philadelphia: University of Pennsylvania Press, 1990.
McGinn, Bernard. "Mysticism and Sexuality." Supplement, *The Way* 77 (1993): 46–54.
———. *The Presence of God: A History of Western Mysticism*. 4 vols. New York: Crossroad, 1991–2005.
McMullen, Dianne Marie. "Melodien geistlicher Lieder und ihre kontroverse Diskussion zur Bach-Zeit: Pietistische kontra orthodox-lutherische Auffassungen im Umkreis des Geist-reichen Gesang-Buches (Halle 1704) von Johann Anastasius Freylinghausen." In *Geist-Reicher Gesang: Halle und das pietistische Lied*, edited by Gudrun Busch and Wolfgang Miersemann, 197–210. Halle: Franckesche Stiftungen; Tübingen: Niemeyer-Verlag, 1997.
Mettele, Gisela. "Erudition vs. Experience: Gender, Communal Narration and the Shaping of Eighteenth-Century Moravian Religious Thought." In Lempa and Peucker, *Self, Community, World*, 187–98.
———. *Weltbürgertum oder Gottesreich: Die Herrnhuter Brüdergemeine als globale Gemeinschaft, 1727–1857*. Göttingen: Vandenhoeck & Ruprecht, 2009.
———. "Die Zirkulation von Wissen in der Herrnhuter Brüdergemeine: Strukturen und Logistik globaler Kommunikation im 18. und frühen 19. Jahrhundert." In *Etappen der Globalisierung in christentumsgeschichtlicher Perspektive / Phases of Globalization in the History of Christianity*, edited by Klaus Koschorke, 215–38. Wiesbaden: Harrassowitz, 2012.
Meyer, Dietrich. *Bibliographisches Handbuch zur Zinzendorf-Forschung*. Düsseldorf: Privately printed, 1987.
———. *Der Christozentrismus des späten Zinzendorf: Eine Studie zu dem Begriff "täglicher Umgang mit dem Heiland."* Bern: Herbert Lang, 1973.
———. "Christus mein ander Ich: Zu Zinzendorfs Verhältnis zur Mystik." *Zeitwende* 54 (1983): 87–101.
———. "Cognitio Dei experimentalis oder 'Erfahrungstheologie' bei Gottfried Arnold, Gerhard Tersteegen und Nikolaus Ludwig von Zinzendorf." In Meyer and Sträter, *Zur Rezeption mystischer Traditionen*, 223–40.
———. "Die Herrnhuter Brüdergemeine als Brücke zwischen radikalem und kirchlichen Pietismus." In Breul, Meier, and Vogel, *Der radikale Pietismus*, 147–58.
———. "The Moravian Church as a Theocracy: The Resolution of the Synod of 1764." In *The Distinctiveness of Moravian Culture: Essays and Documents in Moravian History In Honor of Vernon H. Nelson on His Seventieth Birthday*, edited by Craig D. Atwood and Peter Vogt, 255–62. Nazareth, Pa.: Moravian Historical Society, 2003.
———. "Die Rezeption des Liedguts der Böhmischen Brüder in der erneuerten Brüderkirche." *UF*, no. 67–68 (2012): 51–76.
———. *Zinzendorf und die Herrnhuter Brüdergemeine, 1700–2000*. Göttingen: Vandenhoeck & Ruprecht, 2000.
———. "Zinzendorf und Herrnhut." In *Geschichte des Pietismus*, vol. 2, *Der Pietismus im achtzehnten Jahrhundert*, edited by Martin Brecht and Klaus Deppermann, 3–106. Göttingen: Vandenhoeck & Ruprecht, 1995.

Meyer, Dietrich, and Paul Peucker, eds. *Graf ohne Grenzen: Leben und Werk von Nikolaus Ludwig Graf von Zinzendorf*. Herrnhut: Unitätsarchiv, 2000.

Meyer, Dietrich, and Udo Sträter, eds. *Zur Rezeption mystischer Traditionen im Protestantismus des 16. bis 19. Jahrhundert: Beiträge eines Symposiums zum Tersteegen-Jubiläum 1997*. Cologne: Rheinland Verlag, 2002.

Meyer, Gerhard. "Einführung in die Sichtungszeit." In *Reden während der Sichtungszeit in der Wetterau und in Holland*, by Nikolaus Ludwig von Zinzendorf, vi–xxv. Nikolaus Ludwig von Zinzendorf Hauptschriften 3. Hildesheim: Olms, 1963.

———. "Die Epoche der Wetterau im Rückblick Zinzendorfs und des Herrnhutertums: Ein nicht bewältigtes Generationsproblem der Herrnhuter." In *Londoner Gesangbuch: Alt- und Neuer Brüder-Gesang*, 1*–77*. Nikolaus Ludwig von Zinzendorf Materialien und Dokumente 4. Hildesheim: Olms, 1980.

Miller, Derrick R. "Alexander Volck's Anti-Moravian Polemics as Enlightenment Anxieties." *JMH* 14, no. 2 (2014): 103–18.

———. "Moravian Familiarities: Queer Community in the Moravian Church in Europe and North America in the Mid-Eighteenth Century." *JMH* 13, no. 1 (2013): 54–75.

Moglen, Seth. "Excess and Utopia: Meditations on Moravian Bethlehem." *History of the Present* 2, no. 2 (2012): 122–47.

Moore, Stephen D. "The Song of Songs in the History of Sexuality." *Church History* 69 (2000): 328–49.

Müller, Joseph Theodor. *Geschichte der Böhmischen Brüder*. 3 vols. Herrnhut: Missionsbuchhandlung, 1922–31.

———. *Hymnologisches Handbuch zum Gesangbuch der Brüdergemeine*. Herrnhut: Verein für Brüdergeschichte, 1916.

Neisser, Georg. *A History of the Beginnings of Moravian Work in America*. Edited by William N. Schwarze and Samuel H. Gapp. Bethlehem: Moravian Archives, 1955.

Nelson, Vernon. *John Valentine Haidt: The Life of a Moravian Painter*, edited by June Schlueter and Paul Peucker. Bethlehem: Moravian Archives, 2012.

Nesmith, Tom. "Seeing Archives: Postmodernism and the Changing Intellectual Place of Archives." *American Archivist* 65 (2002): 24–41.

Noller, Matthias. "Die Rezeption der Geschichte der alten Brüder-Unität bei David Cranz: Traditionspflege im Wandel der Zeit." *UF*, no. 67/68 (2012): 15–29.

Noth, Isabelle. *Ekstatischer Pietismus: Die Inspirationsgemeinden und ihre Prophetin Ursula Meyer (1682–1743)*. Göttingen: Vandenhoeck & Ruprecht, 2005.

Parsons, Michael. *Reformation Marriage: The Husband and Wife Relationship in the Theology of Luther and Calvin*. Eugene, Ore.: Wipf and Stock, 2011.

Petry, Ray C. *Late Medieval Mysticism*. Library of Christian Classics 13. Louisville, Ky.: Westminster John Knox Press, 2006.

Peucker, Paul. "Aus allen Nationen: Nichteuropäer in den deutschen Brüdergemeinen des 18. Jahrhunderts." *UF*, no. 59/60 (2007): 1–35.

———. "Beyond Beeswax Candles and Lovefeast Buns: The Role of History in Finding a Moravian Identity." *The Hinge: International Theological Dialog for the Moravian Church* 17, no. 1 (2010): 4–15.

———. "'Blut' auf unsre grünen Bändchen': Die Sichtungszeit in der Herrnhuter Brüdergemeine." *UF*, no. 49/50 (2002): 41–94.

———. "Communication Through Art: The Role of Art in Moravian Communities." In Lempa and Peucker, *Self, Community, World*, 247–66.

———. "Drei Gemälde aus dem Schwestern- und Brüderhaus in Herrnhut." *UF*, no. 51/52 (2003): 131–44.

———. "'Gegen ein Regiment von Schwestern': Die Änderungen nach Zinzendorfs Tod." *UF*, no. 45/46 (1999): 61–72.

———. "Herrnhuter Archive als Aufbewahrungsort Pietistischer Erfahrungen." In *Aus Gottes Wort und eigener Erfahrung gezeiget": Erfahrung—Glauben, Erkennen und Gestalten im Pietismus; Beiträge zum III. Internationalen Kongress für Pietismusforschung 2009*, edited by Christian Soboth and Udo Sträter, 695–705. Hallesche Forschungen 33. Halle: Franckesche Stiftungen, 2012.

———. "The Ideal of Primitive Christianity as a Source of Moravian Liturgical Practice." *JMH*, no. 6 (2009): 7–29.

———. "Inspired by Flames of Love: Homosexuality, Mysticism, and Moravian Brothers Around 1750." *Journal of the History of Sexuality* 15 (2006): 30–64.

———. "In Staub und Asche: Bewertung und Kassation im Unitätsarchiv 1760–1810." In *"Alles ist euer, ihr aber seid Christi." Festschrift für Dietrich Meyer*, edited by Rudolf Mohr, 127–58. Schriftenreihe des Vereins für Rheinische Kirchengeschichte 147. Cologne: Rheinland Verlag, 2000.

———. "In the Blue Cabinet: Moravians, Marriage, and Sex." *JMH*, no. 10 (2011): 7–37.

———. "Kreuzbilder und Wundenmalerei: Form und Funktion der Malerei in der Herrnhuter Brüdergemeine um 1750." *UF*, no. 55/56 (2005): 125–74.

———. "Pietism and the Archive." In *A Companion to German Pietism, 1660–1800*, edited by Douglas H. Shantz. Leiden: Brill, 2014.

———. "Pink, White, and Blue: Function and Meaning of the Colored Choir Ribbons with the Moravians." In *Pietism and Community in Europe and North America, 1650–1850*, edited by Jonathan Strom, 179–97. Brill's Series in Church History 45. Leiden: Brill, 2010.

———. "Selection and Destruction in Moravian Archives Between 1760 and 1810." *JMH* 12, no. 2 (2012): 170–215.

———. "The Songs of the Sifting: Understanding the Role of Bridal Mysticism in Moravian Piety During the Late 1740s." *JMH*, no. 3 (2007): 51–87.

———."Was geschah mit Zinzendorfs 'Grünen Büchern'? Ein Fund in den Beständen des Unitätsarchivs." In *Rezeption und Reform: Festschrift für Hans Schneider zu seinem 60. Geburtstag*, edited by Wolfgang Breul-Kunkel and Lothar Vogel, 309–21. Quellen und Studien zur hessischen Kirchengeschichte 5. Darmstadt: Hessische Kirchengeschichtliche Vereinigung, 2001.

———. "Wives of the Lamb: Moravian Brothers and Gender Around 1750." In Faull, *Masculinity, Senses, Spirit*, 39–54.

———. "Zinzendorf's Plan for a 'Complete History of the True Church of Christ.'" *JMH*, no. 7 (2009): 59–82.

Pfister, Oskar. *Die Frömmigkeit des Grafen Ludwig von Zinzendorf: Ein psychoanalytischer Beitrag zur Kenntnis der religiösen Sublimierungsprozesse und zur Erklärung des Pietismus*. Schriften zur Angewandten Seelenkunde 8. Leipzig: Franz Deuticke, 1910.

Philipp, Franz-Heinrich. "Zinzendorf und die Christusmystik des frühen 18. Jahrhunderts." In *Glaube, Geist, Geschichte: Festschrift für Ernst Benz*, edited by Gerhard Müller and Winfried Zeller, 339–43. Leiden: Brill, 1967.

Plitt, Hermann. *Zinzendorfs Theologie*, 3 vols. Gotha: F. A. Perthes, 1869–74.

Podmore, Colin. *The Moravian Church in England, 1728–1760*. Oxford: Clarendon Press, 1998.

Rambuss, Richard. *Closet Devotions*. Durham: Duke University Press, 1998.

Reichel, Gerhard. *Die Anfänge Herrnhuts: Ein Buch vom Werden der Brüdergemeine; zur Erinnerung an die Gründung Herrnhuts am 17. Juni 1722*. Herrnhut: Verlag der Missionsbuchhandlung, 1922.

———. *August Gottlieb Spangenberg: Bischof der Brüderkirche*. Tübingen: Mohr, 1906.

———. *Zinzendorfs Frömmigkeit im Licht der Psychoanalyse*. Tübingen: Mohr, 1911.

Reichel, Hellmut. "Das Ende der Brüdergemeine Herrnhaag 1750." *UF*, no. 26 (1989): 52–72.

Reichel, Jörn. *Dichtungstheorie und Sprache Bei Zinzendorf: Der 12. Anhang zum Herrnhuter Gesangbuch*. Bad Homburg: Gehlen, 1969.
Reichel, Levin Theodore. "The Early History of the Church of the United Brethren, (Unitas Fratrum) Commonly Called Moravians, in North America, A.D. 1734–1748." *TMHS* 3 (1888): 1–241.
Renkewitz, Heinz. *Hochmann von Hochenau (1670–1721): Quellenstudien zur Geschichte des Pietismus*. Breslau: Maruschke & Berendt, 1935.
———. *Im Gespräch mit Zinzendorfs Theologie: Vorträge aus dem Nachlaß*. Hamburg: Wittig, 1980.
———. "Luther und Zinzendorf." *Neue Kirchliche Zeitschrift* 43 (1932): 156–79.
Ritschl, Albrecht. *Der Pietismus in der lutherischen Kirche des 17. und 18. Jahrhunderts*. 2 vols. Geschichte des Pietismus 2–3. Bonn: Adolph Marcus, 1886.
Roeber, A. G. *Hopes for Better Spouses: Protestant Marriage and Church Renewal in Early Modern Europe, India, and North America*. Grand Rapids, Mich.: Eerdmans, 2013.
———. "The Waters of Rebirth: The Eighteenth Century and Transoceanic Protestant Christianity." *Church History* 79 (2010): 40–76.
Rollmann, Hans. "Spangenberg über die Frömmigkeitssprache der Sichtungszeit in der Labradormission." *UF*, no. 61/62 (2008): 127–29.
Rosenblatt, Helena. "The Christian Enlightenment." In *Enlightenment, Reawakening and Revolution, 1660–1815*, edited by Stewart J. Brown and Timothy Tackett, 285–301. Cambridge History of Christianity 7. Cambridge: Cambridge University Press, 2008.
Rupp, I. Daniel. *History of the Counties of Berks and Lebanon*. Lancaster: G. Hills, 1844.
Schneider, Hans. "Christoph Friedrich Brauer und das Ende des Herrnhaag." In *Bericht der Büdingischen Grafschaft zur Vertreibung der Herrnhuter aus der Wetterau*, edited by Erich Beyreuther and Gerhard Meyer. Hildesheim: Olms Verlag, 1978.
———. "Geheimer Brief-Wechsel des Herrn Grafens von Zinzendorf mit denen Inspirierten." *UF*, no. 49/50 (2002): 213–28.
———. *German Radical Pietism*. Translated by Gerald T. MacDonald. Lanham, Md.: Scarecrow Press, 2007.
———. "Johann Arndt und die Mystik." In Meyer and Sträter, *Zur Rezeption mystischer Traditionen*, 59–90.
———. "Nikolaus Ludwig von Zinzendorf als Gestalt der Kirchengeschichte." In Meyer and Peucker, *Graf ohne Grenzen*, 10–29.
———. "'Philadelphische Brüder mit einem lutherischen Maul und mährischen Rock': Zu Zinzendorfs Kirchenverständnis." In Brecht and Peucker, *Neue Aspekte der Zinzendorf-Forschung*, 11–36.
———. "Der radikale Pietismus im 17. Jahrhundert." In *Geschichte des Pietismus*, vol. 1, *Der Pietismus vom siebzehnten bis zum frühen achtzehnten Jahrhundert*, edited by Martin Brecht, 391–437. Göttingen: Vandenhoeck & Ruprecht, 1993.
———. "Der radikale Pietismus im 18. Jahrhundert." In *Geschichte des Pietismus*, vol. 2, *Der Pietismus im achtzehnten Jahrhundert*, edited by Martin Brecht and Klaus Deppermann, 107–97. Göttingen: Vandenhoeck & Ruprecht, 1995.
———. "Der radikale Pietismus in der neueren Forschung." *PuN* 8 (1982): 15–42; 9 (1983): 117–51.
———. "Understanding the Church: Issues of Pietist Ecclesiology." In *Pietism and Community in Europe and North America, 1650–1850*, edited by Jonathan Strom, 15–35. Brill's Series in Church History 45. Leiden: Brill, 2010.
———. "Zu den Begriffen 'Sichtung' und 'Sichtungszeit.'" *UF*, no. 63/64 (2010): 211–24.
———. "Die 'zürnenden Mutterkinder': Der Konflikt zwischen Halle und Herrnhut." *PuN* 29 (2004): 37–66.

Schrader, Hans-Jürgen. "Zinzendorf als Poet." In Brecht and Peucker, *Neue Aspekte der Zinzendorf-Forschung*, 134–62.
Schuchard, Marsha Keith. *Why Mrs. Blake Cried: William Blake and the Sexual Basis of Spiritual Vision*. London: Century, 2006.
Schulz, Walter. "'Viel Anschein zu mehrerem Licht': Henriette Katharina von Gersdorff, geborene von Friesen, und ihre Bibliothek auf Großhennersdorf." *PuN* 36 (2010): 63–118.
Schutt, Amy C. *Peoples of the River Valleys: The Odyssey of the Delaware Indians*. Philadelphia: University of Pennsylvania Press, 2007.
Seibert, Dorette. "A. G. Spangenberg und die *Idea fidei fratrum* (1778)." *UF*, no. 61/62 (2009): 131–46.
Sensbach, Jon. *Rebecca's Revival: Creating Black Christianity in the Atlantic World*. Cambridge, Mass.: Harvard University Press, 2005.
Sessler, John Jacob. *Communal Piety Among Early American Moravians*. New York: Henry Holt, 1933. Repr., [New York]: [AMS Press], 1971.
Shantz, Douglas H. *An Introduction to German Pietism: Protestant Renewal at the Dawn of Modern Europe*. Baltimore: Johns Hopkins University Press, 2013.
Sheehan, Jonathan. *The Enlightenment Bible: Translation, Scholarship, Culture*. Princeton: Princeton University Press, 2005.
———. "Enlightenment, Religion, and the Enigma of Secularization: A Review Essay." *American Historical Review* 108 (2003): 1061–80.
Smaby, Beverly. "Gender Prescriptions in Eighteenth-Century Bethlehem." In *Backcountry Crucibles: The Lehigh Valley from Settlement to Steel*, edited by Jean R. Soderlund and Catherine S. Parzynski, 74–103. Bethlehem: Lehigh University Press, 2007.
———. "'No One Should Lust for Power . . . Women Least of All': Dismantling Female Leadership Among Eighteenth-Century Moravians." In Gillespie and Beachy, *Pious Pursuits*, 159–75.
———. "'Only Brothers Should Be Accepted into This Proposed Council': Restricting Women's Leadership in Moravian Bethlehem." In *Pietism in Germany and North America, 1680–1820*, edited by Jonathan Strom, Hartmut Lehmann, and James Van Horn Melton, 133–62. Burlington, Vt.: Ashgate, 2009.
Sommer, Elisabeth W. *Serving Two Masters: Moravian Brethren in Germany and North America, 1727–1801*. Lexington: University Press of Kentucky, 2000.
Sorkin, David. *The Religious Enlightenment: Protestants, Jews, and Catholics from London to Vienna*. Princeton: Princeton University Press, 2008.
Sterik, Edita. "Die böhmischen Emigranten und Zinzendorf." In Brecht and Peucker, *Neue Aspekte der Zinzendorf-Forschung*, 97–114.
———. *Mährische Exulanten in der erneuerten Brüderunität im 18. Jahrhundert*. Herrnhut: Herrnhuter Verlag, 2012.
Strom, Jonathan. "Problems and Promises of Pietism Research." *Church History* 71 (2002): 536–54.
Tanner, Fritz. *Die Ehe im Pietismus*. Zürich: Zwingli Verlag, 1952.
Temme, Willi. "From Jakob Böhme via Jane Leade to Eva von Buttlar: Transmigrations and Transformations of Religious Ideas." In *Pietism in Germany and North America 1680–1820*, edited by Jonathan Strom, Hartmut Lehmann, and James Van Horn Melton, 101–6. Burlington, Vt.: Ashgate, 2009.
———. *Krise der Leiblichkeit: Die Sozietät der Mutter Eva (Buttlarsche Rotte) und der radikale Pietismus um 1700*. Arbeiten zur Geschichte des Pietismus 35. Göttingen: Vandenhoeck & Ruprecht, 1998.
Uttendörfer, Otto. "Aus Zinzendorfs Alltagsleben." *Mitteilungen aus der Brüdergemeine* (1939): 55–108.

———. "Neusalz: Vorgeschichte und Geschichte der Brüdergemeine bis zum Anfang ihres Wiederaufbaus." Unpublished manuscript, 1944. Copy at UA (NUO 63.a).
———. *Zinzendorfs Gedanken über den Gottesdienst*. Herrnhut: Gustav Winter, 1931.
———. *Zinzendorfs religiöse Grundgedanken*. Gnadau: Unitätsbuchhandlung, 1935.
———. *Zinzendorfs Weltbetrachtung: Eine systematische Darstellung der Gedankenwelt des Begründers der Brüdergemeine*. Berlin: Furche, 1929.
———. "Zinzendorf und die Entwicklung des theologischen Seminars der Brüderunität." Pt. 1, ZBG 10 (1916): 32–88; pt. 2, ZBG 11 (1917): 71–123; pt. 3, ZBG 12 (1918): 1–78; pt. 4, ZBG 13 (1919): 1–63.
———. *Zinzendorf und die Mystik*. [East] Berlin: Christlicher Zeitschriften Verlag, [1950].
Vogt, Peter. "Ehereligion: Religiös konzeptionierte Sexualität bei Zinzendorf." In *Alter Adam und Neue Kreatur: Pietismus und Anthropologie; Beiträge zum II. Internationalen Kongress für Pietismusforschung 2005*, edited by Udo Sträter et al., 371–80. Tübingen: Max Niemeyer, 2009.
———. "*Ehereligion*: The Moravian Theory and Practice of Marriage as Point of Contention in the Conflict Between Ephrata and Bethlehem." *Communal Societies* 21 (2001): 37–48.
———. "'Er ist Mann': Die Männlichkeit Jesu in der Theologie Zinzendorfs." In *"Der Herr wird seine Herrlichkeit an uns offenbahren": Liebe, Ehe und Sexualität im Pietismus*, edited by Wolfgang Breul and Christian Soboth, 175–209. Hallesche Forschungen 30. Halle: Hallesche Stiftungen, 2011.
———. "'Everywhere at Home': The Eighteenth-Century Moravian Movement as a Transatlantic Religious Community." *JMH*, no. 1 (2006): 7–29.
———. "Geschichte und Aktualität des Akoluthenamts in der Brüdergemeine." *UF*, no. 63/64 (2008): 1–28.
———. "Gloria Pleurae! Die Seitenwunde Jesu in der Theologie des Grafen von Zinzendorf." *PuN* 32 (2006): 175–212.
———. "'Headless and Un-erudite': Anti-Intellectual Tendencies in Zinzendorf's Approach to Education." In Lempa and Peucker, *Self, Community, World*, 107–26.
———. "'Honor to the Side': The Adoration of the Side Wound of Jesus in Eighteenth-Century Moravian Piety." *JMH*, no. 7 (2009): 83–106.
———. "Nicholas Ludwig von Zinzendorf (1700–1760)." In *The Pietist Theologians: An Introduction to Theology in the Seventeenth and Eighteenth Centuries*, edited by Carter Lindberg, 207–23. Malden, Mass.: Blackwell, 2005.
———. "'No Inherent Perfection in This Life': Count Zinzendorf's Theological Opposition to John Wesley's Concept of Sanctification." *Bulletin of the John Rylands University Library of Manchester* 85 (2003): 297–307.
———. "'Philadelphia': Inhalt, Verbreitung und Einfluß eines radikal-pietistischen Schlüsselbegriffs." In *Interdisziplinäre Pietismusforschung: Beiträge zum Ersten Internationalen Kongress für Pietismusforschung 2001*, edited by Udo Sträter, 837–48. Tübingen: Max Niemeyer, 2005.
———. "Spangenberg als Apologet des Grafen von Zinzendorf, 1750–1752." *UF*, no. 61/62 (2009): 75–88.
———. "Zinzendorf's 'Seventeen Points of Matrimony': A Foundational Document on the Moravian Understanding of Marriage and Sexuality." *JMH*, no. 10 (2011): 38–67.
———. "Zinzendorf's Theology of the Sabbath." In *The Distinctiveness of Moravian Culture: Essays and Documents in Moravian History in Honor of Vernon H. Nelson on His Seventieth Birthday*, edited by Craig D. Atwood and Peter Vogt, 205–31. Nazareth: Moravian Historical Society, 2003.
Võsa, Aira. "Johann Georg Gichtels Verhältnis zum anderen Geschlecht in Leben und Lehre." In Breul, Meier, and Vogel, *Der radikale Pietismus*, 361–68.

Wagner, Walter H. *The Zinzendorf-Muhlenberg Encounter: A Controversy in Search of Understanding*. [Nazareth, Pa.]: Moravian Historical Society, 2002.
Wallmann, Johannes. "Bernhard von Clairvaux und der deutsche Pietismus." In Meyer and Sträter, *Zur Rezeption mystischer Traditionen*, 1–23.
———. "Kirchlicher und radikaler Pietismus: Zu einer kirchengeschichtlichen Grundunterscheidung." In Breul, Meier, and Vogel, *Der radikale Pietismus*, 19–43.
———. *Der Pietismus*. Göttingen: Vandenhoeck & Ruprecht, 1990.
Ward, W. R. *Early Evangelicalism: A Global Intellectual History, 1670–1789*. Cambridge: Cambridge University Press, 2006.
———. *The Protestant Evangelical Awakening*. Cambridge: Cambridge University Press, 1992.
———. "The Renewed Unity of the Brethren: Ancient Church, New Sect, or Transconfessional Movement?" In *Faith and Faction*, 112–29. London: Epworth Press, 1993.
Weigelt, Horst. "Zinzendorf und die Schwenckfelder." In Brecht and Peucker, *Neue Aspekte der Zinzendorf-Forschung*, 64–96.
Weinlick, John R. *Count Zinzendorf: The Story of His Life and Leadership in the Renewed Moravian Church*. New York: Abingdon Press, 1956.
Wheeler, Rachel M. "'Der schönste Schmuck': Mahican Appropriations of Moravian Blood and Wounds Theology." *Covenant Quarterly* 63 (2005): 20–34.
Wiesner-Hanks, Merry E. *Christianity and Sexuality in the Early Modern World: Regulating Desire, Reforming Practice*. London: Routledge, 2000.
Winship, Michael P. "Behold the Bridegroom Cometh! Marital Imagery in Massachussetts Preaching, 1630–1730." *Early American Literature* 27 (1992): 170–84.
Wollstadt, Hanns Joachim. *Geordnetes Dienen in der christichen Gemeinde, dargestellt an den Lebensformen der Herrnhuter Brüdergemeine in ihren Anfängen*. Göttingen: Vandenhoeck & Ruprecht, 1966.
Yonan, Jonathan. "Evangelicalism and Enlightenment: The Moravian Experience in England, 1750–1800." D.Phil. thesis., University of Oxford, 2007.
Zimmerling, Peter. *Ein Leben für die Kirche: Zinzendorf als Praktischer Theologe*. Göttingen: Vandenhoeck & Ruprecht, 2010.

# INDEX

Aalen, Leiv, 42
Africa, 12
Africa, 4, 20, 26
African slaves, 26
alchemy, 9, 12
Algiers, 131
Amsterdam, 75, 181, 184
Andresen, 138
Andresen, Johann Heinrich, 49
Anglican Church, 60
Annaberg, 181
anti-intellectualism, 40, 62, 68–71
antinomianism. *See* perfectionism
Arawak Indians, 26
Arbeitskreis für Brüdergeschichte, 43
archives, 7–8, 149, 158, 172, 174–76, 180
Arndt, Johann, 9, 28, 129
Arnold, Gottfried, 3, 12, 16, 29, 62, 69, 109
art, 144
assemblies. *See* classes
Atwood, Craig, 6, 8, 10, 28, 35, 44, 69, 109, 148
Augsburg Confession, 17, 157
August 13, 1727, 15, 17
Augustine, 96

Bähr, David Andreas, 129
Baptists, 149
Barby, 136, 172, 178
Barby, synod of 1750, 54, 56, 58–59, 62, 66, 85, 122, 141, 162, 179
Baumann, Matthias, 129–30
Baumgarten, Siegmund Jacob, 80
Bayle, Pierre, 150
Bayly, Lewis, 72
Becker, Johann Christoph, 105, 114
bed, marital, 30, 76, 88–91, 99, 101, 118, 120, 122
Bedford, 136
Beissel, Conrad, 3, 112, 184
Bengel, Johann Albrecht, 73
Benzien, Thomas, xi–xii
Berbice, 26
Berleburg Bible, 73
Berlin, 50, 72, 97, 127, 129, 135, 182

Bernard of Clairvaux, 28–29, 44, 82–83, 99
Berthelsdorf, 9–10, 14–16, 24–25, 124, 172
Bethlehem, Pennsylvania, xii, 21, 27–28, 30, 40, 53, 67–68, 94, 131, 133, 137, 147–48, 152–54, 184–85
  General Economy, 148, 168
  Moravian Archives, 40, 177
  Moravian Theological Seminary, 38
  single brothers' house, xi–xii, 184
Bettermann, Wilhelm, 28, 41
Beyreuther, Erich, 42–43, 163
Bible, 71–73, 157
Birken, Sigmund von, 55
blood-and-wounds devotion, 6, 14, 26–28, 30, 33, 39, 42, 44, 69, 80, 98, 135, 143–45
Bohemia, 4, 15
Bohemian Brethren. *See* Unity of Brethren
Böhme, Jakob, 9, 184
Book of Ceremonies, 151, 156
Bordelum, 129
Bothe, Heinrich, 72, 96–97, 102, 127, 182–83
Brauer, Christoph Friedrich, 53
Breul, Wolfgang, 20
Britain, 4, 12–13, 26, 39, 49, 53, 178
British Parliament, 5, 49
Brodersen, Christian, 66
Brügglen, 129
Büdingen, 20, 35, 48, 53, 66, 180–81
Buntebart, Br., 126
Burkhardt, Guido, 41
*Busskampf. See* penitential struggle
Buttlar, Eva von, 3, 128
Bynum, Caroline Walker, 27

cabinet. *See* bed, marital
Caillet, François, 50–52, 66, 78, 105, 117, 131, 133, 135–37
Cammerhoff, Friedrich, 38, 68
Caribbean, 4, 12, 26, 53, 152
Caroline (in Ebersdorf), 131
celibacy, 3–4, 107, 129
childlikeness, 61–62, 68–71, 78, 89–92, 118
choirs, 21–23

Christ
  as bridegroom and husband, xii, 23, 60, 83, 86, 92, 98, 107, 112, 117, 119, 122–23, 125–26, 128, 140, 143, 163
  as chief elder, 24–25, 59
  in the grave, 25, 61, 86–88, 101, 111–13
  as mother, 109–10
  union with, 2, 4, 23, 64, 71, 76–78, 80–82, 84, 88, 92, 98, 100–101, 103, 107, 109–10, 115, 117, 119–20, 127–29, 133, 155, 166, 168
Christianity, primitive, 15–16
classes, 23, 118, 120
Clemens, Gottfried, 153
Comenius, Jan Amos, 16–17
Communion, Holy, 25, 84, 88, 115, 117, 151
community, imagined, 26
Congregational Accounts, 136, 176–79
Constantinople, 131
Cook, John, 50–51, 131
Copenhagen, 50, 135
Cranz, David, 33–36, 62, 65, 122, 156–57
Cröger, Ernst Wilhelm, 35, 55, 122
cross-air birds, 30, 64, 66, 68, 74, 76, 98, 165

David, Christian, 14, 181
death. *See* grave
Deghaye, Pierre, 42
Demuth, Sr., 121, 131
diaries, 175–77
diminutives, xiv, 39, 69, 74, 89, 99
Dippel, Johann Conrad, 182
Dober, Leonhard, 20, 160
Dober, Martin, 30
Dresden, 11–12, 20, 48–49, 181
dress, 22, 60, 141

Eberhard, Samuel, 42
Ebersdorf, 11, 13–14, 16, 67, 119, 131
Elisha, 81–82
Eller, Elias, 128
embrace, 81–83, 100, 107, 119, 124–26
Enlightenment, 8, 29, 68, 70, 169
enthusiasm, 10, 28, 33–36, 40, 44, 128, 149–50, 168–69, 174
Ephrata, Pennsylvania, 8, 10, 112, 129, 184
Erbe, Hans-Walter, 43, 78, 180
Erlangen, 51
eroticism, 81–85, 116, 120, 125
eschatology, 13, 26, 31, 69, 92, 105, 113
Ettwein, Johannes, 131–32, 135–37
Ettwein, Johannetta, 132, 135–36

Falkner Swamp, Pennsylvania, 184
fanaticism. *See* enthusiasm

Faull, Katherine, 10, 109, 155
festivities, 6, 25, 35, 37–39, 42, 44, 75, 177
Fogleman, Aaron, 10, 44, 109–10
foot washings, 16, 25, 136
France, 12
Francke, August Hermann, 3, 12, 18
Francke, Gotthilf August, 18
Frank, Johann, 55
Frankfurt am Main, 2, 20–21, 38, 157
Frankfurt an der Oder, 169
freethinkers, 169
French Prophets, 8
Freud, Sigmund, 36
Frey, Andreas, 51, 65, 67, 69, 180, 184–85
Fulneck, 136

Gammern, Br., 138
Gapp, Samuel H., 40
Geller, Friedrich, 65
gender-changing ceremony, 1, 2, 103–7, 113–23, 128, 133
gender, 1, 3, 5–6, 10, 30, 105, 107, 109–12, 115–16, 118, 120, 123, 133, 163, 166, 170, 178
Geneva, 51
genitalia, 81
Georgia, 20
Gerhardt, Paul, 109
Germantown, Pennsylvania, 185
Gersdorf, Henriette Katharina von, 11–12, 14, 18
Gewinn, Br., 72
Gichtel, Johann Georg, 3
Gnadenberg, 132
  synod of 1750, 52, 54, 56, 58, 144, 179
Gnadenfeld, Moravian Theological Seminary, 37, 41
Gnadenfrei, 54, 113, 132–33
Goebel, Max, 128
Gollin, Gillian Lindt, 40, 56
Görlitz, 14
Göttingen, 180
Gottwalt, Johann Daniel, 142
Gracehill, 175
Grassmann, Andreas, 27
grave, 61, 77, 85–89, 101, 116–17. *See also* mortification
Greenland, 4, 12, 20, 26, 156–57
Gregor, Christian, 84, 154, 176
Greven, Philip, 69
Grossglogau, 127
Grosshennersdorf, 11, 14, 18, 47, 72, 150
Gutbier, Br., 121, 131

Haidt, Johann Valentin, 144
Hallart, family, 132

INDEX 245

Halle, 9, 12, 17–19, 80, 130, 132, 166
Hamilton, John Taylor, 38, 40
Hamilton, Kenneth G., 40, 148
Hanover, 48–49
Hart, Christian, 30, 65, 71, 106, 114, 116, 118, 120–22, 131, 133, 183
Hasse, Matthias, 91, 126
Hecker, Andreas Petrus, 183
Heerendijk, 20–21, 184
Heinrich XXIX Count Reuss, 13
Heinrich XXXI Count Reuss, 160
Heintschel, Catharina Elisabeth, 137
Heithausen, Georg Ernst, 88–89
Hellevoetsluis, 47
Hennicke, Count, 48
Herrnhaag, 1–2, 20–21, 25–26, 30, 44, 47, 49–53, 61–62, 65, 67, 69–70, 74–77, 81, 83–86, 88, 90, 93–94, 97, 101, 103–6, 112, 115–28, 130–33, 136, 138, 141, 162, 175–76, 178–82, 184
  end, 35, 38, 53–54
  Lichtenburg, 21, 60, 71, 78, 184
  single brothers' house, 21, 24, 68, 75–79, 89, 125, 177, 184
  250th anniversary, 43
Herrnhut, 4, 9, 11–16, 18–20, 23–26, 37–38, 40, 47–48, 50–52, 54–55, 63, 67, 71–75, 80–81, 83–84, 93, 95, 97, 102, 110, 113, 117, 124–28, 131–33, 135–37, 139, 141–42, 147–48, 150, 152–54, 157, 162, 165, 174–78, 182, 184
  sexual misconduct, 48, 123–24
Herz, Abraham, 127
*Herzel*, 99
Hessel-Robinson, Timothy, 83
Hetzmann, Wenzel, 129
hierarchy, spiritual, 24
historiography, 5–6, 33–45, 55
history, 29–31
Hoburg, Christian, 12
Hochmann von Hochenau, Ernst Christoph, 4, 14
Höffly, Catharina, 97
Hofmann, Carl Gottlob, 48
Höhlchen, Christian von, 108
Hohlchen, Joachim von, 108
Hök, Gösta, 42
Holmes, John Beck, 37
Holy Spirit as mother, xii, 6, 38–39
homosexuality, 37, 116, 124, 126–28
Horch, Heinrich, 55
Hungary, 39
Hunt, Samuel, 49
Hus, Jan, 15
Hütschel (manservant), 123–24

Hutton, Joseph, 39–40
hymn book 1749 (ms.), 96–97, 120, 174, 180
hymn book, twelfth appendix, 56, 95
hymns, 7, 93–103, 136, 153–55, 174
  "It's Thumping," 67, 99, 102
  "Kissing, Kissing Must Be Done," 99, 126
  "That our Mind the Lamb's Resemble," 87
  "What Does a Bird in Cross's Air," 64, 74

imitatio Christi, 23, 38, 115
Inspirationists, 8–9, 18
interim administration (Ratskonferenz), 147–53, 157, 159–61
irrationality. *See* anti-intellectualism
itinerancy, 20–21, 26

Jablonski, Daniel Ernst, 17
Jannasch, Wilhelm, 140–41
Jena, 38, 132, 139
Jenkinson, Hilary, 173
Jerome, 96
Juster, Susan, 116
justification by faith, 2, 19, 28, 67–68, 117

Kemnitz, 73
Ketelaar, Eric, 173
kissing, 68, 78, 81–83, 99–100, 102–3, 119–20, 122, 124–26
Köber, Johann Friedrich, 47–48, 161, 181
Köhler, Br., 66–67
Kohler, Christian, 129
Kohler, Hieronymus, 129
Kölbing, Paul, 41
Königsfeld, 36
Kredzeck (religious leader), 129
Krügelstein, David, 66

Labadists, 9
Labrador, 4
Langguth, Johann. *See* Watteville, Johannes von
language, 26, 33, 37–40, 42, 89–92
Latvia, 26
Lawatsch, Anna María, 112
Leade, Jane, 12–13
Levering, Joseph Mortimer, 38
Lindheim, 62–63, 136
Litany of the Wounds, 6, 27–28, 73, 87–88
literalism, 103, 116, 125
Livonia, 38–39, 91, 126
Livorno, 131
loan words, 26, 89
London, 47–50, 52–55, 59, 85, 95, 107, 113, 119, 131, 133, 135, 140–41, 143, 177, 184
  synod for single brothers, 31, 90, 136

*Losungen*, 199n60
lot, 23, 25, 59, 66, 119, 152–53, 157, 159–60, 179
love feasts, 16, 25, 37, 61, 71, 86, 121, 128
Luedecke, Urban von, 51–52, 136
lust, 3–4, 106, 111–12, 114–15, 128–29, 155, 166–67
Luther, Martin, 3, 27–28, 96
Lutheranism, 2, 9–10, 17–19, 27, 29, 32, 36, 42, 60, 94, 117, 147–48, 164, 166

Malabar Coast, 26
Maria Louise, Princess of Orange, 20
Marienborn, 1, 20–21, 25–26, 30, 52, 54, 62, 75–76, 86, 88, 97, 104–7, 112, 114, 116, 118, 122–23, 130, 133, 143, 178–79, 181, 183–84
 Theological Seminary, 1, 52, 58, 61, 66, 70, 77, 95, 136, 176
marriage, 3–4, 8, 14, 23, 128, 155, 166, 168, 183
marriage, mystical, 60, 83–84, 105, 112, 119, 122, 128, 140, 143
McGinn, Bernard, 28, 82, 112
Merkel, Margarethe, 184
Methodists, 5, 27, 149
Meyer, Dietrich, 29, 44
Meyer, Gerhard, 42, 148
Middletown, New Jersey, 39
Miller, Derrick, 10
missions, 20, 42, 152
Moglen, Seth, 10
Moravia, 11, 14–19, 38
Moravian Church
 leadership, 148–50, 158–61, 163
 renewal, 15–17
 transition, 2, 7, 28, 147–49, 161, 163–64, 169, 171
 mortification, 23, 61, 85–88, 92, 105, 111–17, 123. *See also* grave
Moser, Friedrich Carl von, 157
Moser, Johann Jacob, 119
Mühlenberg, Heinrich Melchior, 72, 130
Müller, Johann Jakob, 27
Müller, Polycarp, 27
mysticism, 5, 9–10, 12, 29, 32, 42, 44, 69, 76, 94, 101, 110, 122, 149
 bridal, 2, 7, 23, 28, 63, 83, 89, 98, 104, 107, 109, 120, 128, 166–68

Native Americans, 5, 152
Nazareth, Pennsylvania, 170
Neisser, Augustin, 11
Nesmith, Tom, 173
Netherlands, 12–13, 20, 74, 95
Neusalz, 54, 121, 132, 135–36
New Born, 129–30, 167
New England, 110, 116
Newton, John, 169

Niesky, 54
Nitschmann, Anna, 24, 47, 119, 130–31, 147, 149–50, 158–59
Nitschmann, David, 20, 169, 181
Nitschmann, Johann, 61, 65, 71, 138, 170
Nonhebel, Philipp Samuel, 97
North America, 4, 26, 37–39, 53, 55, 153, 158
North Carolina, 12

Oekonomatskonferenz, 153
Oesel, 62
Oldendorp, Georg, 157
Oley, Pennsylvania, 129
Order of Fools, 62
order, 25

passivity, 83, 100–101, 111, 126
Peilau, 86
Peistel, Carl Heinrich von, 47–48, 57, 123, 132, 136
penetration, 27, 82–83, 85, 88, 90, 98, 107, 110, 119, 125–27, 137
penitential struggle, 18, 65
Pennsylvania, 3, 12–13, 24, 27, 50, 54, 67, 129–30, 133, 143, 147, 157, 162, 169, 177, 184
perfectionism, 2, 84, 87–88, 92, 103, 105, 115–17, 128–30, 133–35, 143, 166–67
Persia, 26
Petersen, Johann Wilhelm, 12, 20
Petersen, Johanna Eleanora, 12
Petsch, Johannes, 138–39
Pfister, Oskar, 36–37
Philadelphia, Pennsylvania, 181, 184
Philadelphianism, 9, 12–17, 20, 28, 32, 55, 62, 184
Piesch, Anna Johanna, 131, 150
Pietism, 2, 3, 9–10, 17–19, 28–29, 32, 42, 44, 63, 65, 68, 94, 116, 139, 143, 149, 166, 174
 historiography, 10
 radical, 3–5, 8–9, 12–13, 18, 20, 23, 29, 62, 72–73, 84, 166, 168, 171, 174
Pilgerruh, 20–21
pilgrim congregation, 20–21
Pirna, 124
playfulness, 6, 33–36, 42, 56, 61–70, 72, 89, 92, 99, 119, 121, 137, 162, 178
Plitt, Hermann, 36, 41
Plitt, Johannes, 34–36, 56
Poland, 15, 39
Portage, John, 13
prayer meetings, 16, 25
preaching, 177–78
Presbyterians, 83
Puritans, 27–28, 83, 110, 116
purity, 3

Quakers, 149
quarter-hours, 25

Rambuss, Richard, 116
rationalism, 68, 71, 79. *See also* anti-
    intellectualism
Ratskonferenz. *See* interim administration
record keeping. *See* archives
Reformation, 3
Reichel, Gerhard, 37, 41, 158
Reichel, Hellmut, 53
Reichel, Jörn, 56
Reichel, Levin Theodore, 37
Renkewitz, Heinz, 42
Reval, 62–63, 132
Rhode, Anton, 72, 150
Ritschl, Albrecht, 180
Rock, Johann Friedrich, 20
Roeber, A. G., 3
Roman Catholicism, 15, 27
Ronneburg, 20
Ronsdorf, 128–29, 167
Rothe, Andreas, 17
Rubusch, Joachim, 1, 50, 52, 54, 60–65, 67–68, 74–75, 77–79, 83, 86, 90–92, 104–8, 113, 115, 122, 124, 131, 136–39, 179
Rush, Benjamin, 169

Sabbath, 25
Saur, Christoph, 185
Saxony, 20, 39, 48–49, 52
*Schätzel*, 56, 69, 89, 99, 102–3, 108, 119–21, 123, 126, 133
Schellinger, Jacob, 75
Schlözer, Reinhard, 175
Schneider, Hans, 9–10, 12, 15, 18, 55, 72
Schrautenbach, Ludwig Carl von, 33–34, 66
Schröder, Johann Heinrich, 55
Schuchard, Marsha Keith, 10
Schwarzenau Brethren, 9–10
Schweinitz, Ludwig von, 175–76
Schwenckfelders, 14
separatism, 9
Sessler, John Jacob, 39–40
sexual intercourse, 2, 4, 82–83, 107, 121, 123, 128–29, 143, 156
    extramarital, 2–3, 43, 48, 58, 81, 121–24, 126, 128–30, 132, 135, 142, 166–68
    as sacrament, 4, 107, 139, 166, 168
sexuality, 2, 3, 5, 10, 14, 23, 35, 39, 42, 116, 122–23, 141, 155–56, 166
Shakers, 8
Shantz, Douglas, 9–10
Sheehan, Jonathan, 72
side wound, 28, 30, 53, 73–81, 92, 98, 143

sifting time, term, 2, 55–57
Silesia, 14, 16–17, 26, 47, 52, 132, 136
sin, original, 3
singing meetings, 16, 25
singing, 25
Skippack, Pennsylvania, 184
sleep, 23, 77, 98, 100–101, 115–16, 119
Smaby, Beverly, 10
Society of Mother Eva, 3, 8–10, 128, 167
Söhle, Moravia, 14
Song of Songs, 75, 82–83, 88, 96, 99–101, 114, 116, 120
souls, femininity of, 109–11, 113, 123, 143, 163
South America, 12, 26
Spangenberg, August Gottlieb, 33–34, 36, 80, 115, 143–44, 147–49, 153–55, 157–59, 162–63, 184
Spener, Philipp Jakob, 3, 18
spiritualism, 42, 44, 72–73
St. Petersburg, 66, 132, 182
St. Thomas, 20
Stach, Thomas, 49
Stargard, 106, 183
Steinhofer, Friedrich Christoph, 96, 102, 182
Stettin, 183
Stockholm, 49
Stöhr, David, 181
Stöhr, Johann Christoph, 181
Suriname, 20
surplice, 60–61, 78, 86
Suter, Christlieb, 172–73
Sweden, 39
sweetheart. *See Schätzel*
Switzerland, 39
symbols
    bees, 86
    doves, 75, 98
    fish, 75–76
    lion, 76
    magnet, 76
    rock, 76, 88, 98
    swans, 75–76
    table, 76
    water, 76
synods, 179
Synods, General
    of 1764, 148, 151–53, 157, 159–61, 174
    of 1769, 152, 157
    of 1775, 157
    of 1789, 150, 152

Tallinn. *See* Reval
Tarnowitz, 129
Tauler, Johannes, 28
Temme, Willi, 3

theocracy, 25, 159
Töllner, Johann Gottlieb, 169
translations, xiv
Trinity, xi
tunes, 97–98

Unander, Rev., xi–xii
unio Dei. *See* Christ, union with
Unity Elders' Conference, 152, 159, 172–74
Unity of Brethren, ancient, 4–5, 9–10, 15–17, 28, 32
Urb, 91
Uttendörfer, Otto, 132, 176, 179

Vierorth, Anton, 131–32
Vogt, Peter, 10, 70, 74, 76, 109, 162
Volck, Alexander, 48–49, 52, 61, 66–67, 96–97, 102, 180–82
Volck, Anna Margaretha Sophia, 181
Volck, Juliane, 181
Volck, Nicolaus Christoph, 181

Waiblinger, Georg, 157
Wallmann, Johannes, 9
Ward, W. R., 29, 44, 168
warriors, 30, 38
Watteville, Benigna von, née Zinzendorf, 24, 53–54, 110, 143, 158, 162
Watteville, Friedrich von, 95, 122, 158
Watteville, Johannes von, 23–24, 31, 50–51, 53–54, 56–58, 63–64, 68, 74–75, 79–80, 83, 110, 112, 114–16, 121–23, 130–32, 135, 137–39, 141–45, 147–48, 155, 158–62, 177, 179
Weiss, Jonas Paulus, 57, 130, 194n4
West Indies. *See* Caribbean
Wetterau, 20
White Mountain, battle of, 14–15
Wiegner, Christoph, 184
Winston-Salem, North Carolina, 177
Wittenberg, 12, 48
women, 1, 9, 148–52, 159, 168
work, neglect of, 35, 40
World War II, 176

Yonan, Jonathan, 156
Yorkshire, 136
Ysenburg and Büdingen, Count Ernst Casimir zu, 53
Ysenburg and Büdingen, Count Gustav Friedrich zu, 53

Zauchtenthal, Moravia, 14
Zechlau, 129

Zeist, 47, 50, 65, 95, 106–7, 118, 120–21, 126, 133, 137, 160, 174, 183
Zeist, synod of 1746, 62, 110, 158, 163
Zimmerling, Peter, 178
Zinzendorf, Charlotte Justine von, née Gersdorf, 12
Zinzendorf, Christian Renatus von, 1–2, 27, 47–50, 52, 54, 57, 59–64, 66–67, 71, 74–86, 88, 90–93, 95, 103–8, 113–15, 117–19, 122–27, 131, 133–34, 136–42, 158, 162, 165, 167, 174, 177, 179
  "Christ reborn," 90, 139
  preaching, 90, 179
Zinzendorf, Elisabeth von, 69
Zinzendorf, Erdmuth Dorothea von, née Reuss, 11, 14, 24, 54, 63, 123, 138, 170
Zinzendorf, Georg Ludwig von, 12
Zinzendorf, Nikolaus Ludwig von
  banishment, 20
  Bible translation, 73
  biography, 157–58
  on conversion, 18
  death, 2, 24, 145, 147–54, 156, 159, 161, 168–69
  debt, 160
  as "disciple," 24, 159–60
  ecclesiology, 15–16
  entourage, 24
  estate, 4, 11, 159
  family, 50, 59, 160
  green books, 173
  history, 29–30
  historiography, 7, 29, 36–37, 39–45, 148
  ignorance about Sifting Time, 47, 50, 52, 123
  leadership, 2, 24, 59, 159–62
  letter of reprimand, 6–7, 38, 44, 46–53, 57–62, 69, 74, 80–81, 89–90, 121–23, 132–33, 135, 170
  as Lutheran, 42
  on marriage, 3–4, 22–23, 107, 139, 155, 166–67, 178
  and mysticism, 29
  personality, 18
  in Pennsylvania, 24, 55–56, 158, 184
  and Pietism, 9, 17–19
  reaction to Sifting Time, 39, 162–163
  role in Sifting Time, 35–40, 42, 62
  successor, 158–60
  theology of the heart, 69
  and Unity of Brethren, 17
  on women, 150
  works, 153–54, 162–63
  young, 12, 18
Zittau, 12, 16

www.ingramcontent.com/pod-product-compliance
Lightning Source LLC
Chambersburg PA
CBHW021940290426
44108CB00012B/909